Border Ruffians "Going over to wipe out Lawrence."

HISTORY

OF

KANSAS:

FROM

THE FIRST EXPLORATION OF THE MISSISSIPPI VALLEY,

TO

ITS ADMISSION INTO THE UNION:

EMBRACING

A CONCISE SKETCH OF LOUISIANA; AMERICAN SLAVERY, AND ITS ONWARD MARCH; THE CONFLICT OF FREE AND SLAVE LABOR IN THE SETTLEMENT OF KANSAS, AND THE OVERTHROW OF THE LATTER, WITH ALL OTHER ITEMS OF GENERAL INTEREST: COMPLETE, CONSECUTIVE AND RELIABLE.

By J. N. HOLLOWAY, A. M.

LAFAYETTE, IND:
JAMES, EMMONS & CO., JOURNAL BUILDINGS.
1868.

TO

Rev. C. A. Brooke,

A SINCERE FRIEND OF MANKIND,

IRRESPECTIVE OF PARTY, CONDITION OR COLOR,

And a Laborer for Good,

UNDER A GRATEFUL SENSE OF MANY FAVORS,

AS A TOKEN OF HIGH ESTEEM,

THIS VOLUME IS RESPECTFULLY INSCRIBED BY

The Author.

PREFACE.

Kansas has a history which is common with no other State in the Union. The history of Slavery in our country is the history of successive triumphs and continued advances over the will of a majority of our people, until it entered into a hand to hand grapple with Free Labor in Kansas. Here was the battle-field of the combined forces of the "Irrepressible Conflict," and here the question of supremacy between its opposing elements was finally settled. Slavery triumphed in every Territory where she sought to establish her dominion until she provoked, by tearing down the bulwarks of Plighted Faith, a single-handed contest with Free Labor in the settlement of Kansas, upon the principles of Popular Sovereignty.

To the people of this Territory, aided by friends in the Free States, therefore, belongs the honor of first repelling the advances of Slavery, and of forever destroying its power. Slave propagandists felt this, and hence, when the question was decided in Kansas, they turned in their wrath upon the General Government, which had been to Slavery an indulgent and fostering guardian, to take its life, whereby to rid themselves of its control.

Few have fully comprehended the awful character and extent of the desperate conflict in Kansas. Both parties upheld by the pecuniary means and moral support of their respective States, engaged in it with the most intense and inflamed spirit of partisans. Plans, deep, dark and far-reaching, were laid by the great minds of the nation, and found their execution in Kansas. Worse than civil war reigned, worse than its concomitant evils prevailed.

To fully understand the character of the Kansas conflict requires a proper acquaintance with the aggressions of Slavery in the United States upon Freedom, of which the Kansas trouble was but the outgrowth or culmination. I have, therefore, inserted a short sketch of that Institution.

The history of Kansas is a difficult one to write. Though there is an incalculable amount of material which can be gathered together, still facts were so perverted and differently represented by contemporary writers, that the searcher for truth is often lost and puzzled in his investigations. Much, too, of the history of Kansas has never been written. The designs and motives of each party, and many of their plans, can not be found on paper, all of which so essential to a complete history of Territorial struggle, must be gathered from men who are still living, and to whom they are familiar.

There is no complete and consecutive history of Kansas Territory. The books which have been written upon Kansas matters cover but a short space of time, and contain but a partial and disjointed sketches of those times. They were written in great haste for campaign documents, and hence were in many instances highly colored and inaccurate.

Most of the important documents bearing upon Kansas history are scarce and difficult to find. There is no public library or historical society in the State which has made the collection. The writer has been at the trouble and pains to make this collection himself, which he has found more difficult than the labor of writing the book. In a few years this work could not have been done. Documents would have been lost, families moved away, and thus some of the most essential items in the history of Kansas become oblivious.

The UNWRITTEN history of Kansas could never be WRITTEN so well as at the present time, while most of the actors in the early troubles of the Territory are still living. The author has visited those, made their acquaintance, whom he has ever found open and communicative on all subjects, and from whom he has gathered much valuable assistance.

To supply what seemed to be a great public demand has been my design in undertaking the preparation of this volume. I have had but one idea to guide me in its compilation, and that is Truth. By this I have sought to test every word and sentence. I have sought not only to avoid misrepresentation, but also another very common fault into which writers are prone to fall—exaggeration of facts; but I have labored to describe events exactly as they transpired, without underrating or over coloring them. How far I have succeeded in accomplishing this purpose is left to the impartial judgment of the public to decide.

In the prosecution of this work, I have enjoyed many advantages. Totally unconnected with the Territorial difficulties, without any political or personal preferments, my judgment has been wholly free from prejudice and partiality. I have freely consulted with men of all parties and opinions, from all of whom I have gathered much information. Books, files of papers, letters and documents of various kinds have come to me from every quarter. In this way my labors have been greatly facilitated, and I take this opportunity to make a public acknowledgement of these favors, which are the more appreciated as I am a stranger in the State. It would be tedious to mention all who have rendered me much invaluable assistance, but I cannot forbear to name the State Auditor. Mr. Swallow, and State Librarian, Dr. Hounton, who has permitted me the use of the library, as though it were my own; Mr. Barker, Secretary of State and Mr. Clarkson, Clerk in that office, who have allowed me free access to official records; Hon John W. Forman of Atchison, who has furnished me, among other valuable documents, a complete file of the "Squatter Sovereign;" Dr. A. Hunting of Manhattan, who sent me several valuable scrap-books; Hon. G. W. Smith of Lawrence, who furnished me a complete file of the "Herald of Freedom"; Hon. Joel Grover, of Lawrence, who supplied me with some rare documents; Col. C. K. Holliday of Topeka, who has given me many important items; Hon. J. A. Halderman of Leavenworth, through whose influence I obtained access to the Mercantile Library of that city, and the use of its excellent files of old papers; Hon. S. A. Kingman of Atchison, who has assisted me in various ways; Gov. Robinson, to whom I am much indebted, as also to Col. Montgomery, whose assistance and hospitality I have enjoyed; Hon. J. A. Wakefield who wrote out some early reminescences for me; Hon. George Hillyer who furnished me a file of the "Kansas Freeman"; Hon. John Ritchie from whom I obtained valuable official documents; S. M. McDonald and Baker of the "State Record" who have greatly assisted me; Hon. James Christian who has the most valuable library in the Territory. J. N. H.

CONTENTS.

CHAPTER I.

CHAPTER II.

CHAPTER III.

CHAPTER IV.

CHAPTER V.

CHAPTER VI.

CHAPTER VII.—1854.

CHAPTER VIII.—1705-1854.

CHAPTER IX.—1854.

CHAHTER X—1854.

CHAPTER XI—1854.

CHAPTER XII.—1854.

CHAPTER XIII—1855.

CHAPTER XIV—1855.

CHAPTER XV—1855.

CHAPTER XXVIII—1856.

CHAPTER XXIX—1856.

CHAPTER XXX—1856.

CHAPTER XXXI—1856.

HISTORY OF KANSAS TERRITORY.

CHAPTER I.

HISTORY OF LOUISIANA.

As the territory of the State of Kansas is a part of the Louisiana purchase, I will first give a succinct account of the discovery, exploration and settlement of that province; of the many changes in ownership which it underwent, and the final division and organization of its broad domain into territories and states to form integral parts in the American Union.

Forty-four years after the western shores of the Atlantic had been discovered and before any settlements had been effected thereon, the first Europeans traversed the valley of the Mississippi. Ferdinand De Soto, a man of valor, fame, and fortune, headed this expedition. An intimate associate of Pizarro in the conquest of Peru, he shared in the immense ransom of the Inca. Returning to his native land, he enjoyed the admiration and honors of Spain. Charles V. appointed him governor of Cuba, and gave him a grant of Florida. His ambition inflamed by the adulations of the court, his avarice more craving by the taste ot riches, he sought to surpass Cortes in glory and Pizarro in wealth by seeking a new field for fame and riches in America. With six hundred chosen men he disembarked in 1538 at Tampa Bay, in Florida, and began his memorable march through the savage wilds of the interior. After two years of wandering through swamps and brush, over ragged hills and swollen torrents, harrassed on every hand by enraged savages, but with hopes inspired, amid all embarrassments, by the *ignis fatuus* of early adventurers—the El Dorado of North America—he stood upon the banks of the Mississippi, the discoverer of the most majestic river in the world. Crossing this, where the southern boundary of Tennessee touches it, as though it had been a swampd rain, he pressed his vain search for the "gold region," westward through cane-brakes, marshes and tangled forests, perplexed by the murmurings of his followers, until he reached the head waters of the Arkansas, where Fort Gibson was afterwards located, within one hundred miles of the southern boundary of Kansas. Looking out upon the broad expanse of prairie before him, he saw no prospect of the "land of hope." Disappointed and disheartened, the little band of adventurers returned to the banks of the Mississippi. There, on the wet lands of the bottoms, surrounded by weeds and cane-brakes, with no one to administer to the sympathies and wants of the sick, De Soto died of fever. "Thus perished," says Bancroft, "Ferdinand De Soto, the governor of Cuba, the successful associate of Pizarro. His miserable end was the more observed from the greatness of his former prosperity. His soldiers pronounced his eulogy by grieving for his loss; the priests chanted over his body the first requiems that were ever heard on the waters of the Mississippi. To conceal his death, his body was wrapped in a mantle, and, in the stillness of midnight, was sunk in the middle of the stream. The discoverer of the Mississippi slept beneath its waters. He had crossed a large part of the continent in search of gold, and found nothing so remarkable as a burial place." His followers reduced in numbers to three hundred and eleven, after long wanderings, reached a place of safety in Mexico. *

*Some writers discredit the account of De Soto's journey, but I have followed the readings of Bancroft and Schoolcraft. The latter has been over the country west of the Mississippi, and finds it to corroborate the description of it in the alleged account of De Soto's journey.

More than a century elapsed before another European visits the Mississippi valley. The French had settled along the St. Lawrence, and around the Great Lakes. Missionaries with pious zeal were planting the Cross among the Indians and subduing the barbarians unto Christ by the gentleness of Love. The most earnest and successful among these was Father Marquette!

The Indians frequently spoke of a great river at the West, flowing south which they called *Mississippy*, as Marquette wrote it. It was a matter of debate among the French, what course this river pursued to the ocean. Some contended that it continued to flow directly south, and emptied into the Gulf of Mexico; others were of the opinion that it deflected either to the east and discharged itself into the Atlantic, or west, and poured its waters into the Gulf of California.

To settle this difficult question and carry the Gospel to the heathen, Father Marquette determined to make a tour of exploration. Encouraged by the governor of Canada, who gave him M. Joliet as a companion, and five other Frenchmen, he embarked on the 13th of May, 1673, in two bark canoes at Michilimackinac. Reaching Green Bay, the solicitous aborigines besought him with tears to abandon so hazardous an undertaking, portraying to him the frightful dangers of the Meschasebe (Mississippi.) "I thanked them for their good advice," says Marquette, "but I told them I could not follow it, since the salvation of souls was at stake, for which I would be overjoyed to give my life." Ascending Fox River and crossing the portage, they gave themselves to the current of the Wisconsin, and were soon carried into the waters of the Mississippi.

Borne upon this mighty stream, they continued to descend, occasionally halting at Indian villages, smoking the calumet of peace and narrating the story of the Cross, until they reached the mouth of the Arkansas. Here, satisfied that the Mississippi continues its course to the Gulf of

Mexico, and their provisions well nigh exhausted, they resolved to return.

Father Marquette was the first to observe the muddy waters of the *Peketanoni*, as he called the Missouri. He represents it as being a very large river, flowing from the north-west, "on which are prodigous nations who use wooden canoes."* From the Indians he gathered the idea that by following this river to its head waters, and crossing a narrow portage, another stream might be found, flowing down through a large lake to the "Red Sea," or Gulf of California. In the map accompanying his journal he lays down the general course of the Missouri for one hundred miles pretty accurately.

The account of La Hontan's travels through the West, which he dates Feb. 28, 1689, would give him the honor of being the discoverer and explorer of the Missouri, were it entitled to credibility. But it contains so many palpable contradictions and errors that historians refuse to acknowledge its claims.

The next explorer of the Mississippi was the celebrated ROBERT DE LA SALLE. Though of noble family, on being educated a Jesuit, he lost his patrimony. Obtaining an honorable discharge from this order, he came to Canada in 1667 a penniless, yet ambitious adventurer. While the single hearted Marquette was floating upon the western waters, he was engaged in the fur traffic, revolving plans for future achievements. To discover a short route to China across the western continent was his favorite scheme. When he learned Marquette's discoveries, he conceived the design for the future greatness of France and his own glory of colonizing the valley of the Mississippi and connecting Canada and the Gulf of Mexico by a chain of fortifications. What a mighty undertaking for a poor, unknown wanderer! But this idea that sprung from the warm and fertile brain of La Salle ultimately electrified all France. He lays his plans

*Among them were the "Kansas."

before the Governor of Canada who recommends him to the favor of the King. Repairing to the courts of France, he obtains the sanction and encouragement of his sovereign. He returns to Canada and applies himself, like an enthusiast and a philosopher, a skilful financier and an importunate mumper, to the prosecution of his plans. He raises money without security, builds a ship sixty tons burthen, and crosses the waters of Lake Michigan to Green Bay. Returning his barge, laden with furs, to Niagara for the benefit of his creditors, he with others coasts the lake in canoes to the mouth of St. Joseph River where he erects a fort. Ascending this stream he crosses the portage and glides down the Kankakee into the Illinois. He descends with the current of this smooth flowing river as far as Peoria and erects another fort. His means are now exhausted and he is compelled to return, while Henepin, his associate, sets out in a northwest direction and explores the Mississippi for some distance above the mouth of the Wisconsin.

On the 4th of January, 1682, La Salle enters upon his second expedition. Descending the river Chicago, across the portage, down the Illinois, by the 6th of February he glides upon the waters of the Mississippi; yielding to its swift current, occasionally halting to smoke the calumet with the natives, and erecting Fort Prudhomme, on Chicasaw Bluffs, in three months he explores it to its mouth. Here, with due solemnity and in a formal manner, he takes possession of the country, by the name of Louisiana, in behalf of the King of France. Erecting a column with a cross, he has inscribed upon it *Louis the Great, King of France and Navarre, reigns the 9th of April*, 1682. He now resolves to return to Canada, collect a number of emigrants, convey them down the Mississippi and plant a colony at its mouth. His journey back was long delayed by illness, and this plan was never executed. He determines to accomplish his object in a different way. Placing his faithful associate Tonty, in command of Fort St. Louis at Peoria, which by this time was completed, on the 13th of December, 1683, he repairs to France. In 1684, with four vessels and two hundred and eighty-four emigrants, he sets sail from the shores of his native land for the Gulf of Mexico. Early in the following year, he reaches his point of destination. After vainly searching for the mouths of the Mississippi, he anchors his vessels in the Bay of Matagorda and disembarks his little colony upon the sandy shore. But here he experiences sad disasters. One by one, he loses all his vessels by shipwreck and desertion. After making scanty provisions for his colony, he explores the country. He searches for the mouths of the Mississippi and for his lost ship, Belle, but with ill success. He now pursues in ecstacy golden visions for the mines of St. Barbe, but in a few months, he returns in rags and sadness to his dejected colony—diminished by fatal fevers and savage massacres. Cut off from France by the loss of his ships, misfortune constantly attending him, he resolves to seek assistance in Canada. Having made arrangements for his colony during his absence, he sets out for the northern lakes with a company of twenty men. He had not proceeded far when a mutiny sprang up among his followers, and he was the victim of assassination. His little colony which had cost him so much labor, solicitude and misfortune, was soon visited by the Spaniards and all of its members killed, save five, who were spared on account of their youth, and a few men who escaped to the woods and were never heard of more.

During the next five years, France is too much engaged in war to turn her attention to her distant possessions. After the peace of Ryswick, another colony was sent out under her auspices. Early in 1699, Lemoine De Iberville, a distinguished Canadian officer, established a little settlement near the Bay of Baloxi. While exploring one of the mouths of the Mississippi he obtained Tonty's letter to La Salle from the wandering savages. It will be recollected that this was the individual whom La Salle had left in charge of Fort St. Louis on his going to France the last time. Tonty supposing that La Salle had returned with his intended colony to the mouth of the Mississippi, had descended, to visit him. But not being able to find him, Tonty had left this letter in the hands of the natives who had carefully preserved it for thirteen years.

The little daughter of France, thus cast upon the burning sands of the Mexican Gulf, struggled through a miserable infancy. The men, many of whom were of a reckless character, instead of pursuing the slow, but sure way of acquiring a subsistence, wealth and independence, by opening farms and tilling the fertile soil and raising stock, spent their time in roving over the country in search of game and gold mines. Whenever game failed, or supplies from France, the colony was in a suffering condition.

In 1712, France being plunged again in war was unable to lend assistance to her "infant child" across the waters. For the benefit of the colony, she sells the monopoly of Louisiana to Crozat, a merchant prince, who hoped by discovering and working mines, and by opening a traffic with Mexico, to make a wonderful speculation. But in this he was doomed to disappointment. In 1717, having lost his fortune—though he had labored more for his own aggrandizement than the good of the colony—he surrenders his privileges.

But other speculators were not intimidated by the failure of Crozat. Louisiana passed the same year into the hands of the western company. This corporation had absolute sovereignty over Louisiana, except homage and fealty to the King of France. The association was headed by John Law, a notorious gambler and swindler, and was organized just on the eve of his financial glory with a charter for twenty-seven years.

CHAPTER II.

HISTORY OF LOUISIANA CONTINUED—1541-1854.

The company began their work by laboring to increase the settlement of Louisiana. A wonderful interest was awakened in France by artfully circulating reports of the gold and silver mines in the Mississippi valley. The stock of the company was soon in great demand. A company of eight hundred emigrants is shipped over and the city of New Orleans is laid out. Great expectations are awakened both in France and Louisiana of the future greatness and grandeur of the province, and for the first time the pulsations of life begin to throb vigorously in the little colony.

But the prosperity was not real. It was awakened by the financial flush, springing from the erroneous and ephemeral money theory of John Law. The financial gloom having spread over France, it extends to the colony, and the bright prospect vanishes. Louisiana is in but little better condition than when she passed into the hands of the company. The members of the company held their charter until 1733, when, wearied with their burden, surrendered it.

Though the company did not accomplish for the colony all that it and others expected, still it is entitled to credit for what it did. Under its auspices the colony had been increased to 5,000 white and 2,000 black, inhabitants—the latter having been shipped from Africa and sold for one hundred and seventy-six dollars apiece on three years credit. The vast territory had been divided into nine districts and settlements; factories and store-houses had been established in each; the attention of the colonists had been drawn from the unprofitable search for gold, to the importance of agriculture; the culture of rice, indigo and tobacco had been introduced, and figs and oranges were growing in luxuriant abundance; communication and commerce had been opened with the Indies and Canada; in short, the colony had been brought into a condition of self support.

On the reversion of Louisiana to the King, he began the chastisement of the Indians, who had been instigated to deeds of violence by the English and Spaniards. One powerful tribe, the Natches, was utterly annihilated, and the Chicasaws severely punished.

The territory claimed by the French under the name of Louisiana was immense. Beginning to the east, midway between Pensacola and Mobile, the boundary ran north to the head waters of the Ohio. Every rivulet whose waters ran to the Mississippi was claimed by the French. "Half a mile," says Bancroft, "from the head of the southern branch of the Savannah River is a spring, which flows to the Mississippi; strangers who drank of it would say that they had tasted of French waters." Beginning at the south-west on the Rio del Norte and ascending on a line of the ridge that divides it from the Red River, the boundary extended along this ridge to the Gulf of California. On the north-west, the boundary line between the Hudson Bay Company was not fixed. On the north-east it was bounded by Canada.

It must not be supposed that while the French were thus exploring, taking possession of, and settling so vast a country, that the Spaniards and English were wholly ignorant of, or indifferent to, their operations. Both nations had watched the French with a jealous eye and envied their success. The Spaniards had at one time destroyed a settlement at the Isle of Dauphine and frequently harassed the colonists. From the discovery of the continent, England had

2

claimed all territory from sea to sea. In 1684 and 1726 she had purchased all the land laying north-west of the Ohio from the Six Nations, who claimed to hold it. As early as 1724 English settlers were found along the Ohio River.—Upon these grounds England based a claim to this country, and the Governor of Virginia had repeatedly called the attention of the legislators to the importance of protecting their claim against the encroachments of the French.

It was not until 1748 that anything was done by the English to openly assert their right to the territory. It was then resolved that the most effectual way to secure their possessions was to settle them. The Ohio company was organized with a grant of a half a million acres of land and several other companies of a similar nature were formed. These sent out emigrants, established settlements, opened farms, built store-houses and began a traffic with the Indians.

The Governor of Canada learning the movements of the British, caused inscriptions to be made upon plates of lead, setting forth the fact that the territory belonged to France, and had them placed on stakes in different parts of the disputed possessions. But this effort to stay the encroachment of the English proving futile, an irregular warfare was begun between the French settlers and their allies—the Indians—on the one side, and the English settlers on the other, until finally one neighborhood of the latter was utterly destroyed.

Meanwhile the Governor of Canada constructs military roads and forts in different parts of the territory. The executive of Virginia learning of the sad destruction of an English settlement on the banks of the Ohio by the French and their other warlike demonstrations, despatched a messenger (Geo. Washington) to the commander of one of the French forts to inquire what business he had upon his Majesty's domains and require his removal from the territory. This messenger having met with a decided refusal by the French General to comply with these requisitions, an open rupture soon took place between the two nations. The war which followed—commonly known as the French war—I have not space to treat of in detail. It lasted for nine years, first in America, then in Europe, and was terminated, in 1763, by the treaty of Paris.

This treaty ceded from France to England Canada, Nova Scotia and the Island of Cape Breton, with their dependencies; fixed the boundary between the dominions of the two nations by a line drawn along the middle of the river Mississippi from its source to the river Iberville, and from thence by a line drawn along the middle of this river and the lakes Maurepas and Ponchartrain, to the sea, and withdrew all claim on the part of France to any territory east of the Mississippi. The vast territory, thus acquired by England west of the Alleghanies, was divided out among the colonies along the Atlantic coasts and held by them by charters from their mother country until after their independence.

Spain, who had stood aloof from the conflict of the two nations until she had seen the vast territory in America wrested from France, alarmed at the increasing greatness of Britain and the danger of losing her own possessions across the Atlantic, in 1762, determined to make common cause with France, and declared war against England. But by this step she suffered what she sought to avert; for before another year had passed, she, with France, was compelled to treat for peace by relinquishing Florida in favor of England.

But France undervaluing her remnant of Louisiana, ceded it, in 1764, to Spain as a compensation for her loss of Florida. Thus the vast and fertile territory included in Canada and Louisiana, which had awakened dazzling hopes in France by the greatness of its prospects, and which had cost her so much solicitude, expense and misfortune, was swept from her by the fortune of war.

This cession of Louisiana to Spain was not made known

to the inhabitants for a time; but when the rumor reached them, it awakened a general dissatisfaction among the colonists; for they were intensely French, and nothing could be more odious to them than Spanish rule. When Spain did take possession of Louisiana, it was in such a way as to exasperate the excited inhabitants, and the policy she pursued, was one not calculated to win their affection. It was years before the machinery of government was fully established and worked with smoothness.

In 1776, the thirteen colonies east of the Alleghanies declared their separation from England, and by a long and hard struggle maintained it. After the establishment of the general government, they ceded their respective claims to territory in the west, to the sovereignty of the United States. This broad expanse of country lying between the Alleghany mountains and the Mississippi river, once a part of Louisiana, was divided up into districts by Congress, which were organized under territorial government, and, in a constitutional way, successively admitted into the Union as states with the names they now bear.

In this great American revolution, which resulted in the independence of the English colonies, Spain employed about the same tactics as in the former war, but with better success. France had repeatedly solicited her to join the cause of the colonies against Britain, but fearing the effects of their independence upon her adjoining possessions, she observed a strict neutrality, hoping to be able to accomplish more by diplomacy than by a resort to arms. She offered herself as a mediator between the belligerent powers, to which France acceded, but England peremptorily refused to acknowledge the independence of her subjects across the ocean, whereupon Spain joined (1779) heartily in the strife, doing much mischief to Engalnd by her maritime strength. The colony of Louisiana, rejoicing at the opportunity of revenging her suffering during the last war, raised fourteen thousand men, under the command of Galvez, and took possession of the East and the West Floridas. By the treaty of peace which England was compelled to make this time, all the territory east of the Mississippi, below the thirty-first degree of latitude, was ceded to Spain.

The treaty between the United States and Spain in, 1795, conceded to the former the free navigation of the Mississippi, the right of deposit at New Orleans, and fixed the boundary of the two dominions east of the Mississippi on the thirty-first degree of north latitude, deviating slightly from it towards the Atlantic.

From 1793 to 1797 efforts were made by the agents of France and Spain to prevail upon the people of the south-western territory to separate from the United States, and, with Louisiana in connection with these two powers, form an independent government west of the Alleghany mountains. Genet, the Minister of the French Republic, first fermented the idea, and even went so far as to enlist the sympathies and co-operation of the western people. But his government discovering his acts and recalling him, the United States establishing a strong military force in the West, squelched the movement. Garondolet, the governor of Louisiana, sought to attain the same object. He refused to give up certain posts that fell to the United States by the treaty, and embarrassed the navigation of the Mississippi. He sent secret agents into Ohio and Kentucky and sought to bribe over commanders of military posts to his interests; but finding them incorruptible, his project failed.

Therefore, when the United States ascertained through her Minister at Paris, Mr. Livingston, that the whole of Louisiana had been re-troceded to France by the secret treaty of Ildefonso (1800), as might be expected, was greatly alarmed. While impotent Spain had held dominion there, she had experienced great danger; still more was she imperilled when ambitious and powerful France established herself in so strong and commanding position.

The sagacious Jefferson, then President, comprehending the peril of his country's situation, like a wise and skillful statesman, by one of the most celebrated and strategic strokes of American diplomacy, steered the ship of State free of danger. Though the future seemed lowering, the present he augured propitious.—France suffering from a long and disastrous war with England and an impoverished treasury, was in no condition to resist a determined overture from the United States for the possession of Louisiana. Jefferson, accordingly, dispatched instructions to the United States Minister at Paris, to represent to the First Consul that the occupation of New Orleans by France would endanger the friendly relations between the two nations, and, perhaps, even oblige the United States to make common cause with England; as the possession of this city by the former, by giving her the command of the Mississippi, the only outlet to the produce of the Western States, and also the Gulf of Mexico, so important to American commerce, would render it almost certain that the conflicting interests of the two nations would lead to an open rupture. Mr. Livingston, the Minister, was instructed to negotiate not only for the free navigation of the Mississippi, but for the acquisition of New Orleans and the territory itself.

Bonaparte, on receiving these representations from the Minister of the United States, summoned a conference with two of his ministers who had resided in Louisiana, and opened it with these words: "I am fully sensible of the value of Louisiana, and it is my wish to repair the error of the French diplomatists, who abandoned it in 1763. I have scarcely recovered it, before I run the risk of losing it; but, if I am obliged to give it up, it shall hereafter cost more to those who force me to part with it, than to those to whom I yield it. The English have despoiled France of all her northern possessions, and now they covet those of the south. I am determined that they shall not have the Mississippi. Although Louisiana is but a trifle compared with their vast possessions in other parts of the globe, yet, judging from the vexation which they have manifested on seeing it return to the power of France, I am certain that their first object will be to gain possession of it. They will probably commence war in that quarter. They have twenty vessels in the Gulf of Mexico, and affairs in St. Domingo are daily getting worse since the death of Le Clerc. The conquest of Louisiana might be easily made, and I have not a moment to lose in putting it out of their reach. I am not sure but that they have already begun the attack upon it. Such a measure would be in accordance with their habits, and in their place, I should not wait. I am inclined in order to deprive them of all prospects of ever possessing it, to cede it to the United States. Indeed, I cannot say I cede it, for I hardly possess it; and if I wait but a short time, my enemies will leave me nothing but an empty title to grant to the republic I wish to conciliate. They only ask for the city of Louisiana, but I consider the whole colony lost; and I believe in the hands of this rising power, it will be more useful to the political, and even the commercial interest of France, than if I should attempt to retain it."

After inquiring from both for their opinions on the subject and debating the matter for a long time, he dismissed the conference without making known his determination. On the following day, calling his chief minister, he said: "The season for deliberation is over; I have determined to renounce not only New Orleans, but the whole colony. * * * I commission you, therefore, to negotiate this affair with the envoys of the United States. Do not wait for the arrival of Mr. Monroe; but go this very day and confer with Mr. Livingston. Remember, however, I want ample funds for carrying on the war, and I do not want to commence it by levying new taxes. For the last century France and Spain have incurred great expenses in the improvement of Louisiana, for which her trade has never indemnified us. Large sums have been advanced to different companies which have never returned to the treasury. It is fair that I should require payment for these. Were I to regulate my demands by the importance of this territory to the United States, they would be unbounded; but, being obliged to part with it, I shall be moderate in my terms. Still remember, I must have fifty millions of francs and will not consent to take less. I would rather make some desperate effort to preserve this fine country."

After some considerable correspondence between the ministers of the two republics, and quibbling about the price, the purchase was effected by the United States for sixteen million dollars, four millions of which was to be paid to American merchants to indemnify them for losses from French privateers. The treaty was signed on the 3d of May, 1803, and ratified by Congress on the twentieth of the following October; the most essential provisions of which, bearing upon our subject, are here inscribed:

"ARTICLE 1.—Whereas, by the article the third of the treaty concluded at St. Ildefonso, the 9th Vendimiaire, an 9, (October 1, 1800,) between the First Consul of the French Republic and his Catholic Majesty, it is agreed as follows: His Catholic Majesty promises and engages on his part to retrocede to the French republic, six months after the full and entire execution of the conditions and stipulations herein to his royal highness, the Duke of Parma, the colony or province of Louisiana, with the same extent it now has in the hands of Spain, and that it had when France possessed it, and such as it should be after the treaties entered into between Spain and other States; And, Whereas, in pursuance of the treaty, and especially the third article, the French Republic has an incontestable title to the domain and possession of said territory: The First Consul of the French Republic, desiring to give to the United States a strong proof of his friendship, doth hereby cede to the United States, in the name of the French Republic, forever, and in full sovereignty, the said territory and all its appurtenances, as fully and in the same manner as they have been acquired by the French Republic, in virtue of the above mentioned treaty concluded with his Catholic Majesty.

"ARTICLE 3. The inhabitants of the ceded territory shall be incorporated into the Union of the United States, and admitted, as soon as possible, to all the rights, advantages and immunities of the citizens of the United States; and, in the meantime, they shall be maintained and protected in the free enjoyment of their liberty, property, and the religion which they prefer."

Immediately after the accession of Louisiana, the President dispatched Generals Wilkinson and Claiborne to take possession of it in behalf of the United States. On their arrival at

New Orleans the star-spangled banner supplanted the tri-colored flag of France. By an act of Congress the same year, it was divided into two unequal parts: the one extending from the thirty-third degree of latitude to the Gulf of Mexico, under the name of the Territory of Orleans; the other embraced the remaining portion of the cession, and was called the District of Louisiana.

The following year the Territory of Orleans passed under the second grade of government. In those days there were two distinct conditions which organized territory could occupy. In the first they were governed by a governor, judges and secretary, appointed by the President; in the second, besides these officers, they had a council appointed by the President and Senate of the United States, and a House of Representatives, chosen and elected by the people. In 1811 the Territory of Orleans having complied with the necessary requisitions, was constituted a State in the Federal Union, under the name of Louisiana. The Territory of Louisiana was under the jurisdiction of the Governor and judges of Indiana Territory the first year, but in 1805 was admitted to the first grade of government; in 1811 to the second, under the name of Missouri, and in 1820 it was made one of the United States of America.

The narrow skirt of coast along the Gulf of Mexico, below the thirty-first degree of latitude, was ceded to the United States by Spain in 1818, and was annexed to the States immediately above it.

The territories of Texas, Arkansas, Iowa and Minnesota were in turn next organized, formed, and, in the usual way, admitted to the dignity, rights and privileges of independent States.

In 1854, by an act of Congress, the territories of Kansas and Nebraska were organized, a detailed account of which I will give in a subsequent chapter. Before I enter upon this branch of my subject, I desire to disclose the gathering of the storm that burst upon the virgin soil of Kansas; but which, by discreet council, strong arms and brave hearts, was turned back to vent its fury on the nation.

CHAPTER III.

INTRODUCTION AND ESTABLISHMENT OF AFRICAN SLAVERY IN THE UNITED STATES AGAINST THE WISHES OF THE PEOPLE.

African slavery has always met with a spirited, yet compromising opposition from the American people. From the time it first began to attract attention in the English colonies, the earnest prayer and efforts of the inhabitants have been to prevent its extension, and provide for its ultimate extinction. But the history of this foul institution will show that whenever by its growth the bonds of legislation have become too tight, it has broken them; that whenever the patriotic and freedom-loving people of this country have met its advance with a determined resistance, it has, by menacing the existence of the General Government, or brandishing aloft the sword of disunion, compelled them in order to avert the threatened danger, to acquiesce in its demands; that thus it ruled the founders of our Republic and the Congress of the United States, until it challenged a contest with Freedom at the ballot-box in the distant field of Kansas; that here, discarding its chosen weapon, and trampling under foot the sanctity of the ballot-box—the palladium of American liberty—it sought to attain its ends by its usual tactics,—intimidation, force and fraud; that here, Freedom, driven to the very door of her temple, comprehending the real character of the monster with which she had to grapple, fought with the valor and prowess of an angel, combatting Satan and his demons in their approach upon the battlements of Heaven; that, its loathsome and blighting presence driven back from the sacred soil of Kansas, smarting from defeat, with its ungovernable spirit enraged by opposition, it attacked the life of the beneficent government which had fostered its growth through forbearance, and perished from the sword of its own drawing.

The odious distinction of establishing negro slavery in the thirteen colonies belongs to England. Although the Dutch were the first to engage in transporting Africans to the colonies, yet, under their commerce alone, it languished, and slavery thus introduced could easily have been removed by the benevolent spirit of colonial legislation. It was not until after the treaty of Utrecht, under English monopoly, that the slave trade with the colonies acquired its importance. By the decisions of her chief counsellors, York and Talbot, England legalized it; by her sovereignty the American ports were thrown open to the slave trade, and the prohibitions of the colonies against such importation annulled; by her Queens and Lords, the business was carried on and profits shared; by her ministers, a cloak of religion was thrown around its foulness, and they called it a mode to evangelize the heathen; by her merchants it was declared that "negro labor will keep our colonies in due subserviency to their mother country; for while our plantations depend only on planting by the negro, our colonies can never prove injurious to British manufactories, never become independent of their kingdom." In 1702 Queen Anne instructed the governor of New York and New Jersey to "give due encouragement to slave merchants, and in particular to the royal African Company of England." In 1775 the Earl of Dartmouth declares "we can not allow the colonies to check, or discourage in any degree, a traffic so beneficial to the nation." Prior to 1740 England had introduced into the colonies about one hundred and thirty thousand blacks; by 1776 it had increased to three hundred thousand. The population of negro slaves among the thirteen colonies in 1754 stood as follows: New Hampshire, Massachusetts and Maine, 3,000; Rhode Island, 4,500; Connecticut 3,500; New York 11,000; New Jersey

5,500; Pennsylvania and Delaware 11,000; Maryland 4,400; Virginia 116,000; North Carolina 20,000; South Carolina 40,000; Georgia 2,000. Between 1754 and 1776 these numbers must have been greatly augmented, as that was the most flourishing time for slave merchants. We have no means of ascertaining what number there was at the time the colonies declared their independence; but by the census taken in 1790 the population of slaves was returned as follows; New Hampshire 158; Rhode Island 952; Connecticut 2,759; Massachusetts emancipated hers in 1780; New York 21,324; New Jersey 11,423; Pennsylvania 3,737; Delaware 8,887; Maryland 103,036; Virginia 293,-427; North Carolina 100,572; South Carolina 107,094; Georgia 29,264. It must be borne in mind that many had been emancipated by the northern States during and after the Revolution, and others had been taken into new States and Territories.

Thus did England plant "the great evil of Slavery" in the constitution of her colonies; and that in many cases against their earnest and filial remonstrance. Massachusetts always opposed the introduction of slaves from abroad, and in 1701 instructed her representatives "to put a period to negroes being slaves." But the Earl of Dartmouth interposes his edict, "we cannot allow the colonies to check, or discourage, in any degree, a traffic so beneficial to the nation." In 1645 two reputable townsmen of Boston, "sailed for Guinea to trade for negroes." But when it is noised abroad, public sentiment pronounces them malefactors and murderers, and a worthy magistrate denounces their act as contrary to the law of God and the law of the country, "and committed the guilty men for the offense." After advice with the elders and representatives of the people "bearing witness against the heinous crime of man-stealing," ordered the negroes to be restored at the public charge "to their native country, with a letter expressing the indignation of the court" at their wrongs. But Queen Anne admonishes the governor "to give due encouragement to slave merchants." In Virginia slavery built up a landed aristocracy who loved "the institution." But such was the spirit of popular liberty that it demands of the legislature to suppress the importation of slaves. The legislature yielding to some extent to the voice of its constituency levies a tax on each negro imported, but the Governor soon announces that "the interfering interests of the African company has obtained a repeal of that law." Whereupon a statesman of Virginia, despairing of success, declares that "the British government of Virginia constantly checks the attempts of Virginia to put a stop to the infernal traffic." In Georgia from the very first the colonists prohibited the introduction of slaves by law. James Oglethorpe writes, "my friends and I settled the colony of Georgia, and by charter were established trustees. We determined not to suffer slavery there; but the slave merchants and their adherents not only occasioned us much trouble, but at last got the government to sanction them." In New York the Dutch offered to furnish slaves to the colonists, but the rigor of the climate more than the humanity of the people, prevented the rapid growth of slavery there. But notwithstanding the obstacles which the climate interposed, the governor is instructed by royal authority to encourage the importation of negroes. In 1712 Pennsylvania circulates a general petition for the gradual emancipation of slaves by law. In the New England States laws were framed prohibiting the holding of negroes as slaves. Every man owning slaves was required after ten years to emancipate them; and every one failing to comply with this regulation was fined twice the value of each slave thus held. Although this law was not strictly enforced, still it shows the feeling of the colony relative to slavery. Even South Carolina, where slavery is coeval with the settlement on Ashley River, and where it was found to be "very profitable," complains in 1727 of "the vast importation of slaves," and when she seeks to apply a restriction, she is met by a rebuke from the English ministry.

The immortal Declaration of Independence contains a clear and familiar expression of the sentiments of the colonists upon the natural rights of men at that time. That "all men are created equal, with certain inalienable rights" was no new conception of Jefferson; it was the embodiment of the deeply rooted convictions of the American people; an idea that had been fully discussed in their conventions. Even Georgia had, just the year previous, resolved in the Darien committee, "at all times to use our utmost efforts for the manumission of our slaves in this colony upon the most safe and equitable footing for the masters and themselves." The clause in the original draft of the Declaration indicting George III, as the patron and upholder of the African slave trade, which was stricken out to satisfy South Carolina and Georgia, whose people had found slavery "profitable," expresses clearly the feelings of the majority of the colonists in regard to this horrible traffic in human flesh. It reads as follows:

> "Determined to keep open a market where men should be bought and sold, he has prostituted his negative for every legislative attempt to prohibit, or restrain this execrable commerce. And that this assemblage of horrors might want no fact of distinguished dye, he is now exciting those very people to rise in arms against us, and purchase that liberty of which he has deprived them, by murdering the people on whom he also obtruded them; thus paying off former crimes committed against the liberties of one people, with which he urges them to commit against the lives of another."

The first Continental Congress in which the colonists enjoyed, for the first time, an unrestrained legislation, in accordance with the long expressed wish of the country, resolved "that no slaves be imported into any of the thirteen united colonies."

After the Revolution was over, the colonies having achieved their independence, the vast lands lying between the Alleghanies and Mississippi were held by certain members of the Confederacy. As the charters by which these lands were held conflicted; the whole having been won by the common valor of all the colonies; it was agreed, to avoid disputes and settle the matter upon equitable principles, that the colonies, thus holding lands, should cede their right over to the General Government. Accordingly in 1784 Mr. Jefferson reported "An Ordinance for the government of the territory ceded already, or to be ceded, by individual States to the United States; specifying that such territory extends from the 31st to the 47th degree of latitude, so as to include what now constitutes the States of Tennessee, Alabama and Mississippi;" the fifth article of which ordinance declares "that after the year 1800 of the Christian era, there shall be neither slavery nor involuntary servitude in any of the said States"—that is States formed from the said territory. The southern members generally voted against this bill, but it came so near being the fundamental law of the land, thus restricting slavery forever where the mother country had planted it, that it only lacked one vote, occasioned by the absence of a member from New Jersey.

In 1787 the last Continental Congress passed a law prohibiting slavery in the territory north-west of the Ohio River which Virginia had ceded to the United States, and to which other States had relinquished their claims. The prohibition reads as follows:

> "There shall be neither slavery, nor involuntary servitude in the said territory, otherwise than in punishment of crime, whereof the parties shall be duly convicted."

In the constitutional convention that framed the government under which which we now live, the triumph of slavery over the prevailing sentiment of the American people by the same tactics which is successfully employed for the next seventy years, is, for the first time, witnessed. Although our fathers were unable to abolish slavery at once, so great was the magnitude to which it had attained, and so deeply had it rooted itself in the interest of some of the southern colonies, still they expected that the northern states would continue to emancipate their slaves as some of them already had done, and by a prudential legislation to restrict slavery in the southern states, so that for the want of territory it would ultimately become extinct. But after the constitution had been framed, with an utter silence in regard to slavery, except a clause which contained an article against an immediate and absolute prohibition to importing negro slaves, the representatives of Georgia and South Carolina came forward and declared "that their constituents can never accede to a constitution containing such an article;"* that if such a clause is retained they might regard these two States out of the Union. To obviate the objections of these two factious colonies, a compromise was effected, extending the slave trade franchise twenty years, with the implication that at the expiration of that time Congress might prohibit it. Encouraged by the success of their demand, they now make an humble request on the plea of equity, for the rendition of fugitive slaves from one state to another, as a kind of sugar-coat to the constitution for the tender stomachs of the southern colonies. The horror of slave-catching was not then realized by the northern states, the most of whom owned slaves,

*The African trade in slaves had long been odious to most of the states, and the importation of slaves into them had been prohibited. Particular states, however, continued the importation and were extremely averse to any restriction on their power to do so. In the convention the former states were anxious in framing a new constitution, to insert a provision for an immediate and absolute stop to the trade. The latter were not only averse to any interference on the subject, but solemnly declared that their constituents would never accede to a constitution containing such an article. Out of this conflict grew a middle measure providing that Congress should not interfere until 1808. Writings and Times of Madison 111.150.

after some modifications the clause is inserted without much opposition.

In 1789 South Carolina, who had continued to hold her land grants in the West, which covered the territory of the present State of Tennessee, ceded them to the United States on the condition among others "that no regulation made or to be made by Congress, shall tend to emancipate slaves." The western territory held by Georgia, comprising the States of Alabama and Mississippi, was ceded to the Union in 1802, upon about the same condition. There was no alternative but to accept these cessions with their conditions. If the States held the lands, they would plant slavery there themselves, and thus increase their own greatness; and the United States could not secure the territory without the conditions.

Thus has slavery in the infant days of our Republic, by menaces and strategy triumphed over Congress and the will of the majority of our people.

The framers of our Constitution thought that they had laid a legislative coil which would sometime restrict the growth of slavery when they limited slave importation to twenty years; and they were no sanguinary visionists, but based their judgement upon the teachings of history. "In all former ages," says Greeley in his "American Conflict:" "slavery so long as it existed and flourished, was kept alive by a constant or frequent enslavement of captives, or by importation of bondmen. Whenever that enslavement, that importation, closed, slavery began to decline." But American slavery has set at naught the teachings of history and baffled the calculations of statesmen. The acquisition of Louisiana, thus opening a vast territory for the introduction of slaves, and the invention of the Cotton Gin, thus increasing the value of slave labor, rendered the commerce in human flesh as profitable as in the days of the African West India Company. Rapacious avarice unable longer to satisfy its greediness for gain by importation, invents a new system for multiplying human chattels. "Slave-breeding for gain, deliberately proposed and systematically pursued, appears to be among the late devices and illustrations of human depravity. Neither Cowper nor Wesley, nor Jonathan Edwards, nor Granville Sharp, nor Clarkson, nor any of the philanthropists or divines, who, in the last century, bore fearless and emphatic testimony to the iniquity of slave-making, slave-holding and slave-selling seemed to have had any clear conception of it. For the infant slave of the past ages was rather an encumbrance and a burden, than a valuable addition to his master's stock. To raise him, however roughly, would cost all he would ultimately be worth. That it was cheaper to buy slaves than to rear them, was quite generally regarded as self-evident. But the suppression of the African slave-trade, coinciding with the rapid settlement of the Louisiana purchase, and the triumph of the Cotton-Gin, wrought here an entire transformation. When a field hand brought from ten to fifteen hundred dollars, and young negroes were held at about ten dollars per pound, the new born infant, if healthy, well formed, and likely to live, was deemed an addition to his master's wealth of not less than one hundred dollars even in Virginia or Maryland. It had now become the interest of the master to increase the number of births in his slave cabin; and few evinced scruples whereby this result was obtained. The chastity of female slaves was never deemed of much account, even where they were white; and, now that it had become an impediment to the increase of their master's wealth, it was wholly disregarded. No slave girl, however young, was valued lower for having become a mother, without waiting to be first made a wife; nor were many masters likely to rebuke this as a fault, or brand it as a shame. Women were publicly advertised as extraordinary breeders, and commanded a higher price on that account. Wives, sold in separation from their husbands, were imperatively required to accept new partners, in order that the fruitfulness of the plantation might not suffer."

CHAPTER IV.

TRIUMPH OF SLAVERY IN 1820.

As it has been before shown, when the Territory of Orleans was admitted into the Union, under the name of Louisiana, the remaining portion of the Louisiana purchase, heretofore called the Territory of Louisiana, passed to the second grade of government, under the title of Missouri Territory. The population spreading back from each side of the Missouri River, and extending about two hundred miles west of the Mississippi, in 1815 petitioned Congress for the privilege of forming a State government and an admission into the Union on the same footing as the original States. This petition, after having been presented twice in the House of Representatives and ordered to lie on the table, was a third time presented[1] by Mr. Scott, delegate from that territory, and referred to a select committee of which the above named gentleman was made chairman. On the 3d of April Mr. Scott reported a bill in compliance with the petitioners' request which was referred to a Committee of the Whole, but was never acted upon. At the next session of Congress the Speaker, Mr. Clay, presented a petition from the Legislative Council and House of Representatives of the Territory of Missouri, praying that they might be permitted to form a constitution and frame a State government, and be admitted into the Union. The House in Committee of the Whole entered into discussion upon a bill relating to this subject,[2] and after consid-

(1) March 16, 1818. (2) December 18.

ering various amendments, one was proposed by Mr. Tallmadge, of New York, in these words:

"And provided, That the further introduction of slavery or involuntary servitude be prohibited, except for the punishment of crime, whereof the party shall have been duly convicted; and that all children born within said State, after the admission thereof, shall be free at the age of twenty-five years."

This amendment elicited a spirited discussion, but passed the House[3] by a very close vote. The bill on going to the Senate was amended by striking out[4] the restriction clause, and concurred in[5]; but the House adhering to its amendment, it was lost.

The same Congress organized the Territory of Arkansas from the southern part of Missouri, agreeable to a petition from the inhabitants thereof. Attempts were made to apply the slavery restriction to it, but failed, and it was accordingly organized without any reference to slavery.

A glance at the map will reveal the magnitude of this question which affected the two contending parties. It was not merely whether Missouri should be a slave or a free State; but whether the vast expanse of territory extending westward from Missouri across the broad prairies, over the Rocky Mountains, to the Pacific—comprising about one-fourth the area of the United States—should be consecrated to Slave, or Free, labor. This is the way the question was viewed at that time; it was thought that the fate of Missouri would decide that of the territory west and south of it, which then belonged to, or would be acquired afterwards by, the United States.

During the following summer, the interim between the two Congresses, the subject of slavery restriction was agitated all over the country. Public meetings were held and speeches made; conventions were called and resolutions passed in accordance with their sentiments; the whole country was can-

(3) February 13, 1819. (4) February 26. (5) March 2.

vassed by public speakers and flooded with pamphleteers; the press opened its battery and kept up a continual fire; thus the country was agitated until it was fairly ablaze with excitement.

The North opposed the permanent establishment of slavery, from moral and political considerations. It claimed to be actuated by the spirit of the founders of the Republic, who sought by all legislative means to prevent the growth of slavery. It was plain, however, that whatever party obtained Missouri, obtained the balance of power, and there is no doubt that the North sought to obtain it on this account, as well as from other considerations. But such is the construction which mankind put upon the motives of an action, that where there may be an unworthy one, no matter how many good ones, they generally attribute it to the former. The South put, therefore, the very worst interpretation upon the actions of the North, as aiming at political supremacy by an unjust and oppressive legislation.

The position of the anti-restrictionists was a very singular one, if not inconsistent. They bewailed in most eloquent lamentations over the wrongs which slavery inflicted upon the slaves, country and people; conceded the right and duty of Congress to prohibit it from the territories, and to provide, in every constitutional way, for its removal; but now that they had the power to prevent its extension, and, consequently, its growth, they refused to exercise it. But they fought the battle under the banner of State Rights, State Sovereignty, Liberty, and the Right of the people to frame their own institutions, as opposed to Usurpation and Oppression on the part of Congress.

Fresh from the heat of popular discussion, with feelings all aglow with excitement, the members of the XVIth Congress convened.[6] Memorials from the people and Legislature of Missouri bearing evidence of an angry feeling, caused by

(6) December 16, 1819.

their former rejection, were soon presented, and in the House referred[7] to a select committee; in the Senate,[8] to the Judiciary. The committee in the House reported,[9] through its chairman, Mr. Scott, delegate from Missouri, a bill authorizing that territory to form a State constitution and government, without any prohibition of slavery. On motion of Mr. Taylor, of New York, a committee was appointed to inquire into the expediency of prohibiting slavery in all territory west of the Mississippi, of which he was made chairman. But the committee being unable to agree among themselves, in a few days, at the request of the chairman, was discharged.[10] On January 26, 1820, Mr. Taylor proposed an amendment to the Missouri bill, the restrictive provisions of which are as follows:

"And shall ordain and establish that there shall be neither slavery nor involuntary servitude, otherwise than in the punishment of crimes, whereof the party shall have been duly convicted. *And it is provided, also,* That the said provision shall not be construed to alter the condition or civil rights of any person now held to service or labor in said territory."

An animated discussion immediately ensued, which continued, with scarcely any interruption, for twenty-three days.

In the meantime, the bill admitting Maine into the Union, which had passed[11] the House, had a heavy burden thrown upon it in the Senate. The skill and tactics of slavery propagandists were here most strikingly displayed. The committee to whom the bill had been referred recommended[12] its passage, with several amendments, the most important of which was the Missouri bill without restriction. The object was, of course, to enable the latter bill to ride through the House upon that of the former. Strong efforts were made in the Senate to throw it off, or apply to it the restrictive clause, which occasioned a long and protracted discussion.

Both Houses were now intently engaged in stormy debate. Never before, nor since, was there ever such a display, in the

(7) December 8. (8) December 9. (9) December 14. (10) December 28. (11) January 3, 1820. (12) January 6.

halls of Congress, of forensic skill and impassioned eloquence. It was a sublime occasion for the orator. The excited nation were the anxious spectators; the Legislatures of the different States the abettors.[13] The subject was one calculated to call forth no buncombe speech-making; but earnest, heart-warmed sentiments. It was legislating, not for a day, nor a year, upon one section of the country and a few people; but for centuries, over one-fourth of the domain of the United States. In it humanity plead her claim, and the country asked for deliverance from a curse. On the other hand, the rights of a free people were invaded, and Oppression frowned upon them, ready to trample them beneath her iron heel. The beams of sovereignty in a State were to be blotted out, and its greatness and glory abased. Many of the speakers rose to the sublimity of the occasion, and even their opponents melted to tears before their persuasive pleadings. Others descended as far below it, and their speeches are marked by sectional prejudice, vanity and animosity. Both parties were about equally matched in argument, skill and eloquence.

On the part of the Restrictionists it was contended that the founders of our Republic lamented the existence of slavery, as a "great evil," which they could not remove, but hoped, by a wise legislation, that it would ultimately disappear; that they had themselves set the example by the famous ordinance of 1787, which was intended to cover all the territory of the United States, and now, at least, its precedent should have weight; to all of which the Anti-restrictionists fully conceded, but denied that the precedent spoken of should have any weight, as that was done under the Confederacy; and, furthermore, it was unconstitutional, because done after the cession made by Virginia, which declared that the States formed from that territory should be admitted into Union on the footing of the original thirteen States. For constitutional right the Restrictionists point to

(13) Memorials had been received in Congress from the different States, both for and against restriction.

the clause in that sacred document which says, "New States may be admitted by Congress into the Union;" from which they argue that Congress has the right to refuse a State admittance into the Union, and to prescribe the conditions of admission. To which it is replied that the powers of Congress are specified, and those not plainly mentioned in the Constitution are reserved to the States or people; and hence, Congress can gather no powers from inference. They are then directed to another clause in the Constitution, which says that "Congress shall have power to dispose of and make all needful rules and regulations respecting the territories;" to which a reply is given that Missouri is not to be regarded as an open, wild and uninhabited territory but a populous State, with sovereign powers, asking admission into the Union according to the original compact between the States. The clause relating to the powers of Congress to prevent the migration and importation of slaves, in which the term migration is used, the Restrictionists declare, refers to the passage of slaves form States to States, or from States to Territories; but the opposite party demostrate that it refers entirely to the introduction of slaves from abroad. The Restrictionists show that the practice of Congress has been to exact conditions from States before admission into the Union, and point to Illinois, Ohio, Indiana and Louisiana; to which their opponents reply that all such exactions were usurpations, and hence not binding, or entitled to consideration as precedents. The treaty between France and the United States would be adduced by the Anti-restrictionists with an air of triumph, which provided that the inhabitants of Louisiana should be protected in the possession of their property, and that it would be a breach of faith for the United States to emancipate their slaves; to which it is replied that the restriction does not affect the relation of master and slave there now, but merely provides against the introduction of slaves from abroad. It is further contended that this treaty provides that the people of said territory "shall be incorporated into the Union as soon as possible, and admitted to all the rights, advantages and immunities of citizens; to which it is replied that they have already been admitted to all the privileges of citizens in the Union, but admitting a State into the Union formed from that territory was a different thing, for which the treaty made no provision. It is argued that by extending slavery west, the condition of both master and slave would be improved; but it is replied that by extension the growth of slavery is only accelerated, that it is a curse, and the more it is extended, the more country it afflicts. It was asserted that these conditions would be degrading and humiliating to the sovereign State of Missouri; but it is retorted that other States have complied with them and not felt in the least degraded, but were proud of their positions among the sister States, and were unequaled in prosperity and promise.

Such was the way that some of the arguments were put and answered. I will now give a few extracts from speeches although their severance from the closely wrought connection will not show them in their real light. Speaking of the treaty by which Louisiana was obtained and which, it had been argued, would compel Congress to admit Missouri without restriction, Mr. Otis, of Massachusetts, says:

"Still, if in reality our faith, by treaty, was thus plighted, though he should deem the acquisition of the whole territory a vital misfortune, and should think it would have been better for us if the Mississippi was an eternal torrent of burning lava, impassible as the lake which separates the evil from the good, and the regions beyond destined forever to be covered with brakes and jungles, and the impenetrable haunts of the wolf and the panther; yet, he would not advocate a breach of public faith, but he should think it the duty of Congress to recommend a new negotiation with the present beneficent monarch of France, to the end of obtaining his release from the provisions of a treaty so fatal to our best interests."

Here is Mr. Barbour's (of Virginia) apology for the change of sentiment from that which existed at the time of the formation of our Government:

"We are asked why has Virginia changed her policy relative to slavery? That the sentiments of our most distinguished men thirty years past entirely correspond with the course which the friends of restriction now advocate; that Mr. Jefferson has delineated a gloomy picture of the baneful effects of slavery; that the Virginia delegation, one of whom was the late President of the United States, voted for the restriction on the north-western territory.—When it is recollected that the notes of Mr. Jefferson were written during the progress of the Revolution, the mind operated upon its incidents as novel as stupendous, it is no matter of surprise, that the writer who was performing so distinguished a part, should have imbibed a large share of that enthusiasm which such an occasion was so well calculated to produce. With the eye of benevolence surveying the condition of mankind, and a holy zeal for the amelioration of their condition, he gave vent to his feelings in the effusion to which our minds have been called. It is palpable these are the illusions of fancy."

Mr. Scott closed his remarks by warning gentlemen from the North that "they were sowing the seeds of discord in the Union;" that "they were signing, sealing and delivering their own death-warrant;" that "the weapon they were unjustly wielding was a two-edged sword;" that "he considered the question big with the fate of Cæsar, and of Rome." Mr. Walker, of Georgia, said that "he must be badly acquainted with the signs of the times who does not perceive a storm portending, and callous to all the better feelings of our nature who does not dread the bursting of that storm." Mr. Cobb, of the same State, declares that "if they (Restrictionists) persist the Union will be dissolved;" that "they were kindling a fire which all the waters of the ocean cannot put out, which seas of blood can only extinguish." Mr. Colston, of Virginia, accuses Mr. Livermore, of New Hampshire, "of speaking to the galleries, and by his language, endeavoring to excite a servile war," and ended by saying that "he was no better than Arbuthnot, or Ambrister, and deserved no better fate." Mr. Jones rings in the chorus, "although Missouri be an infant, she reposes on the laps of eleven mothers, that if even Missouri succumbs to this humiliating condition, her name will be written in characters of blood."

On the 18th of February, the Missouri bill, which had been appended to the Maine bill was passed in the Senate with Mr. Thomas' amendment prohibiting slavery from the territories north of 36°-30° north latitude, except that included in the aforesaid State. It then passed to the House, which refusing to concur in the amendments on the 1st of March passed the Missouri bill with the restrictive clause of Mr. Taylor. This passed in the Senate by striking out the amendment of the House and inserting that of Mr. Thomas.

In the meantime a committee of conference had been appointed which now reports, recommending to the Senate to recede from its amendment of the Maine bill, and to the House to concur in the amendment of the Senate to the Missouri bill. The House thereupon accepted the amendment of the Senate by 90 yeas and 87 nays. This was the *Missouri Compromise.* It was decidedly a Southern measure, originated by a man who had opposed restriction, and only received 14 votes from northern men, and all the votes of the South.

Some of those from the North who voted for it did so to quiet the agitation and to avert what they feared would be the consequence—the disruption of the Government—which had been so frequently threatened in debate.

The following is Mr. Thomas' amendment, generally called the Missouri Compromise:

"*And be it further enacted,* That in all that Territory ceded by France to the United States under the name of Louisiana, which lies north of thirty-six degrees thirty minutes north latitude, excepting only such part thereof as is included within the limits of the State contemplated by this act, slavery and involuntary servitude, otherwise than in the punishment of crime, whereof the party shall have been duly convicted, shall be and is hereby forever prohibited; *Provided always,* That any person escaping into the same, from whom labor or service is lawfully claimed in any State or Territory of the United States, such fugitive may be lawfully taken and conveyed to the person claiming his or her labor or service as aforesaid."

On the authority thus obtained the people of Missouri proceeded the following summer to frame a constitution and organize a State government, and at the meeting of the next Congress this State presented herself in her constitutional robe for admission into the Union. The Senate after some debate passed a resolution admitting her; but the House on account of the following clause refused her admission:

"It shall be the duty of the General Assembly, as soon as may be, to pass such laws as may be necessary to prevent free negroes and mulattoes from coming to, or settling in, this State, under any pretext whatever."

There was also a clause forbidding the General Assembly from emancipating slaves without the consent of their owners All of these, together with the general spirit of the Constitution, were regarded as a menace and a strike at those who favored restriction. The clause given above was plainly unconstitutional. The Constitution of the United States ordains that "the citizens of each State shall be entitled to all the privileges and immunities of the citizens of the several States;" and negroes and mulattoes in some States are citizens. The excitement ran very high in Congress and seemed to threaten more danger than at any previous time; but the difficulty was finally adjusted by passing a bill to admit Missouri whenever she should legitimately expunge the above odious clause.

This condition Missouri soon complied with and her admission into the Union was declared by a proclamation of the President.

CHAPTER V.

TRIUMPH OF SLAVERY IN THE ANNEXATION OF TEXAS.

The boundaries of Louisiana were always vague and uncertain, and the treaty by which the United States acquired it left them still indefinite. The consequence was, as might have been expected, difficulties soon arose with Spain in regard to the eastern and western boundaries of this province. The French always alleged that Louisiana extended to the Rio Grande; whereas the Spaniards, with an equal show of reason, contended that it did not extend quite to the Sabine. According to the provisions of the treaty of St. Ildefonso, Spain ceded to France " the province with the same extent it now has in the hands of Spain, and that it had when France possessed it, and such as it should be after other treaties entered into between Spain and other States." By the treaty of Paris, France ceded to the United States all the right and title she had thus acquired to Louisiana, leaving the question of boundaries to be settled with Spain.

Thus matters remained *in statu quo*, although Spain continued to hold both Floridas and claimed the Sabine as the western boundary of Louisiana, until 1819, when a treaty was effected between the two nations, after a protracted correspondence and negotiation. Through this treaty the United States acquired undisputed possession of all the territory west of the Mississippi by renouncing her claim to Texas.

This was a Southern move, and it was difficult at first to

understand the motive which actuated it. Why slavery should be willing to give away such a beautiful and extensive country as Texas when she could just as easily have retained it and the Floridas too, was a query which but few in the North could solve. But it was a political scheme of the South, whereby she might secure the co-operation of the North in the election of a pro-slavery President, The agitation of the Missouri question had so united the North against slavery extension in the south-west that the slavery propagandists well knew, if this was made an issue in the Presidential election, they would be defeated. So in order to keep in power, they rid themselves of this troublesome question by giving away Texas, knowing that the could get it again whenever they wanted it.

In the meantime Mexico had established her independence, which was recognized by the United States, and consequently Texas passed under her dominion.

Soon afterwards a little colony was established in Texas at Austin, by a few restless adventurers and desperadoes from the United States. In 1827 and 1829 attempts were made on the part of our government to purchase Texas of Mexico, but without success. The people of this little colony considerably increased by emigrants from the United States, under the leadership of the notorious Sam Houston, who, it is thought, was sent there by the Southrons, for that purpose, in 1833 framed a State Constitution and in three years afterwards declared their independence. War necessarily ensued; Houston was made commander by the colony of its forces; and after two victorious battles, Texas asks to be annexed to the United States. But on account of our friendly relations with Mexico, the request could not, with any show of consistency, be granted until the independence of that province should be more fully established. The slave States, therefore, mustered aid and sympathy for the few struggling freemen (?) in this little Republic. Money, men and arms with provisions and ammunition, were sent to them by the friends of slavery.

Texas thus maintained her independence until 1845, when she was annexed to the United States upon the following provision among others: "*Third*, New States of convenient size, not exceeding four in number, in addition to the said State of Texas, and having sufficient population, may hereafter, by the consent of said State, be formed out of the territory thereof, which shall be entitled to admission under the provisions of the Federal Constitution; and such States as may be formed out of that portion of said territory lying south of thirty-six degrees thirty minutes north latitude, commonly known as the Missouri Compromise line, shall be admitted into the Union with or without slavery, as the people of each State asking admission may desire. And in such State or States as shall be formed out of said territory north of said Missouri Compromise line, slavery or involuntary servitude (except for crime), shall be prohibited." (A. S. Papers.)

It must not be supposed that this bill of annexation was passed without any opposition, thus introducing slavery into, and fastening it upon, so vast a region of country. On the other hand, its passage was violently contested, and several attempts were made to either divide the territory between slave and free labor, or prohibit the former altogether. But the influence of the Administration, the sanctity with which the Missouri Compromise line was held by the North, and the fear that Texas would form an alliance with some European power that would endanger our Union, prevailed.—The most injurious feature connected with this bill is that it secured the recognition of Congress to the extension of the territory of Texas from the mouth of the Rio Grande to its source—near a thousand miles beyond the legitimate boundary of that province. Thus slavery was virtually extended over this broad domain where it had been prohibited by the laws of Mexico twenty years before. Thus was the strength and resources of our glorious government which our fathers had consecrated to liberty and justice, made the efficient means for the extension of the wrongs and pollutions of human slavery over a vast expanse of unsullied territory. War with Mexico followed the annexation, consuming a hundred million of the nation's wealth, and the lives of thousands of her brave sons. All for what? For the extension of human slavery!

Immediately after the war began, the Mexicans having suffered a severe defeat, and the President thinking that their feeble and divided republic could now begin to realize her utter inability to cope with the arms of the United States, presumed that she would rather accept a monied overture for Texas than run the chances of losing it by war. The President, Mr. Polk, therefore represents this matter to Congress, asking that a considerable sum be placed at his disposal to effect this object, at the same time stating that he thought he could not only secure the territory this side of the Rio Grande, but also a vast scope of country beyond it. A bill was accordingly drawn up, agreeable to his request, and had for a time every indication of success.

But the question arose among those who were opposed to the extension of slavery what should be the condition of this territory as to Free or Slave labor. They knew heretofore that slavery had laid claim to all the territory of the United States on the plea of pre-occupancy; but will slavery covet the soil where it never existed and where the laws of the country from which it was obtained forbid it? Many of the northern democrats who had before been disposed to be tolerant towards slavery, now began to think that they had reached the utmost limits of a virtuous forbearance. An amendment was therefore prepared and offered by Mr. Wilmot to the following effect:

"*Provided*, That as an express and fundamental condition to the acquisition of any territory from the Republic of Mexico by the United States, by virtue of any treaty that may be negotiated between them, and to the use by the execution of the monies herein appropriated, neither slavery nor involuntary servitude shall ever exist in any part of said territory, except for crime, whereof the party shall be duly convicted."

With this amendment, commonly known as the Wilmot Proviso, the bill passed the House, but was lost in the Senate on account of the Proviso. Thus the President was left without any means to negotiate a treaty by which much suffering and many thousand precious lives might have been spared. But this would have thwarted the very design which had occasioned the war—the acquisition of more territory for slavery.

It was about this time that the doctrine of Popular Sovereignty was advanced. First conceived in the brain of Calhoun, it was first enunciated by General Cass when about to be used by the Democratic party as a candidate for the Presidency. The great argument, prior possession, against prohibiting slavery from the territories heretofore urged, had now failed, for the condition of territory was exactly reversed from what it had been formerly. This territory had never been polluted by slavery. But, to meet the exigency of the situation, a new dogma is brought forward that Congress has no right to prevent the citizens of the United States from taking with them their property (slaves) into the territories and determining there their local institutions for themselves. This doctrine, so new and strange to the Democratic party, was not popular at first, for their Baltimore convention which nominated Cass for President, voted it out of their platform by an overwhelming majority.

After the peace with Mexico an attempt was made in the 30th Congress to organize the territories acquired from this Power and submit the question of slavery to the adjudication of the Supreme Court, its pulse having been previously felt upon the constitutionality of Popular Sovereignty. This bill passed the Senate, but was killed in the House by a motion of Alexander H. Stephens, of Georgia. Various attempts were made in the 29th and 30th Congresses to organize the territories of California and New Mexico, both for and against slavery, but all were unsuccessful.

At the first session of Congress in 1850 efforts for organizing these territories were resumed. The doctrine of Popular Sovereignty (though not by that name) was forcibly announced by such spirits as Jefferson Davis, W. L. Yancy and J. M. Mason, and the Missouri Compromise was held up as a sacred compact between the Restrictionists and Anti-Restrictionists in the division of territory; whereas it was framed near thirty years before the United States had acquired this territory, and could relate only to the partition of that of the Louisiana purchase. After considerable debate and the defeat of several bills for the organization of the territory of New Mexico and the admission of California into the Union, whose people had framed a Constitution and presented herself for this purpose, the whole subject was referred to a Committee of Thirteen, of which Mr. Clay was constituted chairman. The report of this committee formed the basis of a Compromise between the two contending parties, in the following words:

"1. The admission of any new State or States formed out of Texas to be postponed until they shall hereafter present themselves to be received into the Union, when it shall be the duty of Congress fairly and faithfully to execute the compact with Texas, by admitting such State or States.

"2. The admission forthwith of California into the Union, with the boundaries which she has proposed.

"3. The establishment of Territorial Governments, without the Wilmot Proviso, for New Mexico and Utah, embracing all the territory recently acquired from Mexico, not contained in the boundaries of California.

"4. The combination of these two last measures in the same bill.

"5. The establishment of the western and northern boundaries of Texas, and the exclusion from her jurisdiction of all New Mexico, with the grant to Texas of a pecuniary equivalent; and the section for that purpose to be incorporated in the bill admitting California, and establishing Territorial Governments for Utah and New Mexico.

"6. More effectual enactments of law to secure the prompt delivery of persons bound to service or labor in one State, under the laws thereof, who escape into another State; and

"7. Abstaining from abolishing slavery, but, under a heavy penalty, prohibiting the slave-trade, in the District of Columbia."

The "pecuniary equivalent" spoken of in this report to be given to Texas for her claim on the Territory of New Mexico, was rendered by the House and concurred in by the Senate, $10,000,000. And, yet, Texas never had the least shadow of a claim on said Territory. It was first obtained from Mexico by the arms of the United States and afterwards paid for by her money. Slavery gained by this Compromise not only the vast region of Texas and ten million dollars, but the continuance of its existence in the District of Columbia, more stringent laws for slave-catching, the territories of New Mexico and Utah opened to its grasp by the newly ordained doctrine of Popular Sovereignty, and a basis by which to uproot the Sacred Compromise of 1820. What a monstrous Compromise! And, yet, the North made these reluctant concessions, to still agitation, to escape the threat of disunion by satisfying the craving demands of the South.

CHAPTER VI.

KANSAS-NEBRASKA ACT—A SLAVERY TRIUMPH.

By the compromise measure of 1820 slavery was *forever* prohibited north of thirty-six degrees thirty minutes north latitude from the territory of the Louisiana purchase, except that portion included in the State of Missouri. As this Compromise was a Southern movement and maintained by Southern votes, it would seem that they were most fairly and solemnly bound to this compact. The opponents of slavery extension were bitterly opposed to the Compromise, because it yielded up the extensive domain of Missouri to slavery; whereas the spirit and teachings of our Government demanded an inhibition of this curse; but after it was legitimately approved of by the legislative councils of the nation, they regarded it with that veneration which is due to a law of the land.

The first infraction of this Compromise occurred in 1836 when a triangular piece of territory, lying between the then existing boundary of the State of Missouri and the Missouri River, was annexed to the former. The original western boundary of Missouri was a line drawn due north and south from the point where the Kansas River enters the Missouri. This was an exceedingly fertile tract of country, from which was formed seven counties of largest size and capable of sustaining the densest population, which numbered in 1860, 70,505 souls. This work was effected so quickly and dextrously by Colonel Benton that it attracted little attention at the time.

Petitions were received at the first session of the thirty-second Congress (1851-2) for organizing the territory west of Missouri, but no action was taken upon them. At the next session Mr. Willard P. Hall, of Missouri, introduced a bill[1] in the House to organize the same territory, together with that west of Iowa, under the name of *Platte*, which was referred to the Committee on Territories. From this Committee a report was presented[2] organizing the same territory under the name of Nebraska. This, on going to the Committee of the Whole, encountered a strong Southern opposition and was reported[3] back to the House with a recommendation for its rejection. After the failure of a motion to lay it on the table, the bill passed by 98 yeas to 43 nays. On arriving[4] in the Senate it was referred to the Committee on Territories, of which Mr. Stephen A. Douglas was chairman. From this committee it was reported without amendment, but was never acted upon though several unsuccessful efforts were made to have it taken up in the latter days of the session. Thus the Southern members stoutly refused to organize this territory at that time, which, in the next Congress, was an object that they earnestly sought to accomplish. But it is a note-worthy fact that the existence and validity of the Missouri Compromise had not, as yet, been questioned, and no one had discovered that the legislation of 1850 had superceded that of 1820; the only objection urged being that it would infringe upon the rights of the Indians to organize this territory.

In the thirty-third Congress (1853-4), agreeable to a previous notice, Mr. Dodge, of Iowa, introduced[5] a bill into the Senate to organize the Territory of Nebraska without any reference to slavery, which, after being read twice, was referred to the Committee on Territories, from which it was reported back by the chairman, Mr. Douglas, with various amendments. In the report of Mr. Douglas, which accompanied the bill, although he raised the question as to the con-

(1) Dec. 2, 1852. (2) Feb. 2, 1853. (3) Feb. 10. (4) Feb. 11. (5) Dec. 14. 1853.

stitutionality of the Missouri Compromise, he refrained from passing judgment upon it himself, and no where intimated that the legislation of 1850 had rendered it inoperative. The seat of government was located at Fort Leavenworth, and "all questions pertaining to slavery in the Territories and new States formed therefrom," it suggested that agreeable with the legislation of 1850, should be left to the decision of the people residing therein, through their appropriate representatives. The bill, with the report and amendments, was ordered to be printed.

Mr. Dixon gave notice[6] that when the bill should come up for consideration he would offer an amendment to the following effect:

"That as much of the 8th section of 'An act approved March 6, 1820, entitled 'An act to authorize the people of Missouri Territory to form a constitution and a State government and for the admission of such a State into the Union on an equal footing with the original States, and to prohibit slavery in certain Territories' as declares in all that territory ceded by France to the United States, under the name of Louisiana, which lies north of thirty-six degrees thirty minutes north latitude, slavery and involuntary servitude otherwise than in the punishment of crime, whereof the party shall have been duly convicted, is forever prohibited,' shall not be so construed as to apply to the territory contemplated by this act, or to any Territory of the United States, but that the citizens of the several States and Territories shall be at liberty to take and hold their slaves within any of the Territories of the United States, or of the States to be formed therefrom, as if the said act, entitled as aforesaid and approved as aforesaid, had never been passed."

This first stroke at the sacred Compromise which had quieted the storm of 1820, and which had been regarded for thirty-four years as lasting as time, fell like a thunder bolt upon the Senate and the nation. The blast of strife was thus sounded by the expiring breath of Plighted Faith. Slavery

(6) January 16, 1855.

no longer seeks to disguise its foulness, or apologize for its existence; but vaunteth itself as an institution of our fathers, wholesome to society, and sanctioned by religion. Disdaining all legislative restrictions and trampling under foot all compromises whereby it has hitherto secured tolerance, it arrogates to itself the prerogatives of a full grown monster and dictates to the nation its demands.

Even the ambitious Stephen A. Douglas was startled at the unexpected report. He had congratulated himself that he had rendered such signal service to the South by questioning the validity of the Missouri Compromise and virtually removing its interdiction to slavery that it could only be rewarded by placing him in his long sought for position—the Presidency. Ambition, though baffled and apparently defeated, never despairs, but proceeds to consult the unprincipled Oracle of Success. Mr. Douglas resolves to go so far beyond the one who thus outbid him, that the spoils of his achievements shall be all that the insatiable cravings of slavery can demand. He therefore draws up a bill almost entirely unlike any of the preceding ones. Instead of organizing one, he now proposes to organize two Territories, the first to include that Territory lying between Missouri and the Rocky Mountains, north of thirty-seven degrees north latitude, to be called Kansas; the second, the remaining portion of what was contemplated by the former bills, called by the name of Nebraska. He moved the southern boundary up to thirty-seven degrees north latitude in order that it might coincide with the boundary between the Osages and Cherokees. The question of slavery was left to be decided by the people of said Territories through their appropriate representatives. The section providing for electing a Delegate is amended by adding to the words "that the Constitution and all the laws of the United States which are not locally inapplicable shall have the same force and effect within the said Territory as elsewhere in the United States," the following:

"Except the 8th section of the act preparatory to the admission of Missouri, approved March 6, 1820, which was superceded by the legislation of 1850, commonly called the Compromise Measure, and is declared inoperative.

The bill thus reported by Mr. Douglas was debated at length in the Senate The arguments employed by the disputants were the same as those employed in the similar discussion of 1820 with two additional ones. The *Restrictionists* now had besides all their other arguments, the Missouri Compromise, *forever* prohibiting slavery from the territory in question, which had been regarded as sacred for more than a score and a half of years. The *Anti-Restrictionists* had the famous doctrine of Squatter Sovereignty, which, claiming for itself absolute orthodoxy, utterly repudiated all quondam legislation not in harmony with it, disdained precedents and overswept every logical barricade.

On the 15th of February Mr. Douglas moved that the clause, declaring that the Restriction of 1820 superceded by the legislation of 1850, be stricken out, and in lieu thereof, had inserted the clause of similar nature now found in the Ordinance. Mr. Chase then moved to have the following added:

"Under which the people of the Territories through their appropriate representatives, may if they see fit, prohibit the existence of slavery therein."

But this motion was lost by 36 nays to 10 yeas. Thus the people of these territories which had been shielded from slavery by the compromise of 1820, were not allowed by this act to exclude slavery if they wished. On motion of Mr. Badger, of North Carolina, the following amendment was added.

"*Provided*, That nothing herein shall be construed to revive or put in force any law or regulation which may have existed prior to the act of 6th of March, 1820, either protecting, establishing, abolishing or prohibiting slavery."

This motion elicited considerable discussion, many contending that it infringed upon the principles of non-intervention by Congress.

Mr. Clayton, of Delaware, attached the following provision:

"*Provided* That the right of suffrage and of holding office shall be exercised only by citizens of the United States."

Mr. Chase then proposed to strike out the second section and insert a provision for dividing the territory into election precincts, appointing places of election, etc., so that the people could choose their own Governor and Legislators. But the motion was defeated by 30 nays to 10 yeas.

The bill on coming from the Committee of the Whole was concurred in[1] by the Senate.

In the House Mr. Richardson, of Illinois, Chairman of the Committee on Territories, reported a bill[2] for organizing Nebraska and Kansas Territories, similar to that reported in the Senate by Mr. Douglas.

This bill was referred to the Committee of the Whole on the state of the Union, which was regarded as equivalent to its rejection. No further action was taken upon it until the 8th of May, when other bills on the calendar were laid aside and it taken up; whereupon Mr. Richardson offered the Senate bill as a substitute. An effort was made on the 11th to have the debate upon the subject close on the following day at 12 o'clock M., which occasioned a violent and protracted session of thirty-six hours. It was afterwards fixed that the debate should close on the 20th of May. During the discussion which followed, various attempts were made to insert a clause in the bill giving to the people of the territory the right to prohibit slavery therein through their appropriate representatives if they saw fit. On the 22nd of May, Mr. Stephens, of Georgia, made a skillful parliamentary move-

---

1, March 3. 2 Jan, 31.

ment by which the bill was quickly forced through. He moved that the enacting words of the bill be stricken out, which has precedence of all motions to amend, and is regarded as equivalent to the rejection of a measure. The vote upon this motion was immediately pressed, which resulted in 103 ayes and 22 noes; many of its opponents refusing to vote. Thereupon the Committe arose and reported its action to the House which refused to concur in the amendment, striking out the enacting clause. Mr. Richardson then moved an amendment by which all after the enacting clause was stricken out and in lieu thereof introduced the Senate bill (except Mr. Clayton's amendment) and demanded the previous question. The amendment was accordingly passed; the bill engrossed, read a third time and adopted by 113 yeas to 100 nays. The Congressional Globe says:

"[The announcement of the vote was received with prolonged clapping of hands, both in the House ad Galleries and cries .of "Order! Order!"]

" The Speaker—Unless order is preserved, the Chair will order the galleries to be cleared."

"Mr. Stuart of Michigan—(in his seat), The trouble is not in the galleries."

This bill passed the House as an original bill of that body, and was sent to the Senate for concurrence. An unsuccessful attempt was now made to reinsert Mr. Clayton's amendment excluding foreigners from certain civil privileges. In the course of the debate which ensued Senator Atchison, of Missouri, said:

"Mr. President, I voted for the amendment of the Senate bill proposed by the Senator from Delaware, but I must say now that I concur with the Senator from Georgia. I have not, however, changed my opinion, which I entertained then, that none but American citizens, native-born or naturalized, should be entitled to the right of suffrage or hold office either in the States or Territories of this country. But, Sir, there is a higher principle involved in this measure. There is no constitutional question in my opinion involved in voting either for or against this amendment. It is a mere question of policy and that question of policy I am willing to yield for the sake of a higher principle entertained in this bill. Sir, I would vote for this bill, although there might be not only one, but one thousand obnoxious principles contained in it. I would vote for it because it blots out that infamous,—yes, sir, I think it a proper term to use—that infamous restriction passed by the Congress of 1820, commonly called the Missouri Compromise, passed when the State which I now in part have the honor to represent, asked admission into the Union of these States, and it was made a condition, an infamous condition, that slavery should be excluded from all the territory acquired from France, then called Louisiana, north of 36° 30′ north latitude. Yes, Sir, if this bill contained one thousand obnoxious priniples, with the repeal of that infamous 'Compromise,' as it is called, I should vote for it. When this is done we shall have achieved what, after thirty years of struggle,.has only been consummated at this session."

This exhibits the feeling with which slavery propagandists regarded the Missouri Compromise—a restriction which they had solemnly and voluntarily applied to slavery themselves in order that they might gain other ends. But after they had secured all the advantages of these concessions on the part of of Free Labor, they break down the barrier of plighted faith and demand all that they had of their own accord surrendered up.

The bill which passed the Senate on the 25th and received the signature of the President on the 30th of May, 1854, will be found in the following chapter:

It is very evident that the scheme of organizing two terriries instead of one, was designed to keep up the balance of power between the northern and southern States. The latter who saw that no reasonable objection could be interposed sooner or later against the organization of Nebraska, which must necessarily be a free Territory, determined, in order to preserve the equilibrium of power, to divide it into two territories, one of which would, as necessarily, by the repeal of the Missouri Compromise, come into the Union as a Slave State. That this was the real design and understanding of those who originated and supported the Nebraska-Kansas Bill is fully shown by what followed.

CHAPTER VII.

AN ACT TO ORGANIZE THE TERRITORY OF KANSAS.

SECTION 19. *And be it further enacted,* That all that part of the territory of the United States included within the following limits, except such portions thereof as are hereinafter expressly exempted from the operations of this act, to wit: beginning at a point on the western boundary of the State of Missouri, where the thirty-seventh parallel of north latitude crosses the same; thence west on said parallel to the eastern boundary of New Mexico; thence north on said boundary to latitude thirty-eight; thence following said boundary westward to the east boundary of the Territory of Utah, on the summit of the Rocky Mountains; thence northward on said summit to the fortieth parallel of latitude; thence east on said parallel to the western boundary of the State of Missouri; thence south with the western boundary of said State, to the place of beginning, be, and the same is hereby created into a temporary government by the name of the Territory of Kansas, and when admitted as a State or States, the said Territory, or any portion of the same, shall be received into the Union with or without slavery, as their constitution may prescribe at the time of their admission; *Provided,* That nothing in this act contained, shall be construed to inhibit the government of the United States from dividing said Territory into two or more Territories, in such manner and at such times as Congress shall deem convenient and proper, or from attaching any portion of said Territory to any other State or Territory of the United States; *Provided further*, That nothing in this act contained shall be construed to impair the rights of person or property now pertaining to the Indians in said Territory, so long as such rights shall remain unextinguished by treaty between the United States and such Indians, or to include any territory which by treaty with any Indian tribe is not, without the consent of said tribe, to be included within the territorial limits or jurisdiction of any State or Territory; but all such territory shall be excepted out of the boundaries, and constitute no part of the Territory of Kansas, until said tribe shall signify their assent to the President of the United States to be included within the said Territory of Kansas, or to affect the authority of the government of the United States to make any regulation respecting such Indians, their lands, property, or other rights, by treaty, law, or otherwise, which it would have been competent to the government to make if this act had never passed.

Sec. 20. *And be it further enacted*, That the executive power and authority in and over said Territory of Kansas, shall be vested in a Governor, who shall hold his office for four years, and until his successor shall be appointed and qualified, unless sooner removed by the President of the United States. The Governor shall reside within said Territory, and shall be commander-in-chief of the Militia thereof. He may grant pardons and respites for offenses against the laws of said Territory, and reprieves for offenses against the laws of the United States, until the decision of the President can be made known thereon; he shall commission all officers who shall be appointed to office under the laws of said Territory, and shall take care that the laws be faithfully executed.

Sec. 21. *And be it further enacted*, That there shall be a Secretary of said Territory, who shall reside therein, and hold his office for five years, unless sooner removed by the

President of the United States; he shall record and preserve all the laws and proceedings of the Legislative Assembly hereinafter constituted, and all the acts and proceedings of the Governor in his executive department; he shall transmit one copy of the laws and journals of the Legislative Assembly, within thirty days after the end of each session, and one copy of the executive proceedings and official correspondence semi-annually, on the first days of January and July in each year, to the President of the United States; and two copies of the laws to the President of the Senate and to the Speaker of the House of Representatives, to be deposited in the libraries of Congress; and in case of the death, removal, resignation or absence of the Governor from the Territory, the Secretary shall be, and is hereby authorized and required, to execute and perform all the powers and duties of the Governor during such vacancy or absence, or until another Governor shall be duly appointed and qualified to fill such vacancy.

SEC. 22. *And be it further enacted,* That the legislative power and authority of said Territory shall be vested in the Governor and a Legislative Assembly. The Legislative Assembly shall consist of a Council and House of Representatives. The Council shall consist of thirteen members, having the qualifications of voters, as hereinafter prescribed, whose term of service shall continue two years. The House of Representatives shall, at its first session, consist of twenty-six members, possessing the same qualifications as prescribed for members of the Council, and whose term of service shall continue one year. The number of representatives may be increased by the Legislative Assembly, from time to time, in proportion to the increase of qualified voters; *Provided,* That the whole number shall never exceed thirty-nine. An apportionment shall be made, as nearly equal as practicable, among the several counties or districts, for the election of the Council and Representatives, giving to each section of the Territory representation in the ratio of its qualified voters, as nearly as may be. And the members of the Council and House of Representatives shall reside in, and be inhabitants of, the district, or county or counties, for which they may be elected, respectively. Previous to the first election, the Governor shall cause a census, or enumeration of the inhabitants and qualified voters of the several counties and districts of the Territory, to be taken by such persons, and in such mode as the Governor shall designate and appoint; and the person so appointed shall receive a reasonable compensation therefor. And the first election shall be held at such time and places, and be conducted in such manner, both as to the persons who shall superintend such election and the returns thereof, as the Governor shall appoint and direct; and he shall, at the same time, declare the number of members of the Council and House of Representatives to which each of the counties or districts shall be entitled under this act. The persons having the highest number of legal votes in each of said council districts for members of the Council, shall be declared by the Governor to be duly elected to the Council; and the persons having the highest number of legal votes for the House of Representatives, shall be declared by the Governor to be duly elected members of said House; *Provided*, That in case two or more persons voted for shall have an equal number of votes, and in case a vacancy shall otherwise occur in either branch of the Legislative Assembly, the Governor shall order a new election; and the persons thus elected to the Legislative Assembly, shall meet at such place and on such day as the Governor shall appoint; but thereafter, the time, place and manner of holding and conducting all elections by the people, and the apportioning the representation in the several counties or districts, to the Council and House of Representatives, according to the nnmber of qualified voters, shall be prescribed by law, as well as the day of the commencement of the regular sessions of the Legislative Assembly; *Provided*, That no session, in any one year, shall exceed the term of forty days, except the first session, which may continue sixty days.

SEC. 23. *And be it further enacted*, That every free white male inhabitant above the age of twenty-one years, who shall be an actual resident of said Territory, and shall possess the qualifications hereinafter prescribed, shall be entitled to vote at the first election, and shall be eligible to any office within the said Territory; but the qualifications of voters, and of holding office, at all subsequent elections shall be such as shall be prescribed by the Legislative Assembly; *Provided*, That the right of suffrage and of holding office shall be exercised only by citizens of the United States and those who have declared on oath their intention to become such, and shall have taken an oath to support the Constitution of the United States, and the provisions of this Act; *And provided further*, That no officer, soldier, seaman or marine, or attached to troops in the service of the United States, shall be allowed to vote or hold office in said Territory, by reason of being on service therein.

SEC. 24. *And be it further enacted*, That the legislative power of the Territory shall extend to all rightful subjects of legislation, consistent with the Constitution of the United States and the provisions of this Act; but no law shall be passed interfering with the primary disposal of the soil; no tax shall be imposed upon the property of the United States; nor shall the lands or other property of non-residents be taxed higher than the lands or property of residents. Every bill which shall have passed the Council and House of Representatives of the said Territory, shall, before it becomes a law, be presented to the Governor of the Territory; if he approve, he shall sign it; but if not, he shall return it with his objections to the House in which it originated, who shall enter the objections at large on their journal, and proceed to reconsider it. If, after such reconsideration, two-thirds of that House shall agree to pass the bill, it shall be sent, together with the objections, to the other House, by which it shall likewise be reconsidered, and if approved by two-thirds of that House, it shall become a law. But in all such cases, the votes of both Houses shall be determined by yeas and nays, to be entered on the Journal of each House, respectively. If any bill shall not be returned by the Governor within three days —Sundays excepted—after it shall have been presented to him, the same shall be a law in like manner as if he had signed it, unless the Assembly, by adjournment, prevent its return, in which case it shall not be a law.

SEC. 25. *And be it further enacted*, That all township, district and county officers, not herein otherwise provided for, shall be appointed or elected, as the case may be, in such manner as shall be provided by the Governor and Legislative Assembly of the Territory of Kansas. The Governor shall nominate, and by and with the advice and consent of the Legislative Council appoint all officers not herein otherwise provided for; and in the first instance the Governor alone may appoint all said officers, who shall hold their offices until the end of the first session of the Legislative Assembly; and shall lay off the necessary districts for members of the Council and House of Representatives, and all other officers.

SEC. 26. *And be it further enacted*, That no member of the Legislative Assembly shall hold, or be appointed to any office which shall have been created, or the salary or emoluments of which shall have been increased while he was a member, during the term for which he was elected, and for one year after the expiration of such term, but this restriction shall not be applicable to members of the first Legislative Assembly; and no person holding a commission or appointment under the United States, except postmasters, shall be a member of the Legislative Assembly, or shall hold any office under the government of said Territory.

SEC. 27. *And be it further enacted*, That the judicial power of said Territory shall be vested in a Supreme Court, District Courts, Probate Courts and in Justices of the Peace.—

The Supreme Court shall consist of a Chief Justice and two Associate Justices, and two of whom shall constitute a quorum, and who shall hold a term at the seat of government of said Territory, annually, and they shall hold their offices during a period of four years, and until their successors shall be appointed and qualified. The said Territory shall be divided into three judicial districts, and a District Court shall be held in each of said districts by one of the justices of the Supreme Court, at such time and places as may be prescribed by law; and the said judges shall, after their appointments, respectively reside in the district which shall be assigned them. The jurisdiction of the several courts herein provided for, both appellate and original, and that of the Probate Courts and Justices of the Peace, shall be as limited by law; *Provided*, That Justices of the Peace shall not have jurisdiction of any matter in controversy when the title or boundaries of land may be in dispute, or where the debt or sum claimed shall exceed one hundred dollars; and the said Supreme and District Courts, respectively shall, possess chancery as well as common law jurisdiction. Each District Court or the judge thereof, shall appoint its clerk, who shall also be the register in chancery, and shall keep his office at the place where the court may be held. Writs of error, bills of exception and appeals may be allowed in all cases from the final decision of said District Courts, to the Supreme Court, under such regulations as may be prescribed by law; but in no case removed to the Supreme Court, shall trial by jury be allowed in said court. The Supreme Court or the justices thereof, shall appoint its own clerk, and every clerk shall hold his office at the pleasure of the court for which he shall have been appointed. Writs of error and appeals from the final decision of said Supreme Court shall be allowed, and may be taken to the Supreme Court of the United States, in the same manner and under the same regulations as from the Circuit Courts of the United States, where the value of the property or the amount in controversy, to be ascertained by the oath or affirmation of either party or other competent witnesses, shall exceed one thousand dollars; except that *in all cases involving title to slaves*, the said writs of error or appeals shall be allowed and decided by said Supreme Court, without regard to the value of the matter, property or title in controversy; and except, also, that a writ of error or appeal shall also be allowed to the Supreme Court of the United States, from the decision of the said Supreme Court created by this act, or any judge thereof, or of the District Courts created by this act or any judge thereof, upon any writ of habeas corpus, involving the question of personal freedom; *Provided*, That nothing herein contained shall be construed to apply to or effect the provisions of the "Act respecting fugitives from justice, and persons escaping from the services of their masters," approved Feb. twelfth, seventen hundred and ninety-three, and the "Act to amend and supplementary to said act," approved September eighteenth, eighteen hundred and fifty; and each of the said District Courts shall have and exercise the same jurisdiction, and in all cases arising under the Constitution and laws of the United States as is vested in the Circuit and District Courts of the United States; and the said Supreme Courts of the said Territory and the respective judges thereof, shall and may grant writs of habeas corpus in all cases in which the same are granted by the judges of the United States in the District of Columbia; and the first six days of every term of said courts arising under the Constitution and laws,, and writs of error and appeal in all cases shall be made to the Supreme Court of said Territory, the same as in other cases. The said clerk shall receive the same fees in all such cases which the clerks of the District Courts of Utah Territory now receive for fimilar services.

SEC. 28. *And be it further enacted*, That the provisions of the act entitled "An act respecting fugitives from justice, and persons escaping from the service of their masters," approved

Feb. twelfth, seventeen hundred and ninety-three, and the provisions ef an act entitled "An act to amend, and supplamentary to the aforesaid act," approved September eighteenth, eighteen hundred and fifty, be and the same is hereby declared to extend to and to be in full force within the limits of the said Territory of Kansas.

SEC. 29. *And be it further enacted,* That there shall be appointed an attorney for said Territory, who shall continue in office for four years, and until his successor shall be appointed and qualified, unless sooner removed by the President, and who shall receive the same fees and salary as the attorney of the United States for the present Territory of Utah. There shall also be a marshal for the Territory, appointed, who shall hold his office for four years, and until his successor shall be appointed and qualified, unless sooner removed by the President, and who shall execute all processes issuing from the said courts when exercising their jurisdiction as circuit and district courts of the United States; he shall perform the duties, be subject to the same regulations and penalties, and be entitled to the same fees as the marshal of the district court of the United States for the present Territory of Utah, and shall, in addition, be paid two hundred dollars annually, as a compensation for extra services.

SEC. 30. *And be it further enacted,* That the Governor, Secretary, Chief Justice and Associate Justices, Attorney and Marshal, shall be nominated, and by and with the advice and consent of the Senate, appointed by the President of the United States. The Governor and Secretary to be appointed as aforesaid, shall, before they act as such, respectively take an oath or affirmation before the District Judge or some Justice of the Peace in the limits of said Territory, duly authorized to administer oaths and affirmations by the laws now in force therein, or before the Chief Justice or some Associate Justice of the Supreme Court of the United States, to support the Constitution of the United States, and faithfully to discharge the duties of their respective offices, which said oaths, when so taken, shall be certified by the person by whom the same shall have been taken; and such certificate shall be received and recorded, by the said Secretary, among the executive proceedings; and the Chief Justice and Associate Justices, and all other civil officers in said Territory, before they act as such, shall take a like oath or affirmation before the said Governor or Secretary, or some Judge or Justice of the Peace of the Territory, who may be duly commissioned and qualified, which said oath or affirmation shall be certified and transmitted by the person taking the same, to the Secretary, to be by him recorded as aforesaid; and, afterwards, the like oath or affirmation shall be taken, certified and recorded, in such manner and form as may be prescribed by law. The Governor shall receive an annual salary of two thousand five hundred dollars. The Chief Justice and Associate Justices shall receive an annual salary of two thousand dollars. The Secretary shall receive an annual salary of two thousand dollars. The said salaries shall be paid quarter-yearly, from the dates of the respective appointments, at the treasury of the United States; but no such payment shall be made until said officers shall have entered upon the duties of their respective appointments. The members of the Legislative Assembly shall be entitled to receive three dollars each per day, during their attendance at the sessions thereof, and three dollars each for every twenty miles travel in going to and returning from the said sessions, estimated according to the nearest usually traveled route; and an additional allowance of three dollars shall be paid to the presiding officer of each House, for each day he shall so preside. And a chief clerk, one assistant clerk, a sergeant-at-arms and door-keeper, may be chosen for each House; and the chief clerk shall receive four dollars per day, and the said other officers three dollars per day during the session of the Legislative Assembly; but no other officers shall be paid by the United States; *Provided*, That there shall be but one session of the Legislature annually, unless, on an extraordinary occasion, the Governor shall think proper to call the Legislature together. There shall be appropriated annually, the usual sum to be expended by the Governor, to defray the contingent expenses of the Territory, including the salary of a clerk of the executive department; and there shall also be appropriated annually, a sufficient sum to be expended by the Secretary of the Territory, and upon an estimate to be made by the Secretary of the Treasury of the United States, to defray the expenses of the Legislative Assembly, the printing of the laws and other incidental expenses; and the Governor and the Secretary of the Territory shall, in the disbursement of all moneys intrusted to them, be governed solely by the instructions of the Secretary of the Treasury of the United States, and shall, semi-annually, account to the said Secretary for the manner in which the aforesaid moneys shall have been expended; and no expenditure shall be made by said Legislative Assembly for objects not specially authorized by the acts of Congress making the appropriations, nor beyond the sums thus appropriated for such objects.

SEC. 31. *And be it further enacted,* That the seat of government of said Territory is hereby temporarily located at Fort Leavenworth; and that such portions of the public buildings as may not be actually used and needed for military purposes, may be occupied and used under the direction of the Governor and Legislative Assembly, for such public purposes as may be required under the provisions of this act.

SEC. 32 *And be it further enacted,* That a delegate to the House of Representatives of the United States, to serve for the term of two years, who shall be a citizen of the United States, may be elected by the voters qualified to elect members of the Legislative Assembly, who shall be entitled to the same rights and privileges as are exercised by the delegates from the several other Territories of the United States to the said House of Representatives; but the delegate first elected shall hold his seat only during the term of Congress to which he shall be elected. The first election shall be held at such times and places, and be conducted in such manner as the Governor shall appoint and direct; and at all subsequent elections, the times, places and manner of holding the election, shall be prescribed by law. The person having the greatest number of votes shall be declared, by the Governor to be duly elected, and a certificate thereof shall be given accordingly. That the Constitution, and all laws of the United States which are not locally inapplicable, shall have the same force and effect within the said Territory of Kansas as elsewhere within the United States, except the eighth section of the act preparatory to the admission of Missouri into the Union, approved March sixth, eighteen hundred and twenty, which being inconsistent with the principle of non-intervention by Congress with slavery in the States and Territories, as recognized by the legislation of eighteen hundred and fifty, commonly called the compromise measures, is hereby declared inoperative and void; it being the true intent and meaning of this act not to legislate slavery into any Territory or States, nor to exclude it therefrom, but to leave the people thereof perfectly free to form and regulate their domestic institutions in their own way, subject only to the Constitution of the United States; *Provided*, That nothing herein contained shall be construed to revive or put in force any law or regulation which may have existed prior to the act of the sixth of March, eighteen hundred and twenty, either protecting, establishing, prohibiting or abolishing slavery.

SEC. 33. *And be it further enacted*, That there shall hereafter be appropriated, as has been customary for the Territorial governments, a sufficient amount, to be expended under the direction of the said Governor of the Territory of Kansas, not exceeding the sums heretofore appropriated for similar objects, for the erection of suitable public buildings at the seat of government, and for the purchase of a library, to be kept at the seat of government for the use of the Governor, Legislative Assembly, Judges of the Supreme Court, Secretary, Marshal and Attorney of said Territory, and such other persons, under such regulations, as shall be prescribed by law.

Sec. 34. *And be it further enacted,* That when the lands in the said Territory shall be surveyed under the direction of the government of the United States, preparatory to bringing the same into market, sections numbered sixteen and thirty-six in each township in said Territory, shall be, and the same are hereby reserved for the purpose of being applied to schools in said Territory, and in the States and Territories hereafter to be erected out of the same.

Sec. 35. *And be it further enacted,* That until otherwise provided by law, the Governor of said Territory may define the judicial districts of said Territory, and assign the Judges who may be appointed for said Territory to the several districts; and also appoint the times and places for holding courts in the several counties or sub-divisions in each of said judicial districts, by proclamation, to be issued by him; but the Legislative Assembly, at their first or any subsequent session may organize, alter or modify such judicial districts and assign the Judges, and alter the times and places of holding the courts, as to them shall seem proper and convenient.

Sec. 36. *And be it further enacted,* That all officers to be appointed by the President, by and with the advice and consent of the Senate, for the Territory of Kansas, who, by virtue of the provisions of the laws now existing, or which may be enacted during the present Congress, are required to give security for the moneys entrusted with them for disbursement, and shall give such security at such time and place and in such manner as the Secretary of the Treasury may prescribe.

Sec. 37. *And be it further enacted,* That all treaties, laws, and other engagements made by the government of the United States with the Indian tribes inhabiting the Territories embraced within this act, shall be faithfully and rigidly observed, notwithstanding any thing contained in this act; and that the existing agencies and superintendencies of said Indians be continued with the same powers and duties which are now prescribed, except the President of the United States may, at his discretion, change the location of the office of the Superintendent.

Approved, May 30, 1854.

CHAPTER VIII.

ANTIQUITIES OF KANSAS.—1705-1854.

Kansas cannot boast of a remote antiquity. Her soil never became the scene of stirring events until of late years. Her level and far-reaching prairies afforded but little temptation to the early adventurer. No ideal gold mine or opulent Indian city were ever located within her boundary.

The name Kansas, signifying *smoky*, is derived from the chief river running from the east through the centre of the State; the name of the river having been derived from that of the tribe of Indians inhabiting its borders towards its mouth. It is variously spelled by early writers, *Cansan*, *Kanson*, *Kanzas*; but since the organization of the Territory it has been written *Kansas*. The Kansas Indians are sometimes called Kaws—a nick-name given them by the French.

In 1705 the French explored the Missouri River as far as the mouth of the Kansas. They were kindly received by the natives, and were soon engaged in a profitable trade with them, which they continued to carry on for more than a century afterwards. These were the first Europeans that beheld the soil and river of Kansas.

In 1719 M. Dutisne, a young French officer, was sent out with a party by Beinville, Governor of Louisiana, on an exploring expedition. He ascended the Mississippi as far as the Sabine river, and thence traveled westward over a rocky, broken and timbered country, about three hundred miles as near as he could judge, until he came to the principal vilage of the *Osages*. As he describes the village, it was then situated on a hill, five miles from the Osage River, and contained about one hundred cabins. These Indians spent but a small part of their time at the village, being engaged in the chase at a distance.

Traveling thence to the north-west one hundred and twenty miles, he visits the *Panoucas*. They lived on the prairie which abounded in buffaloes, in two villages of about one hundred and thirty cabins. They had three hundred fine horses which they prized very highly. Then he advanced westward four hundred and fifty miles to the Paonis,[2] a very brave and warlike nation. Here he takes formal possession of the country in the name of his King by erecting a cross with the arms of France, Sept. 27th, 1719. He now turns back and directs his march to the Missouri River, three hundred and fifty yards from which he discovers the village of the *Missouries*. Thus so early the French have discovered and explored the Territory of Kansas, and had opened a lively traffic with the Indians, which was kept up for a century afterwards.

The Spaniards, who always repelled with alacrity every western advance of the French, having driven them from Texas, determined to have command of the Missouri River before their rivals had permanently established themselves upon its border. They had heard of M. Dutisne's tour through the territory and knew that success required celerity. They sought by possessing themselves of the Missouri River, to command its waters and enjoy its commerce by restricting the French on the Illinois side of the Mississippi. Their object was first to conquer the Missouries who lived upon the banks of that river, and who were friendly to the French, and establish there a colony. The Pawnees, who dwelt west of the aforesaid Indians, were at war with them, and the Spaniards hoped to enlist tke former as allies in the undertaking.

---

1. Supposed to be the Pawnees. 2. This tribe cannot be identified.

Massacre of the Spaniards.

Accordingly a numerous caravan set out from Santa Fe in 1720 to take possession of the country along the Missouri and establish upon its borders a colony. They first sought the Pawnee villages in their march, but losing their way, they unfortunately fell in with the Missourie s whose destruction they had planned. Mistaking them for the Pawnees, they made known their designs, and solicited their co-operation. The Missouries manifesting not the least astonishment at this unexpected visit and startling communication, requested time to assemble their warriors. In forty-eight hours two thousand assembled in arms. They attacked the Spaniards in the night and killed the whole party except one priest who escaped on horseback and returned to Santa Fe, where the records of this account are preserved.

This battle occurred a little below Fort Leavenworth, on the banks of the Missouri.

The French apprised of this bold undertaking of the Spaniards in advancing almost one thousand miles from their possessions into this unexplored country, resolved to establish a fortification in that direction. Accordingly M. de Bourgmont was dispatched with a considerable force, who ascended the Mississippi and Missouri Rivers to an island in the latter above the mouth of the Osage River a short distance, and established on it Fort Orleans.

At this time the Padoucas, who lived north-west of the Missouries, were at war with the latter and their allies, the Kansas, Ottoes, Osages and Iowas. The above mentioned officer in 1724, made an extensive exploration from Fort Orleans to the north-west, accompanied by a few soldiers and some friendly Indians, for the purpose of establishing friendship among the native tribes and opening and strengthening trade with them. Setting out on the 3d of July, he returned on the 5th of November, having successfully accomplished his object.

Lewis and Cark in 1804 made an expedition up the Missouri and across to the Pacific under the direction of the Government. They encamped at the confluence of the Kansas and Missouri Rivers and spent two days. Here they found plenty of game. Somewhere near Atchison, they discovered the remains of an old French fort and village. A little farther up they found a house and a trading-post but met with no white people. A negro cook with them excited the curiosity of the Indians.

The first steamboat that passed Kansas on the waters of the Missouri was the *Western Engineer* in 1819, under the command of Major S. H. Long. He, with a corps of Topographical Engineers, went on a tour of observation up to the Yellow Stone. "The boat was a small one with a stern wheel and an escape pipe so contrived as to emit a torrent of smoke and steam through the head of a serpent with a red, forked tongue from the bow." This was designed to imitate a powerful serpent, vomiting fire and smoke, and lashing the water into a foam with its tail, in order to strike terror among the Indians. Tradition says that they thought it was a "maniteau" which had come to destroy them.

The fur trade was early prosecuted along the Missouri River. In this extensive and lucrative traffic Kansas must have participated largely. During the fifteen years previous to 1804 the value of furs annually collected at St. Louis is estimated at $203,750. James Pursley was the first hunter and trapper to traverse the plains between the United States and New Mexico (1802), and consequently the first Anglo-American to behold the soil of Kansas. General William H. Ashley in 1823 fitted out his first trapping expedition to the mountains. He discovered the South Pass and thus opened the highway to Oregon and California. For forty years the fur trade averaged from two to three hundred thousand dollars annually. The last named gentleman alone between the years 1824 and 1827 sent fur to St. Louis to the value of $180,000.*

Peck's Annals of the West.

In the spring of 1823 the great Santa Fe trade from Missouri originated at Franklin, now Booneville, in Howard County, where the first enterprise was planned and outfit procured. It being an experimental trip, the stocks conveyed were slender, comprising a cheap class of goods, which were carried on pack mules and in wagons. This expedition proving a success, and awakening bright prospects of wealth, it was repeated the following year on a more extensive scale. In 1825 the Government, having its attention directed to this new channel of commerce by Colonel Benton, employed Major Sibley to survey and establish a wagon road from the Missouri State line to Santa Fe, which has been a great thoroughfare of travel ever since. The trade increased slowly but gradually during the next twenty-two years, the value of its exports averaging from $50,000 to $100,000 per annum.

The Indian tribes through whose territory the trains had to pass soon became very troublesome. They would suddenly swoop down upon the unsuspecting encampment of the transporters, drive off their draft animals, rob the wagons and frequently destroy lives. As but few traders in those days started out with more than two or three wagons, considerations of safety suggested a general rendezvous, from which point they could all start together and afford each other mutual protection. A spot well timbered and watered was selected for this purpose, which has ever since been known as "Council Grove." The caravans that thus collected here, numbered hundreds of wagons and thousands of mules, horses and oxen, and their departures over the Plains noted in the papers through the States.

The town of Independence, Missouri, was formed soon after the opening of this overland traffic and became the principal outfitting post. From 1832 to 1848 it held this commercial ascendancy and its merchants accumulated vast fortunes. In 1834 the first stock of goods was landed a little below Kansas City, at Francis Chouteau's log warehouse, destined for the New Mexico trade. From that time Kansas City and Westport continued to acquire more and more of this overland commerce, so that by 1850 they had secured its complete monopoly.

According to the record kept by Messrs. Hays & Co. at Council Grove, there were engaged in the New Mexico trade in 1860, 5,984 men; 2,170 wagons; 464 horses; 5,933 mules; 17,836 oxen. The wagons were loaded with fifty-five hundred pounds each on an average, making an aggregate of six thousand tons! The capital employed in carrying on this transportation for this season alone was not far from two million dollars!

To protect this trade and the western frontier from the depredations of the Indians the Government in 1827 posted a portion of the Third Regiment of United States troops, numbering about 200 men, where Fort Leavenworth now stands, under command of Major Baker. This post was named after the Colonel of this regiment, Henry H. Leavenworth. It was at first called a cantonment and the title of Fort was not applied until 1832. For several years after its establishment the troops were so greatly afflicted by disease that in 1829 it was temporarily reduced—the most of the troops being sent upon the prairies. In 1830 the Sixth Regiment of Infantry superseded the Third; and in 1835 it was commanded by the Third Division of Dragoons under Colonel Dodge, who, in 1845, made an expedition to Pike's Peak and back, in which he cultivated the friendship of the Prairie Indians.* Fort Leavenworth attracted but little attention until the breaking out of the war with Mexico and the gold excitement in California when it became a great outfitting post for western travel and trade.

Soon after the admission of Missouri as a State into the Union, large cessions of land were secured to the United States from the natives west of that State. The Government then conceived the design and perfected a plan for the trans-

*American State Papers.

fer of all eastern tribes of Indians to the west of the Mississippi. Tribe after tribe was thus led to migrate westward, so that by the middle of the Nineteenth Century not a tribe remained in the States. Thus up to the time of the organization of this Territory, the lands of Kansas were held and inhabited solely by Indians, white people being forbidden by the terms of the treaties to settle on them without the consent of the former. This was literally the *Indian Territory*, and it was the design of the General Government to make it the permanent home of the Red Man.

Fort Scott was made a military post in 1841 to hold the Indians in check. A few Government buildings were erected, which were sold in 1855 for two or three hundred dollars a piece. The American Fur Company formerly had a post there.

From 1843 to 1850 General Fremont made repeated tours through this Territory.

The first train that ever crossed the Plains, over the Rocky Mountains, to the Pacific coast, was conducted in 1844 by Mr. Neil Gillem. He set out from Buchanan County, Missouri, with fifty wagons and one hundred men, and went to Oregon. The following year the Mormons assembled near Atchison preparatory to crossing the Plains. They made this their place of rendezvous for all companies going to Salt Lake for several years thereafter. They erected a house here afterwards and opened a farm, which is to this day known as the Mormon farm.

In 1845 the Mexican war broke out and Fort Leavenworth became the gathering point for soldiers and the shipping point for military stores, destined for Mexico. It was across the prairies of Kansas that General Kearney made his celebrated march to Santa Fe. Immediately after the termination of this war gold was discovered in California, and the tide of fortune seekers rolled across this soil. Kansas City, Fort Leavenworth and St. Joseph were the principal points at which the emigrants united into vast caravans, miles in length, bound for the land of wealth. In 1849, thirty thousand, and in 1850 sixty thousand, persons crossed the Plains on their journey to the Golden Gate, the chief portion of whom crossed the prairies of Kansas.

As this kind of prairie travel and commerce is passing away, it is thought proper to insert an excellent description of it by one with whom it was perfectly familiar:

"The wagons, after receiving their loads, severally return to the camping places, until all belonging to the train are assembled. At that 'the order of march' is given. A scene then ensues that baffles description. Carriages, wagons, men, horses and mules and oxen, appear in chaotic confusion. Men are cursing, distressing mulish outcries, bovine lowing, form an all but harmonious concert, above the desonances of which the commanding tone of the wagon master's voice only is heard. The teamsters make a merciless use of their whip, fists and feet. The horses rear, the mules kick, the oxen baulk. But gradually order is made to prevail and each of the conflicting elements to assume its proper place. The commander finally gives the sign of readiness by mounting his mule, and soon the caravan is pursuing its slow way along the road.

"The trains reveal their approach at a great distance. Long before getting in sight, especially when the wind carries the sound in the right direction, the jarring and croaking of the wagons, the 'gee-ho' and 'ho-haw' of the drivers, and the reverberations of the whips, announce it in the most unmistakable manner. The traveler coming nearer, the train will by degrees rise into sight, just as ships at sea appear to emerge from below the horizon. The wagons being all in view, the train, when seen a few miles off, from the shining white of the covers, and the hull-like appearance of the bodies of the wagons, truly looks like a fleet sailing with canvass all spread, over a seeming sea. A further advance will bring one up with the train master, who always keeps a mile for so ahead, in order to learn the condition of the roads, leaving the immediate charge of the train to his assistant. On arriving up with the caravan itself, one will pass from twenty-five to seventy-five high-boxed, heavy-wheeled wagons, covered with double sheets of canvass, loaded with from fifty to sixty hundred pounds of freight, and drawn by from five to six yoke of oxen, or five spans of mules each. One driver for every wagon is attached to the train. From four to ten extra hands also accompany it, to fill possible vacancies. One or more mess wagons, under the superintendence of cooks likewise form a part of the cortege, the whole being under the supreme command of the wagon master and his assistant. As to cooks the crew of the prairie fleet, after having traveled on the Plains a week or two, outshine the deck hands of our steamboats altogether. When 'under sail' the prairie schooners usually keep about thirty yards from each other, and as each of them, with its animate propelling power, has a length of eighty or ninety feet, a large train requires an hour to pass a given point."

CHAPTER IX.

A SURVEY OF THE BATTLE-FIELD AND THE CONTESTANTS BEFORE THE CONFLICT.

When the Nebraska-Kansas Bill passed Congress, Kansas contained not a town or settlement of whites. The only inhabitants within its boundaries except Indians, were a few traders, missionaries and Indian agents. The western limits of Missouri were, a few years previous, regarded as the outer verge of civilization, and the domain of Kansas as a part of the great American Sahara, over which farms, towns and cities could never spread—fit only for the nomadic wanderings of the savage, the prowlings of the wolf and the range of the buffalo, It was marked on the map—"Great American Desert," as a desolate and sterile waste. And there was little in it to excite the cupidity and jealousy of bordering States, as it was covered for one hundred miles back with reserves for Indians, guaranteed to them in perpetuity for homes by the general Government—the policy of pro-slavery legislation whereby the territory bequeathed to Freedom was rendered inaccessible for settlement.

During the California emigration, the Eastern and Middle States became more familiar with this country. Travellers in passing through it were struck with its richness, beauty and grandeur, and wrote back glowing descriptions of it. Many that traversed its soil, were the first emigrants to this Territory. But nothwithstanding these lights thrown upon the "Far West," most people east of the Mississippi knew nothing of Kansas by name in 1854, and were required to purchase new maps to ascertain its location.

The people of Missouri from the first favored the organization of the Territory west of their State, on the principle of self-interest. Hon. Willard P. Hall, representative from Missouri, introduced the first bill for that purpose. Senator Atchison opposed it at the first session of the thirty-second Congress, but favored it at the second on account of the instructions of his constituents.

The Missourians had not the least idea or expectation but that when it "come in," as they expressed it, it would come in as Free Territory, until the question of repealing the Missouri Compromise was raised by pro-slavery politicians.

The birth-day and parentage of this design cannot be definitely determined. Both Atchison and Douglas claimed its paternity. One thing, however, is certain that early in 1853, the former in the city of Weston on a goods-box made a speech in which he said "he would oppose the admission of Nebraska into the Union as a Free State with the last drop of his blood; he would oppose the Missouri Compromise to his last breath; he would have that odious Missouri Compromise repealed, which made men either give up their negroes, or give to ——— Northern cattle the finest farms in Nebraska. American citizens should be privileged to go where they pleased and carry their property with them, whether that property was furniture, mules or niggers. On that question, when it should come up, he pledged himself to be faithful; that the Missouri Compromise should be repealed. What will you do if the Missouri Compromise is not repealed? Will you sit down here at home, and permit *the nigger thieves, the cattle,* the vermin of the North to come into Nebraska and take up those fertile prairies, run off your negroes and depreciate the value of your slaves here? I know you well; I know what you will do; you know how to protect your own interests; your own rifles will free you from such neighbors and secure your property. You will go in there if necessary with bayonets and with blood. But we will repeal the Compromise. I would sooner see the whole of Nebraska in the bottom of hell than see it a Free State."

Mr. Atchison continued to make similar speeches to the above during the summer of 1853 over Western Misouri. He denounced Hon. Thos. H. Benton, the best friend and purest statesman Missouri ever had, as a traitor to his State and an abolitionist, because he opposed the repeal of the Missouri Compromise. This Cataline of the Border continued his harrangues until the feelings of the people were all aflame with prejudice and hatred towards persons from the free States.

Those unacquainted with the inhabitants of the Border at that time cannot well comprehend how that public sentiment could so easily be swayed and shaped by drunken, vulgar and inflammatory speeches. First were the native Missourians, who were a singular class of people and have not perhaps, their prototypes in the world—certainly not in the United States. Their fathers were chiefly renegades from the Eastern States, who had fled to escape the just desert for crimes committed. They inherited all the vices of their ancestors, and had learned many new ones. They were incredulous and suspicious of strangers and easily excited against them. When enraged they were as furious as a mad dog and as cowardly and unmanly as a jackal. They had no *conclusions*, but only *beliefs*. They never know anything but by rumor. They had few ideas and opinions of their own, but gather them from their leading men. No matter how clearly a stranger might demonstrate a truth to them they would not believe it. No matter how absurd a proposition advanced by one of their favorite leaders might be, they would embrace it as coming from the Oracle of Truth. Utter stangers to principles, they were never happier than when in meanness. Loud in their professions of law and order, there was not a week passed during which robberies, murders and disturbances were not committed. Whenever an individual became unpopular in community, he was accused of all kinds of mis-doings and evil designs, warned to leave–which failing to observe, he was attacked by a mob, his property destroyed, and lucky he was if he escaped with his life. Infatuated plebians; Proud of the appellation of "*Sovereigns*," which the courting politician of the Border flung out like Roman largesses among them, their enslavement was worse than that of the contemned African. Whiskey was held in high esteem by all classes, and celebrated lecturers on temperance were frequently insulted by continued threats and horrid oaths during their discourses. On a certain occasion at one of the chief towns of the Border, a celebrated champion in the temperance cause was grossly insulted by a ruffian rushing up and pulling his nose in the midst of his lecture, while the audience applauded the outrage. The following day the city papers lavishingly complimented the perpetrator of the offense and offered in imposing capitals a reward of one cent for the "absconded lecturer."

Of native Missourians there were two classes—the wealthy and the poor—holding about the same relation to each other as did the planters and the poor whites of the South. The poor were much the more numerous; but being ignorant and pecuniarily dependent upon their wealthy neighbors, they were the pliant tools of the latter. It is remarkable that Missouri though having as large a school fund as any State in the Union, has had no system of public schools until recently.

Both classes of native Missourians along the Border were at that time alike unscrupulous, ungenerous and ignoble. The wealthy, highly aristocratic, possessed all the cravings to rule of Southern slave masters. Though full of blarney and suavity, with the exterior polish of gentlemen, they would not shrink from any measure to attain their ends. Many of them had become very wealthy from the commerce of the prairies. The above remarks apply entirely to native born Missourians—regular, genuine "Pukes."

With both of these elements were mingled a large number

from the free and slave States, the first of whom generally adopted in a great measure the habits, peculiarities and prejudices of the Missourians and became their boon companions, during the Kansas troubles, though possessing a great deal of native manliness; while the other in most instances retained their former feelings and principles, and were the staunchest free State men and greatest sufferers during the Kansas conflict.

There were also a peculiar, though powerful, class along the Border, composed chiefly of native Missourians, who might justly be termed the loungers and loafers. They accompanied trains across the Plains, went on hunting expeditions, and had generally been through the Mexican war. They were a powerful class—the military of the Border. They formed the mobs, did the stealing and a good share of the drinking. They were ever ready for adventure, any thing wild and daring.

The wealthy and aristocratic were enlightened and viciously refined. They were the prime movers in every public measure, possessing not only the influence and consideration of the slave master, but, also, the train master; they by a little strategy and caution controlled the rabble and the poor class of inhabitants. It has been said that many of this class did not approve of the unjust measures to make Kansas a Slave State. While this is true in some cases, it must also be remarked that they enjoy the odious honor of being the instigators of the outrages which followed, and many of them vied with the rabble in the grossness of their conduct and the atrocity of their acts. Those who laid claims to respectability and honor and who had been so reputed before the Territorial troubles, where they entered into the strife, entirely lost sight of their manhood and plunged into the excesses of infamy and outrage. Many of these individuals since the political elements became still, have reinstated themselves in the esteem and confidence of society. But while it is becoming that society should throw a mantle of oblivion over their past misconduct, it is the painful duty of the faithful historian to exhibit the past in its real light.

Individuals who heartily disapproved of the course pursued by the Missourians dared not raise their protest against it for fear of personal violence or destruction of their property. In cases where the blind and hot-headed policy pursued, was mildly rebuked, happy was the offender against public sentiment if his life and property did not pay the forfeit.

Such was the character of the elements into which the fiery and inflammatory appeals of Hon. D. R. Atchison were thrown. He understood their character and knew well how to prepare them for the coming struggle. As he figured conspicuously in the early part of the Territorial history of Kansas and has been rather a remarkable man, a short account of his life is here given.

David R. Atchison was born in Fayette County, Kentucky, on the 11th day of August, 1807. His father was an industrious farmer of influence in his neighborhood. David at an early age was put into a grammar school, from which he was transferred to Transylvania University, where he graduated. In 1828 he began the study of law as a student in Lexington Law School, where he remained for two years.

After having thus finished his school preparation he emigrated to Clay County, then the extreme border of Missouri. Adapting himself at once to the society of the frontier, ambitious of distinction, he soon became a person of notoriety in that section of the country. In 1834 he was elected to the lower House of the State Legislature, and in 1838 was again elected to the same position. He was, during this session of the Legislature, chosen Major-General of the Militia that were to operate against the Indians. Although he never saw any active service, he ever afterwards retained the title of General. In 1840 he was beaten as a candidate for the Legislature by a small majority, and in 1841 was elevated to the bench of the Platte Judicial Circuit. After filling this position with credit for two years, he was then chosen by Governor Reynolds to fill the vacancy in the United States Senate, occasioned by the death of Dr. Lewis Lynn. In 1844 he was elected to the same position by the State Legislature, and re-elected in 1849.

Mr. Atchison, being President of the Senate at the time of the death of Hon. William R. King, the Vice-President elect, became ex-officio Vice-President of the United States.

In 1851, when the question of organizing the Nebraska Territory was broached in the United States Senate, Mr. Atchison opposed it. At the next session, however, of the same Congress he favored it, though the validity of the Missouri Compromise had not yet been questioned. But it was his intention and that of his constituents to introduce slavery into this Territory regardless of prohibitions. He could not, however, satisfy his Southern friends of his success in the undertaking, and the bill failed.

In the summer of 1853 he boldly announced himself in favor of the repeal of the Missouri Compromise, and preached in the purest orthodoxy the principles of Popular Sovereignty. And consequently the following winter in the Senate he was a warm supporter of the Kansas-Nebraska bill.

He aspired to the Presidency of the United States, and for some time had his name in the Border papers as a candidate. He ran for the United States Senate at the March election in 1855, but was badly defeated. The year after his defeat he spent the most of his time in Kansas leading the Platte County Rifle Company, whose exploits will be duly recorded. After the defeat of slavery in Kansas he retired to his farm about seven miles from Weston, Missouri, where he yet resides, taking no part in politics.

In the fall of 1853, therefore, the people of Western Missouri resolved that Kansas should be a Slave State at all hazards. The question of making it a Slave State was then for the first time raised, and that, too, by a gentleman who understood that the Missouri Compromise would be repealed.

The minds of the people had been prepared for the struggle; the pecuniary interest of the wealthy demanded it; the dependent poor, obsequious to the rich, stood ready to do their bidding, and all prided themselves in maintaining the institutions and honor of Missouri.

When the Missouri Compromise was repealed the impression was made upon the minds of the people of north-west Missouri that the organization of the Territories and the removal of the slavery restriction was a kind of "compromise measure" by which there was an implicit understanding that Kansas should be a Slave State. This was the prevailing, natural, and, in many instances, the sincere and honest impression which pervaded pretty generally the minds of all classes on the Border. This fact may serve to palliate, in some degree, their subsequent conduct.*

The people of the Free States who were the first to favor the organization of Nebraska Territory, never dreamed that an effort would be made to introduce slavery therein until the session of the thirty-third Congress the following winter. There were two large parties in the Middle and Eastern States opposed to Slavery, both radical in principle, but one favoring a prudent, the other a fanatical policy. One opposed the extension and growth of Slavery by all Constitutional means; the other believed the ends would justify the means of its total abolition. Both were equally opposed to yielding Kansas to Slavery, and both resolved to rescue her from its grasp.

---

*From Dr. J. H. Strongfellow's testimony before the Congressional Committee, the following is taken:

"At the time of the passage of that bill, and prior to that time, I never heard any man in my section of Missouri express a doubt about the nature of the institutions that would be established here, provided that the Missouri restriction was removed: and I heard of no combination of persons, either in public or private, prior to the time of the organization of the Emigrant Aid Society, and, indeed, for months afterwards, for the purpose of making united action to frustrate the designs of that society in abolitionizing or making a free State of Kansas. The conviction was general that it would be a Slave State. The settlers who come over from Missouri after the passage of the bill, as far as I know, generally believed that Kansas would be a Slave State."

The friends of Free Labor defeated and overwhelmed in Congress, resolved to renew the conflict on the distant fields of Kansas. Though borne down by an unjust and unfair legislation, they determined "to possess the goodly land" by emigration and settlement—the very mode prescribed by Congress.

The devotees of Slavery entered upon this struggle with many advantages. The Organic act was skillfully framed with this end in view. Slavery was already in the Territory and had been for many years, in violation of the laws of the United States. The Government officials, missionaries and traders among the Indians held slaves and had sought to impress the native inhabitants with its attractions, some of whom held slaves.* It was regarded by the friends of slavery, and conceded by its opponents, that the Organic act establishing the Territory, recognized the right to hold slaves in the same; and that neither the people nor the Territorial Legislature could prohibit slavery; that power was alone possessed· by the people when they were authorized to frame a State Government "It was contended that the removal of the Slavery restriction virtualty established slavery in the Territory." The whole weight and influence of the General Government was ready to be employed in the interest of Slavery. Every officer in the Territory was to be appointed by the President. Missouri lying contiguous to this Territory, enabled her people to pass easily and quickly over and lay out their claims, preparatory to emigrating. It was not in the line of emigration from the Free States, being too far south; whereas up the Mississippi and Missouri the tide of slave emigration had been for years pressing.

Thus stood the sectional parties when the "Irrepressible

These facts are gathered from old settlers. Joe Parks, a chief among the Shawnees and Choeteau, near Westport, each owned three slaves. Revs. Messrs, Perry and Johnson, missionaries among the Delawares and Shawnees, owned several apiece.—S laves must bave been held here twenty years previous to 1854,

Conflict," which had been waged since the childhood of the Thirteen Colonies, was transferred from the Legislative Halls of the nation to the fair and virgin prairie of Kansas, to be renewed with the fury and desperateness of the death grapple.

CHAPTER X.

PRO-SLAVERY EMIGRATION AND EMIGRANT AID SOCIETIES.

In the early part of May before the Territory was thrown open to settlement, the people from the western border of Missouri began coming over and locating their claims upon the best sites in the country. They would mark them with stakes, or four poles thrown quadrangularly upon the ground, as the initium of a cabin, and then return to their homes —some to prepare to emigrate, others merely to watch and hold their newly acquired possessions. Thus they continued to scatter themselves over the best country of Eastern Kansas, in many instances disregarding the Indian title by which the lands were held, until almost every gentleman in Western Missouri had a claim upon which he had moved, intended to move, or designed to hold.*

Immediately after the intelligence of the passage of the Nebraska-Kansas Act was communicated to Western Missouri, some of the leading politicians in that quarter crossed over into Kansas and held meetings among the Squatters.— At one held on Salt Creek, June 10th, 1854, the following Preamble and Resolutions were adopted:

"*Whereas*, We, the citizens of Kansas Territory, and many

*In the Democratic Platform published in Liberty, Missouri, of June 8th, 1854, we find the following:

"We learn from a gentleman lately from the Territory of Kansas, that a great many Missourians have already set their 'meg' in that country, and are making arrangements to 'darken the atmosphere' with their negroes. This is right; let every man that owns a negro go there and settle, and our northern brethren will be compelled to hunt further north for a location."

other citizens of the adjoining State of Missouri, contemplating a Squatter's home on the plains of said Territory, are assembled at Salt Creek Valley for the purpose of taking such steps as will secure safety and fairness in the location and preservation of claims.

Therefore, be it resolved;

"1st, That we are in favor of a *bona fide* Squatter Sovereignty, and acknowledge the right of any citizens of the United States to make a claim in Kansas Territory, ultimately with the view of occupying it.

"2nd, That such claim, when made, shall be held inviolate so long as a *bona fide* intention of occupying it is apparent, and for the purpose of protecting and defending such claim, we agree to act in concert, if necessary to expel intruders.

"3d, That every person of lawful age who may be at the head of a family, who shall mark out his claim of 160 acres, so that it may be apparent how the same lies, and proceed with reasonable diligence to erect thereon a cabin or tent, shall be deemed to have made a proper claim.

"4th, That any person marking out his claim shall be deemed to have forfeited it unless he commences his cabin, or pitches his tent within two weeks thereafter, unless the same be on lands which prohibit it by military or Indian reservations.

"5th, That all persons now holding claims shall have two weeks from this day, in which to make the improvements contemplated by the foregoing resolutions.

"6th, No person shall be protected by the Squatter Association who shall hold in his own right more than one claim.

"7th, That a citizen of the Territory be appointed as register of claims, who shall keep a book in which he shall register the name and description of all squatters, and their claims, and the dates of making the same, for which registration he shall be allowed the sum of fifty cents for each claim, to be paid by the claimant.

"8th, That we recognize the institution of Slavery as always existing in this Territory, and recommend to slave-holders to introduce their property as early as possible.

"9th, That we will afford protection to no abolitionists as settlers of Kansas Territory."

These resolutions were soon after adopted by similar meetings in different places over Eastern Kansas.

It must be here noted that the term *"abolitionists"* meant any person from a Free State, as subsequent facts will show. Thus so early, perhaps before a single emigrant from a free State had entered the Territory, the people of the Border had resolved to afford them no protection, which as proven by following events, signified that they would not be allowed to settle in Kansas. This was the first public meeting of Anglo-Americans assembled, and the first resolutions passed in this Territory.

The first attempt at founding a city in the Territory was that of Leavenworth. On the 13th of June an organization of thirty-two persons, composed of pro-slavery and free State men, was perfected in Weston, Missouri. They had two days previous secured the claim to two quarter sections of land where the city now stands. This was divided into one hundred and seventy-five shares that sold at first for $250 a piece. Over $4,000 were spent during the summer in clearing off the tangled growth of hazel brush and laying the ground off in lots and blocks. The title was not secured to the town site until three years afterwards. Geo. W. Gist was the first President and H. Miles Moore the first Secretary of the Board of Directors. Its political character has always been very much mixed; but no city in the West, after the title to the town site was perfected, has made more rapid improvement. In 1857 Hon. H. J. Adams, the first free State Mayor, was elected.

In July Atchison was laid out by an association formed of gentlemen from Platte County, Missouri. It was named in honor of Hon. David R. Atchison, then in the zenith of his glory. The first sale of lots took place on the 21st of September, and the little daughter nestled among the hills. Peter T. Abell was President and Ira Norris Secretary of the first Board of Directors. It was incorporated by the first

Legislature. Until 1857 it was the most violent pro-slavery town in the Territory.

While slavery propagandists were thus attending to the settlement of Kansas, the friends of Free Labor were not unemployed. The fierce agitation in Congress had already directed the attention of the people in the Northern States to this Territory. The press all over the land set forth glowing descriptions of its loveliness, fertility and future greatness, and urged upon the people to emigrate thither at once, avail themselves of the vast advantages of that new country and secure it from the curse of slavery. To facilitate, expedite and increase emigration, societies were formed by which many of the difficulties and embarrassments attending emigrants to so new and unsettled a country were removed. As the Missourians have sought to excuse their conduct by the action of these societies, it is thought proper to present here a short account of their origin, design, nature and mode of operating.

Foremost and conspicuous among these stands the New England Emigrant Aid Society. In the month of March, 1854, Mr. Eli Thayer circulated a petition for the incorporation, by the General Court of Massachusetts, of the above mentioned society, the object of which, as stated in the charter that was granted, was for directing emigration westward and aiding in providing accommodations for emigrants after arriving at their places of destination." Its capital was limited to five million dollars. This charter was signed by the Governor on the 26th of April and immediately took effect. The persons named in it met on the 4th of May and appointed a committee to report a plan of organization. As the report of that committee sets forth the internal machinery of that company and the motives and designs of those who originated and worked it, a copy of it is here inserted:

REPORT.

"The objects of this corporation are apparent in its name. The emigration to America from Europe introduces into our ports a very large number of persons, eager to pass westward. The fertility of our western regions and the cheapness of the public lands, induce many of the native born citizens of the old States, also, to emigrate thither. At the present time public and social considerations of the gravest character render it desirable to settle the Territories west of Missouri and Iowa, and these considerations are largely increasing the amount of westward emigration.

"The foreign arrivals in America last year were four hundred thousand seven hundred and seventy-seven. In the same year the emigration to the Western States of Americans and foreigners must have amounted to much more than two hundred thousand persons. The emigration thither this year will be larger still; and from the older Western States large numbers are removing into new territory.

"Persons who are familiar with the course of movement of this large annual throng of emigrants, know that under the arrangements now existing, they suffer at every turn. The frauds practiced upon them by 'runners' and other agents of transporting lines, in the State of New York, amount to a stupendous system of knavery, which has not been broken up, even by the patient endeavors of the State officers, and by very stringent State legislation. The complete ignorance as to our customs in which the foreign emigrant finds himself, and in more than half the foreign emigration, his complete ignorance of our language, subjects him to every fraud and to constant accident. It is in the face of every conceivable inconvenience that the country receives every year four hundred thousand foreigners into its seaports, and sends the larger portion of them to its western country.

"The inconveniences and dangers to which the pioneer is subject, who goes out alone, or with his family, only in making a new settlement, are familiar to every American.

"The Emigrant Aid Company has been incorporated to protect emigrants, as far as may be, from such inconveniences. Its duty is to *organize emigration to the West, and bring it into a system.* This duty which should have been attempted long ago, is particularly essential now, in the critical position of the Western Territories.

"The Legislature has granted a charter with a capital sufficient for these purposes. This capital is not to exceed $5,000,000. In no single year are assessments to a larger amount than ten per cent. to be called for. The incorporators believe that if the company be organized at once, as soon as the subscription to the stock amounts to $1,000,000, the annual income to be derived from that amount and the subscriptions, may be so appropriated as to render most essential service to the emigrant, to plant a free State in Kansas, to the lasting advantage of the country, and to return a very handsome profit to the stockholders upon their investment.

"1. The emigrant suffers when he goes alone into his new home. He suffers from the frauds of others, from his own ignorance of the system of travel, and of the country where he settles, and again from his want of support from neighbors, which results in the impossibility of any combined assistance, or of any division of labor.

"The Emigrant Aid Company will relieve him from all these embarrassments by sending out emigrants in companies and establishing them in considerable numbers. They will locate them where they please on their arrival in their new home, and receive from the Government their titles. The Company propose to carry them to their homes more cheaply than they could otherwise go, to enable them to establish themselves with the least inconvenience and to provide the most important prime necessities of a new colony. It will provide shelter and food at the lowest prices after the arrival of emigrants, while they make their arrangements necessary for their new homes. It will render assistance which the information of its agents can give, and by establishing emigrants in large numbers in the Territories, it will give them the power of using, at once, those social influences which radiate from the church, the school and the press, in the organization and development of a community.

"For these purposes it is recommended, first, that the Directors contract immediately with some one of the competing lines of travel for the conveyance of twenty thousand persons from Massachusetts to that place in the West which the Directors shall select for their first settlement.

"It is believed that passage may be obtained, in so large a contract, at half the price paid by individuals. We recommend that emigrants receive the full advantage of this diminution of price, and that they be forwarded in companies of two hundred, as they apply, at these reduced rates of travel.

"2. It is recommended that at such points as the directors shall select for places of settlement, they shall at once construct a boarding house or receiving house, in which three hundred persons can receive temporary accomodations on their arrival; and that the number of such houses be enlarged as necessity may dictate. The new comers or their families may thus be provided for in the necessary interval which elapses while they are making their selection of a location.

"3. It is recommended that the directors procure and send forward steam saw-mills, grist-mills and such other machines as shall be of constant service in a new settlement, which cannot, however, be purchased or carried out conveniently by individual settlers. These machines may be leased, or run by the company's agents. At the same time, it is desirable that a printing press be sent out, and a weekly newspaper established. This would be the organ of the company's agents, would extend information regarding its settlements, and from the very first an index of that love of freedom and of good morals which it is to be hoped, may characterize the State now to be formed.

"4. It is recommended that the company's agents locate and take up for the company's benefit, the section of land in which the boarding houses and mills are located and no others. And further, that whenever the Territory shall be organized as a free State, the directors shall dispose of all their interests there, replace by the sales the money laid out, declare a dividend to the stockholders, and

"5. That they select a new field and make similar arrangements for the settlement and organization of another free State of this Union.

"II. With the advantages attained by such a system of effort, the Territories selected as the scene of operations, would, it is believed, at once fill up with free inhabitants.— There is reason to suppose that several thousand men of New England origin, propose to emigrate under the auspices of some such an arrangement this very summer. Of the whole emigration from Europe, amounting to some four hundred thousand persons, there can be no difficulty in inducing some thirty or forty thousand to take the same direction.— Applications from German agents have already been made to members of the company. We have also intimations in correspondence from the free States of the West of a wide spread desire there among those who know what it is to settle a new country, to pass on, it such an organization can be made, into that now thrown open. An emigrant company of those intending to go has been formed in Worcester county, and others in other States.

"In view of the establishment by such agencies of a new free State in that magnificent region, it is unnecessary to dwell in detail, on the advantages which this enterprise holds out to the country at large.

"It determines in the right way the institutions of the unsettled Territories in less time than a discussion of them has required in Congress. It opens to those who are in want in the Eastern States a home and a competence, without the suffering hitherto incident to emigration. For the Company is the pioneer, and provides, before the settler arrives, the conveniences which he first requires. Such a removal of an over-crowded population is one of the greatest advantages to Eastern cities. Again, the enterprise opens commercial advantages to the commercial States, just in proportion to the population which it creates of freemen, who furnish a market to our manufactories and imports. Whether the new line of States shall be free States or slave States is a question deeply interesting to those who are to provide the manufactories for their consumption. Especially will it prove an advantage to Massachusetts, if she create the new State by her foresight, supply the first necessities to its inhabitants, and open in the outset communications between their homes and her ports and factories."

The report then sets forth how the investments of the Company will bring handsome returns to the stockholders, and concludes as follows:

"It is impossible that such a region should not fill up rapidly. The Massachusetts Emigrant Aid Company proposes to give confidence to settlers by giving system to emigration, by dispelling the fears that Kansas will be a slave State. The Company will remove the only bar which now hinders its occupation by free settlers. It is to be hoped that similar companies will be formed in other free States. The enterprise is of that character that for those who first enter it, the more competition the better.

"It is recommended that the first settlement made by the directories shall receive the name of that city in this commonwealth which shall have subscribed most liberally to the capital stock of the company in proportion to its last decimal valuation, and that the second city be named by the next city so subscribing."

The organization was never perfected under this charter, nor stock issued on account of some provisions of the law being objectionable to capitalists. On the 13th of June, the company organized under private articles of association, of which Amos Lawrence, John S. Williams and Eli Thayer were constituted Trustees. It then proceeded to operate as suggested in the foregoing report.

The articles under which this company was organized not proving satisfactory on account of the individual liablity to which it subjected the directors, on application a charter was obtained from the Legislature of Massachusetts under the title of the "New England Emigrant Aid Society." The object of the society, as set forth in this charter, was "for directing emigration westward and aiding in providing accommodations for the emigrants after arriving at their places of destination." Its capital stock was limited to one million dollars. It was under this charter that the Society operated.

The Emigrant Aid Society of New York and Connecticut organized on the 18th of July, 1854, under a charter granted by the Legislature of the former State. A board of twenty-seven Trustees controlled its affairs, who appointed an executive committee of three for immediate action. The capital stock was limited to $5,000,000, to be raised in shares of five dollars each. Its objects were the same as the former company.

About the same time, the Union Emigration Society was organized at Washington "by such members of Congress and citizens generally who were opposed to the repeal of the Missouri Compromise, and the opening of Nebraska and Kansas to the introduction of slavery." This society appointed agents in several States to organize auxiliary societies and to call the attention of the people to its movements.

Other societies of a similar character were formed in different parts of the free States, but these were the most important. None of them ever accomplished much or carried out its programme, except the New England.

The primary and chief object of these societies was to make Kansas a free State by settling her lands with a population adverse to slavery. The question occurs were the design and character of this action wrong on the part of the people opposed to the extension of this institution of the South? There can certainly be nothing objectionable in the design of promoting emigration to this newly opened Territory with a view of securing it to Free Labor. The idea of ventilating the great Eastern cities by removing its surplus population to the inviting fields of industry in the West, and of opening the channel for the vast tide of foreign emigration in the same direction, is worthy of a philanthropist. To do this for the purpose of accomplishing an ulterior object, divests the action of its beautiful garb of benevolence, but leaves it clad in its original vestment of justice, and opposition by all lawful measures to the extension of slavery. The act of Congress, therefore, referring "the vexed question of slavery" to arbitrament by the two conflicting interests of our Union in settling Kansas, called into being these societies and legalized their purpose. It is not the design in this place to examine and see whether these societies did any thing unjust or improper, but merely to inquire into the rightfulness of their motive and plan of operation. The works which they did will all be examined in the order of events.

CHAPTER XI.

FREE STATE EMIGRATION.—HOSTILE PREPARATIONS AND THE BEGINNING OF DIFFICULTIES.

About the first of July emigration began to arrive from the north-western free States. A little settlement thus effected in the neighborhood of the present City of Lawrence, having assembled on the first of August at Judge Miller's on what was then called "Back Bone Ridge," for the purpose of enacting squatter regulations, was suddenly interrupted by the intrusion of a band of Missourians under the leadership of an Indiana lawyer by the name of Dunham, who also acted as their spokesman. Seeing that they were unable to effect anything on account of the presence of these invaders, the free State men adjourned the meeting. The Missourians hurrying out of the house to "liquor," the convention arranged it to retire for a short time until the former disappeared. In the course of a couple of hours the little band of free soilers collected again, resumed their deliberations, adopted a constitution and by-laws and elected officers under them. Hon John A. Wakefield was constitutued Chief Justice, and Brier W. Miller, Recorder.

Under this simple and primary government, justice and equity were dealt out to all parties; unanimity and good will pervaded the little community. At one time having met at the call of the Executive Committee, to remodel their constitution, the Missourians again presented themselves to take part in the proceedings. For a time violence seemed imminent, but by a committee of conference a pacification was effected. The Missourians were permitted to take part in the election of officers, with the understanding that the incumbent of the Chief-Justiceship should be retained. Thus Squatter Sovereignty reigned in tranquility for two months when it was superseded by Frank Pierce's democracy.[1]

Hon. Charles H. Branscombe, now member of the Missouri Legislature from St. Louis, having been sent out in July by the New England Emigrant Aid Society to select a site for its first settlement, chose[2] the present beautiful location of Lawrence for that purpose. The first emigrants under the auspices of that Company, about thirty in number, arrived in the Territory the first of August, and laid the foundations for the first free state city of Kansas. When this little colony first encamped on the town site, but one man and his family occupied it, and some two or three Missourians had claims upon it. The New England party having succeeded in purchasing all prior improvements and claims, took possession of the town site. Having thus established themselves, they scatter out and selected in the neighborhood a quarter section of land apiece for their claims. Soon afterwards[3] a second and larger party, numbering sixty or seventy, arrived under the supervision of Dr. Charles Robinson and Gen. S. C. Pomroy. At this time the Lawrence association was formed on the principle of Squatter Sovereignty. Their numbers were soon increased by the arrival of the third and fourth parties.—The infant city, wrapped in the swaddling of grass, thatch and canvass, was known by the name of Waukarusa, New Boston, and by the Missourians, Yankee Town, until at a meeting of the Association[4] it took to itself the name of its benefactor—*Lawrence* (Amos A.) The colonists first dwelt in tents, pitched upon Mt. Oread and in the valley north of it; the largest of which was a place of general rendezvous. They were in this situation of primitive simplicity when first visited by the

(1) The author gathered this account from Mr. Wakefield himself. S. N. Wood was Secretary of those meetings. (2) July 17. (3) Two weeks. (4) Oct 6th.

Missourians. They soon applied themselves to the construction of rude homes for the coming winter. The "Pioneer Boarding House" was erected, consisting of two long rows of poles some distance apart at the base, and brought together at the top. These rafters were then thatched with prairie grass. The building, therefore, was all "roof and gable."—"This was the principal hotel of the new 'city'—the seed from which the Free State Hotel, Eldridge House No. 1, and Eldridge House No. 2 have sprung. The private dwellings were mostly log, pole and thatch houses."

The tide of emigration from the free States continued to flow in all the fall, settling various parts of the Territory, founding towns and making claims. They spread far back in the Territory and established themselves in little neighborhoods in the choicest parts of the country.

The city of Topeka was founded by Colonel C. K. Holliday, M. C. Dickey, F. W. Giles and six or seven others, in December, and, perhaps, did not number over twenty-five persons that year. In the spring they obtained a full share of the newly arrived emigrants, and the Constitution Hall, the Topeka House and several stores were erected. Topeka from the first centered her hopes upon the capital and has labored with commendable persistency to secure it. The word Topeka is of Indian origin, signifying "potato," or as the wags say, "small potatoes." It was first suggested by Mr. Webb, Secretary of the New England Emigrant Aid Society.

Manhattan, at the junction of the Big Blue and the Kansas Rivers, was first settled by a portion of the fourth New England party. Their numbers were greatly strengthened in the spring by a company from Cincinnati, Ohio, called the Manhattan Company, which gave name to the town. It is beautifully situated and has always been noted for its steady prosperity.

Grasshopper Falls was selected as a town site by Mr. Frazier. It is so named from the falls of a few feet in the Grasshopper Creek at the place where it is located. Other towns were laid out this fall, but these are the principal and the only ones that ever acquired any considerable importance.

Of the number of free state men who emigrated to the Territory this summer and fall perhaps five hundred came under the auspices of the New England Emigrant Aid Society. The existence of this Aid Society doubtless facilitated emigration, by scattering information respecting the Territory over the land, by calling the attention of the people to the importance of settling Kansas in order to prevent the extension of slavery, and by the assurance which they gave that mills, school houses and churches would be erected to accommodate the new country. Beyond this the work which they did towards peopling Kansas was insignificant. The only advantages which the New England Emigrant Aid Company furnished those who came under its immediate auspices, were the reduction of the fare about $5.00 and affording them the pleasure of a large company. The consequence was most people preferred to come independent of it. Not a cent was ever given by the company towards paying a single emigrant's fare; not a guarantee ever given that any person would be supported free after arriving in the Territory.

It was the deep pervading feeling in the North that Kansas ought to be rescued from slavery which awakened this emigration. The body of them came independent of any association, upon their own resources, to peaceably and legitimately establish free institutions in this land.

Other Aid Societies labored to increase emigration to Kansas, but none of them labored as systematically and upon as extensive a scale as the New England Emigrant Aid Society. None preserved their organization intact and continued their operations until the close of the Kansas difficulties, except the one above mentioned. None organized this fall, established a colony or formed a settlement, except the New England. It was pre-eminently the largest and most thoroughly organized of all similar companies and accomplished more than all others combined. It sent out under its auspices as many as

2,000 persons. It built mills and school houses, thus strengthening the towns of Lawrence, Topeka, Ossawattomie, and a few others. In time it received town shares for the investments made. At Kansas City it built a hotel and likewise the Free State Hotel at Lawrence, which was destroyed. The company never employed over $100,000 in its expenditures, and was nothing more nor less than what it styled itself, "The New England Emigrant Aid Society," not sending, but assisting emigrants to Kansas, and extending the help of capital to better their condition after their arrival.

The first influx of free state men spread alarm among the slavery propagandists of the Border. They readily saw that they would be utterly unable to legitimately compete with the vast numbers coming from the Eastern, Middle and Northwestern States. The bright hallucination that had lit up the prospects of slavery in Kansas and rendered the people of north-western Missouri jubilantly wild, was now darkened by the swarms of "Northern cattle" that had just begun to settle in the Territory, and the coming of which vague rumor had described "as countless as the stars."

The knights of slavery disappointed, though not dismayed, resolved to terrify others from coming by threats and bluster, and persecuting those already arrived. The Platte Argus sounds the alarm thus:

> "It is now time to sound the alarm. We know we speak the sentiments of some of the most distinguished statesmen of Missouri when we advise that counter organizations be made both in Kansas and Missouri to thwart the reckless course of the abolitionists. We must meet them at their very threshhold and scourge them back to their caverns of darkness. They have made the issue and it is for us to meet and repel them."

It was now determined to excite the populace, to influence the noted rabble of the Border, until they are fit and willing for any work of barbarism. The Emigrant Aid Societies were represented as gathering the paupers of the great eastern cities and hiring them to come out to Kansas to disturb the institutions of Missouri, to make it a free State in defiance of law and order. The press was filled with stories of fugitive slaves being run off from other States by abolitionists, meetings were held at the various towns in the first two tiers of counties, at which the most inflammatory speeches were made. The first of these, held at Weston, adopted the following resolution:

"*Resolved*, That this association will, whenever called upon by any of the citizens of Kansas Territory, hold itself in readiness together to assist and remove any and all emigrants, who go there under the auspices of the Emigrant Aid Societies."

At another meeting assembled at Liberty, Clay County, the following preface and resolutions were passed:

"Therefore, we, the citizens of Clay County, believing self-preservation to be the first law of nature, and learning that organizations have been effected in the Northern States for the purpose of colonizing the Territory of Kansas with such fanatical persons as composed the recent disgraceful mob in the city of Boston, where a United States officer, for simply attempting to obtain justice for a Southern citizen, was shot down in the streets; and learning, too, that these organizations have for their object the colonization of said Territory with 'eastern and foreign paupers,' with a view of excluding citizens of slave-holding States, and especially citizens of Missouri, from settling there with their property; and, further, to establish a trunk of the under-ground railroad, connecting with the same line, where thousands of our slaves shall be stolen from us, in thwarting their attempts upon our rights, we do

"*Resolve*, That Kansas ought of right to be a slave State, and we pledge ourselves to co-operate with the citizens of Jackson County, and the South generally, in any MEASURE to accomplish such ENDS."

Other meetings held at various places adopted about the same resolutions.

The Platte *Argus* having advertised $200 reward for the detection and seizure of Eli Thayer, President of the New England Emigrant Aid Society, the Democratic Platform, in noticing it, says: "We hope that the individual may be found and meet with just such a course of treatment as one of his sort deserves—hanging!!"

The same paper, in speaking of A. Guthrie, who had written some letters to the East encouraging emigration, remarks, "We would hate to see an American hung without the benefit of clergy or jury. But is there not some way to punish this traitor? Is *drowning* too good for him?"

In the latter part of July the Platte County Self-Defensive Association was formed at Weston, with Gen. B. F. Stringfellow as Secretary. Its constitution contained a preamble and nine articles, the substance of which was:

All free negroes must be expelled from the country.

No traffic between whites and slaves was to be permitted.

No slaves were to be permitted to hire their own time.

The Association was to try and punish all abolitionists.

That we hereby mutually pledge ourselves, our honor and purses to bring to an immediate punishment any person guilty.

That we appoint six presidents, and wherever any person is found his case shall be referred to one of these presidents, and any other two subscribers hereto, whose concurrent judgment shall be final, and we pledge our persons to defend the same and our purses to indemnify.

About one thousand persons affixed their signatures to this constitution. It was an immense Lynch Court, with six judges and one thousand detectives; from the judgment of one of its judges and two of its members, there was no appeal. It has not its example in history, unless it be the famous Jacobin Club of France. At their first meeting the following resolutions were passed:

"That we, the members of the Platte County Self-Defensive Association, do solemnly pledge ourselves to go at the call of our brethren, who are across the river in Kansas, and drive out from their midst the abolition traitors.

"2. That we recommend to citizens of other counties, and especially those bordering on Kansas Territory, to adopt similar regulations to those of this Association, and to indicate their readiness to co-operate in the objects of the first resolution."

Dr. George Bayliss, a man of small and feeble frame, the author of these resolutions, and who had formerly been Professor of Anatomy in the Louisville and Cincinnati Colleges, remarking upon them, said:

"I can not fight much, but I pledge you I will go with you, and you shall have all my skill as a surgeon for your wounded and dying."

Colonel Peter T. Abell, in speaking on the resolutions, said:

"I am ready to go the first hour it shall be announced that the emigrants have come, and with my own hand help hang every one of them on the first tree."

General Stringfellow having been called upon to express himself, denounced all who labor for their daily bread as slaves and prostitutes. It is justice to remark that he afterwards denied making such assertions.*

Gen. B. F. Stringfellow is a Virginian by birth, and a lawyer by profession. He is a man of more than ordinary ability, and with the exception of the part he took in the Kansas troubles, has always been noted as a high-toned gentleman and an excellent citizen. In 1849 he joined in law partnership with Col. P. T. Abell, at Weston, Mo., between whom

*The following are the sentiments set forth by General Stringfellow, as certified to by seventeen respectable citizens:

All who labor for their daily bread and are dependent on their labor for subsistence are slaves! All females who labor for their daily bread are whores! and have been so from the days of Abraham. He further remarked in this immediate connection, that should Kansas come in as a free State, he would leave this State; he would not allow his daughters and sons to associate with them; he would go where his color was respected and where he could bring up his sons honorable men and his daughters virtuous women.

ever since has existed the closest friendly and business relation. During the Kansas troubles the General continued to reside ta Weston, taking an active and lively interest in the affairs of the Territory. After the Slavery issue was abandoned in 1857, he meditated moving to Memphis, Tenn., and visitedthat city with that end in view. But from some cause, instead of moving to Memphis, he went to St. Louis, Mo., where in connection with Col. Abell, his partner, he opened his law office. Remaining there until 1860, he removed to Atchison, Kansas, where he has continued ever since in the practice of his profession, honored and respected by all with whom he mingles.

Dr. J. H. Stringfellow, the General's brother, was the more violent of the two and is frequently confounded with the latter. In 1854 he settled in Atchison and was senior editor of the Squatter Sovereign. He was wanting in the manliness and intellectual ability of his brother, and was the most ultra and rabid pro-slavery man that *lived* in the Territory. The Doctor remained in Kansas until 1855, when, the contest having been abandoned, he returned to Virginia. During the recent war some of the Kansas boys visited him at his residence and found him very hospitable and apparently glad to see them.

It was some time in the fall, perhaps as late as October, when Secret Societies began to be generally formed in western Missouri for the avowed object of extending slavery into Kansas. They had a constitution and by-laws, signs, grips and pass-words, as other secret societies generally have. They were sworn to assist in extending slavery into Kansas *by all lawful means*, and to afford each other mutual protection—especially while in the Territory. They wore a piece of ribbon in the coat button-hole as a badge of membership or affiliation, which entitled them to the protection of the order. Different orders had various names, as "Blue Lodge," "Social Band," "Friend's Society," "The Sons of the South," &c. They had existed for years in the old slave States, always looking to the interest of slavery, and there were previous to this date, organizations of this order in Missouri.—They formed a union of all the friends of slavery, and combined efforts in carrying out their measures. They had different degrees, the common class being admitted only to the first. Through these Societies the political leaders had immediate access to, and control of the masses. In them passions were inflamed, plans revealed, and whiskey drank.—Their plan of operation was to send men into the territory to watch free state men, and report promptly; to keep a vast number of men in readiness to lend assistance at a moment's notice to those in the Territory; to organize an army to go over and vote, and collect money to pay their expenses. The members under heavy penalties were forbidden to reveal the secrets of the Society. These lodges performed the most efficient services in controlling the Territorial elections.—They were equal to a line of numerous military posts extending two counties deep along the Border, the men of which could be concentrated at a given signal.

Such were the stupenduous arrangements that the Missourians made in the fall of '54 to conquer Kansas by overawing or expelling northern men and deterring future emigration. The avowed apology which they have given for their conduct was to counteract the workings of the Eastern Emigrant Aid Societies. And, yet, most of these steps and measures were taken before the first party of thirty under the auspices of these societies had begun their journey to Kansas. Almost all the emigration had come free and unconnected with the "monied institutions" of the East. It was not, therefore, the action of these societies altogether that led the Missourians to such desperate measures; but the real cause is to be found in the fact that they were alarmed and enraged lest the unexpected influx of free state emigration would render uncertain the darling institution of Slavery in Kansas; and these measures would have been the same had there been no emigrant aid societies. The direct effects of these societies were as a drop in the ocean in the settling of Kansas with freemen. It is but a flimsy apology whereby many of the intelligent and seemingly honest men of Missouri have sought to excuse their conduct. It is the plea of justification afterwards so eloquently made in the halls of Congress, and which blinded the eyes of many in the North to the real nature of the struggle in Kansas. The action of these societies was maliciously employed to inflame the ignorant masses against emigrants to Kansas and prepare them for the barbarous outrages which it now becomes our painful duty to begin to relate and which have long since sunk their instigators into shame and contempt.

In a few days after the organization of the Self-defensive Association, they seized Thomas A. Minnard, Esq., formerly a sheriff in Iowa, a man of wealth and irreproachable character. He had begun to build a house in Kansas and had declared that he would vote for Kansas to be a free State. He was tried, condemned as an abolitionist and ordered to leave the country in twenty-four hours or receive fifty lashes on the bare back. He had helped to elect Franklin Pierce President and was an admirer of the Kansas-Nebraska bill. But he had resolved as a freeman to exercise his franchise in making Kansas a free State, for which he was inhospitably driven into the wilds of Kansas with a sick family where he had not yet completed his shelter.

An old citizen of that place was then seized, tried without proof except a negro's testimony, and condemned as an abolitionist. With the hair shaved from the right half of his head he was ordered to leave the country within forty-eight hours or receive one hundred and fifty lashes on the bare back!

The Rev. Frederick Starr was then arraigned before the tribunal for the offense of teaching the negroes to read, and riding in a buggy with a "negro wench!" Mr. Starr was a graduate of Yale College, and had quietly labored among the people of Weston for seven years, never weary in well doing. He pleaded guilty of the two charges but showed that he had obtained permission of the master to instruct the negro and that the second was in accordance with the custom of the country to take servants in the carriage. Being unable to find any grounds to convict him of misdemeanors and succeeding only in rendering themselves ridiculous before a crowded house of both ladies and gentlmen, they acquitted him.

But this Association did not stop with trying abolitionists, and driving men from the country because of their opinions. It sought, also, to control the business of the country by requiring all classes of trade to patronize only those who were favorable to slavery, by prescribing for the merchants to make their purchase in slave holding cities. But the tyrany of this organizid mob soon became insufferable, and there was a sudden, spontaneous and general uprising of the outraged community against it. A public meeting of the people of Weston was called at which the following preamble and resolutions were adopted, and one hundred and seventy-four citizens of that town affixed their signatures to them:

"*Whereas*, Our rights and privileges as citizens of Weston, Platte County, Missouri, have been disregarded, infringed upon and greviously violated within the last few weeks by certain members of the Platte County Self-Defensive Association; And, whereas, the domestic quiet of our families, the sacred honor of our sons and daughters, the safety of our property, the security'of our livings and persons, the good name our fathers left us, the good name of us all, and the city of our adoption, are each and all disrespected and and vilely aspersed, and contemptuously threatened with mob violence; wherefore it is imperatively demanded that we in mass meeting assembled, cn this the 1st day of September, 1854, do make prompt, honorable, effective and immediate defense of our rights and privileges as citizens of this glorious Union; Therefore,

"*Resolved*, 1. That we whose names are hereunto affixed are order loving and law abiding citizens.

"2. That we are *Union men*; we love the South *much*, but we love the Union *better*; our motto is, "The Union first, Union second, and Union forever."

"3. That we disapprove Bayliss' resolution as containing nullification, disunion and disorganizing sentiments.

"4. That we as consumers invite and solicit our merchants to purchase their goods wherever it is most advantageous to the buyer and to the consumer.

"5. That we hold *every man* as entitled to *equal respect and confidence* until his conduct proves him unworthy of the same.

"6. That we understand the Douglas bill as giving all the citizens of this Confederacy equal rights and equal immunities in the Territories in Kansas and Nebraska.

"7. That we believe in the *dignity of labor*. It does not necessarily detract from the moral or intellectual character of man.

"8. That we are competent to judge who shall be expelled from our community and who shall make laws for our corporation.

"9. That mere suspicion is not a ground of guilt. Mob law can only be tolerated when all other laws fail, and then only on proof of *guilt*.

"10. And, lastly that certain members, the leaders of the Platte County Self-Defensive Association, have proclaimed and advocated and attempted to force measures upon us contrary to the foregoing principles, which measures we do solemnly disavow and disapprove and utterly disclaim as being diametrically opposed to common and constitutional law, and as having greatly disturbed and well nigh destroyed the order, the peace and the harmony of our community; and as being too well calculated to injure us in our property and character at home and abroad, we will thus ever disavow and disclaim."

The power and reign of the Self-Defensives in Weston were now at an end. "Three times did they order the inoffensive blacks to leave the city and county, and when at the third command an armed band of outlaws were coming to drive them out, the citizens armed themselves with loaded rifles to meet them, and the assailants forebore to enter the town." They removed their headquarters from place to place at the remonstrance of the citizens, and were by October almost entirely superseded by the "Blue Lodges" in their operations.*

Scarcely had the little colonists spread their tents upon the grassy sward at Lawrence before the Missourians sought to drive them from their resting place. They came in wagons with "music," flags and whisky, to the number of about one hundred and encamped on the north side of the ravine running through the west part of what is now the city of Lawrence. They grounded their action upon the alleged fact that a certain tent stood on a claim which belonged to their number, and demanded its removal, and threatened in case it was not removed they would remove it themselves. To which the reply was given: "If you molest our property you do it at your peril." The pro-slavery men then informed the emigrants that they might have until morning to remove the tent *peaceably*, and retired to drink, shoot and carouse at their encampment.

All night the colonists kept out a guard to prevent a surprise from the Missourians. Morning came, and the invaders increased by fifty fresh arrivals. They sent over the demand: "The tent must be taken down and all their effects gathered together preparatory to leave by two o'clock," and "that the abolitionists must leave the Territory never to return to it." The free state men mustered about sixty persons and drilled them before the tent with arms. At ten o'clock the solemn assurance was sent, "They could have another half hour to remove *that tent* and get ready to leave," after which, if they did not comply, every one of them would be "put to the bowie knife." "That was in earnest." The half hour sped quickly by, and another messenger appears with the communication that they dreaded the effusion of blood and hoped to avoid it, and for this reason another hour would

*The author gathers the material for an account of this organization chiefly from the letter of Rev. F. Starr, in the New York Tribune, November 5, 1854, and from "Three Years on the Border," by an Episcopal clergyman. They were both reliable men, eye witnesses to the scenes, and wrote their accounts at the time the events transpired.

be given for the tent's removal. The hour elapsed, the Border Ruffians mustered their forces, but no attack was made. They got into a dispute and wrangle among themselves whether to attempt to remove the tent or not—some warmly favoring it, others timidly opposing it. Thus they continued to parade and debate until near sundown, when they broke up their encampment and left with the warning to the colonists that they would return within a week with a thousand men and "wipe them out."

So ended the first invasion of Lawrence, bloodless and harmless, prevoking only laughter from those assailed.

CHAPTER XII.

INAUGURATION OF GOVERNMENT.

For the first four months after the opening ot Kansas for settlement there was no general government over the Territory; but squatters in various localities would get together and adopt rules and regulations to which all would subscribe. By these rules all questions pertaining to claims were settled, and a record of them kept. Peace and harmony prevailed among the settlers, and there was no difficulty, only when some wandering Missourians would seek to disturb free state men in the possession of their claims. People were intent in the construction of their new homes, and the question of slavery attracted little attention. Presses began to be introduced of a stamp that would have done honor to an older country. Prosperity and good will existed among all classes. But the mischief-makers in Missouri were busy at their work, soon, indeed, to disturb the growth and harmony of the rising State.

The following officers were appointed by the President to organize and administer government in Kansas: Andrew H. Reeder, of Pennsylvania, Governor; Daniel Woodson, of Virginia, Secretary; Samuel D. Lecompte, of Maryland, Chief Justice; Sanders W. Johnson, of Ohio, and Rush Elmore, of Alabama, Associate Justices; J. B. Donaldson, of Illinois,

Marshal; Andrew J. Isaacs, of Louisiana, District Attorney; John Calhoun, of Illinois, Surveyor General of Kansas and Nebraska; S. Cunningham, of Missouri, Superintendent of Indian Affairs.

Governor Reeder was born in Easton, Northampton County, Pennsylvania, on the 12th day of July, 1807. He received a thoroughly classical and legal education, and was admitted to the bar in 1828. By diligence and untiring perseverance he steadily advanced to a position of eminence among the first lawyers of the State. Though always a warm advocate of the principles of the Democratic party, he never sought political preferment, but confined himself to his profession with enthusiastic attachment. He was a man of fine appearance, straight figure and slightly inclined to obesity. Of genial disposition, profound reverence for right and incorruptable virtue, he would have made an excellent Governor where excellence is esteemed. Adoring the beautiful theories of Democracy, he knew nothing of its practical workings.' Such was the man first led for immolation upon the gubernatorial altar of Kansas—"a victim without spot or blemish."

The appointment of Mr. Reeder met with the hearty approval of the Democratic press throughout the land. The South had confidence in Mr. Pierce, and felt sure that he understood the man of his selection; the North hoped from Mr. Reeder's character that justice would be administered in the Territory. All felt safe that the Governor would have much influence in determining the institutions of the future State and the eyes of the nation were upon him.

On arriving at Leavenworth he met with a warm reception from the towns-people. Stepping from the Polar Star upon the levee he was greeted by a vast concourse of citizens, a speech of welcome and a national salute from the Fort. His response was that of a pure statesman to a confiding people, in which he said: "By preserving unimpaired the purity of the ballot-box and deciding there, as freemen should, the question which the nation has properly referred to it, each man calmly, fearlessly and dispassionately expressing his opinion in casting his vote in conformity with the dictates of his conscience and understanding, and by bowing submissively to the will of the majority, when properly ascertained, we shall have done our whole duty and may expect to reap its pleasant fruits."

Mr. Reeder immediately made an extensive tour through the Territory to ascertain the character, condition and wants of the people, and was every-where met with the same cordial welcome. On returning to Fort Leavenworth in two weeks, he applied himself to districting the inhabited portion of the Territory preparatory to an election for Delegate to Congress. He soon issued[2] his proclamation for this purpose by which the judges of the election were required under oath that they would reject the votes of all non-residents who they should believe had come into the Territory for the mere purpose of voting. He defined the word "resident" as used in the Organic Act to mean "the actual dwelling or inhabiting in the Territory, to the exclusion of any other present domicile or house coupled with the present *bona fide* intention of permanently remaining for the same purpose."

This proclamation was not at all palatable to the slavery propagandists and from this time henceforth Mr. Reeder was in disfavor with them. In a few days some two or three hundred Missourians crossed[3] over in wagons and on horseback to hold a convention at Leavenworth. In this convention Mr. Reeder was denounced as favoring the free soilers and abolitionists by not calling an election for members of the Territorial Legislature. They saw that they were fast losing ground by the increasing emigration from the free States, and hence desired an election that they might get control of the legislative affairs of Kansas before

(2) November 10. (3) November 15.

they lost the balance of power. They, therefore, appointed a committee to urge upon him his duty in this direction. The cômmittee presented themselves to Governor Reeder as representing a convention composed of actual residents of Kansas Territory, and handed him a memorial from that body soliciting him to call an election for members of the Legislature. But Mr. Reeder was not to be deceived, and requested of them the proceedings of the convention to which they alluded. This they haughtily and peremptorily refused.

Mr. Reeder replied in a written document to these memorialists that if they had been actual residents of the Territory their petition would have met with a respectful consideration; but, though their committee refused to furnish him a copy of their proceedings that he might know the character of the convention, he had ascertained from other sources that it was composed chiefly of persons from Missouri whose wishes had no claims upon his consideration. He then proceeded to rebuke them for their misconduct and closed with a hope that the people from a neighboring State would not meddle with the affairs of the Territory.

There were three candidates in the field for Delegate to Congress. Hon. John A. Wakefield was the avowed free State candidate. He was a Virginian by birth, no politician, a sincere, honest old man. He was not learned in schools, but possessed a large share of practical common sense, and would have well represented the interests of the Territory. General J. W. Whitfield was the pro-slavery candidate. He was a resident of Jackson County, Missouri, a tall Tennesseean of rather good appearance. With his moderate abilities he possessed a good share of cunning. He was nominated by the convention of his fellow-citizens in Leavenworth to which we alluded above. He afterwards found a position in the rebel army. Hon. Robert P. Flenneken was an independent candidate who came out with Governor

Reeder on purpose to run at the election. He was shrewd, ambitious and vain; left immediately after his defeat.

There was but little interest taken in the election by the settlers; many of them having just arrived in the Territory, were busy providing for winter. The issue of slavery was not generally made, most of the people feeling that the delegate would have little to do in deciding this question. So spoke Judge Flenneker and Gen. Whitfield; by which means they obtained free state votes. They both professed to be in favor of leaving this question to the people of the Territory to settle, and who could object to that? Wherever the issue was made the free state votes were divided between Wakefield and Flenneken—Whitfield getting a few of this class.

The election took place the 29th fo November. Atchison and Stringfellow through the agency of the secret societies had prepared the Missourians for their work. The former in a public speech which he made a few weeks previous to the election in Platte county, eloquently exhorted them to go over and do their duty by voting.[4] In one half the districts there was little or no fraudulent voting; in the other half there 1729 illegal votes cast. At Lawrence the day previous to the election, the Missourians came on horseback and in wagons, with guns, bowie knives, revolvers and whiskey, and encamped near town. Early next morning having gathered around the house where the polls were to be kept, two of the judges not appearing, they selected two from their crowd to fill the vacancies and voted. "In order to make a pretense of right to vote, some persons of the company kept a pretended register of Squatter claims,

(4) Speech of General Atchison, Nov. 6: "When you reside in one day's journey of the Territory, and when your peace, your quiet and your property depend upon your action, you can without an exertion, send five hundred of your young men who will vote in favor of your institutions. Should each county in the State of Missouri only do its duty, the question will be decided quietly and peaceably at the ballot-box. If we are defeated then Missouri and the other Southern States will have shown themselves recreant to their interests and will deserve their fate."—Platte Argus.

on which any one would enter his name, and then assert that he had a claim in the Territory. When the polls closed they mounted their horses and wagons and cried out "All aboard for Westport and Kansas City." With thirty-five legal votes there were polled two hundred and twenty-six illegal ones. In the 4th District, forty miles from Missouri, out of one hundred and sixty-one votes polled, one hundred and thirty-one were those of non-residents. In a very remote settlement called "110," seventy-five miles west from the border, there were six hundred and four votes polled, of which only twenty were legal.[5] In Marysville, where only seven legal votes were polled, there were two hundred and thirty-eight fraudulent ones. Some of the leading men of Missouri, comprising merchants, doctors and lawyers, were recognized among these ballot-box stuffers. There were the Judges of Buchanan and Cass Counties, the City Attorney of St. Joseph and a noted lawyer from Independence. Of the total number of legal votes cast General Whitfield received a plurality. He was declared duly elected by the Governor and obtained his seat in Congress. There was

(5) ABSTRACT OF ELECTION, NOVEMBER 29, 1854.—FROM REPORT OF CONGRESSIONAL COMMITTEE.

DISTRICTS.	Place of Meeting.	Whitfield.	Wakefield.	Flenncken.	Scattering.	Total.	Legal Votes.	Illegal Votes.
First	Lawrence,	46	188	51	15	300	300	....
Seco d	Douglas	235	20	6	....	261	35	226
Thi d	Stinson's	40	....	7	....	47	47	....
Fourth	Dr. Chapin's	140	21	21	....	161	30	131
Fifth	H. Shemai's	63	4	15	....	82	30	52
Sixth	Ft. Scott	105	....	....	....	105	25	80
Seventh	"110"	597	....	7	....	604	20	584
Eighth	Council Grove	16	....	....	....	16	16	....
Ninth	Reynold's	9	....	31	....	40	40	....
Tenth	Big Blue Cross	2	6	29	....	37	37	....
E eventh	Marysvil e	237	....	3	5	245	7	238
Twe fth	arton's Store	31	9	....	1	41	41	....
Thirteenth	Osawkie	69	1	1	....	71	71	....
Fourteenth	Herding's	130	....	23	....	153	103	50
Fifteenth	Penseno	267	....	39	....	306	100	206
Sixteenth	Leavenworth	232	....	80	....	312	150	162
Seventeenth	Shawnee Agency	49	....	13	....	62	62	....
Total		2258	248	305	22	2833	1114	1729

but little need of this intermeddling on the part of Missouri to elect a pro-slavery man. The free state men disorganized, scattered over a vast territory, divided in reference to the choice of Delegate, not regarding the question of slavery at stake, indifferent as to the result, would likely have been beaten without votes from Missouri. Had the election been on the issue of slavery, the result would have been doubtful; but most probable, as the Missourians feared, in favor of Mr. Wakefield. Although Mr. Whitfield dextrously avoided making slavery an issue in his canvass, his election was immediately heralded by his friends as a victory achieved in the interest of slavery.

Such were the first practical exemplifications of Popular Sovereignty. A doctrine incubated by General Cass in 1848, it was afterwards attired in such a beautiful and attractive garb as to charm the nation. But its success on the field of practice was prevented by its own friends and itself rendered ridiculous before the world.

In the meanwhile Justices of the Peace were appointed in various localities, before whom differences could be adjusted, criminals arraigned and bound over to the higher court. About the first of January the Territory was divided into three Judicial Districts and a Justice assigned to each. Hon. Samuel D. Lecompte had jurisdiction over the north-eastern portion; Hon. Rush Elmore the south-eastern, and Hon. S. W. Johnson the remaining portion of the Territory. Preliminary courts were to be held on the first of March, and the regular term to begin in April.

CHAPTER XIII.

ELECTING TERRITORIAL LEGISLATURE.

This winter proved a remarkably mild and pleasant one which greatly favored the new settlers. They continued their improvements uninterrupted by cold.

In order to make a proper apportionment of representation, preparatory to calling an election, the Governor caused the census to be taken in the Territory during January and February. This work was undertaken without any public announcement of the fact, which highly incensed the people of the Border. Had such knowledge been imparted to them it was their design to cross over and be enumerated. In this, they were disappointed and the census returns were sent in as accurate as could be under the circumstances.—From them it appears there were 5,128 males, 3,383 females, 2,805 voters and 3,469 minors in the Territory at that time. From the same report we learn that there were 408 of foreign birth, 7,161 natives of the United States, 151 negroes and 192 slaves, making a total population of 8,601 souls.

The following anecdote is obtained from Mr. Phillip's "Conquest of Kansas:"

"As a census taker approached a log cabin some three miles from Atchison, a woman with violent gesticulations and loud voice came running across the prairie; 'Are you the man that takes the censum?[1] 'Yes, Ma'm; What do

(1) In many places pro-slavery men would prepare a list of those living in Missouri and endeavor by threats to have the census-taker insert them.

you want?' 'Why, ride to Atchison just as quick as you can and take the censum; there are two men in my house with my husband; they are expecting you, and they are to get you talking and detain you while one rides to Atchison to tell them that you are coming, so that the people from Missouri can come over and get in the censum. So ride there quick and my husband wont know that you have come along.' He passed on to Atchison and took the census."

For months the Missourians and pro-slavery men had been railing at Gov. Reeder for not calling an election for members of the Territorial Legislature. They charged him him with being in league with the "Abolition Societies" of the East and with deferring the election, that they might carry it by the vast influx of imported voters in the spring. They threatened to depose him by assassination, or petition his removal. Others desired to elect a new Governor at the coming election and solicit his appointment by the President. Unheeding their outcries and menaces, he perseveringly labored for the good of the Territory. What need was there for such haste in electing a Legislature?—Peace and quiet prevailed throughout the Territory, and courts were established where all differences could be adjusted. Had Mr. Reeder designed to favor the free state party by delaying the election, he certainly would have fixed it a little later in the season, as eastern emigration could not reach here before the last of April. He really favored the Missourians whose spring emigration could arrive in March by appointing the election to be held at the time he did.

Five days after the census returns were perfected,[1] the Governor issued his proclamation for an election of members to the Council and House of the Territorial Legislature, to take place on the 30th of March.

The free state men determined to be more organized this

---

(1) March 8th.

time, and make a manful contest at the polls. There was no disguising the fact that slavery was the real issue in this election. The Free State party was organized, speakers appointed to canvass the country and awaken the people to the importance of the interests at stake; primary conventions were held and candidates nominated, in short all the paraphernalia of a political campaign was exhibited. Every one telt that the destinies of the State were to be decided.

But the earnest and peaceful effort of these isolated freemen were doomed to meet a crushing opposition. The people of the Border no longer concealed their intention to come over and vote. The pro-slavery newspapers in Kansas invited and urged them to come. False and inflammatory rumors were circulated through all Western Missouri concerning vast "hordes of paupers and abolitionists" being carried to Kansas on every boat by the Emigrant Aid Societies in order to control the election. The secret societies were put into requisition and every arrangement and provisions made for the conquest of Kansas unto Slavery.

At a pro-slavery mass meeting in Platte City November 5th, 1855, Hon. D. R. Atchison addressed the people, and among other things said:

"We must and will make Kansas a Slave State, *peaceably* if we can, and at the point of the bayonet if we must."

Rev. Leander Kerr, who read a poem and an address denouncing the free state settlers in Kansas, said:

"Go then (to Kansas) as men, as patriots, as Christians, and do your duty to yourselves, *your country* and your God."

Gen. B. F. Stringfellow, to remove all scruples of legality in the conduct of Missourians going over to vote, delivered the following argument upon it:

"If the very day of his returning is not fixed, if he is uncertain, he is in strictest law a 'resident' and an 'inhabitant.'

"By the Kansas act every man in the Territory on the day of election is a loyal voter, if he has not fixed a day for his return to some other home.

"Every man has a right to go to Kansas for such purposes as he pleases.

"The presence of a voter is all the proof of residence he is required to give. If present it is necessary to show he has not a right to vote."

As these invasions and stuffing of the ballot-box by the Missourians have no precedent in the history of our country, and so strikingly exemplify the doctrine of Popular Sovereignty, which repealed the Missouri restriction on the plea of injustice and unconstitutionality, a full account of the second invasion is here inserted from the report of the committee appointed by Congress to investigate it.

"By an organized movement which extended from Andrew County in the north to Jasper County in the south, and as far eastward as Boone and Cole Counties, Missouri, companies of men were arranged in irregular parties and sent *into every council district in the Territory, and into every representative district but one.* The members were so distributed as to control the election in each district. They went to vote, and with an avowed design to make Kansas a Slave State. They were generally armed and equipped, carried with them their own provisions and tents, and so marched into the Territory. The details of this invasion from the mass of testimony taken by your committee are so voluminous that we can here state but the leading facts elicited.

FIRST DISTRICT—LAWRENCE.

"The company of persons who marched into this district were collected in Ray, Carrol, Howard, Boone, LaFayette, Randolph, Macon, Clay, Jackson, Saline and Cass Counties in the State of Missouri. Their expenses were paid; those who could not come, contributing provisions, wagons, &c. Provisions were deposited for those who were expected to come to Lawrence, in the house of William Lykins, and were distributed among the Missourians after they arrived there. The evening before, and the morning of the day of the election, about 1,000 men from the above named counties arrived and camped in a ravine a short distance from town, near the place of voting. They came in wagons (of which there were over 100), and on horse-back, under the command of Colonel Samuel Young, of Boone County, Missouri, and of Clairborn F. Jackson, of Missouri. They were armed with guns, pistols, bowie knives, and had tents, music and flags with them. They brought with them two pieces of artillery loaded with musket balls. On their way to Lawrence some of them met Mr. N. B. Blanton, who had been appointed one of the judges of the election by Governor Reeder, and, after learning from him that he considered it his duty to demand an oath from them as to their place of residence, first attempted to bribe him, and then threatened him with hanging, in order to induce him to dispense with that oath. In consequence of these threats he did not appear at the polls the next morning to act as judge.

"The evening before the election the Missourians were called together before the tent of Clairborn F. Jackson, and speeches were made to them by Colonel Young and others, calling for volunteers to go to other districts where there were not Missourians enough to control the election, as there were more at Lawrence than were needed there. Many volunteered to go, and on the morning of the election several companies, from 150 to 200 each, went off to Tecumseh, Hickory Point, Bloomington and several other places. On the morning of the election the Missourians came to the place of voting from their camp in bodies of 100 at a time. Mr. Blanton not appearing another judge was appointed in his place, Colonel Young claiming that as the people of the Territory had two judges it was nothing more than right that the Missourians should have the other one to look after their interests; and Robert A. Cummings was elected in Blanton's stead, because he considered every man had a right to vote if he had been in the Territory but one hour.

"When the voting commenced the question of legality of a vote of a Mr. Page was raised. Before it was decided Colonel Samuel Young stepped up to the window where the votes were received and said he would settle the matter. The vote of Mr. Page was withdrawn and Colonel Young offered to vote. He refused to take the oath prescribed by the Governor, but swore he was a resident of the Territory, upon which his vote was received. He told Mr. Abbot, one of the judges, when asked if he intended to make Kansas his future home, that it was none of his business; that if he were a resident then, he should ask no more. After his vote was received he got up on the window-sill and announced to the crowd that he had been permitted to vote, and they should all come up and vote. He told the judges that there was no use in swearing the others, as they would all swear as he had done. After the other judges had concluded to receive Colonel Young's vote, Mr. Abbot resigned as judge of the election, and Mr. Benjamin was elected in his place.

"The polls were so much crowded until late in the evening, that for a time when men had voted they were obliged to get out by being hoisted upon the roof of the building where the election was being held, and pass out over the house. Afterwards, a passage way through the crowd was made by two lines of men being formed, through which the voters could get up to the polls. Colonel Young asked that the old men be allowed to go up first and vote, as they were tired with the traveling and wanted to get back to camp.

"The Missourians sometimes came up to the polls in procession two and two and voted.

"During the day the Missourians drove off the ground some of the citizens—Mr. Stearns, Mr. Bond and Mr. Willis. They threatened to shoot Mr. Bond, and a crowd rushed after him, threatening him; and as he ran from them some shots were fired at him as he jumped off the bank of the river and made his escape. The citizens of the town went over in a body late in the afternoon, when the polls had become comparatively clear, and voted.

"They said they came to the Territory to elect a Legislature to suit themselves, as the people of the Territory and persons from the East and the North wanted to elect a Legislature that would not suit them. They said they had a right to make Kansas a slave State, because the people of the North had sent persons out to make it a free State. Some claimed that they had heard that the Emigrant Aid Society had sent men out to be at the election, and they came to offset their votes; but the most of them made no such claim. Colonel Young said that he wanted the citizens to vote, in order to give the election some show of fairness. The Missourians said there would be no difficulty if the citizens did not interfere with their voting; but they were determined to vote peaceably if they could, but vote anyhow. They said each one of them was prepared for eight rounds without loading and would go the ninth round with the butcher knife. Some of them said that by voting they would deprive themselves of the right to vote in Missouri for twelve months afterwards. The Missourians began to leave the afternoon of the election, though some did not go home until next morning. In many cases when a wagon load had voted they immediately started for home. On their way home they said that if Governor Reeder did not sanction their election they would hang him.

"The citizens of the town of Lawrence as a general thing were not armed on the day of election, though some had revolvers, but not exposed as were the arms of the Missourians. They kept a guard about the town the night after the election, in consequence of the threats of the Missourians, in order to protect it.

SECOND DISTRICT—BLOOMINGTON.

On the morning of the election, the judges appointed by the Governor appeared and opened the polls. Their names were Harrison Burson, Nathaniel Ramsey, and Mr. Ellison. The Missourians began to come in early in the morning, some 500 or 600 of them in wagons and carriages, and on horseback, under the lead of Samuel J. Jones, then postmaster at Westport, Missouri; Claiborne F. Jackson and Mr. Steeley, of Independence, Missouri. They were armed with double-barreled guns, rifles, bowie-knives and pistols, and had flags hoisted. They held a sort of an informal election off at one side, at first for Governor of Kansas Territory, and shortly afterwards announced Thomas Johnston, of Shawnee Mission, elected Governor. The polls had been opened but a short time, when Mr. Johnson marched with the crowd up to the window and demanded that they be allowed to vote, without swearing as to their residence.—After some noisy and threatening talk, Claiborne F. Jackson addressed the crowd, saying that they had come there to vote; that they had a right to vote if they had been there but five minutes, and he was not willing to go home without voting; which was received with cheers. Jackson then called upon them to form into little bands of fifteen or twenty, which they did, and went to an ox wagon filled with guns, which were distributed among them, and proceeded to load some of them on the ground. In pursuance of Jackson's request, they tied white tape or ribbons in their button-holes, so as to distinguish them from the "abolitionists." They again demanded that the judges should resign, and upon their refusing to do so, smashed in the windows, sash and all, and presented their guns and pistols to them, threatening to shoot them. Some one on the outside cried out to them not to shoot as there were pro-slavery men in the house. During this time the crowd repeatedly demanded to be allowed to vote without being sworn, and Mr. Ellison, one of the judges, expressed himself willing, but the other two judges refused; thereupon a body of men headed by Sheriff Jones, rushed into the judges' room with cocked pistols and drawn bowie-knives in their hands, and approached Burson and Ramsey. Jones pulled out his watch and said he would give them five minutes to resign in, or die. When the five minutes had expired and the judges did not resign, Jones said he would give them another minute and no more. Ellison told his associates if they did not resign there would be one hundred shots fired in the room in less than fifteen minutes, and then snatching up the ballot-box ran out into the crowd, holding up the ballot-box and hurrahing for Missouri. About that time Burson and Ramsey were called out by their friends, and not suffered to return. As Mr. Burson went out he put the ballot poll books in his pocket, and took them with him, and as he was going out Jones snatched some papers away from him, and shortly afterwards came out himself holding them up, crying "Hurrah for Missouri!" After he discovered they were not the poll-books, he took a party of men with him and started off to take the poll-books from Burson. When Mr. Burson saw them coming he gave the books to Mr. Minberger and told him to start off in another direction, so as to mislead Jones and his party. Jones and his party caught Mr. Minberger, took the poll-books away from him, and Jones took him up behind him on a horse and carried him back a prisoner. After Jones and his party had taken Minberger back, they went to the house of Mr.

Ramsey and took Judge John A. Wakefield prisoner, and carried him to the place of election and made him get up on a wagon and make a speech; after which they put a white ribbon in his button-hole and let him go. They then chose two new judges and proceeded with the election.—They also threatened to kill the judges if they did not receive their votes without swearing them, or else resign.—They said no man should vote who would submit to be sworn; that they would kill any man who would offer to do so; "Shoot him;" "cut his guts out," &c. They said no man should vote this day unless he voted an open ticket, and was all right on the goose; and if they could not vote by fair means, they would by foul. They said they had as much right to vote if they had been in the Territory two minutes as if they had been in the territory two years, and they would vote. Some of the citizens who were about the window when the crowd of Missourians marched up there, upon attempting to vote were driven back by the mob, or driven off. One of them Mr. J. M. Mace, was asked if he would take the oath; and upon his replying that he would if the judges required it, he was dragged through the crowd away from the polls, amid cries of "kill the damned nigger thief," "cut his throat," "tear his heart out," &c. After they got him to the outside of the crowd, they stood around him with cocked revolvers and drawn bowie-knives, one man putting a knife to his breast so that it touched him; another holding a cocked pistol to his ear, while another struck at him with a club. The Missourians said they had a right to vote, if they had been in the Territory but five minutes. Some said they had been hired to come there and vote, and got a dollar a day, and by God they would vote or die there.

SIXTEENTH DISTRICT.

"For some time previous to the election, meetings were held and arrangements made in Missouri to get up companies to come over to the Territory and vote; and the day before, and the day of the election, large bodies of Missourians from Platte, Clay, Ray, Carrol, Clinton and Saline Counties, Missouri, came into this district and camped there. They were armed with pistols, bowie knives, and some with guns and rifles, and had badges of hemp in their button-holes and elsewhere about their persons. On the morning of the election there were from 1,000 to 1,400 persons on the ground. Previous to the election the Missourians endeavored to persuade the two free state judges to resign, by making threats of personal violence to them; one of whom resigned on the morning of the election, and the crowd chose another to fill his place. But one of the judges—the free state judge—would take the oath prescribed by the Governor, the other two deciding they had no right to swear any one who offered to vote, but that all on the ground were entitled to vote. The only votes refused were some Delaware Indians, some thirty Wyandott Indians being allowed to vote. One of the free state candidates withdrew in consequence of the presence of the Missourians, amid cheering and acclamation by the mob. During the day the steamboat New Lucy came down from Weston, Missouri, with a large number of Missourians on board, who voted, and then returned on the boat. The Missourians gave as a reason for thus coming over to vote, that the North had tried to force emigration into the Territory, and they wanted to counteract that movement. Some of the candidates, and many of the Missourians, took the ground that, under the Kansas-Nebraska act, all who were on the ground on the day of election were entitled to vote, and others, that laying out a town and taking a lot, or driving down stakes, even on another man's claim, gave them a right to vote, and one of the members of the Council, R. R. Rees, declared in his testimony that he who should put a different construction upon the law must be either a knave or a fool. The free state men generally did not vote at that election, and no newly arrived emigrants were there.

EIGHTEENTH DISTRICT.

"Previous to the election, General David R. Atchison, of Platte City, Missouri, got a company of Missourians, and, passing through Weston, Missouri, went over into the Territory. He remained all night at the house of Arnett Groams, and there exhibited his arms, of which he had an abundance. He proceeded to the Nemaha or 18th district. On his way he and his party attended a nominating convention in the 14th district, and proposed, and caused to be nominated a set of candiates in opposition to the wishes of the pro-slavery residents of the district. At that convention he said that there were 1,100 coming over from Platte County, and if that wasn't enough they would bring 5,000 more; that they came to vote and would vote, or kill every G—d d—d abolitionist in the Territory.

"On the day of election the Missourians under Atchison, who were encamped there, came up to the polls in the 18th district and voted, taking the oath that they were residents of the district. The Missourians were all armed with pistols and bowie knives, and said there were sixty in their company. But seventeen of the votes given there were given by citizens of the district. The whole number of votes was sixty-two. R. L. Kirk, one of the candidates, came into the district from Missouri about a week before the election and boarded there. He left after the election, and was not at the time a legal resident of the district in which he was elected. No protest was sent to the Governor on account of threats made against any who should dare to contest the election.

"The following table embodies the result of the examination of your committee in regard to this district. In some of the districts it was impossible to ascertain the precise number of legal votes cast, and especially in the 14th, 15th and 16th districts. In such cases the number of legal and illegal votes cast is stated after a careful re-examination of all the testimony and records concerning the election.

TAKEN FROM THE ABSTRACT OF THE ELECTION RETURNS OF THE 30TH OF MARCH,

PLACE OF VOTING.	Pro-slavery Votes.	Free State Votes.	Scattering.	Total.	Total Legal Votes.	Total Illegal Votes.	By Census.	
							No. persons resident.	No. Voters.
Lawrence	781	253	....	1034	232	802	369	962
Bloomington	318	12	11	341	30	316	199	519
Stinson's	366	4	2	372	32	338	101	282
Dr. Chapman's	78	2	....	80	15	65	47	177
Bull Creek	377	9	....	386	13	380	....	....
Pottawattamie	199	65	....	564	75	191	....	....
Big Sugar Creek	74	17	7	98	32	59	442	1407
Little Sugar Creek	34	70	....	104	104	....	....	....
Ft. Scott	315	35	....	350	100	550	253	812
Isaac B. Titus'	211	23	....	234	25	209	53	118
Council Grove	17	17	....	37	37	....	39	83
Pawnee	23	52	....	75	75	....	36	86
Big Blue	27	42	....	69	48	21	63	151
Rock Creek	2	21	....	23	23	....	....	....

TAKEN FROM THE ABSTRACT OF THE ELECTION RETURNS OF THE 30TH OF MARCH—CONCLUDED.

PLACE OF VOTING.	Pro-slavery Votes.	Free State Votes.	Scattering.	Total.	Total Legal Votes.	Total Illegal Votes.	By Census.	
							No. persons resident.	No. Voters.
Marysville	328	....	....	328	7	321	24	36
St. Mary's	4	7	....	11	11	....	....	....
Silver Lake	12	19	2	33	33	....	78	144
Hickory Point	233	6	....	239	12	230	96	284
Doniphon	313	30	3	346	....	....	....	....
Wolf Creek	57	15	6	78	200	530	334	1167
Burr Oak	256	2	48	306	....	....	....	....
Hays	412	....	5	417	80	337	208	873
Leavenworth	899	60	5	964	150	814	385	1183
Green Spring	43	16	....	59	59	....	50	150
Moorestown	48	14	....	62	17	45	28	99
Total	5427	791	89	6307	1410	4908	2905	8601

These extracts afford a fair sample of border invasion. At many of the other precincts it was equally as bad. Thus we see an army of almost 5,000 men, fully equipped, marched into the Territory under the leadership of the distinguished men of Missouri—Hon. David R. Atchison, United States Senator and *ex officio* Vice President, Hon. M. J. Oliver, likewise Senator, and afterwards a member of the Investigating Committee, by whom these facts were elicited, Hon. Claiborn F. Jackson, afterwards Governor of Missouri, and many others of like stamp, for the avowed purpose of controling the election; and the only justification they could offer for their conduct was that they had *heard* the Emigrant Aid Societies were going to ship in voters.

The invasion of Kansas was a popular movement in Western Missouri, participated in by all classes of society. With the exception of a few leaders, who were doubtless behind the curtain, most of them acted sincerely and conscientiously, believing that the measures thus adopted were called out and fully justified by the action of the Emigrant Aid Societies. Old men and young men, the robust and infirm, the conscientious and reckless, the educated and illiterate, all joined heartily in this movement to make Kansas a slave State.

"The only persons emigrated into the Territory under the auspices of this company in 1855, prior to the election in March, were a party of one hundred and sixty-nine persons, who came under the charge of Dr. Charles Robinson.

"In this party there were sixty-seven women and children, They came as actual settlers, intending to make their homes in the Territory, and for no other purpose. They had about their persons but little baggage, usually sufficient clothing in a carpet sack for a short time. Their personal effects, such as clothing, furniture, &c., were put into trunks and boxes, and for convenience in selecting and cheapness in transporting, were marked, 'Kansas party baggage; in care of B. Slater, St. Louis.' Generally this was consigned as freight, in the ordinary way, to a commission merchant. This party had, in addition to the usual allowance of one hundred pounds to each passenger, a large quantity of baggage on which the respective owner paid the usual extra freight. Each passenger or party paid his or their own expenses, and the only benefit they derived from this society, not shared by all the people of the Territory, was the reduction of about seven dollars in the price of fare, the convenience of traveling in a company instead of alone, and the cheapness and facility of transporting their freight through regular agents. Subsequently many emigrants, being either disappointed with the country, or its political condition, or deceived by statements made in newspapers, and by agents of the society, became dissatisfied and returned, both before and after the election, to their old homes. Most of them are now settlers in the Territory. Some few voted at the election in Lawrence, but the number was small. The names of these emigrants have been ascertained, and thirty-seven of them are found on the poll books. This company of peaceful emigrants, moving with their household goods, was distorted into an invading horde of pauper abolitionists, who were, with those of a similar character, to control the domestic institutions of the Territory, and then overrun those of the neighboring State.

"The entire emigration in March, 1855, is estimated at

five hundred persons. They came on steamboats up the Missouri River in the ordinary course of emigration. Many returned for causes similar to those before stated, but the body of them are now residents. The only persons of those who were connected by proof with the election, were some who voted at the Big Blue precinct, in the 16th District, and at Pawnee, in the 9th District."

The time of holding the election was not known to the first emigrant party until they reached St. Louis.

Although the free state men had determined to make every honest effort to secure Kansas from the curse of slavery at the ballot box, still, on the day of the election, seeing that there was no hope in attempting to compete with all Missouri, they in many instances gave up the struggle, and did not vote at all, their candidates withdrawing from the unfair contest. Of the 2,905 names of legal voters in the census table, only 831 were found on the poll books.

Had the election been a fair one, in which every legal voter among the actual settlers, and none others, had participated, it would have resulted in the election of seven members of the Council in favor of making Kansas a free State, three opposed to it and three doubtful. Under like circumstances the House would have been composed of fourteen free state members, seven slave state and seven doubtful ones.

The City Attorney of St. Joseph, in giving his testimony before the Investigating Committee, in reference to the motive of the Missourians in coming over and voting, said :

"It is my intention, and the intention of a great many other Missourians now resident in Missouri, whenever the slavery issue is to be determined upon by the people of this Territory in the adoption of the State Constitution, to remove to this Territory in time to acquire the right to become legal voters upon that question. The leading purpose of our intended removal to the Territory, is to determine the domestic institutions of this Territory when it becomes a State, and we would not come but for that purpose, and would never think of coming here but for that purpose. I believe there are a great many in Missouri who are so situated."

It was plainly the duty of Governor Reeder to have set aside this election as fraudulent and irregular. The Organic Act empowered him so to do; he was fully aware of the enormous frauds perpetrated; the free state men urged the subject upon him, pledging him protection and support. Such a step on the part of Governor Reeder would have thwarted the efforts of the Missourians to force a government upon the people of Kansas, and might have averted the fierce conflict which ensued.

But the members of the Legislature thus elected immediately demanded of Mr. Reeder certificates of election, as required by the Organic Act, threatening him with assassination in case of refusal. With pistols cocked and pointed at his breast, he examined the election returns, and painfully witnessed the evidences of fraud. He hesitated and wavered; he scarcely knew what to do. As he hesitated he was more sorely pressed; as he wavered danger was more thickly menaced. He faltered, gave way, issued the certificates, and thus, so far as he could, legalized the election. It was a sad misstep, and grew out of the want of sufficient fearless and undaunted firmness.

But few protests against the election frauds reached Mr. Reeder before he issued the certificates, the people being remote and ignorant, in many instances, of the proper remedy, or intimidated by the threats of pro-slavery men. Without deciding upon his power to cast aside elections for illegality or fraud, thus going behind the returns, he set aside the election in six districts on account of informalities in the returns, and ordered a new election in the same.

The pro-slavery men were highly incensed at Mr. Reeder in daring thus far to question the legality of their proceedings. They held their meetings, and decided not to pay any attention to the newly ordered election in every district except at Leavenworth. They declared that the Governor had no right to decide upon the legality of an election, but was bound to issue certificates according to the election returns.

The contested election came off on the 22d of May, and free state men were elected unanimously, except at Leavenworth, where about five hundred Missourians came over and "played their old game."

CHAPTER XIV.

THE CONSEQUENCE.

The free state men keenly felt the outrages committed upon them by the people of Missouri. The whole North was deeply moved and incensed at these glaring acts of injustice and oppression. All felt the danger and weakness of these isolated emigrants thus over-ridden in Kansas. All began to understand the desperate, reckless character of the men who led and composed these invaders. The designs and plans of slavery propagandists in subduing Kansas and planting slavery there at every hazard, began to be discernable. Dark and ominous clouds, foreboding a bursting storm, began to lower over the beautiful fields of this Territory. All felt that a storm was gathering and dreaded the bursting of that storm.

The free state men demeaned themselves under such indignities and acts of violence with the forbearance of christians and the coolness of patriots. They believed in a just God that would rectify their wrongs and looked to the general Government as His appointed deliverance. They could not but hope that the United States would extend its strong arm of protection over the infant Territory from the oppression of a neighboring State for which they most filially petitioned Congress. They could not believe that those who had so eloquently declaimed against intervention in the affairs of a Territory by Congress, would be the first to excuse and apologize for like conduct on the part of a State.

Thus feeling, believing and hoping, they determined to suffer and wait in patience.

The people of the Border were jubilant over their triumph. The pro-slavery newspapers went into ecstacies on receiving the news. The Platte Argus declared "it must be admitted that they—the Missourians—have conquered Kansas. Our advice is let them hold it or die in the attempt." The Squatter Sovereign resounds, "OUT WITH THE GUN! 'WE HAVE MET THE ENEMY AND THEY ARE OURS!' WE HAVE ACHIEVED A GLORIOUS VICTORY." Meetings of congratulations were held in various Border counties, at which the perpetrators of these outrages were complimented for their patriotic achievements.

In all these newspaper announcements, in all the public meetings, called by the news of the election, an exhortation was made "not to let the good work stop but carry it on until every abolitionist (alias free state men) was exterminated from the Territory. Many means could be devised whereby these unbearable nuisances could be removed; but the most effectual method that occurs to our mind is to inflict instant punishment upon the offender. We are not, except in extreme cases, an admirer of Judge Lynch's code of practice, nor of self-constituted powers, but under the circumstances we opine the organization of a Vigilance Committee throughout the Territory, for the protection of slave property, would not only be a judicious policy but one fully justifiable in the premises. As a first step the town of Lawrence should be rid of its pestiferous inhabitants."

Thus sustained by the press and public sentiment, the mobatic spirit knew no bounds. Mr. Reeder, who went to Washington soon after the election, was threatened with lynching if he returned to the Territory. A convention was accordingly called by the people of Platte County, Missouri, to be held at Leavenworth on the 28th of May, for the purpose of taking into consideration the question of deposing Governor Reeder and electing a new Governor.

This movement was doubtless designed to intimidate Mr. Reeder and hasten his resignation; at least the convention never met. From this time dates the mobatic reign of terror in north-west Missouri and in Kansas.

On the 14th of April the mob collected in Parkville and destroyed the printing press of the "Industrial Luminary." They first paraded it in the streets with a white cap drawn over its head, then carried it to the Missouri River and threw the press into its waters. It was their intention to tar and feather Messrs. Park and Patterson, the editors, but the former was absent and the latter was saved from their fury by the affectionate interposition of his wife. This paper supported Mr. Benton and opposed Mr. Atchison and his friends, by which it had incurred their displeasure. After the election in Kansas Territory, it mildly condemned the course of the Missourians. The followers of Atchison, perhaps, inspired by their chief, decreed its destruction, and were not long in carrying out their purposes. After having accomplished their work, they passed resolutions requesting the two editors to leave the country under severe penalties in case of refusal. They also forbade all ministers of the Northern branch of the Methodist church from preaching in that vicinity.

In a few days afterwards meetings held at Liberty and Weston endorsed the action of the mob at Parkville, and extended the resolution in reference to Methodist preachers to all ministers from free States, or those who were not known to be friendly to slavery. They resolved that "every person who shall in any manner speak or publish doctrines or sentiments calculated to bring reproach upon the institution of negro slavery, 'shall be expelled from the country.'" In accordance with the above resolutions, several pious, devoted and talented ministers of the Gospel were compelled to leave the State on account of their opinions.

On the last day of April, at a squatter meeting in Leavenworth, an altercation took place between a Mr. Clark and a

Mr. McCrea, which resulted in the latter's shooting the former in self-defense. As one of these was pro and the other anti-slavery, it awakened party excitement and furnished grounds for further acts of violence. McCrea was pursued, fired upon and wounded—was taken to the fort prisoner, where he was retained a long time—finally escaped and went to Texas. At a meeting assembled on the evening following this homicide, a committee was appointed to wait upon a young attorney, William Phillips, Esq., to notify him to leave the Territory. They accused him of being accessory to the murder of Clark, and of having perjured himself in swearing to a protest against the election held there on the 30th ultimo.

The same crowd assembled on the following Thursday, which was but an adjourned meeting of the former. The committee appointed to wait upon Mr. Phillips reported that he had left agreeable to the notice given, and was discharged. A vigilance committee of thirty members was then appointed "to watch and observe all persons producing disturbances to the quiet of our citizens," with authority to expel the same from the Territory. This meeting "was eloquently addressed" by the Chief Justice of the Territory.

The Vigilance Committee, on learning in the afternoon that Mr. Phillips was in town, proceeded immediately to his house. On his declaring to them that he would not leave the Territory, they took him to Weston, shaved one side of his head, tarred and feathered him, rode him on a rail through the streets, and finally had him sold at auction by a negro.

At a meeting held in Leavenworth a few days afterwards, of which a prominent member of the Legislature elect was president, the following resolutions were adopted:

"1st. That we heartily endorse the action of the committee of citizens, that shaved, tarred and feathered, and rode on a rail and had sold by a negro, William Phillips, the moral perjurer.

"2d. That we return our thanks to the committee for faithfully performing the trust enjoined upon them by the pro-slavery party.

"3d. That the committee be now discharged.

"4th. That we severely condemn those pretended pro-slavery men who, from mercenary motives, are now calling upon the pro-slavery party to submit without further action.

"5th. That in order to secure peace and harmony to the community we now solemnly declare that the pro-slavery party stand firmly by and carry out the resolutions reported by the committee appointed for that purpose on the '*memorable 30th*.'"

The wonderful difference between the two conflicting elements in the Territory at that time is remarkable. The pro-slavery men, impetuous, aggressive and overbearing, sought by all possible means to embroil the opposite party into difficulties. The free state men, cool, prudent and sagacious, "as harmless as doves and as wise as serpents," acted entirely upon the defensive, and avoided, as much as possible, all troubles. The former were blustering and mercenary, the latter quiet and unobtrusive. The former claimed as their right the very thing which had been referred to the decision of the ballot-box; the latter only claimed the right which their Government guaranteed them of assisting to give shape to that decision. The one was wild with excitement, blinded by prejudice, rough and profane, supported by the adjoining State, strong in numbers and wealth. The other quiet, intelligent, refined and devotional, were far removed from friends, liable to be crushed at any moment by the furious and threatening Ruffians of the Border. The press of one sent forth slang, vituperation, misrepresentation and inflammatory appeals, fit fuel for civil war; that of the other denounced all acts of violence, and appealed to men's better natures to abstain from engendering strife.

CHAPTER XV.

FIRST TERRITORIAL LEGISLATURE.

Gov. Reeder having issued a proclamation for convening the Legislature at Pawnee, started for the East. While there he visited Washington and had protracted interviews with the President, in which he set before the Executive the true state of affairs as they had transpired in the Territory and the course which he had pursued. The President seemingly sanctioning Mr. Reeder's official conduct, told him, however, that heavy pressures were being made for his removal, and that there was great personal danger attending his return to the Territory from the ill feeling of pro-slavery men on the Border. The President, thereupon, advised him to resign; as an inducement to such a step, offered him another appointment. Mr. Reeder refused to resign his position on the grounds that it would be dishonorable for him, for the sake of personal safety, to abandon the people of the Territory in their present perilous and unhappy condition. The President then proposed that Mr. Reeder should make out a detailed account of the transactions in the Territory and set forth his official conduct and views in regard to Kansas matters, and he would assume the responsibility to remove Mr. Reeder on the plea that it was necessary in order to allay public excitement in Kansas and on the Border; at the same time he would fully exonerate the Governor from the charge of being instrumental in producing that excitement, and express his approbation of Mr. Reeder's conduct and views. To this proposition Mr. Reeder assented—providing that they could agree upon the terms of the correspondence. He accordingly prepared a statement of events and his official action in regard to them, with the reasons which controlled him and his general views upon Kansas troubles, and submitted the paper to the President. After various modifications they could not succeed in reaching an agreement in regard to its character. Failing in this arrangement, there was nothing left but for each to accept the responsibilities of his own acts. The President then remarked "Well, I shall not remove you on account of your official action; if I remove you at all, it will be on account of your speculations in the lands of the Territory;" but said "he thought that all these matters might be arranged in such a manner as to promote his private interests if he would voluntarily vacate his office." Mr. Reeder feeling himself insulted at the proposition, indignantly turned from the President and left him in silent contempt. He immediately repaired to the Territory where he arrived on the 24th of June. Shortly after his return he was violently assaulted at Leavenworth by Gen B. F. Stringfellow, and while his attention was turned in another direction, was knocked down by this pugilist.

The Legislature elected by the people of Missouri, many of whom were then residents of that State, convened at Pawnee on the 22d day of July. Caucuses of the pro-slavery members had been held the day previous (Sunday), and their mode of proceedure determined. Secretary Woodson called the bodies to order and presided over them until temporarily organized. Judge Johnson administered the oath of office to the members. Thomas Johnston was elected President of the Council and Dr. J. H. Stringfellow Speaker of the House.

Both branches of the Legislature proceeded immediately to purge themselves of free state members. The free soilers offered their protest against such actions on the part of the House, but in vain. From the committee on credentials, Mr. Mathias reported "that the Governor of the Territory of Kansas had not the exclusive power to prescribe the manner and form by which the first election for the first Territorial Legislative Assembly of the said Territory of Kansas should be conducted and passed upon; but that a fair construction of the 22d section of the said Organic Act leads them—nay drives a majority of your said committee, to the conclusion that no particular form of the oath which the judges of said election took was necessary, and that no particular form of the return of the said election by the said judges was necessary in order to legalize the said election; but that such oaths and such returns as are usual for judges of election in the several States to take, perform and return, is all that the Organic Act requires. And a majority of your committee believe and are of the opinion that from the original papers filed in the office of the Secretary of the Territory, and of other papers and evidence which were before them, that the oaths and returns and all other acts, taken, done and performed by the judges appointed by his excellency, A. H. Reeder, Governor of the Territory of Kansas, to hold and conduct the election for members of the first Territorial Assembly, were in the usual form, at all events as effectual and as legal and binding as if the said oaths and returns had been in the form prescribed by the Governor in his proclamation, verbatim et literatim."

Mr. Houston of the same committee offered a minority report denying the right of the House of Representatives to go behind the certificates of election from the Governor, held by the members, and determine the legality of the grounds upon which they had been issued; that the mere fact of a member holding such a certificate was a sufficient guarantee that he was entitled to his seat in that body. He said:

"To assume the contrary proposition is to assert that this legislative body exists before it can have a legal existence. Whatever latitude may be taken in State legislation with reference to contested elections, they can form no precedent for us, for the plain reason that while government is formed and complete, ours is in a forming state, and therefore incomplete.

"In regard to the right of the Governor to order a new election, the organizing object to be accomplished, the intention of Congress which pervades the bill, together with the express language of the bill, declaring that when a vacancy shall otherwise occur he shall call a new election—make it perfectly clear that he possessed the right to order a new election, and compelled him to do so. Hence the members holding certificates by virtue of that election, have a clear right to their seats in this House."

John Hutchinson, Esq., made a logical and eloquent speech of two hours' length against the majority report of the committee. Thereupon the Speaker, Dr. Stringfellow, remarked that "though the House had no objections to indulging the members in free speech, it might, perhaps, shorten their remarks in some degree if they knew that their speeches would not change a single vote."

The members to be ousted by the report of the majority offered the following protest:

"We, the undersigned members of the House of Representatives of Kansas Territory, believing the Organic Act organizing said Territory gives this House no power to oust any member from this House who has received a certificate of election from the Governor; that this House can not go behind an election called by the Governor, and consider any claims based on a prior election. We would, therefore, protest against such a proceeding, and ask this protest to be spread upon the journal of this House.

"John Hutchingson,
"William Jessee,
"Augustus Wattles,
"E. D. Todd."

On motion the majority report of the committee was adopted with only one dissenting voice, and the members elected at the March election took their seats, and those elected in May were expelled, except those from Leavenworth, who retained their seats; as at this precinct pro-slavery men took part in the new election and re-elected the same candidates who were successful at the general election.

In the Council, on motion of Judge Wakefield, the Committee on Credentials was instructed to call upon the Governor for the testimony on which he had set aside the election of the 30th of March, 1855, in the 2d and 3d Council Districts.

The chairman, Mr. Coffey, accordingly called upon the Governor and received affidavits setting forth the manner in which the Missourians had unlawfully invaded the polls and elected the members of the Legislature instead of the actual settlers. Judge Wakefield then took the poll books and called the attention of Mr. Coffey to the names of some well known citizens in Westport, and asked him if he knew those gentlemen. On his replying that he did, the Judge asked him what he thought of their coming over to Kansas to elect members of the Legislature. "Perfectly right, perfectly right," he responded, "Missouri has as good a right to vote as Massachusetts."

On the 4th of July the Committee on Credentials reported in favor of excluding Messrs. Wakefield and Wood, and admitting in their stead those elected at the first election. M. F. Conway had previously sent in his resignation. The expelled members then presented the following protest:

"We, the undersigned, members of the first Legislature of the Territory of Kansas, from the 2d and 3d Council Districts, elected on the 22d of May, 1855, agreeable to the Governor's proclamation to fill vacancies in said districts, wherein the people on the 30th of March, 1855, were deprived of the right of choosing members from those districts, by force of arms.

"We respectfully ask leave to enter our solemn protest against being denied our seats in this Assembly, for the following reasons:

"1st. We are the choice of the people of said districts.

"2d. The Governor has declared us duly elected.

"3d. He is the only officer that the Organic Act of Congress gives the power to investigate elections and declare who are legally elected members, until election laws are passed by the Legislature, taking this power from the Governor.

"We maintain that his certificates entitle us to seats in this Legislature."

There was not a single free state man left now in the Legislature, except Mr. S. D. Houston. He, in consequence of the flagrant acts of both bodies, subsequently resigned.

On the second day after the meeting of the Legislature a bill was passed locating the seat of government temporarily at Shawnee Manual Labor School. Within three days the Governor returns it with his veto and objections. They then passed it over his veto and adjourned to the above named place. The Governor based his argument against this action of the Legislature on the grounds that the Organic Act vested in him the right to fix the temporary seat of government, and that the Legislature only had power to locate it permanently.

The design of Mr. Reeder in calling the Legislature together away out at Pawnee was to remove it from the influence of the Border. The people there had solicited it, had went to considerable pains to prepare accommodations for the members, and had expected it. The ground upon which the Legislature predicated its action in changing the place of its sitting was, that the hotel and hall accommodations were insufficient. But these were said by free state men to be ample; that every convenience and arrangement were made for their comfort.

According to adjournment the Legislature convened at Shawnee Mission on the 16th of July. Here they entered upon the laborious task of enacting laws for Kansas. But they greatly facilitated this work by adopting transcripts of the Missouri code. All general laws passed were of this character. They were enacted by a short explanatory clause of the terms contained in them. Thus "State" was made to mean "Territory;" "County Court," "Board of Commissioners," and "Circuit Court," "District Court." If they had attempted to pass new laws it would have consumed all their time in reading them; for the book containing their acts is a large octavo of more than one thousand pages. With the exception of some oppressive laws of their own manufacture they enacted the best code of laws the Territory or State ever enjoyed.

One of the most remarkable features about these legislative enactments was that all officers in the Territory, legislative, executive and judicial, were to be appointed by the Legislature, or by some officer that had been appointed by it. These appointments were to continue until after the general election in October, 1857. There was to be no regular session of the Legislature in 1856, but the members of the House were to be elected in the fall of that year, and there was to be a general election the following year. The new Legislature was not to meet until the first Monday in January, 1858. Thus, indeed, the enslavement of the people of Kansas was complete. They could have no control over the legislative, executive or judicial affairs of the Territory until by the natural progress of population the government thus inaugurated by their oppressors should be superseded by that of a State government. Every attorney admitted to practice in the courts, every officer elected or appointed in the Territory, every candidate to be eligible for the election in 1856 to the House of Representatives, must swear to support the Fugitive Slave Law. There were two classes of persons excluded from the elective franchise, who were entitled to it under the Organic Act; those who could not swear to support the Fugitive Slave law and foreigners who had only declared their intentions to become citizens. All others, though they had not been in the Territory one hour and intended to return the next, provided they had paid one dollar tax to the sheriff who was required to be at the polls to receive it, were entitled to vote. All jurors should be selected by the sheriff, and no person conscienciously opposed to slavery could sit as jurors in a trial pertaining to slaves.

They enacted laws punishing offenses against slave property and persons decoying slaves from their masters which would have disgraced the darkest age and outstripped the cruelest despotism. A copy of these is subjoined to the next chapter.

Soon after the removal of the Legislature from Pawnee, several bills were sent to the Governor for his approval.—But he returned them stating that he could not yield his assent to any of their enactments as he no longer regarded them as a legal body.

Being solicitous about the legality of their proceedings they referred them to the Supreme Court, then sitting at that place. The validity of several laws passed by the Legislaislature were submitted to its decision, and a majority of the judges agreed to entertain the question. It is entirely irregular and extra-judicial for courts to pass judgement upon a law before any case comes before them under that law. But the Supreme Court of Kansas Territory was so eager to declare an opinion upon the laws of the Bogus Legislature, that they entertain them abstractly considered, and find them founded in the principles of Justice. In a lengthy document, they sustain the Legislature in their course of action and highly compliment their talents and character. It is proper to remark that one of the members of the judicial bench, S. W. Johnson refused to have anything to do with the matter thus brought before them.

The members of the Legislature emboldened by this decision, proceeded to memorialize the President for the removal of Mr. Reeder. They charged him with fraudulent land speculations, a want of interest in the affairs of the Territory, of being allied with the Abolitionists, and treating the the Legislature of the Territory with contempt. They dispatched a messenger to carry this memorial to Washington. But before he reached his destination, the Administration had already determined upon the removal of Mr. Reeder, who was officially notified to that effect.

CHAPTER XVI.

CAUSES OF REEDER'S REMOVAL CONSIDERED.

The causes alleged for the removal of Governor Reeder were "speculating in town lots, convening the Legislature on a United States military reserve, and of speculating in Kaw lands." But the *real* cause was that he had not been obsequious to slave propagandists.

The eastern boundary of Fort Riley, as made by the survey in the summer of 1854, was on One Mile Creek, one mile east of the fort. Below this, for several miles, stretched a beautiful valley, upon which the officers of the fort, in imitation of their superiors at Fort Leavenworth, together with several free state men, proposed to build a town. They laid it out and called it Pawnee, after the Indian tribe that once owned the lands. It was considered by those at that time, that such a movement, if successful, would be a great advantage to the fort and surrounding country, by calling settlers there. Colonel Montgomery, the commander of the post, was the leader in the enterprise. The town was laid out with the knowledge and consent of the authorities at Washington, in the fall of 1854.

Such was the condition of affairs there when Governor Reeder took a share in the town by paying the usual prices. He having determined to have the Legislature meet there, the inhabitants had erected several hotels for the accommodation of the members.

Jeff. Davis, on receiving complaints from Missouri, caused another military commission to make a survey, which again reported One Mile Creek as the Eastern boundary of the reserve. A map of this survey was prepared and sent to the Department, with red lines showing where the boundaries would be to exclude Pawnee, and blue lines showing where they would be to include Pawnee. The Secretary of War, seeing the town still excluded, took a pen, drew a red line around it, and wrote on it, "Accepted within the red lines," took it to the President and secured his signature to it. He then issued orders for the removal of the inhabitants from that part of the reserve. This order remained a dead letter until the fall of 1855, when Major Cook arrived at Fort Riley, with one thousand dragoons, from Texas. He, upon seeing the order, immediately, but politely, informed the inhabitants that they must effect their removal or he would be compelled, with reluctance, to do it for them. Most of the townsmen complied with this requisition, but a few persisted in remaining. After being repeatedly warned to remove, their houses were finally assailed by the soldiers, torn down, and the inmates left exposed to the inclement blasts of winter.

Such, indeed, is the history of the ill-fated Pawnee, the first capital of Kansas. Such was the town referred to in the charge against Mr. Reeder "in speculating in town lots," and such the military reserve where he called the Legislature to meet. At Leavenworth the town was laid off and settled contrary to the most sacred treaties, but all such irregular proceedings were "winked at," because the leading property holders were pro-slavery men.

The half-breed Kaw lands extended along the north side of the river from Lecompton a short distance above Topeka, twenty-three miles in length and one in width. The owners of these lands could not sell them without the sanction of the general Government. A company, of which Governor Reeder was one, made arrangements to buy a portion of this land at $4.00 per acre whenever the President's consent should be obtained. As this was never secured the whole thing failed. This was the half-breed Kaw land speculation for which Mr. Reeder was removed. The Delaware land, immediately adjoining these, was sold soon after for only $1.50 per acre. So it seems the "speculation" would not have proven very lucrative if the purchase had been made.

The conduct of Mr. Reeder in Kansas is beautiful and praiseworthy. He shaped his actions by principle and not by the influence of party. Indeed, he knew no party in the performance of his duty, and has been truly styled "the great non-committal." He acted and stood by himself because all others acted from political motives and looked to party triumph. With his eyes intently fixed upon the great and equitable principle of Popular Sovereignty, with ears deaf to contumely and applause, he labored only to see his principles impartially carried out. The consequence was he had few warm and substantial friends among either party. The free state men only admired him for many things, while the pro-slavery men despised him, not because he did not act in accordance with the principles of Squatter Sovereignty, but because he would not act as they wished him. His position was a trying one upon principle. A devoted Democrat himself, holding his office at the pleasure of a Democratic administration, surrounded by political friends who received him with outstretched arms, he had every influence to bend him from the convictions of duty; whereas there was little to gain in favoring free state men who in those days were held in the most abject contempt. But one act stains his administration, and that is his issuing certificates of election to the Missouri members of the Legislature.

One might suppose from the frequent accusations of speculation in lands that he was mercenary. While it can not be denied that, like Pennsylvanians in general, he liked a "good turn," yet his pecuniary transactions in the territory were the most equitable and honest. He never owned but little real estate in Kansas.

Let the people of this Territory cherish the memory of its first Governor, who in the days of its weakness and trials was "faithful among the faithless found." Let aspiring young men imitate his adherence to principle, and posterity will award them their just meed of praise.

Although the members of the Legislature were willing to petition Mr. Reeder's removal for alleged land speculations, they did not deem it unbecoming in themselves to indulge in worse transactions. According to their enactment that empowered the Legislature to appoint officers in the Territory, they proceeded to create offices and elected their own members to fill them, unmindful of their constituency in Missouri. In this way W. P. Richardson was made Major-General, and W. G. Stickler, Wm. Barber and Captain Sutler, Brigadier-Generals of the Territorial Militia. In the same manner pro-slavery Sheriffs, Constables, Judges, and Justices of the Peace were constituted. They created joint stock companies with extraordinary privileges, chartered prospective railroads, all the advantages of which charters and corporate franchises were chiefly conferred upon themselves. They located the capital at Lecompton, where a large sum of public money was to be expended. But the advantages shared by the members of the Legislature in this speculation were never fully known.

Such conduct as this by the members of this quasi-Legislature was very reprehensible in the eyes of their Missouri constituents. Many of the latter, who had spent time and money to carry the election, justly regarded themselves entitled to a part of the profits, and expressed great dissatisfaction at this speculative and official monopoly of the Legislature.

On the removal of Mr. Reeder, the Governorship was tendered to Hon. John L. Dawson, of Pennsylvania, who declined it. Hon. Wilson Shannon, of Ohio, was then appointed Governor and accepted the position. He was born February 24th, 1802, in Belmont County, Ohio, and remained at home while a boy, assisting his mother in obtaining a livelihood. At the age of sixteen he entered Athens College, where he remained a year; thence he was removed to Transylvania University, at Lexington, Kentucky, where he remained two years. He then settled in St. Clairsville and began the study of law.

In 1832 Mr. Shannon was nominated by the Democratic party for Congress, and although he ran ahead of his ticket at home and in a strong Federal county, he was defeated by a few votes in the district. In 1833 he was nominated for Prosecuting Attorney, and was elected by 1,100 majority, and in 1835 re-elected without opposition. In 1838 he was nominated by the Democratic party for Governor of Ohio, and elected by about 6.000 votes over Mr. Vance, a strong man of the Federal party. The same party again nominated him in 1840 for Governor, but he was defeated at the election by Mr. Corwin by about 16,000 votes; but in 1842, receiving the nomination the third time, he was elected over the same competitor by nearly 3,500 majority. In 1844 he favored the nomination of General Cass for the Presidency and received his appointment as Minister to Mexico. Resigning his position as Governor of Ohio, he entered upon his arduous mission and performed his work with credit and honor. By the middle of the year the relations between Mexico and the United States became very critical, all intercourse having been suspended and Mr. Shannon unable to effect anything more with the Government, asked and obtained permission to return home, which he did, and engaged in his profession. In 1852 he was elected to represent his district in Congress, and was consequently there during the Kansas-Nebraska contest in which he voted for the repeal of the Missouri Compromise.

After Mr. Shannon resigned as Governor of Kansas, he settled at Lawrence, to which place he moved his family, and where he still resides, engaged in the practice of law, respected and esteemed by all the citizens.

The following are the enactments of the Shawnee Legislature to punish offenses against slave property:

"*Be it enacted by the Governor and Legislative Assembly of the Territory of Kansas*, as follows:

"SEC. 1. That every person, bond or free, who shall be convicted of actually raising a rebellion or insurrection of slaves, free negroes or mulattoes, in this Territory shall suffer death.

"SEC. 2. Every free person who shall aid or assist in any rebellion or insurrection of slaves, free negroes or mulattoes, or shall furnish arms or do any overt act in furtherance of such rebellion or insurrection, shall suffer death.

"SEC. 3. If any free person shall, by speaking, writing or printing, advise, persuade or induce, any slaves to rebel, conspire against or murder any citizen of this Territory, or shall bring into, print, write, publish or circulate, or shall cause to be brought into, printed, written, published or circulated, or shall knowingly aid or assist in the bringing into, printing, writing, publishing or circulating in this Territory, any paper, book, magazine, pamphlet or circular, for the purpose of exciting insurrection, rebellion, revolt or conspiracy on the part of the slaves, free negroes or mulattoes, against the citizens of the Territory, or any part of them, such person shall be guilty of felony and suffer death.

"SEC. 4. If any person shall entice, decoy or carry away out of this Territory any slave belonging to another, with intent to deprive the owner thereof of the services of such slave, or with intent to effect or procure the freedom of such slave, he shall be adjudged guilty of grand larceny, and, on conviction thereof, shall suffer death, or be imprisoned at hard labor for not less than ten years.

"SEC. 5. If any person shall aid or assist in enticing, decoying or persuading, or carrying away, or sending out of this Territory, any slave belonging to another, with intent to procure or effect the freedom of such slave, or with intent to deprive the owner thereof, shall suffer death, or be imprisoned at hard labor for not less than ten years.

"SEC. 6. If any person shall entice, decoy or carry away out of any State or Territory of the United States, any slave belonging to another, with intent to procure or effect the freedom of such slave, or to deprive the owner thereof of the services of such slave, and shall bring such slave into this Territory, he shall be adjudged guilty of grand larceny, in the same manner as if such slave had been enticed, decoyed or carried away out of this Territory, and in such case the larceny may be charged to have been committed in any county of this Territory, into or through which such slave shall have been brought by such person, and, on conviction thereof, the person offending shall suffer death, or be imprisoned at hard labor for not less than ten years.

"Sec. 7. If any person shall entice, persuade or induce any slave to escape from the service of his master, or owner, in this Territory, or shall aid or assist any slave in escaping from the service of his master, or owner, or shall aid, assist, harbor or conceal, any slave who may have escaped from the service of his master, or owner, he shall be deemed guilty of felony, and punished by imprisonment at hard labor for a term of not less than five years.

"Sec. 8. If any person in this Territory shall aid or assist, harbor or conceal, any slave who has escaped from the service of his master, or owner, in another State or Territory, such person shall be punished in like manner as if such slave had escaped from the service of his master or owner in this Territory.

"Sec. 9. If any person shall resist any officer while attempting to arrest any slave who may have escaped from the service of his master, or owner, or shall rescue such slave when in custody of any officer, or other person, or shall entice, persuade, aid or assist, such slave to escape from the custody of any officer, or other person who may have such slave in custody, whether such slave shall have escaped from the service of his master, or owner, in this Territory, or in any other State or Territory, the person so offending shall be guilty of felony, and punished by imprisonment at hard labor for a term of not less than two years.

"Sec. 10. If any marshal, sheriff, or constable, or the deputy of any such officer, shall, when required by any person, refuse to aid or assist in the arrest and capture of any slave that may have escaped from his master or owner, whether such slave shall have escaped from his master in this Territory, or any State or other Territory, such officer shall be fined in a sum not less than one hundred nor more than five hundred dollars.

"SEC. 11. If any person print, write, introduce into, or circulate, or cause to be brought into, written, printed or circulated, or shall knowingly aid or assist in bringing into, printing, publishing or circulating within this Territory, any book, paper, pamphlet, magazine, handbill or circular, containing any statements, arguments, opinions, sentiment, doctrine, advice, or inuendo, calculated to produce disorderly, dangerous or rebellious disaffection among the slaves of the Territory, or to induce such slaves to escape from the service of their masters, or to resist their authority, he shall be guilty of felony, and be punished by imprisonment at hard labor for a term of not less than five years.

"SEC. 12. If any free person, by speaking or writing, assert or maintain that persons have not the right to hold slaves in this Territory, print, publish, write, circulate, or cause to be introduced into the Territory, written, printed, published, and circulated in this Territory, any book, paper, magazine, pamphlet, or circular, containing any denial of the right of persons to hold slaves in this Territory, such person shall be deemed guilty of felony, and punished by imprisonment at hard labor for a term of not less than five years.

"SEC. 13. No person who is conscientiously opposed to holding slaves, or who does not admit the right to hold slaves in this Territory, shall sit as a juror on the trial of any prosecution for any violation of any of the sections of this act.

"This act to take effect and be in force from and after the 15th day of September, A. D. 1855.

"J. H. STRINGFELLOW, Speaker of the House.

"Attest, J. M. LYLE, Clerk.

"THOMAS JOHNSON, President of the Council.

"Attest, J. A. HALDERMAN, Clerk."

"AN ACT TO PUNISH PERSONS DECOYING SLAVES FROM THEIR MASTERS.

"*Be it enacted by the Governor and Legislative Assembly of Kansas Territory:*

"SEC. 1. If any person shall entice, decoy, or carry away out of this Territory, any slave belonging to another, with intent to deprive the owner thereof of the services of such slave, or with intent to effect or procure the freedom of such slave, he shall be adjudged guilty of grand larceny, and on conviction thereof shall suffer death.

"SEC. 2. If any person shall aid or assist in enticing, decoying, or persuading, or carry out of any State or Territory, any slave belonging to another, with intent to effect or procure the freedom of such slave, he shall be adjudged guilty of grand larceny, and on conviction thereof suffer death.

"SEC. 3. If any person shall entice, decoy, or carry away, out of any State or Territory of the United States, any slave belonging to another, with intent to procure or effect the freedom of such slave, or to deprive the owner thereof of the services of such slave, and shall bring such slave into this Territory, he shall be adjudged guilty of grand larceny, in the same manner as if such slave had been enticed, decoyed, or carried away out of this Territory; and in such case the larceny may be charged to have been committed in any county of this Territory, into or through which such slave shall have been brought by such person, and on conviction thereof the person offending shall suffer death."

CHAPTER XVII.

FREE STATE MOVEMENTS.

Never in the history of the world, even in those days when might made right, were there such bare-faced and audacious acts of civil oppression inflicted upon a community as those we have just recited. By the enactments of a Legislature elected by invaders, the condition of the people of this Territory was far worse than that of our revolutionary fathers. This Legislature had every thing in its power, and had provided for its own perpetuity in the qualifications of its electors. It appointed the State and county officers, levied taxes and gagged the mouths of freemen and a free press, that a word might not be said against "the sum of all villainies."

They had earnestly besought the General Government for protection. They had humbly entreated the President of the United States to issue a proclamation denouncing the conduct of the invaders, and calling upon all good citizens of Missouri and other States to discountenance and disown their acts; to urge upon the United States officers in the Territory—sixteen in number—to disfavor and oppose such proceedings. The effect of such a proclamation from the Chief Executive would have been wonderful. But how did he answer their entreaties? He proceeded to remove the only friend they had among the Federal appointees, and for the simple reason that he was their friend, inasmuch as he sought to protect their rights as freemen.

While these unparalleled outrages were being committed upon the people of Kansas, they proved themselves equal to the trials and responsibilities of the hour. While the clouds of oppression hovered over them the fires of liberty were kindled. The spirit of '76 descended and imbued them with prudence and courage. While Justice had gone to sleep in the gathering darkness, Resistance to Tyranny was abroad in the land.

Despairing of any interposition of the general Government to drive back their oppressors, and protect them in the enjoyment of their rights, they began to cast about to see what course was best to pursue. As early as the 8th of June a meeting of the citizens was held at Lawrence, agreeable to the call of "sundry citizens" "to take into consideration matters of general interest pertaining to the Territory." This convention issued a call, inviting the representative districts in the Territory to send five delegates each to a convention, to be held in the same place, on the 25th of June, "to take into consideration the relation of the people of this Territory to the Legislature about to convene at Pawnee." This convention assembled at the time and place designated, and organized by electing Judge J. A. Wakefield chairman. They resolved to discard all minor differences, and make freedom in Kansas the only issue; that they have a right to regulate their own domestic affairs, and, by the help of God, will do it; that they are not bound to observe any law passed by the Legislature about to assemble; that to the threats of war made by the neighboring State of Missouri, they respond, "WE ARE READY."; "that a free state Central Committee be appointed, and that each election district be entitled to one member, and each election district having two councilmen shall be entitled to two members."

On the 27th of June, the "National Democracy" assembled at Lawrence, of which Colonel James H. Lane was made chaiaman. This convention seems to have been composed of life-long Democrats, who had not yet fully broken loose from the entanglements of party. They resolved that "the best interests of Kansas require an early organization of the Democratic party upon truly national ground;" that they fully endorse the Democratic platform of 1852; that they kindly request citizens of adjoining States to let them alone; that they can not permit the "purity of the ballot box to be polluted by outsiders, or illegal voting from any quarter." The Committee on Resolutions was E. Chapman, C. W. Babcock, Dr. James Garvin, J. S. Emery and Hugh Cameron.

A meeting of the expelled free state members of the Legislature, and other citizens, was held at Lawrence on the 11th of July, of which Judge John A. Wakefield was chairman. Addresses were made by Messrs. G. W. Smith, John Hutchingston, John O. P. Wood, Rev. M. Nute, Dr. C. Robinson C. Stearns and Wm. Jessie. Most of the speakers favored recommending to the people to call a constitutional convention, frame a constitution and apply at the next Congress for admission into the Union. Dr. Wood opposed this, but urged an organization to be made to defend the ballot box. This convention called a mass meeting of the free state citizens of the Territory of Kansas, at Lawrence, on the second Tuesday in August, "to take into consideration the situation of the Territory in reference to its government."

The first general mass convention assembled at Lawrence on the 14th of August, and continued in session two days. Hon. Philip C. Schuyler was made president, with several vice-presidents. Dr. Robinson, chairman of the committee on resolutions, reported a series of resolves, which called forth a lengthy and animated discussion. By these resolutions the convention denounced the Legislature then in session at Shawnee Mission, as having its origin in fraud and "derogatory to the integrity and respectability of the Federal authority;" that they repudiate its authority and pledge themselves to resist its enactments; that they favor a convention to form a State Constitution preparatory to admission into the Union.

There were some in the convention with whom it was hard to let go from the coat tail of the Federal administration. They opposed anything that reflected unfavorably upon it. Though they denounced the Missouri outrages at the March election, they were adverse to coming in conflict with the Government thus inaugurated. Foremost among these was Colonel James H. Lane, who declared "Frank Pierce would give his right arm to-day to insure freedom in this Territory." "That he would prefer to see Kansas a free State in preference to seeing it a slave State."

Others favored more radical measures than these, such as recommending military organizations for self-protection and open resistance to the laws of the Shawnee Legislature.

This convention was the first meeting of the conflicting elements of old parties, such as Whig, Democratic and Abolition, seeking to harmonize upon some plan of action to rid themselves of the oppression thrust upon them by Missouri, and for making Kansas a free State. It is not to be wondered at, then, that there was a difference of views and policies in such a heterogeneous body. It seemed during the first day that the convention would result only in driving free state men farther from each other and the interest of freedom lost in the weakness and folly of dissension.

The intervening night between the two days that the convention was in session, acted as a wonderful sedative upon its members. The little group of freemen—all patriots, all opposed to oppression and in favor of making Kansas a free State, but honestly differing in regard to the best means to employ in effecting their object—were brought together by a free, frank and conversational interchange of opinions. Heart spoke to heart, and eye to eye, until one common feeling pervaded every breast. The radicals receded some and the conservatives advanced, until all met in harmonious unanimity.

The following day the convention proceeded with its deliberations in the most pacific manner. The resolutions, after undergoing some amendments, the most ultra expressions having been stricken out, were unanimously adopted. It was resolved, also, to solicit the Territorial Central Committee, which had previously taken action upon the subject, to call a "Free State Convention of five delegates to each Representative from the several Representative Districts, to be elected on the 25th day of August, to meet in convention at Big Springs on the 5th day of September next, for the purpose of taking such action as the exigency of the times may demand."

In the meantime agreeable to a call published about a week* previous, signed "Many Citizens," "to take into consideration the propriety of calling a Territorial Convention preliminary to the formation of a State Government and other subjects of interest," a convention of the citizens of Kansas Territory, *irrespective* of party, met on the afternoon of the 15th of August. Dr. A. Hunting was elected president. Mr. G. W. Smith, chairman of the committee on business, reported a resolution calling a convention of three delegates for each Representative from the several Representative Districts in Kansas, to meet at Topeka on the 19th of September, "then and there to consider and determine upon all subjects of public interest, and *particularly* upon that having reference to the speedy formation of a State Constitution with an intention of an immediate application to be admitted as a State into the Union of the United States of America." This was really the starting point in fixing the capital at Topeka. It was brought about through the influence of Mr. C. K. Holliday in the committee of business, Mr. G. W. Smith voting with him and Dr. C. Robinson in favor of Lawrence.

A Ratification Convention was held that evening, at which the president, Mr. C. K. Holliday, declared, "There

---

*Some say that this call was made on the day previous, and the circumstances would seem to indicate that such was the case.

is not a dissatisfied mind in all this assembly with the result of the recent deliberations."

The Territorial Delegate Convention which organized the Free State Party, assembled at Big Springs at the designated time. Judge G. W. Smith was chosen permanent chairman. It very fully represented the Territory, consisting of upwards of one hundred members. Five committees of thirteen members each were appointed whose duties were as follows: "1st. To report a platform for the consideration of the convention; 2d. To take into consideration the propriety of a State organization; 3d. To consider the duty of the people as regards the proceedings of the late Legislature; 4th. To devise action on the coming Congressional election; 5th. On miscellaneous business." The following report, submitted by Colonel Lane from the committee on platform, was adopted:

"WHEREAS, The Free State Party of the Territory of Kansas, about to originate an organization for concert of political action, in electing our own officers and moulding our institutions; AND WHEREAS, It is expedient and necessary that a platform of principles be adopted and proclaimed to make known the character of our organization, and to test the qualifications of candidates and the fidelity of our members; AND WHEREAS, We find ourselves in an unparalleled and critical condition—deprived by superior force of the rights guaranteed by the Declaration of Independence, the Constitution of the United States, and the Kansas Bill; AND WHEREAS, The great and overshadowing question, whether Kansas shall become a free or a slave State, must inevitably absorb all other issues, except those inseparably connected with it; AND WHEREAS, The crisis demands the concert and harmonious action of all those who from principal or interest, prefer free labor to slave labor, as well as of those who value the preservation ot the Union and the guarantees of republican institutions by the Constitution, therefore

"*Resolved*, That setting aside all the minor issues of partisan politics, it is incumbent upon us to proffer an organization calculated to recover our dearest rights, and into which Democrats and Whigs, native and naturalized citizens, may freely enter without any sacrifice of their respective political creeds, but without forcing them as a test upon others. And that when we shall have achieved our political freedom, vindicated our rights of self-government and become an independent State of the Union, when these issues may become vital as they are now dormant, it will be time enough to divide our organization by these tests, the importance of which we fully recognize in their appropriate sphere.

"*Resolved*, That we will oppose and resist all non-resident voters at our polls, whether from Missouri or elsewhere, as a gross violation of our rights, and a virtual disfranchisement of our citizens.

"*Resolved*, That our true interests, socially, morally and pecuniarily, require that Kansas should be a *free State;* that free labor will best promote the happiness, the rapid population, the prosperity and the wealth of our people; that slave labor is a curse to the master and the community, if not to the slave; that our country is unsuited to it, and that we will devote our energies as a party to exclude the institution, and to secure for Kansas the constitution of a free State.

"*Resolved*, That the best intererts of Kansas require a population of free white men, and that in the State organization we are in favor of stringent laws excluding all negroes, bond or free, from the Territory; that nevertheless such measures shall not be regarded as a test of party orthodoxy.

"*Resolved*, That the *stale* and ridiculous charge of abolitionism, so industriously imputed to the Free State Party, and so persistently adhered to, in spite of all the evidence to the contrary, is without a shadow of truth to support it, and that it is not more appropriate to ourselves than it is to our opponents, who use it as a term of reproach, to bring odium upon us, pretending to believe in its truth, and hoping to frighten from our ranks the weak and timid, who are more willing to desert their principles than they are to stand up under persecution and abuse with a conscientiousness of right.

"*Resolved*, That we will discountenance and denounce any attempt to encroach upon the constitutional rights of the people of any State, or to interfere with their slaves, conceding to their citizens the right to regulate their own institutions, and to hold and recover their slaves, without any molestation or obstruction from the people of Kansas."

This report elicited a warm discussion. Many were in favor of a more radical platform, and were particularly opposed to those clauses alluding to slavery and abolitionists. They were generally eastern men. On the other hand there were many who despised the name of "abolitionist," and were opposed to negroes being in Kansas in any shape or form. They had not been educated to a high standard of human rights. They were chiefly western men and Democrats, some of whom were Missourians. There can be no doubt that the prevailing element in this Territory at that time, as it was then all over the free States, was not only hostile to slavery, but bitterly hostile to the negro. It was thought, too, that many of the Missourians, in the Territory who could have no interest in slavery, but who could not bear the idea of being "abolitionists" would be gained by this conservative platform.

It was argued by a majority of the convention that such a conservative and liberal platform would commend itself both to Congress and the inhabitants of the Territory, thus enabling them to accomplish the real object of their union—exclusion of slavery from Kansas. It was, indeed, a policy whereby a verbal concession ot principle was made on the part of some, with a view of obtaining a position to more fully vindicate and carry out their principles; but at the same time this platform embodied the sentiments and feelings of a majority of the people in the Territory at that time.

The Committee on State Organization reported that in their opinion the movement was "untimely and inexpedient." Its members were H. B. Brock, J. M. Yates, R. G. Elliott, R. Mendenhall, H. M. Hook, E. Castle, J. Hamilton, H. J. Stout, A. Bowen, S. D. Houston, J. M. Arthur and Isaac Wollard. After a spirited discussion, the report was rejected by a substitute offered by Mr. Hutchingson, that the Convention fully endorse "the People's Convention of the 14th ult., for a delegate convention of the people of Kansas Territory, to be held at Topeka on the 19th inst., to consider the propriety of forming a State constitution," &c.

Mr. J. S. Emery, from the Committee having charge of the legislative matters of the Territory, made the following eloquent report:

"*Resolved*, That the body of men who, for the past two months, have been making laws for the people of our Territory, moved, counselled and dictated to by the demagogues of Missouri, are to us a foreign body, representing only the lawless invaders who elected them, and not the people of the Territory, that we repudiate their action as the monstrous consummation of an act of violence, usurpation and fraud, unparalleled in the history of the Union, and worthy only of men unfitted for the duties and regardless of the responsibilities of Republicans.

"*Resolved*, That having by reason of numerical inferiority and want of preparation, been compelled to succumb to the outrageous oppression of armed and organized bands of the citizens of a neighboring State—having been robbed by force of the right of suffrage and self-government, and subjected to a foreign despotism, the more odious and infamous that it involves a violation of compacts with sister States, more sacred and solemn than treaties—we disown and disavow with scorn and indignation the contemptible and hypocritical mockery of a republican government into which this infamous despotism has been converted.

"*Resolved*, That this miscalled Legislature, by their reckless disregard of the Organic Territorial Act, ana other Congressional legislation, in expelling members whose title to seats was beyond their power to annul, in admitting members who were not elected, and in legislating at an unauthorized place—by their refusal to allow the people to to select any of their own officers, many of whom were unquestionable residents of Missouri at that time—by leaving us no elections save those prescribed by Congress, and therefore beyond their power to abrogate, and even at these selling the right of suffrage at our ballot-boxes to any non-resident who chooses to buy and pay for it—by compelling us to take an oath to support a law of the United States, invidiously pointed out—by stifling the freedom of speech and of the press, thus usurping the power forbidden to Congress, libelled the Declaration of Independence—violated the Constitutional Bill of Rights, and brought contempt and disgrace upon our Republican institutions at home and abroad.

"*Resolved*, That we owe no allegiance or obedience to the tyrannical enactments of this spurious Legislature—that their laws have no validity or binding force upon the people of Kansas, and that every free man among us is at full liberty, consistent with all his obligations as a citizen and a man, to resist them if he chooses so to do.

"*Resolved*, That we will resist them primarily by every peaceable and legal means in our power, until we can elect our own Representatives and sweep them from the Statute Book, and that as the majority of our Supreme Court have so far forgotten their official duty—have so far cast off the honor of a lawyer and the dignity of a Judge as to enter clothed with the judicial ermine into a partisan contest, and by extra-judicial decisions giving opinions in violation of all propriety, having prejudged our case before we could be heard, and have pledged themselves to the outlaws in advance, to decide in their favor, we will therefore take measures to carry the question of the validity of these laws to a higher tribunal where Judges are unpledged and dispassionate—where the law will be administered in its purity, and where we can at least have the hearing before the decision.

"*Resolved*, That we will endure and submit to these laws no longer than the best interests of the Territory require, as the least of two evils, and will resist them to a bloody issue as soon as we ascertain that peaceable remedies shall fail, and forcible resistance shall furnish any reasonable prospect of success; and that in the meantime we recommend to our friends throughout the Territory the organization and discipline of Volunteer Companies and the procurement and preparation of arms.

"*Resolved*, That we cannot, and will not, quietly submit to surrender our great 'American Birth Right'—the elective franchise—which, first by violence, and then by chicanery, artifice, weak and wicked legislation, they have so effectually attempted to deprive us of, and that we with scorn repudiate the 'election law,' so-called, and will not meet with them on the day they have appointed for the election, but but will ourselves fix upon a day for the purpose of electing a delegate to Congress."

Several efforts were made to amend this report, but it was finally received and endorsed.

By the report of the Committee on Congressional Delegate, the time of holding the election was changed from the time specified by the Legislature to the 9th of October; that the rules and regulations prescribed for the March election should govern this election, except the returns, which, by the "people's proclamation" subsequently issued, were to be made to the "Territorial Executive Committee." The reasons for fixing the time on the 2d Tuesday in October, were to avoid recognizing the right of the late Legislature to call an election, and to obviate the obnoxious oath to support the slave code; furthermore, if they should vote at the time designated by the Legislature, there would be no guaranty that they could have a fair expression of their choice.

The Committee on Miscellaneous Business, in their report, defended Governor Reeder from the charges made against him as the cause of his removal, and eulogized his conduct. The Convention nominated him candidate for delegate to Congress by acclamation.

There were some very touching scenes to be witnessed in the two days' sitting of this convention. It was hard for them all to unite upon a common platform. It was thought for some time that the attempt would prove a failure, and the cause of freedom be lost on that account. At this critical crisis Judge Smith arose and began a speech of great earnestness and feeling. With his white locks trembling in the wind, and tears streaming down his furrowed cheeks, he besought them in the spirit of a patriarch and a patriot, to cast aside all minor differences, and to unite in one common struggle towards rescuing Kansas from the vile dominion of slavery.

Mr. Reeder, in response to his nomination, made a most moving and feeling speech. The following is the closing of it as reported in the proceedings of the meeting:

"He spoke long and eloquently upon the importance that no rashness should endanger the Union we all love and cleave to. He did not consider the correct public sentiment of the South as indorsing the violent wrongs which had been perpetrated by Missourians in our Territory, and that being so, he waited to hear their rebuke. Should it not come, and all hope of moral influence to correct these evils be cut off, and the tribunals of our country fail us, while our wrongs still continue, what then? Will they have grown easier to bear by long custom? God forbid that any lapse of time should accustom freemen to the duties of slaves, and when such fatal danger as that is menaced, then is the time to

" 'Strike for our altars and our fires,
Strike for the green graves of our sires,
God and our native land.'

"As he paused there was for an instant a deep silence as when a question of life or death is being considered—every man drew a long breath, but the next instant the air was rent with cries, 'Yes, we will strike,' 'White men can never be slaves,' 'Reeder!' 'Reeder!' 'Nine cheers for Reeder and Right!' During his speech he had been constantly interrupted by shouts and shaking of hands, but now the enthusiasm was ungovernable; the crowd gathered around him with the warmest greetings."

A committee of three was appointed to wait on Governor Shannon and present him a copy of the proceedings of this meeting, composed of General S. C. Pomeroy, Colonel J. H. Lane and Geo. W. Brown.

The Delegate Convention to consider the expediency of taking preliminary steps towards forming a State Constitution with a view of applying for admission into the Union, assembled at Topeka on the 19th of September, and continued in session two days. New elements had been worked into the Free State party by this time in consequence of the liberal spirit pervading the Big Springs convention, and other excellent gentlemen are found co-operating in the State movement, such as H. Miles Moore, M. W. Delahay, &c. The first day was consumed in organizing. On the following morning a committee of eighteen was appointed to set forth in an address to the world the grievances of the people of Kansas. In the afternoon the following resolutions among others were unanimously adopted:

"*Therefore, Resolved*, By the people of Kansas Territory in Delegate Convention assembled, That an election shall be held in the several election precincts of this Territory, on the second Tuesday in October next, under the regulations and restrictions hereinafter imposed, for members of a convention to form a constitution, adopt a bill of rights for the people of Kansas, and take all needful measures for organizing a State government, preparatory to the admission of Kansas into the Union as a State.

"*Resolved*, That a committee of seven be appointed by the chair, who shall organize by the appointment of a chairman and secretary. They shall keep a record of their proceedings and shall have a general superintendence of the affairs of the Territory so far as regards the organization of a State government, which committee shall be styled 'The Executive Committee of Kansas Territory.'

"*Resolved*, That said convention shall be held at Topeka on the fourth Tuesday of October next, at 12 o'clock M. of that day."

Colonel James H. Lane was made chairman of this Executive Committee, and J. K. Goodin secretary. The other members were C. K. Holliday, M. J. Parrott, P. C. Schuyler, G. W. Smith and G. W. Brown.

CHAPTER XVIII.

FREE STATE MOVEMENTS—CONTINUED.

The "People's Proclamation," signed by most of the qualified voters of the Territory, was issued, calling an election on the second Tuesday of October, to choose a delegate to represent them in Congress. After prescribing an oath for the judges and the qualifications of electors, they referred the details and control of the election to the Executive Committee appointed by the Convention at Topeka.

Immediately followed a proclamation, emanating from the chairman of this Executive Committee, calling for an election of delegates to the convention for forming a State Constitution, on the same day that the election for delegate to Congress was held, and prescribing the usual regulations for an election.

The question of forming a State Government and resisting the enactments of the bogus Legislature, was the all-absorbing topic of conversation in those days. It was discussed in numerous local conventions, talked over at home gatherings, preached from the pulpit and mingled in petitions to God. Pious men prayed, and wicked men swore, over it; politicians plotted and patriots thought. All other business, all other channels of thought, were for the time abandoned, and the watchword became, "A FREE STATE; OPPOSITION TO TYRANNY BY PEACEABLE MEASURES FIRST; WHEN THEY FAIL, BY FORCE." It was a question of as serious concern, and as deep interest, to the Squatters in Kansas as that which affected our Revolutionary Fathers in the dark days when it "tried men's souls."

It was argued and confidently felt that if the settlers would harmoniously enter upon these measures, that Congress would recognize their action as the legitimately expressed will of the inhabitants of this Territory; would repudiate the Shawnee Legislature and its proceedings, admit the delegate of the people to Congress, and receive them into the Union under the constitution of their own making. And they had good reasons to expect such a result if justice had not entirely abandoned the legislative halls of the nation. Their actions were certainly in accordance with the true spirit of Squatter Sovereignty. Their constitution was such that even the liberal minded slaveholder would not object to it, except that it did not perpetuate slavery in the State. Their actions and declarations of principles were extremely conservative. And even the great champion of. Squatter Sovereignty, Hon. S. A. Douglas, afterwards admitted that it was the greatest blunder of his life in not favoring their petitions.

The election of delegate to Congress, under the appointment of the Shawnee Legislature, took place on the first of October. There being no other candidate, General J. W. Whitfield, who had been nominated at Shawnee Mission while the Legislature was in session, was unanimously elected, and received certificate of the same from Governor Shannon. There were, at least, as many as two thousand illegal votes polled at this election, making two-thirds the total number cast. The Missourians took but little interest in it, as they knew that the free state men did not intend to contest it.

Governor Reeder was unanimously elected for the same position by the Free State Party. He received twenty-eight hundred and sixteen votes. In several precincts no vote was allowed to be taken. Pro-slavery men did not participate in the election, and offered no disturbance, except in a few places.

About this time occurred an amusing incident, to the chagrin and disadvantage of the people at Leavenworth. The bogus Legislature, among the many things it did, had divided the Territory into counties; but in consequence of the hurry and burden of business, had neglected, in several instances, to locate the county seats, which was the case with Leavenworth County, and accordingly an election by its citizens was called to decide that question. There happened to be three rival towns which contended for the honor of the county seat. Two were intensely pro-slavery; Kickapoo, about ten miles above, and Delaware, eight miles below, Leavenworth. Both were prospectively great in the eyes of those interested at that time, but both have long since ceased to be known. Leavenworth contained a majority of free state men, with a large minority of pro-slavery men; but by being situated so near the border, the latter generally ruled. Its citizens, of course, all desired the county seat, and confidently expected it. They, therefore, made but little effort at the election, feeling that their local interest would poll the majority of votes in favor of their town. The other two contestants knew their cause was hopeless in a fair election, but they resolved to profit by their recent instructions in ballot box frauds. The matter was laid before the people of Platte County, among whom Leavenworth was reputed as an "abolition stink hole," and they agreed to help their friends across the river in this dilemma. On the day of the election Leavenworth polled about five or six hundred votes, all legal. Between Weston and Kickapoo a steam ferry boat was kept running all day, pouring in voters from Missouri, until they polled at the latter place eight hundred and fifty ballots for the county seat; whereas the total number of legal voters in that precinct did not exceed one hun- and fifty. At Delaware they went still farther. Besides conveying voters across the river in a chartered steamer for one day *only*, they kept it up after they had learned the result at Kickapoo, until they had polled nearly nine hundred votes, only fifty of which were legal. For this purpose they had kept the polls open three days. The first authority to whom these returns were made decided in favor of Kickapoo, declaring that keeping the polls open for three days was an "unheard of irregularity." "Kickapoo was jubilant, Leavenworth was sore. Her pro-slavery men were grieviously indignant. So long as this kind of operation had been directed against the 'abolitioners' it was fair; but now they began to realize a touch of Squatter Sovereignty, as enunciated in the Kansas-Nebraska bill. The Leavenworth *Herald* whose editor had been a member of the bogus Council of the Shawnee Mission, began to print moral lessons and homilies on the tendencies of these things. All the respectable, which means the property holding, pro-slaslavery men about Leavenworth, looked solemn."

"The Kickapoo *Pioneer*, a fire-eating, pro-slavery paper, taunted Mr. Easton, of the Leavenworth *Herald*, of his sudden conversion to the 'purify-the-polls' doctrine, and finished a somewhat sarcastic article by asking, 'Who elected you to the Legislature?' This was severe but fair. In the dilemma the *Herald* got off the following interesting morsel, being a part of a glorious article two columns long:

"'Much has been said by the abolition presses throughout the country about 'armed invasions of Kansas by the Border Ruffians of Missouri,' but, as we then asserted and still assert, they were acting solely in self-defense; and history will tell of the purity of their purpose and of the justice of the *cause they vindicated.* They came here actuated by the noblest of human sentiments, determined to ward off a blow which was aimed against their institutions and against their peace. As such, with open arms we welcomed them; and, when victory crowned our common efforts, and the black flag of abolitionism trailed in the dust, how grateful were the feelings we experienced to those who had rallied with us to a hand-to-hand encounter with the aggressive foes.

"'But did any pro-slavery man in or out of Kansas for a moment imagine that, by reason of such elections, Kansas had surrendered unconditionally, and that Missouri had made the conquest of the Territory for the use and benefit of Platte County, upon her border? and, worse than this, to be made the plaything and the puppet of a few demagogues and hucksters in Weston and Platte City? The idea is simply absurd.'

"Absurd though it might be, it still was a 'fixed fact.' Kickapoo had to bite the dust before the sovereign will of the 'majority.' The election was referred to a court which decided in favor of Delaware. This was, at least, consistent; for, as all the pro-slavery courts, which means all the courts in the Territory, had decided in favor of bogus authority, it was not going to do to establish so dangerous a precedent as setting aside an election on account of any irregularity."

The Topeka Constitutional Convention, from the object it had in view, and from the circumstances under which it assembled, was one of the most important bodies of men ever convened in Kansas. It was composed of the chief men among the free soilers from all parts of the Territory. They had emigrated from every State in the Union, and represented every political party, religious sect, habit of life, prejudice, dogma and principle that exist in the United States. There were Republicans, Democrats, Whigs and Abolitionists—all freesoilers. Every occupation had its representative; the farmer, the teacher, the doctor, the preacher and the lawyer. They occupied every grade of intelligence and age; from the illiterate to the learned, from the young to the old. Some were pious and some were not so much so; some were temperate, others indulged when they felt like it. There were the young and the ambitious, who, while they sought to advance the cause of freedom, equally hoped to advance themselves. There were those who had entered upon the conflict to defend the principles involved. They were no politicians, but men of sound sense and sterling worth, who sought no preferment, but expected to retire to private life when the contest should end. There were politicians, experienced and adroit in pulling the wires, who had come here to retrieve or better their political fortune. They thought by judiciously framing the ship of State with reference to the political elements with which it had to contend, to safely ride themselves into office. They were unscrupulous as regards principles and advised the surrendering of a portion of them, like mariners do with their cargo in a storm, to prevent the shipwreck of their hopes. The members of the convention were, *indeed*, what they purported to be—THE REPRESENTATIVES OF A PEOPLE *that had recently emigrated from all parts of the nation, bringing with them their characteristic peculiarities and provincialisms.*

Fifty-two members had been elected, but only forty took part in the deliberations. Their daily proceedings were officially published in a small sheet from the press of the "Kansas Freeman." Mr. E. C. K. Garvey was editor—a short, thick, hump-shouldered Irishman. The convention had all the attendants of a legislative body. There were caucuses, committee meetings, electioneering, button-hole fingering and speech making. Newspaper reporters were admitted to a seat within the bar, and sent the proceedings of the convention to all parts of the country. A chaplain opened their sessions with prayer, and humbly invoked the "wisdom that cometh from above." Parties, oyster suppers, concerts and lectures afforded amusements.

The citizens were especially courteous and clever, as they hoped to secure the capital of the rising State.

The members of the Convention were generally conservative, the Democrats having a slight majority, and about as many from the western as from the eastern States. The vote upon striking out the word "white" from the Constitution stood 7 yeas to 24 nays, as follows:

Yeas—Brown, Crosby, Hillyer, Hunting, Knight, Robinson, Schuyler.

Nays—Arthur, Burson, Curtiss, Cutler, Delahay, Dodge, Hunt, Klotz, Lane, Latta, Landis, McDaniels, McWhenny, Parrott, Roberts, Sayle, Smith, Thomson, Tutton, Wakefield, Hicks, Emery, Gooden, Holliday, Graham.

On a resolution "approving the principles of Squatter Sovereignty, and non-intervention by the people of the States as well as Congress in the local affairs of the Territories and States," the vote stood 17 yeas to 15 nays.

The Convention did not come to a test vote upon the exclusion of free negroes from the Territory, but compromised the matter by a resolution providing for a submission of the question to a vote of the people, which should act as instruction to the State Legislature. Thus the odious "black law" had no place in the Constitution, but a majority of the delegates were probably in favor it. The great argument employed in its favor was that unless some such provision should be made, Missouri would burden the State with her worn out, infirm and worthless negroes.

The Convention was in session sixteen days, and moulded the first Constitution of the State. There was nothing remarkable in the document itself; but the circumstances under which it was framed rendered it illustrious. Nevertheless, it formed the model by which the other two free state Constitutions were shaped, which are in reality only amendments of that instrument. It provided that "there shall be no slavery in the State, nor involuntary servitude, unless for a punishment of crime," and that the first Legislature should provide for the enforcement of this article on or before the 4th of July, 1857. The boundaries of the State were the same as those prescribed in the act organizing the Territory. All male Indians who had adopted the customs of the whites should be allowed to vote. The question of excluding from the State free negroes and mulattoes occasioned much discussion. The General Assembly should be composed of sixty Representatives and twenty Senators, who should receive $4,00 per day for their services. There was no Superintendent of Public Instruction provided for, and educational provisions were generally defective. Topeka was made the temporary capital, twenty votes being cast for it, and sixteen for Lawrence. The first General Assembly was to locate the permanent seat of government. There can be no convention to form a new Constitution, nor can this be amended until after 1865. The Constitution was to be submitted to the people on the 15th of December, 1855 for their ratification or rejection. At the same time the general banking law was to be voted upon, and if adopted was to stand as a part of the Constitution. In case the Constitution was ratified at the election, the Executive Committee should call an election for State officers and for Representative in Congress. The first General Assembly was to meet on the 4th of July, 1856. Election districts were arranged, rules and regulations for the election the 15th of December were prescribed by the Convention. The Territorial Executive Committee, appointed on the 19th of November, was empowered to superintend the State organization at the coming elections, to issue scrip, not to exceed twenty-five thousand dollars, to meet all necessary expenses, and the first Assembly was to provide for the redemption of this scrip. Late on Saturday night, (November 10th,) the members of the Convention subscribed their names to the Constitution in the following order:*

Robt. Klotz, merchant, Pa.; Pawnee, Dem., Pa., 35.

M. J. Parrott, S. C., Leavenworth, Dem., Ohio.

M. W. Delahay, lawyer and editor, Md., Leavenworth, Dem., Ala., 37.

W. R. Griffith, teacher, Ia., Rep., Bourbon Co., Pa.

G. S. Hillyer, farmer, Ohio, Grasshopper Falls, Whig, Ohio, 35.

*Explanation—The words and abbreviations opposite each name designate successively as follows: 1, profession; 2, nativity; 3, residence at time of convention; 4, politics; 5. State emigrated from to Territory; 6, age.

William Hicks, farmer, Pa., Dayton, Dem., Ind., 33.
S. N. Latta, lawyer, Ohio, Leavenworth, Whig, Iowa, 39.
John Landis, farmer, Ky., Doniphan, Dem., Mo., 28.
H. Burson, farmer, Virginia, Bloomington, Whig, Ill., 36.
W. Stewart, farmer, Ky., Ocena, Dem., 42.
J. M. Arthur, farmer, Ind., Sugar Creek, Dem., Ind., 38.
J. L. Sayle, farmer, Ill., Kickapoo, Rep., Iowa, 37.
Caleb May, farmer, Ky., Ocena, Dem., Mo., 40.
S. McWhinny, farmer, Ohio, Prairie City, Dem., Ill., 45.
A. Curtiss, lawyer, N. Y., Bloomington, none, Ky., 32.
A. Hunting, physician, Mass., Manhattan, Rep., R. I., 61.
R. Knight, clergyman, England, Lawrence, Free State, Mass., 43.
O. C. Brown, farmer, N. Y., Ossawattomie, Free Soiler, N. Y., 44.
W. Graham, physician, Ireland, Prairie City, Democrat, Tenn., 39.
Morris Hunt, lawyer, Ohio, Lawrence, Whig, Ohio, 27.
J. H. Nesbit.
C. K. Holliday, lawyer, Pa., Topeka, Dem., Pa., 28.
David Dodge, lawyer, N. Y., Leavenworth, Democrat, N. Y., 25.
J. A. Wakefield, lawyer, S. C., Bloomington, Whig, Iowa, 59.
W. Y. Roberts, farmer, Pa., Washington, Dem., Pennsylvania, 41.
G. W. Smith, lawyer, Pa., Franklin, Whig, Pa., 50.
J. G. Thomson, saddler, Pa., Topeka, Dem., Pa., 55.
G. A. Cutler, physician, Tenn., Doniphan, Free Soiler, Mo., 23.
J. K. Goodin, lawyer, Ohio, Clear Lake, Dem., Ohio, 31.
J. M. Tutton, clergyman, Tenn., Bloomington, Democrat, Mo., 33.
Thomas Bell.
R. H. Crosby, merchant, Maine, Ocena, Rep., Min., 21.
P. C. Schuyler, farmer, N. Y., Council City, Rep., 50.

C. Robinson, physician, Mass., Lawrence, Independent, Mass., 37.

M. F. Conway.

J. S. Emery, lawyer, Maine, Lawrence, Democrat, N. Y., 26.

J. H. Lane, lawyer, Ky., Lawrence, Dem., Ind., 33.

CHAPTER XIX.

VARIOUS EVENTS.

The emigration from the free States was very large during the spring and summer. More than five hundred came in under the auspices of the New England Emigrant Aid Societies. Pennsylvania sent many of her industrious, persevering and enterprising children. Ohio, Indiana, Illinois, Michigan, Wisconsin and Iowa, poured in an energetic and sturdy class of pioneers. Many went far back into the Territory, and selected choice sites for their homes.

The various towns laid out the fall before received their respective proportions of the incoming population. Many new town sites were located, but none of these ever acquired any importance. New and more substantial buildings were erected; large hotels, saw mills, churches and school houses were prepared for the accommodation of the public.

There might be many amusing items written relative to the laying out and settlement of Kansas towns. Each one had its "blowers" and drummers along the Border. Here would be one expatiating on the merits of Leavenworth, another of Lawrence, while a third would prove to a demonstration that Pawnee would be the emporium of the West. Towns were laid out, represented on paper, their praises sounded, which never had any existence only on paper, and were known as "paper towns." Doniphon, Delaware, Kickapoo, Lecompton and Tecumseh maintained a struggling infancy, and then perished. The towns of Kansas grew slowly at first, and it was not until the troubles subsided that their growth was accelerated.

Many of the new emigrants were utterly unfit for the arduous life on the frontier. They were chiefly young men of no fixed habits of life, who had come as on a pleasing adventure to the land of which there was then so much talk. They seemed never to have thought of the many hardships, privations and denials concomitant with a new country ; so on arriving here and not finding the advantages and luxuries, they returned in disappointment, cursing the country as barren of all the comforts of life. Others came from cities, and were alike unaccustomed to the inconveniences to which they found themselves necessarily subjected, while another class came merely to prospect, with the expectation of emigrating if suited with the country. These classes of new comers generally made but transient stays in the Territory. They hurried back to their old pleasant homes, feeling that there were but few charms for them in pioneer life. Those of them who dared to weather the hardships to which they found themselves exposed, only procrastinated their return. The troubles and sickness which soon broke out, repaid their temerity with fresh suffering, and, sometimes, with mourning. The consequence was that very many of the eastern emigrants, this spring and summer, found no permanent lodgment upon our prairies, but migrated back to their old peaceful and congenial abodes.

To add to the many hardships with which settlers in a new country have to contend, disease spread among them. The summer being an exceedingly dry one, it was difficult to obtain water. Few wells had been dug, and the only water that could be secured in many instances, was taken from stagnant pools in the beds of creeks, covered with a yellow slime. Hard labor, improper diet, unwholesome drink and general filthiness invited the visits of epidemics. Cholera and fever vied with each other in ravaging the unhappily situated people of their only enjoyment—health.

Until the arrival of Governor Shannon after Governor Reeder was removed, Secretary Daniel Woodson acted as Governor. He was a tall, slender, and rather handsome Virginian of about thirty years. He was once editor of the "Lynchburg Republican" in his native State. He was pro-slavery from taste and not principle. Although there was nothing apparently bad in the man, he was utterly wanting in that essential quality of an executive officer—which we sometimes express by "backbone." With pro-slavery feelings, he was well calculated to be used as a tool by Border politicians. No sooner had Gov. Reeder turned the powers of the Executive over to the Secretary than he began signing the bills passed by the bogus Legislature.

A convention, composed of delegates from twenty-five counties, was held on the 12th of June, at Lexington, Missouri, for the purpose of taking into consideration the interests of their ward in Kansas. The chief men of the Border were there in grave council for two days and nights. In it the principles of nullification were clearly set forth. Said the orator of the day, "A minority have not the right to revolt against any constitutional measure that may be enacted, but that minority have the right to resist any act of Congress that has not the sanction of the Constitution." Their attention was chiefly directed to the proceedings of the Emigrant Aid Societies, which they bitterly denounced in their speeches and resolutions. They petitioned the Legislature to retaliate on free States "by discriminating against their sales and manufactures" in Missouri, and to suppress "the circulation of abolition or freesoil publications, and the promulgation of abolition or freesoil opinions." A committee was appointed to prepare and issue an address to the people of the United States "setting forth the history of the Kansas excitement and the views and actions of our people thereon." This address was a weak and puerile production, full of misrepresentations and tirades against the Aid Societies. Their chief complaint against these organizations was that they tended to divert the natural course of emigration so as to make Kansas a free State against the wishes and interests of Western Missouri.

The invasions of the 30th of March and the continued threatening and armed demonstrations of the Missourians, suggested to the free state men some kind of military organization for self-defense. Accordingly a secret order of a military character was introduced, (the Kansas Legion,) similar to the Blue Lodges of Missouri, with this exception —its object was solely defensive, while that of the latter was offensive. Its design was to labor by all lawful means to make Kansas a free State, and to protect the ballot-box from invasion. There was nothing wrong in the Society itself, nor in its object, or means employed to attain that object. It never extended far over the Territory. There were, however, several "encampments" at different places. It was secret in its character, and the members took an obligation in accordance with the nature and design of the society. It was found to be too cumbrous and unwieldy, and soon fell into disuse. Many of its members became dissatisfied with its unnecessary obligations to secrecy. Its cumbersome machinery was never put into practical operation.

This is the society which Pat Loughland claimed to expose. He was a chubby Irishman of some ability, who lived at Doniphan. He was first pro-slavery, then free state. Having been chosen a delegate to the Big Springs Convention, he attended it and took an active part in its proceedings. At this time he was initiated into the Order. On returning to Doniphan, for some mercenary consideration, he made his exposition, which was published in the "Squatter Sovereign." The ritual as published in that paper, declared the object of the society to be the same as stated above. The pro-slavery presses made a great ado about this society as exposed. Hon. Stephen A. Douglas arraigned it in the United States Senate as a monster of iniquity. And yet it was only a local and secret organization of a few oppressed freemen, designed solely for self-defense.

As the Kansas Legion fell into disuse, independent military companies were kept up in different localities. The threatening condition of the country required some such measures. The Missourians having finished their law making for the people of Kansas after sixty days of labor, having had the validity of their enactments duly tested by the Supreme Court and signed by the acting Executive, they were anxious to see them enforced. Accordingly every opportunity was watched by the official emissaries of the Shawnee Legislature to entangle free state men in the dark mazes of their voluminous laws. Efforts were made to get up street broils, whereby some freesoiler would be led to retaliate upon their insolence, and thus subject himself to arrest at their hands. Then in case of concerted resistance they would dispatch to Missouri for a horde of their brothers to come to their assistance and bring down summary vengence upon the unruly people.

But the free state men had adopted a policy which, for a time, entirely frustrated the designs of these officials. They had determined to avoid, as far as possible, any conflict with the Territorial laws, and, at the same time, not recognize their legality or authority. They resolved to quietly and peaceably demean themselves as good citizens without any reference to the enactments of the Legislature. They had nothing to do with its pretended courts of justice or officers, but conducted and carried on their business, and righted their differences according to their own rules and regulations. These remarks apply only where the free state element predominated; in other places free soilers were compelled to recognize, in some degree, the "bogus laws."

Particularly are the remarks in the last two paragraphs applicable to the citizens of Lawrence and vicinity. Repeated personal attacks were made upon them singly, when unarmed, in and out of town, and every opportunity was taken to harass and brow beat them. In consequence of this state of affairs, another society was organized,* whose proceedings were secret, but its existence was intended to be known. Its design was to guard the free state movement, and insure its success by affording personal protection to free state men, and being prepared for any assault from the Missourians, either upon their conventions, homes or towns. It was military in its character, defensive in its object, and confined itself almost exclusively to Lawrence. This is the society which Dr. A. J. Francis exposed to the Grand Jury. It fell into disuse soon after the ratification election in December. The leading free state men were members of it. Its members were required to keep about their persons and homes arms and ammunition, and be ready to hurry to the rescue of any brother endangered. It was the policy of the free state men thus to preserve and guard their state movement, and at the same time not come in conflict with the Territorial authorities, until the Government which they had thus inaugurated should be recognized by Congress as the legitimate one, and that of their oppressors repudiated. It was thought that Congress could be prevailed upon to admit them as a State, and in case their application should be rejected, they could still preserve their State government out of the Union as other Territories had done before.

In the month of August several outrages were committed upon inoffensive persons by a mob. A gentleman from Cincinnati, by the name of J. W. B. Kelley, having made some remarks at Atchison which were construed to reflect upon the institution of slavery, the ruffian Thomason, twice the size of the former, jumped upon him and almost beat him to death. A meeting of the citizens was called and the act publicly sanctioned and applauded. The following resolutions were passed:

*About the middle of September.

"*Resolved*, 1st. That one, J. W. B. Kelley, hailing from Cincinnati, having upon sundry occasions denounced our institutions, and declared all pro-slavery men ruffians, we deem it an act of kindness to rid him of such company, and hereby command him to leave the town of Atchison one hour after being informed of the passage of this resolution, never more to show himself in this vicinity.

"*Resolved*, 2d. That in case he fails to obey this reasonable command, we inflict upon him such punishment as the nature of the case and circumstances may require.

"*Resolved*, 3d. That other emissaries of this 'Aid Society' now in our midst, tampering with our slaves, are warned to leave, else they, too, will meet the *reward* which their nefarious designs so justly merit—*hemp*.

"*Resolved*, 4th. That we approve and applaud our fellow townsman, Grafton Thomason, for the castigation administered to said J. W. B. Kelley, whose presence among us is a libel upon our good standing and a disgrace to our community.

"*Resolved*, 5th. That we recommend the good work of purging our town of all resident abolitionists, and after cleansing our town of such nuisances shall do the same for the settlers on Walnut and Independence Creeks, whose propensities for cattle stealing are well known to many.

"*Resolved*, 6th. That the chairman appoint a committee of three to wait upon said Kelley and acquaint him with the action of this meeting.

"*Resolved*, 7th. That the proceedings of this meeting be published that the world may know our determination."

It was further agreed that copies of these resolutions be made out and circulated for the signatures of all the townsmen, and all who refused to sign them should be reckoned and treated as abolitionists.

On the 16th of August Rev. Pardee Butler, of the Christian Church, who lived about twelve miles from Atchison on his claim, happened in this city waiting for a boat to go east on business. Robert S. Kelley was postmaster, and likewise assistant editor of the "Squatter Sovereign." Meeting Mr. Kelley at the post-office, Mr. Butler informed him he would have some time since become a regular subscriber to his paper had he not disliked the spirit of violence which characterized it. Mr. Kelley replied, "I look upon all free soilers as rogues, and they ought to be treated as such." Mr. Butler responded, "I am a free soiler, and expect to vote for Kansas to be a free State." "I do not expect you will be allowed to vote," was the reply. Mr. Butler then retired to the hotel, and there was no further disturbance that night. The following morning Mr. Kelley entered Mr. Butler's boarding house and demanded of him to sign the resolutions above quoted in regard to Mr. Thomason. The rest of the story is given in Mr. Butler's own words:

REV. PARDEE BUTLER ON A RAFT.

"I declined to subscribe to these resolutions. I commenced reading the resolutions aloud. Robert S. Kelley finally interrupted me and demanded I should sign them. I rose up; walked down stairs into the street; here they stopped me and demanded, 'will you sign?' I refused, when they seized me and dragged me to the river, cursing me for a damned abolitionist, and saying they were going to drown me. When we arrived at the bank, Mr. Kelley painted my face with black paint, marking upon it the letter 'R.' The company had increased to some thirty or forty persons. Without any trial, witness, judge, counsel or jury, for about two hours, I was a sort of target at which were hurled imprecations, curses, arguments, entreaties, accusations and interrogatories.

"They constructed a raft of three cotton wood saw logs, fastened together with inch plank nailed to the logs, upon which they put me and sent me down the Missouri River. The raft was towed out to the middle of the stream with a canoe. Robert S. Kelley held the rope that towed the raft. They gave me neither rudder, oar nor anything else to manage my raft with. They put up a flag on the raft with the following inscription on it: 'Eastern Emigrant Aid Express.' 'The Rev. Pardee Butler again for the underground railroad.' 'The way they are served in Kansas.' 'For Boston.' 'Cargo insured, unavoidable danger of the Missourians and the Missouri River excepted.' 'Let future emissaries from the North beware.' 'Our hemp crop is sufficient to reward all such scoundrels.' They threatened to shoot me if I pulled the flag down. I pulled it down, cut the flag off the flag staff, made a paddle of the flag staff, and ultimately got ashore about six miles below."

The writer does not think that Mr. Butler is correct about the inscription on the flag, if his impressions are not false. A horse was represented on the flag at full speed with Mr. Butler upon him; a negro was clinging behind him, while Mr. Butler was represented as exclaiming, "To the rescue, Greeley, I've got a negro!" Over the painting was printed in large letters, "Eastern Abolition Express." The other side of the flag bore the following inscription, "From Atchison, Kansas Territory." "THE WAY THEY ARE SERVED IN KANSAS."

On the 25th of October a fatal rencounter took place between Pat Laughland and Samuel Collins near Doniphan. It will be recollected that the former gentleman is the man who had made the *expose* of the secret association of the free state men. He had been petted and dandled by pro-slavery men until he had become extremely insolent towards the opposite party. The gentleman with whom he had the fatal affray was a free state man and a member of the society whose working and character Laughland had exposed. Much bitter feeling prevailed in the neighborhood between the two factions.

Mr. Collins, with several other friends, happening to meet Laughland at a saw-mill, a quarrel ensued. In the midst of the excitement one of the latter's friends fired a shot at the former, which he returned without effect. Laughland continued his insulting remarks, when Collins advanced upon him with his drawn gun. Laughland drew his revolver, fired and killed him. A conflict ensued between the friends of each in which shots were exchanged, bowie knives used and several badly hurt.[1] Laughland was taken to Atchison and employed as salesman in a store after he recovered from a wound he received in the affray.

Governor Shannon's appointment was viewed with distrust by the slave propagandists. The "Squatter Sovereign" said: "Mr. Shannon *may* be a reliable man; we *hope* he is; but coming as he does from a State that produces a Giddings, a Wade and a Chase, we can not but regard him with suspicion." "If we know the feelings of the people of Kansas Territory, we can safely state that the point has now arrived, at which forbearance ceases to be a virtue, and the further attempts of the President and Cabinet to saddle an abolitionist upon us for a ruler, will not be tolerated, but resisted even unto death." They desired the President to appoint Mr. Woodson, who had proven "all sound on the goose,"[2] and a very placid tool, or at least some man from a slave State. On the other hand, for those very same reasons for which pro-slavery men disfavored the appointment of Mr. Shannon, the free state men hoped that, like Reeder, he would be disposed, at least, to act impartially in the administration of justice.

But the new Governor had no sooner arrived on the Border than he committed himself decidedly to the interest

---

(1) Accounts of this disturbance vary considerable. (2) A phrase applied by the Missourians to those who were decidedly in favor of making Kansas a slave State.

of slavery. He received a public reception at Kansas City, and was escorted by members of the Legislature to Westport. In the evening he addressed a large audience from the front of the Harris House. His remarks were very acceptable, which was a good evidence that they were "all sound on the goose." The "Squatter Sovereign," in giving a summary of his remarks, said: "Those who heard him assure us that he was eminently felicitous in his remarks, and made the best possible impression on the minds of his hearers. He did not let fall a word which a pro-slavery man, or any other right minded man would wish to have changed; nor did he leave unsaid any thing necessary to a full understanding of his position. He recognized, in its fullest extent, the legality of the Legislative Assembly, and the binding force of its enactments, which he pledges himself to see executed with all his power and authority. He spoke of the deep interests which the Missourians have evinced in the institutions of Kansas, and declared that it was nothing more than natural that people divided only by an ideal line, and clearly allied by the ties of kindred, intimate acquaintance and personal friendship, should desire to have their institutions as near assimilated to each other as possible." He next attended a political meeting, at which General J. W. Whitfield was to make his opening speech of the canvass as delegate to Congress. Here the Governor spoke again, and declared that "he would mildly but firmly, resist every attempt, come from what quarter it may, to introduce higher law doctrines, or in other words, anarchy and confusion into the Territory."*

At a meeting of a few pro-slavery men at Leavenworth on the 3d of October a committee was appointed to prepare an address to the law and order people of Kansas. The members of this committee were Andrew Isaacs, John A.

*The author is aware that Mr. Shannon denied many of the statements attributed to him in his speech at Westport by the free state presses; but this account is taken from an intensely pro-slavery paper, and it is presumed, therefore, reliable.

Halderman, D. J. Johnson, W. G. Mathias, R. R. Rees, L. F. Hollingsworth and D. A. N. Grover. This address urged upon "the lovers of law and order" to oppose all attempts to resist the code of laws recently enacted by the Territorial Legislature, and declared it treason to oppose them. It also called for a grand convention of all the people of this class to assemble at Leavenworth on the 14th of November.

The object of this movement was to quiet down all peaceable citizens who cared for little beyond the improvement of their claims, into submission to the laws of the foreign Legislature. They very clearly saw that they could not always force the citizens to acknowledge and obey them. It had been concocted by the officers and politicians in the Territory and on the Border with a view to frustrate the free state movement, after which the people seemed to be running.

The convention met and the celebrated "Law and Order Party" was organized. It was slimly attended, composed chiefly of pro-slavery men of Leavenworth and Missouri. Governor Shannon was elected chairman and made quite an eloquent speech in favor of obedience to law. He was reported delegate from Douglas County, where he did not then reside. It was a most unbecoming and imprudent act, if not indecent and highly reprehensible, in entering such a mock convention of law and order, accepting the leadership, and calling upon them, the most lawless and reckless in the whole country, most of whom were Missourians, to assist in preserving order. He denounced the movement of free state men as treasonable, and that it must be crushed.

General Calhoun, the Surveyor General, made an intensely partisan speech. It was filled with vituperation and low slang. Pro-slavery journals eulogized it for weeks afterwards.

Upon General Calhoun's taking his seat, Mr. Parrott rose

to speak, but was prevented by various motions of other members. After making repeated calls for the attention of the chair he was finally recognized. He began his speech, but was constantly interrupted by groans and hisses and cries of "put him out." Finally Dr. Stringfellow slyly whispered to him that the crowd did not wish to hear a free state man speak. Mr. Parrott claimed to reverence the law, but the law and order men would not listen to him simply because he was a *free state man.* Judge Lecompte was there and endorsed Mr. Calhoun's speech. Daniel Woodson joined in the chorus for "law and order." Thus the Governor, Secretary, Chief Justice and Surveyor General held conspicuous places in this "law and order" assembly. Says one speaker, "We must enforce the laws, though we resort to the force of arms; trust to our rifles and make the blood flow as freely as do the turbid waters of the Missouri that flows along our banks."

CHAPTER XX.

BEGINNING OF THE WAKARUSA* WAR.

During the summer and fall there were frequently disputes in reference to claims by different parties, which sometimes resulted in personal violence and bloodshed. This was especially the case whenever the two conflicting political elements sought the occupancy of the same neighborhood or grounds. Wherever there was a choice locality the first immigrants, of course, laid claim to it. These would frequently consist of free and slave state men. Each would seek to introduce and gather around them immigrants of their own political faith. The grounds being unsurveyed, no courts of justice at hand, inflamed by political excitement, angry contentions and collisions were of frequent occurrence.

An instance of this character took place at Hickory Point, about ten miles south of Lawrence, on the Santa Fe road, which led to what is termed the Wakarusa war. Hickory Point was a beautiful site of timber and prairie. The first settlers were chiefly from Indiana, but, as in many other cases, some of the original occupants had left their claims and returned to the States. Several Missourians came in

*This is the name of a large creek running south of Lawrence about four miles. It is so named from an Indian legend, which says that a maiden, during a great freshet, sought to cross it on horse back. As she proceeded across, the waters became deeper and deeper, until her body was half immersed, when she exclaimed, "Wakarusa!" (hip deep.) Though she crossed in safety, still the savages, from this occurrence, named the stream Wakarusa.

and took those claims thus forfeited according to Squatter laws, and fraudulently seized others. Among those who thus came in, was Franklin Coleman.

Difficulties soon ensued between the new comers and the old settlers, which were increased by the return of the original claimants of those lands forfeited by absence. Each party sought to strengthen and increase its numbers. The leader among the free state men, Jacob Branson, had encouraged a young man by the name of W. Dow to settle upon an unoccupied claim.

The pro-slavery men would commit trespasses upon the premises of the free soilers, by cutting their timber, burning lime kilns, and appropriating lumber to their own use. Such acts of depredation Coleman committed upon the premises of Dow. The latter determined not to allow this, and notified Coleman that he must stop his trespasses.

On the morning of the 21st of November Mr. Dow went from his boarding place, Mr. Branson's, to a blacksmith shop a short distance off, and while there was abused and threatened by some pro-slavery men. As he started to return home, one of those who had been most violent in denouncing Dow, raised his gun to shoot him, but his courage failed in the murderous act, and he dropped his weapon. On his way home Mr. Dow fell in company with Mr. Coleman. They conversed together until they arrived opposite Coleman's house. Here they separated; one turned to go up to the house, the other continued in the road; but in a moment Dow was startled by the snap of a gun. He turned round and beheld Coleman putting a fresh cap upon his gun. While the innocent man, with arms upraised towards heaven, implored mercy, Coleman deliberately leveled his piece and, with a sure aim, fired. The whole discharge of slugs and buckshot entered Dow's breast and neck, and he fell backwards upon the ground—dead.

The murderer fled to Westport, where, after consultation

with his friends, in compliance with their suggestions, he proceeded to surrender himself up to Governor Shannon. But this official being absent, he threw himself into the custody of S. J. Jones. This latter person had been appointed Sheriff of Douglas County by the Territorial Legislature, although he lived in Westport and was acting postmaster there. He had the appearance of a gentleman, but in those days when Border respectability sunk to the depth of villainy, he was the most consummate rogue. He faithfully served his party in contemptible meanness, for which his name will ever stink in the annals of history. He was about thirty years of age, six feet high, of light complexion, and highly esteemed among his friends as a man of courage and energy. He was the *acting* postmaster at Westport when appointed Sheriff, which office he filled until the spring of 1857. He was soon after appointed collector at El Paso in New Mexico, where he still resides.

Although pro-slavery men were aware of the murder a few moments after it was committed, they refused an act of charity to the dead. The body laid by the roadside until dusk, before the friends of the deceased were aware of the disaster.

The neighborhood in which the deed was committed was filled with excitement and indignation at the sad occurrence. At the funeral, two days afterwards, it was agreed to hold a meeting on the following Monday, to investigate the circumstances relative to the recent outrage. This meeting convened at noon on the spot where Dow was killed. S. F. Tappan and S. N. Wood, of Lawrence, and Mr. Abbot, of the Wakarusa, were present. They appointed a committee "to ferret out and bring the murderers and accomplices to condign punishment." Resolutions extending condolence to the friends of the deceased, and condemning the outrage, were passed. About one hundred men were in attendance. A proposition was made to burn Coleman's house, only a few steps off, which was strongly disapproved by the majority. Some one cried out, "All in favor of burning Coleman's house, form a line." Against this many remonstrated, and especially those from Lawrence. Abbott said, "Let us prevent them if they should try to do it." Only two made the attempt. They rushed up, burst open the door, and set the house on fire. S. N. Wood and others hurried up and put the fire out. This gentleman then addressed the meeting, declaiming against such conduct, and moved a resolution in accordance with that sentiment. This house and one or two others were burned the next morning. Some of the pro-slavery families, fearful that violence would be offered them, fled to Missouri.

From the facts brought to light, it was believed that this murder was not prompted by anger or revenge, but proceeded from the pro-slavery spirit to destroy and scare off free state men.

At the suggestion of Governor Shannon, Jones set out with the prisoner for Lecompton. On arriving at Franklin he met with two of Coleman's neighbors. There he entered upon the execution of a deep plot concocted at Shawnee Mission, to involve the citizens of Lawrence in the Hickory Point difficulties, in such a way as to array them against the Territorial government. He induced one of Coleman's friends—Buckley—to go before Esquire Cameron—of recent appointment by the Board of Commissioners—and swear out a peace-warrant for the arrest of old man Branson. On the strength of this writ Jones summoned a posse of ten men, which was afterwards increased to about forty, and proceeded to Hickory Point. Arriving at the residence of Jacob Branson at a late hour of the night, he and his posse forcibly burst open the door, and with pistols cocked, claimed the old man as their prisoner. "Don't you move, or I'll blow you through," said Jones. They took him out of the house, set him on a mule, and started in the direction of Lawrence. A young lad staying at Branson's gave the alarm to the neighbors.

As Jones and his posse passed up the Wakarusa, on his way to Branson's, he was discovered by the free state men, who were returning from the meeting at Hickory Point. S. F. Tappan actually rode among them unawares, and learned from them their destination and object. He, thereupon, hurried back to warn his friends who were at Mr. Abbot's, about half a mile from Blanton's bridge. Messrs. S. N. Wood and Abbot mounted their horses and hurried up to give Branson warning, but on arriving there they found that the arrest had already been made, and learned the particulars of it. Turning to leave, Mrs. Branson inquired where they were going. "To save your husband or die," was the reply. They started in pursuit of Jones, but not being able to find any trail of him, they returned to Mr. Abbot's where they found several persons from Hickory Point. They numbered in all fifteen men, as follows: S. N. Wood, J. B. Abbot, Paul Jones, Philip Hupp, Minor Hupp, Philip Hutchingson, T. Nichols, Jonathan Keney, Elanore Allen, Carlos Holloway, Rev. Julius Eliot, John Smith, Edward Carlos, Wm. Ears, A. Rowley. Only one of these was from Lawrence. They had eight Sharp's rifles and a few pistols.

While deliberating upon the course to pursue, word was given that Jones and his troops were coming. The free state men immediately filed across the road. When the advancing party spied them they sought to shy around, but were prevented by the extending line of the intercepting force. Whereupon Jones shouted out:

"What's up?"

S. N. Wood—"That's what we should like to know."

Abbot—"Is Mr. Branson there?"

Branson—"Yes, I am here, a prisoner."

Wood—"If you want to be among your friends come over here."

Several to Branson—" If you move we will shoot you."

Hupp (a Hoosier)—"Shoot and be d—d."

Wood—" Come on, let them shoot if they dare. Gentlemen," (addressing the posse) "shoot but one gun at Mr. Branson, and not a man of you will be left alive."

Branson—" I will do as you say."

Company—" Come on, come on."

Branson then crossed over to the rescuing party.

Wood (stepping forward and taking hold of the bridle)—" Whose mule is this?"

Branson—" It is theirs."

Wood (turning the mule and hitting it a kick)—" Go back to your friends."

Jones—" My name is Jones; I have a warrant to arrest old man Branson, and I *must serve it*."

Wood—" We know of no Sheriff Jones in Kansas, nor in Douglas County, and what is better, we never intend to know him. We know of a postmaster in Missouri named Jones."

" Jones—" I have a warrant to arrest Branson, and *must do it*."

Wood—" If you *must* arrest him, go at it. I am Branson's attorney; if you have a warrant for him, let me see it."

Jones—" I have one, but do not see proper to show it at present."

After parleying thus for about an hour, the valiant Sheriff and his posse faced about and hastened, by a circuitous route, to Franklin. He left with threats that he would raise the Territorial militia to enforce the laws. During this altercation, six more persons joined the free state party, two of whom lived in Lawrence—S. F. Tapan and S. C. Smith.

The rescue of Branson was violent and irregular, and can only be excused by the violent and irregular manner of his arrest. His neighbors, already excited and inflamed by the recent murder, were not prepared to brook the midnight as-

"Rescue of Branson."

sault upon one of their most peaceable and oldest citizens. To aggravate the offense still more, the Sheriff had never exhibited any authority by which the arrest was made, nor stated the cause of it. The excited and indignant farmers hurried to the rescue of one of their number, from what they imagined to be a ruffian mob.

The rescued and rescuers passed on to Lawrence, where they aroused the citizens. The drum and fife rang out on the stillness of the night, and the awakened inmates of the little city hastened to ascertain the cause of so unusual a demonstration. The squad of rescuers drew up before Dr. Robinson's house, and Mr. Branson stepped out and told the story of his wrongs.

Early on the following day, a public meeting was held to counsel together upon the events that had just transpired, and the course to be pursued with reference to them. All knew and felt that the drama was not finished. By the more youthful and passionate it was at first resolved to resist every attempt at arrest by the Territorial authorities. But discretion and prudence prevailed over excitement and rashness. As Lawrence had nothing to do with the rescue or any of the late disturbances at Hickory Point, it was thought best that she should not assume the responsibilities of them. It was known that the Missourians were but too ready to find an excuse for an attack upon the town. From the threats that Jones had made to the rescuers, from the information derived from other sources and what they knew of the character of the Missourians, all felt that an invading horde would soon be upon them.

It was finally decided that Lawrence should have nothing to do with the recent irregular proceedings; that Branson and those connected with the rescue should leave the town. Thus every pretext for an attack upon the place was removed. It was thought proper, however, that some measures of self-defense should be taken, and the following committee of ten persons was appointed to provide for the protection of the town against armed aggression: G. P. Lowery, chairman, G. W. Hutchingson, C. Robinson, G. W. Deitzler, C. W. Babcock, G. W. Brown, R. Morrow, J. Miller, A. H. Mallory, J. S. Emery. It was the express understanding that this committee was to provide, not for the purpose of aggression nor to shield any person from deserved punishment, but to protect the town against armed invaders then assembling around Lawrence.

It was the design, it is thought, on the part of pro-slavery men to have taken Branson to Lawrence, where they expected he would be rescued by the citizens, which would furnish a good pretext for its demolition. Long before this time the place had been threatened—in fact, from the first week that the pioneer emigrants pitched their tents upon the town site, border ruffians menaced it. There is no doubt that the arrest of Branson was a plot by which to involve the colonists in open conflict with the Territorial Government, or compel them to a recognition of the bogus laws.

Sheriff Jones, somewhat thwarted in his design by the unexpected movement of the free state men, on returning to Franklin, in his wrath, sent a dispatch to Colonel Boone, of Westport, Missouri, at the same time remarking, "That man is taking my dispatch to Missouri, and by G—d I'll have revenge before I reach Missouri." In the course of an half hour he wrote a dispatch and sent it to the Governor, of which the following is a copy:

"DOUGLAS COUNTY, K. T., Nov. 27, 1855.

"SIR:—Last night I, with a posse of ten men, arrested one Jacob Branson, by virtue of a peace warrant regularly issued, who, on our return, was rescued by a party of forty armed men, who rushed upon us suddenly from behind a house upon the roadside, all armed to the teeth with Sharp's rifles.

"You may consider an open rebellion as having already commenced, and I call upon you for three thousand men to carry out the laws. Mr. Hargis, the bearer of this letter, will give you, more particularly, the circumstances.

"Most respectfully, SAMUEL J. JONES,
"Sheriff of Douglas County."

"To his excellency, William Shannon, Governor of Kansas Territory."

Where Mr. Jones expected the Governor to procure three thousand men, does not appear from the letter. There was no organized militia in the Territory. The Shawnee Legislature had appointed three officers for the militia, but beyond that there had been no militia organization effected. The Governor, on receiving the dispatch, sent the following to Mr. Richardson:

"HEADQUARTERS SHAWNEE MISSION,
"K. T., Nov. 27, 1855.

"WILLIAM P. RICHARDSON, *Major General:*

"SIR:—Reliable information has reached me that an armed military force is now in Lawrence, or in that vicinity, in open rebellion against the laws of this Territory, and that they have determined that no process in the hands of the Sheriff of that county shall be executed. I have received a letter from S. J. Jones, the Sheriff of Douglas County, informing me that he had arrested a man under a peace warrant placed in his hands, and while conveying him to Lecompton, he was met by an armed force of some forty men, who rescued the prisoner from his custody, and bid open defiance to the laws. I am also duly informed that a band of armed men have burned a number of houses, destroyed personal property, and turned whole families out of doors. This has occurred in Douglas County. Warrants will be issued against these men, and placed in the hands of Mr. Jones, the Sheriff of that county, for execution, who has written to me demanding three thousand men to aid him in preserving peace and carrying out the process of the law.

"You are hereby ordered to collect together as large a force as you can in your division, and repair without delay to Lecompton, and report yourself to S. J. Jones, Sheriff of Douglas County. You will inform him of the number of men under your control, and render him all the assistance in your power, should he require your aid in the execution of any legal process in his hands. The forces under your command are to be used for the sole purpose of aiding the Sheriff in executing the law, and for none other.

"I have the honor to be, your obedient servant,

"WILSON SHANNON."

A similar dispatch was sent to General Strickler at Tecumseh.

Meanwhile Colonel Boone had been busy rallying the Missourians. He issued an inflammatory appeal to the people, stating that not only had Branson been rescued from the hands of the Sheriff, but that pro-slavery men in the Territory were every-where fleeing for their lives, and that their houses were burnt down and the inmates driven upon the open prairies. The excitement soon spread all over Western Missouri. The Blue Lodges were put into requisition. Men were called upon in every town and neighborhood to join a company and hurry to the assistance of their brethren in Kansas; that the great battle was to be fought in which if they were defeated the cause would be lost. Those that could not go themselves were compelled to contribute towards defraying the expenses of those who volunteered and would go. At Liberty, Missouri, two hundred men and one thousand dollars were raised in one day "to assist Jones." The following dispatch was sent out from Independence, signed by some of the leading citizens of the place:

"Jones will not make a movement until there is a sufficient force in the field to insure success. We have not more than three hundred men in the Territory. You will, therefore, urge all who are interested in the matter to start immediately for the seat of war. There is no doubt in regard to having a fight, and we all know that many have complained because they were disappointed heretofore in regard to a fight. Say to them, now is the time to show game, and if we are defeated this time, the Territory is lost to the South."

The day after the occurrence, L. J. Eastin, Brigadier-General of the 2d Brigade of the Kansas Militia, issued an order, calling the militia of his brigade to meet on the first day of December at Leavenworth, "armed and equipped according to law, and to hold themselves in readiness, subject to the order of Major-General W. P. Richardson." The following is the appeal as was printed upon the same hand-bills, which were circulated through the counties across the river in Missouri:

"TO ARMS! TO ARMS!

"It is expected that every lover of law and order will rally at Leavenworth, on Saturday, December 1st, 1855, prepared to march at once to the scene of rebellion, to put down the outlaws of Douglas County, who are committing depredations upon persons and property, burning down houses and declaring open hostility to the laws, and have forcibly rescued a prisoner from the Sheriff. Come one, come all! The laws must be executed. The outlaws, it is said, are armed to the teeth, and number one thousand men. Every man should bring his rifle, ammunition, and it would be well to bring two or three days' provisions. Let the call be promptly obeyed. Every man to his post and do his duty. MANY CITIZENS."

In a few days Governor Shonnon issued the following proclamation, which was sent to various pro-slavery towns, but no others:

"PROCLAMATION.

"WHEREAS, Reliable information has been received that a numerous association of lawless men, armed with deadly weapons, and supplied with all the implements of war, combined and confederated together for the avowed purpose of opposing, by force and violence, the execution of the laws of this Territory, did, at the county of Douglas, on or about the 26th of this month, make a violent assault upon the

Sheriff of said county, with deadly weapons, and did overcome said officer, and did rescue from his custody, by force and violence, a person arrested by virtue of a peace-warrant, and then and there a prisoner, holden by said Sheriff, and other scandalous outrages did commit in violation of law.

"AND WHEREAS, Also, information has been received that this confederate band of lawless men did, about the same time, set fire to and burn down a number of houses of peaceable and inoffensive citizens, and did destroy a considerable amount of personal property, and have repeatedly proclaimed that they would regard no law of this Territory, resist by force of arms all officers, and those aiding and those assisting them in the execution of the laws, or any process issued in pursuance thereof;

"And WHEREAS, also I have received satisfactory informamation that this armed organization of lawless men have proclaimed their determination to attack the said Sheriff of Douglas County, and rescue from his custody a prisoner, for the avowed purpose of executing him without a judicial trial, and at the same time threatened the life of said Sheriff, and other citizens.

"Now, therefore, to the end that the authority of the laws may be maintained and those concerned in violating them brought to immediate and condign punishment; that the Sheriff of Douglas county may be protected from lawless violence in the execution of lawful warrants and other processes in his hands, I, Wilson Shannon, Governor of said Territory, have issued this, my proclamation, calling on all well disposed citizens of this Territory to rally to the support of the laws of their country, and requiring and commanding all officers, civil and military, and all other citizens of this Territory, who shall be found within the vicinity of these outrages, to aid and assist, by all means in their power, in quelling this armed organization, and to assist the said Sheriff and his deputies in recapturing the above named prisoner, and aid and assist him in the execution of all legal processes in his hands. And I do further command that the District attorney for the district in which these outrages took place, and all other persons concerned in the administration or execution of the laws, cause the above offenders, and all such as aid or assist them, to be immediately arrested and proceeded with according to law.

"Given under my hand and the seal of this Territory, this 29th day of November, in the year of our Lord, eighteen hundred and fifty-five.

"[L. S.] WILSON SHANNON.

"By the Governor.

"D. WOODSON, Secretary of the Territory."

Secretary Woodson, understanding the pro-slavery plan to conquer Kansas better than the Governor, and desiring to serve the cause all he could, wrote to Senator Atchison as follows:

"DEAR GENERAL:—The Governor having called out the militia, this is to inform you to order out your division and and proceed forthwith to Lecompton. The Governor not having the power, you can call out the Platte County rifle company, as our neighbors are always ready to help us. Do not implicate the Governor, whatever you do.

"DANIEL WOODSON."

It is doubtful whether the Secretary ever wrote this, but it was penned by somebody, sent to Platte City and read to a large public meeting, and it had the effect to bring over the Platte County Riflemen, with their distinguished leader.

CHAPTER XXI.

WAKARUSA WAR.

The people of Missouri were not long in responding to the call of their fellow-citizen, Mr. Jones, for help. On the 29th of November, only two days after the word had been sent, a company of about fifty, from the neighborhood of Westport and Independence, arrived and encamped at Franklin, about four miles below Lawrence. These were the first reinforcements that came to the relief of the Sheriff. For several days from this time companies almost constantly arrived. In Clay County they seized the arms from the United States arsenal, rifles, swords, revolvers, three 6-pounders, ammunitions, &c. For two or three counties back from the western line of Missouri, troops were sent fully equipped and expecting a fight. In three days more the Sheriff of Douglas County mustered a posse of about fifteen hundred men. Said Governor Shannon, "Missouri sent not only her young men, but her gray-headed citizens were there. The man of seventy winters stood shoulder to shoulder with the youth of sixteen. There were volunteers in that camp who brought with them not only their sons, but their grandsons, to join, if need be, in the expected fray. Every hour added to the excitement, and brought new fuel to the flame."

The main force was encamped near Franklin, in the Wakarusa bottom, and was known as the "Wakarusa Encampment." The other wing of the army was in position near Lecompton, under the joint command of Strickler and Richardson. These forces were chiefly from Platte and Buchanan Counties, Missouri. There were about fifty pro-slavery residents among them, principally Kickapoo Rangers. At no time in all the encampments of the invading forces were there more than eighty residents of the Territory. Opposite Lawrence, on the north side of the Kansas River, some two hundred riflemen from Platte County were stationed, under the command of Hon. D. R. Atchison, who had come in response to Secretary Woodson's call.

The object of the pro-slavery Generals in thus surrounding the town was to prevent the escape of those for whom the Sheriff had writs to arrest, and to cut off all communication with the beleagued city. The intervening country between the encampments, was constantly scoured by mounted patrols.

The editors of the "Squatter Sovereign" both entered upon the crusade and left their press idle. Here are their words when on the eve of the expedition:

"In view of the exciting state of affairs, the Governor of Kansas has called out the Militia to execute the laws. Men are hourly passing our office with their guns on their back, going to the assistance of the officers of the law. A large company with two pieces of artillery have started from Atchison county. As both of the editors of this paper are going to the seat of war, we have no time to enter further particulars. We anticipate blood-shed, and *we, the junior, expect to wade waist deep in the blood of the abolitionists.*"

Meanwhile active preparations were going on at Lawrence for the reception of the armed host. The rescuers who lived at Hickory Point had returned home. Messrs. S. N. Wood, S. F. Tappan and S. C. Smith, all of whom lived at Lawrence, and who were connected with the rescue, and Branson, remained. When it was ascertained that a force was gathering on the Wakarusa, in order not to jeopardize the safety of the town for their protection, all those concerned in the rescue, who lived at Lawrence, were requested to leave. This was evidently a very prudent and judicious measure, as Lawrence had taken no part in the rescue, and was in no way responsible for it; besides it would leave an attack upon the town wholly unjustifiable.

The Committee of Safety first organized the citizens into guards, from fifteen to twenty in a squad, by enrolling them and taking the places of their residence, in order to call them out at any moment. By this measure the people were enabled to pursue their daily engagements, and be ready to fly to arms at a given signal.

The Committee of Safety, as affairs grew more threatening, sent the following call for assistance through the Territory:

"FELLOW-CITIZENS:—We, whose names are annexed hereto, having been appointed a Committee of Public Safety by the citizens of Kansas, assembled at Lawrence, for the purpose of defending it from threatened invasion by armed men now quartered in its vicinity, hereby deem it necessary to call upon you to come to our aid fully prepared for any emergency. [Signed,] COMMITTEE OF SAFETY.

"LAWRENCE, K. T., December 4, 1855."

The news of the invasion and the designs of the Missourians to destroy Lawrence, spread over the country, and free state men from every quarter, rushed to the assistance of the threatened people. They came in squads and companies; the one from Topeka, numbering one hundred men, was the largest. On the 2d of December, a delegation from Leavenworth arrived, to expostulate with the citizens and to council peace. But they found that they had entirely misapprehended the position of the assailed—that they were strictly on the defensive. This delegation brought the Governor's proclamation, and fuller accounts of the gathering forces from Missouri. The proclamation, which was filled with gross misrepresentations and misstatements, awakened deep indignation. A committee was appointed to answer it, in behalf of the people, which reported as follows:

"That the allegations contained in the proclamation aforesaid are false in whole and in part; that no such a state of facts exist in this community; that if such representations were ever made to Governor Shannon, the person or persons who made them have grossly deceived him; that no association of lawless men armed with deadly weapons has been formed in this community for the purpose of restraining the laws of the country, trampling upon the authority of its officers, destroying the property of its peaceable citizens, or molesting any person in this Territory, or elsewhere in the enjoyment of their rights."

The Executive of the United States was invoked to lend protection by the following dispatch:

"*To his Excellency, the President of the United States:*

"Sir:—We, the citizens of Kansas Territory, notify you that the city of Lawrence is besieged by armed men from a neighboring State, committing depredations upon the unoffending citizens of said Territory, stopping and arresting persons, and seizing the property of travelers, threatening the destruction of said city and its inhabitants. The lawless assemblage, it is claimed, is here under the authority of Wilson Shannon, Governor of said Territory. We trust you will take such steps as will remove this armed horde from our borders, and restore peace to our people.

"Marcus J. Parrott,
"J. H. Lane,
"J. S. Emery.

"Lawrence, December 4, 1855."

The following letter was sent to Colonel Sumner at Fort Leavenworth, signed by the Committee of Safety:

"Sir: We, the Committee of Public Safety, appointed by the citizens of Kansas Territory, assembled at Lawrence, being beleagued by a body of armed who have marched here from a neighboring State, and who are threatening the town of Lawrence with destruction, and our citizens with immediate death, as well as committing all manner of depredations upon unoffending travelers on the highway, all of which is being done without our being able to understand the cause of provocation, therefore, if consistent with your discretion and duty, we request of you a sufficient force from your command to quell this riot, and prevent further invasion of our peace and safety."

The following memorial was prepared and sent to Congress:

"*To the Honorable the United States Senate and House of Representatives in Congress assembled:* Your memorialists, citizens of the United States, and residents of Kansas Territory, respectfully represent unto your Honorable body, that, without any justifiable cause whatever, Governor Shannon has caused to be issued a proclamation, and under it military orders have been issued, calling upon the militia of Kansas and Missouri to meet at certain points within the Territory, armed and equipped, and to march against certain portions of our people and territory. Copies of such proclamation, military orders, and a letter from Daniel Woodson, Secretary of the Territory, to Lucien J. Eastin, editor of the 'Kansas Herald,' are herewith inclosed, from which it will be seen that your memorialists are exposed to the authorized march of a military force from Missouri, who are arresting our citizens, and committing depredations on persons and property, only known in cases of war between hostile countries. Devoted, as we are, to the Constition and the Union, and estimating neither as secondary to slavery, we earnestly invoke the interposition of Congress so far as to send for persons and papers to substantiate the truth of our statements herewith inclosed.

[Signed by a very large number of the citizens of Kansas.]

"Kansas Territory, Dec. 5, 1855."

Meantime Lawrence was put in an attitude of self-defense. The Committee of Public Safety appointed Dr. Charles Robinson commander-in-chief of all the forces, and Colonel J. H. Lane second in command. The following are the companies under their different commanders: Lawrence Stubbs,

Lyman Allen; Bloomington, Samuel Walker; Wakarusa. Abbott; Ottowa Creek, Shore; Palmyra, McWhenny; Pottowattomie, John Brown, who came with his four sons. arms and ammunition. Many citizens came in not belonging to any company, until the forces numbered about 1,000 men, 800 of whom were enrolled and under drill.

Every house was filled with soldiers. The Free State Hotel was used for barracks, in which several hundred men were quartered and fed. This large body of men were provisioned by the voluntary contributions of the citizens.

General Lane superintended throwing up the fortifications and gave directions for their construction. The first and largest redoubt was erected on Massachusetts Street. near the crossing of Pinckney Street. It was circular, made of hewed timber, against which was thrown up a strong earth embankment with a deep entrenchment surrounding it, and was about five feet high, and four feet wide on top. This fortification was under the command of Judge G. W. Smith, who held the rank of Colonel for the defense of Lawrence. It was designed as a retreat for women and children in case of an attack.

The second redoubt was on Massachusetts Street, near Henry, under the direction of J. A. Wakefield, who held a commission of Colonel for the defense of Lawrence. "This had bastions, and it was the design to have planted the cannon here, it having a good range of the open prairie in every direction.

The third was a circular redoubt erected on an elevation a little north of Henry Street, between Massachusetts and New Hampshire Streets, under the direction of Colonel Morris Hunt. The fourth was also a circular earth redoubt erected under the superintendence of Colonel C. K. Holliday, a few rods south of Fort Wakefield, with the view of meeting an attack from Mt. Oread, should one be made, which was within the range of Sharp's rifles. The fifth was on Kentucky Street, commanding an entrance from a ravine on the west.

Lawrence was thus suddenly changed into a military encampment filled with armed soldiers, and surrounded by fortifications. A brass cannon was procured from Kansas City in disguise by Mr. Buffum. Mrs. S. N. Wood and Mrs. G. W. Brown conveyed into town a quantity of ammunition from the country through the enemy's lines under crinoline cover. Many of the ladies were engaged in making cartridges while the men watched and drilled.

Free access was had to the city at all times and by all persons. The leaders of the invading forces would frequently come in and reconnoitre without being disturbed. Sheriff Jones, when in town once, was asked what he was going to do with the troops on the Wakarusa; to which he replied, "I'll show you when I get ready." He made no attempts to arrest any person. S. N. Wood went up and shook hands with him one day and invited him home to dine.

The pro-slavery men, learning of the determined spirit and strength of the free state men, feared to make an attack. Brigadier-General Eastin wrote, therefore, to Governor Shannon as follows:

"Governor Shannon:

"Information has been received here direct from Lawrence, which I consider reliable, that the outlaws are well fortified at Lawrence with cannon and Sharp's rifles, and number at least one thousand men. It will, therefore, be difficult to dispossess them.

"The militia in this portion of the State are entirely unorganized, and mostly without arms.

"I suggest the propriety of calling upon the military at Fort Leavenworth. If you have the power to call out the Government troops, I think it would be best to do so at once. It might overawe these outlaws and prevent bloodshed.

T. J. Eastin,

"Brig.-Gen. Northern Brigade K. M."

The Governor at once telegraphed to Washington, representing to the President the recent difficulties in the Territory, and soliciting authority to call to his relief the United States troops. He also sent a dispatch to Colonel Sumner at Fort Leavenworth to hold himself and command in readiness in case the orders should be received, to which he obtained the following judicious reply:

"HEADQUARTERS FIRST CAVALRY,
FORT LEAVENWORTH, December 1, 1855.

"GOVERNOR:

"I have just received your letter of this day. I do not feel that it would be right in me to act in this important matter until orders are received from the Government. I shall be ready to move instantly when I receive them. I would respectfully suggest that you make your application extensively known at once, and I would countermand any orders that may have been given for the movement of the militia until you receive the answer. I write this in haste.

"With much respect, your obedient servant,

"E. V. SUMNER,
"Colonel First Cavalry."

The Governor immediately adopted the suggestions of Colonel Sumner, and sent letters to Sheriff Jones and General Richardson to that effect. As both letters were in substance the same, only the one to Jones is here given:

"EXECUTIVE MANSION,
SHAWNEE MISSION, K. T., Dec. 2d, 1855.

"SIR: I am in receipt of Colonel Sumner's reply to my dispatch, in which he informs me that he will be ready at a moment's warning to move with his whole force, if desired, on the arrival of his orders from Washington. My telegraphic dispatch to the President must have reached its destination by this time, and an answer should soon come to hand. I have no doubt but that the authority I have requested—to call upon the United States troops—will be granted. Under these circumstances you will wait until I obtain the desired orders, before attempting to execute your writs. This will save any effusion of blood, and may have a moral influence hereafter, which would prevent any further resistance to law; for when these lawless men find that the forces of the United States can be used to preserve order, they will not be so ready to adopt an opposite course. And, if necessary, steps will be taken to station an adequate number in the disturbed district to protect the people against mob violence, and to secure the fulfillment of the laws.

"You will retain a sufficient force to protect yourself and guard your prisoner. Any thing beyond this had better remain at a distance, until it can be ascertained whether their aid will or will not be needed. The known deficiency in arms, and all the accoutrements of war, which must necessarily characterize the law-abiding citizens who have rushed to your assistance in the maintenance of order, will invite resistance from your opponents, who are well supplied with arms. It would be wrong, therefore, to place your men in a position where their lives would be endangered, when we shall, in all probability, have an ample force from Leavenworth in a few days.

"Show this letter to Major-General Richardson, and also to General Eastin, who, as I am advised, have gone to your aid. Their destination is Lecompton, but they will join you wherever you are. Their forces are but small, and may be required for your protection until advices are received from Washington.

I send you, with this, a communication to General Richardson, which you will please deliver to him at as early a day as practicable. As I refer him to this my letter to you, for my views, you will permit him to read it. Let me know what number of warrants you have, and the names of the defendants. I shall probably accompany Colonel Sumner's command.

"Yours, with great respect,

"WILSON SHANNON.

"Sheriff Jones, Lecompton."

The Sheriff did not like the idea of the United States troops interposing, and thus spoiling the plot he had laid for the destruction of Lawrence. He, therefore, replied to the Governor as follows:

"CAMP AT WAKARUSA, December 3, 1867.

"*His excellency, Governor* WILSON SHANNON:

"SIR:—In reply to your communication of yesterday I have to inform you that the volunteer forces now at this place and at Lecompton, are getting weary of inaction. They will not, I presume, remain but a short time longer, unless a demand for the prisoner is made. I think that I shall have a sufficient force to protect me by to-morrow morning. The force at Lawrence is not half so strong as reported. I have this from a reliable source. If I am to wait for Government troops, more than two-thirds of the men now here will go away very much dissatisfied. They are leaving hourly as it is. I do not, by any means, wish to violate your orders, but I really believe that if I have a sufficient force, it would be better to make the demand.

"It is reported that the people of Lawrence have run off those offenders from that town, and, indeed, it is said they are now all out of the way. I have writs for sixteen persons, who were with the party that rescued my prisoner. S. N. Wood, P. R. Brooks and Samuel Tappan are of Lawrence, the balance from the country around. Warrants will be placed in my hands to-day for the arrest of G. W. Brown, and probably others in Lecompton. They say that they are willing to obey the laws, but no confidence can be placed in any statement they may make.

"No evidence sufficient to cause a warrant to be issued has as yet been brought against those lawless men who fired the houses.

"I would give you the names of the defendants, but the writs are in my office at Lecompton.

"Most respectfully yours,

"SAMUEL J. JONES.

"Sheriff of Douglas County."

General Richardson replied to the Governor, urging that the people of Lawrence should be made give up their arms. He began to feel that their shadowy pretext was not sufficient for assailing and destroying the town, or else he was afraid to undertake it while the free state men had arms in their hands. He knew very well that this demand would be resisted, and that if complied with the free state men would be left at the mercy of the Border Ruffians. He earnestly solicited authority to make this demand as the only effective mode to compel obedience to the laws.

Governor Shannon having received, in reply to his, a dispatch from the President, assuring him that authority should be sent to use the United States troops in the enforcement of the laws, as soon as the orders could be made out and transmitted from the War Department, communicated this intelligence to Colonel Sumner, and requested his assistance on the strength of it. Colonel Sumner at first agreed to march with his troops to the assistance of the Governor, but upon more mature reflection, declined to move until his orders from Washington should arrive.

About this time the chief men of Lawrence resolved to open communications with Governor Shannon. Accordingly a letter was written, of which the following is a copy:

"*To His Excellency*, WILSON SHANNON, *Governor of Kansas Territory:*

"SIR: As citizens of Kansas Territory, we desire to call your attention to the fact that a large force of armed men from a foreign State have assembled in the vicinity of Lawrence, are now committing depredations upon our citizens, stopping wagons, opening and appropriating their loading, arresting, detaining and threatening travellers upon the public road, and that they claim to do this by your authority. We desire to know if they do appear here by your authority, and if you will secure the peace and quiet of the community by ordering their instant removal, or compel us to resort to some other means and to higher authority."

SIGNED BY COMMITTEE.

Messrs. G. P. Lowery and C. W. Babcock were selected to bear this letter to the Governor, and to make further verbal statements. On the fifth of December they set out for Shawnee Mission, where after repeated interruptions by the Missouri guards, they safely arrived, and obtained an interview with his Excellency. They explained to him that the

Territorial laws had nothing to do with the excitement and dangers threatening Lawrence; that they were getting ready at that place to fight for their lives, and the only question was whether he would be the *particeps criminis* to their murder, or the murder of somebody else, should they all be slaughtered. They explained to him that the rescue, upon which he based his proclamation, took place a number of miles from Lawrence; that there were but three persons living in Lawrence who were alleged to have had any thing to do with it, and that these had left the town and were not there at all; that from what they could judge of the intentions of the force on the Wakarusa, at Lecompton and in the country about, from their own declarations, they intended to destroy the town for a thing in which its people had had no part or parcel.

The Governor at first declared that the people of Lawrence had burned sixteen houses of pro-slavery men and driven their families from the country; to which it was replied that the two or three houses which had been burnt were ten miles from Lawrence, and those of its citizens engaged in the rescue were in town at the time these were burnt; that the pro-slavery men with their families had left these houses of their own accord before the burning of them occurred, and that they very probably set them on fire themselves. The Governor then referferred to the many resolutions and threats that free state men had made at their conventions that they would not obey the Territorial laws, and would resist them; to which it was replied that they had never resolved to resist them until all peaceable measures should fail to enable them to throw off the yoke of oppression.

The Governor, from the misrepresentations sent him, and the want of acquaintance with the people of Lawrence, and free state men generally, which he had never sought to acquire, had misapprehended the condition of things in and about this town. He was surrounded, too, by evil advisers who coveted the destruction of Lawrence, and with characteristic failing, gave way to the influence about him. Let not posterity judge his conduct too harshly. He was evidently in favor of making Kansas a slave State, and was disposed to favor pro-slavery men. But he, by no means, desired to destroy or injure free state men. There was nothing blood thirsty about him, and his soul recoiled with horror at the idea of a deadly collision between the parties at Lawrence. From what he had been recently informed, he saw that an assault upon the town would be totally uncalled for; and, as he says, "affairs in Lawrence and vicinity were fast coming to a crisis"—he felt that the moment for him to act understandingly, and to avoid bloodshed, had ar-arrived. He, therefore, "determined to repair to the scene of difficulties immediately, in person."

The Governor, on arriving at the Wakarusa camp, was convinced more than ever, from what he beheld, that something must be done quickly in order to prevent an effusion of blood. He found the Missourians there, sure enough, in multitudes, from youth to old age. He found, too, that "those men came to the Wakarusa camp to fight; they did not ask peace; it was war—war to the knife. They would come; it was impossible to prevent them." He "found a disposition, which appeared to be almost universal, to attack Lawrence." He resolved upon his course and entered upon the praiseworthy, yet thankless, part of a mediator.

He called together in conference thirty or forty of the leading men from both pro-slavery camps, and laid before them the plan which he wished them to pursue. He only found one person who would accede to it. The most of them "would hear of nothing less than the destruction of Lawrence and its fortifications, the demolition of its printing presses, and the unconditional surrender of the arms of its citizens; others, more moderate, expressed a willingness to be satisfied if the free state party would give up their Sharp's rifles and revolvers. Under these circumstances the conference broke up at midnight, having accomplished nothing beyond the interchange of opinions on either side."

The Governor discovered a fixed purpose on the part of pro-slavery men to attack the town, and in order to avert such a sad calamity, he resolved to make another attempt to secure the immediate interposition of the United States forces. He, therefore, wrote the following letter:

"WAKARUSA, December 6th, 1855.

"COLONEL SUMNER, *First Cavalry U. S.:*

"SIR: I send you this special dispatch to ask you to come to Lawrence as soon as you possibly can. My object is to secure the citizens of that place, as well as others, from a warfare which, if once commenced, there is no telling where it will end. I doubt not that you have received orders from Washington, but if you have not the absolute pressure of this crisis is such as to justify you with the President, and the world, in moving with your force to the scene of difficulties.

"It is hard to restrain the men here (*they are beyond my power, or at least soon will be*) from making an attack upon Lawrence, which, if once made, there is no telling where it may terminate. The presence of a portion of the United States troops at Lawrence would prevent an attack—save bloodshed, and enable us to get matters arranged in a satisfactory way, and at the same time secure an execution of the laws. *It is peace, not war, that we want*, and you have the power to secure peace. Time is precious—fear not that you will be sustained.

"With great respect,

"WILSON SHANNON."

How different the language of this letter to the one previously sent to the same commander. It was then to operate *against* Lawrence that he wanted troops; it was now to *protect* it from the frenzy of a mob. It was then *war*, but now *peace*, which was wanted to preserve law and order.

The Missourians, informed of this step taken by the Governor, determined to intercept the dispatch at Kaw River Crossing. Their object in doing this was "to prevent the arrival of the United States troops, who, they feared, would restrain them from attacking Lawrence. By gaining time they expected to make the assault before any force could be brought to mediate between the conflicting parties." The Governor, informed of the plot by General Strickler, dispatched a courier at 2 o'clock A. M. by an unusual route, who safely conveyed the letter to Colonel Sumner.

The Colonel replied that he regretted extremely that he was compelled to disappoint Mr. Shannon; that the more he reflected upon the matter the more he was of the opinion he should not interpose without orders; that he stood ready to march by night or by day when these should arrive. He suggested that the pro-slavery men might be induced to pause a short time by being told that orders were momentarily expected from the General Government, and that "there was little doubt but that these orders framed from an enlarged view of the the whole difficulty, would give general satisfaction, and settle the matter honorably to both parties."

The following letter to General Richardson, from J. C. Anderson, member of the bogus Legislature, will show the determination and desperation of the forces encompassing Lawrence:

"*Major General* WILLIAM P. RICHARDSON:

"SIR:—I have reasons to believe, from rumors in camp, that before to-morrow morning the *black flag* will be hoisted, when nine out of ten will rally around it, and march without orders upon Lawrence. The forces at Lecompton camp fully understand the plot, and will fight under the same banner.

"If Governor Shannon will pledge himself not to allow any United States officer to interfere with the arms belonging to the United States now in their possession, and, in case there is no battle, order the United States forces off at once, and retain the militia, provided any force is retained, all will be well, and all will obey to the end, and commit no depredation upon private property in Lawrence.

"I fear a collision between the United States soldiers and the volunteers, which would be dreadful.

"Speedy measures should be taken. Let me know *at once—to-night—and I fear that it will then be too late to stay the rashness of our people.*

"Respectfully, your obedient servant,

"J. C. ANDERSON."

On the 6th of December, Gen. S. C. Pomeroy was dispatched to carry important messages to the States, and to solicit aid and protection for the free state men in Kansas. His departure was immediately made known in the camp at Franklin, and a party sent to intercept him. When he had nearly reached the Quaker Mission, they overtook him, and asked him, "Where are you going?" "To our Mission," was the reply. Gen. Pomeroy represented himself as Rev. Moses Brown, a Baptist clergyman, collecting funds for the Indian Missión. He asks, "Will you arrest a clergyman traveling in the Territory to propagate the Gospel?" The party was about to let him go, thinking that they were mistaken, when a little Irishman spoke: "Be the powers of mud, Mister Brown, it's myself thinks ye'r old Pomr'y, but ave you ain't the same we'll take you to the camp on the Wakarusa Creek, and make you chaplain, for a divil a set of spalpeens wants a chaplain worse than the b'hoys." They accordingly took him over to the encampment, where, after some suffering, his condition was relieved by General Atchison. His dispatches were all taken, and afterwards published in the pro-slavery papers.

The chiefs of the Delawares and Shawnees about this time came into Lawrence, and proffered the assistance of their warriors to the Committee of Safety. They were kindly thanked for their offer, but it was declined until it should be known that the Missourians had employed similar forces. George W. Clark, however, did bring a company of Pottowatomies to the Border Ruffian camp at Lecompton. On their way thither, as they passed through Topeka, they declared that they would return with an abolition scalp on each shoulder.

CHAPTER XXII.

THE MISUNDERSTANDING.

At this point in the history of this war a most tragic and sad event occurred. The blood of Dow had aroused the God of War, and it required that of another from the pure and innocent to appease him.

Thomas W. Barber lived on a farm about seven miles south-west of Lawrence. He was a sober-minded, honest, industrious and peaceable man. He was beloved by all his neighbors and all his friends, being one of such gentle and quiet disposition as to call forth the esteem and affection of all who mingled with him. He was a lover and an admirer of stock, and was enthusiastically devoted to farming.

He had no family but a tender and loving wife, who had always been attached to him with the fondness of a girlish love and the strength of matured affection. In him seemed to center her pleasure and sunshine, with whom no society was so pleasant, from whom no separation was so miserable. When his absence from home was protracted, she would grow anxious about his safety, and would watch his return with constant solicitude. When he returned, she would greet him as though a year had elapsed since they were together.

When Lawrence was invested with armed bands, Barber determined to go to its assistance. His wife seemed to have a presentment that harm would befall him should he go, and hence earnestly insisted on his staying at home. But he was a firm free state man, and could not bear the idea of remaining away when his friends stood so much in need of help. He finally prevailed in securing her consent, and on starting, while clinging endearingly to him, she exclaimed, "Oh, Thomas, if you should get shot I would be all alone indeed: remember I have no child, nothing in the wide world to fill your place."

He hurried to the rescue of his friends of Lawrence, where, remaining for a few days, he concluded to return to visit his home. On starting back he bid the boys "good bye," saying that he "would be back in the morning." Accompanied by his brother Robert, and Mr. Thomas M. Pierson, he set out for home, himself unarmed.

The open country south and south-west of Lawrence was constantly scoured by mounted patrols at that time, who would stop and search every party that sought to pass over it. When, therefore, the Barbers and company had traveled out on the California road about four miles from town, just as they were in the act of turning off to the left to proceed more directly to their homes, they perceived some fourteen horsemen approaching the trail from the right. Two of this number suddenly spurred up their horses and rapidly approached the highway. By taking a more direct route, and traveling faster, they came in ahead of the Barbers, on the by-road leading to their homes. When they had approached within a few yards of each other, one of the assailants demanded:

"Where are you going?"

Thomas W. Barber—"We are going home."

Assailant—"Where are you from?"

Barber—"We are from Lawrence."

Assailant—"What is going on in Lawrence?"

Barber—"Nothing in particular."

Assailant—"Nothing in particular, hey? We have orders from the Governor to see the laws executed in Kansas."

Barber—"We have disobeyed no laws."

Assailant, (pointing towards his party)—"Then turn and go with us."

Barber—"We won't do it."

Assailant, (spurring up his horse)—"You won't hey?"

The latter then drew his pistol and discharged it at Barber. At the same time the other assailant fired a shot. Robert Barber drew his revolver and fired three times without effect. The assailants then passed a few words between each other, wheeled their horses and rode away. The main body of the horsemen were in full sight during the affray, about four hundred yards off, standing as spectators. Thomas W. Barber then turned to his two comrades, saying, "Boys, let us be off." The three started at full gallop towards their homes. After riding about one hundred yards, Thomas said to his brother, "That fellow shot me," and smiled. His brother asked, "Where are you shot?" With a melancholy smile upon face, he pressed his hand upon his right side. His brother then remarked with much feeling, "It is not possible, Thomas." To which he replied with a sickly smile, "It is." After uttering these words he dropped the reins and reeled in the saddle. His brother caught him and steadied him for nearly a hundred yards, and then eased him upon the ground. Halting the horses, he dismounted and bent over the fallen body of his brother. He felt his pulse, but, alas, it was still—Thomas was dead. While Robert and Pierson were consulting by the fallen brother, they perceived the main body of horsemen, who had been standing at a distance, advancing. Fearing that they would meet the same fate, they mounted their horses and galloped on.

George W. Clark, the agent of the Pottowottomie Indians, and Mr. Burns, a merchant of Weston, were the assailants. Both claimed the honor of killing Barber, but it has generally been awarded to the former. The writer, however, was informed by a most respectable member of the pro-slavery party that, in his opinion, Burns committed the

29

inhuman act. Be this as it may, both were equally guilty in the distinguishe'd drama.

This pro-slavery patrol was made up of prominent Territorial officials. Such as Brigadier-General W. P. Richardson, Judge Cato, General G. W. Clark, Indian agent, Judge Wood, one member of the Legislature, &c. They were spectators to the whole affray, rode up and beheld the body of murdered Barber, then passed on to confer with Governor Shannon about requiring free state men to give up their arms.

Intelligence was soon communicated to Lawrence, and a carriage was dispatched to bring in the body. The wife knew nothing of the sad transaction, until the following day, when a conveyance was sent to bring her to town. Upon arriving at the house where Mrs. Barber lived, the driver unthoughtedly shouted out, "Thomas Barber is killed." The tidings fell upon the listening ears of the widow. She, rushing to the door, with a wild air cried, "Oh! God! what do I hear?" and shrieked in frantic agony. Sh'e was immediately taken to Lawrence in a carriage. While on the road she was with difficulty confined to her seat, while she rent the air with her heart-broken wails and lamentations. Reaching the hotel at Lawrence, entering the room where the cold, stiff form of her husband lay, and bending over it, she exclaimed, "They have left me, a poor forsaken creature, to mourn all my days. Oh, my husband! They have taken from me all that I held dear—one whom I loved better than I loved my own life."

Efforts had been made to conceal the knowledge of Barber's death from the soldiers, but the sobs and shrieks of the heart-stricken woman soon revealed the fact. The young men, on hearing it, were almost beyond control. They were for rushing immediately upon the camp of the ruffians and driving them from the country. The company to which Barber belonged entered into a conspiracy to leave town without orders, and spread havoc and destruction among them. This plot was discovered, and prudently put down by General Robinson.

On the same morning that this affecting scene was witnessed in Lawrence, Governor Shannon sent notice that he was waiting for an escort at Franklin, to accompany him to that place. Ten leading free state men were selected, with Mr. G. P. Lowry for leader, as a deputation for this purpose. The Governor, in company with Colonel Boone, of Westport, Colonel Kearney, of Independence and Colonel Strickland, from Missouri, was duly conducted into Lawrence. He was taken, with his staff, into the room of the Committee of Safety. As they passed up to the upper floor in the Free State Hotel, their gaze fell, through a half opened door, upon the silent form of Barber. To the question, "what does this mean?" the reply was, "Oh, it is our yesterday's loss."

General Robinson and Colonel Lane conducted the negotiations on the part of the free state men. The whole matter was fully explained to the Governor. The interview lasted about an hour, which resulted in the admission from the Governor that he had *misunderstood* the conduct and feeling of the people of Lawrence. He stated that Mr. Jones had made certain representations to him which he was satisfied were incorrect. He told them it was impossible to close the negotiations that day on any terms fair for them, and satisfactory to those in the pro-slavery camp. He expressed a desire that a kind of a treaty should be drawn up, expressive of the views and feelings of both parties. He urged that the free state men should give up their arms as a condition of peace, which was positively declined.

The Governor returned to the pro-slavery camp and continued his work of conciliation. He there learned of the plot to raise the black flag and march upon Lawrence, whereupon he immediately issued the following order:

"WAKARUSA, December 8th, 1855.

"*Major-General* RICHARDSON:

"SIR:—You will repress all movements of a disorderly character, and take no steps except by order from me. If any unauthorized demonstrations should be made upon Lawrence, you will immediately use your whole force to check it, as in the present state of negotiations an attack upon Lawrence would be wholly unjustifiable.

"Your obedient servant,

"WILSON SHANNON."

A similar order was issued to General Strickler. Early in the morning the Governor collected some prominent men from the camp. It was suggested that a committee of thirteen Captains should be selected from the pro-slavery men to meet a similar deputation from Lawrence, that evening, at Franklin, to frankly interchange opinions, and seek, if possible, to arrive at some amicable adjustment of the threatening difficulties. This proposition was finally conceded to after a protracted debate, many refusing any conditions of peace other than the surrender of arms on the part of the free state men.

The Governor, with a lighter spirit, returned to Lawrence. In the meantime, on the evening previous, the free state men had discussed and adopted a plan upon which they desired the existing difficulties settled. This was presented to the Governor on his arrival, which, after several verbal modifications, he approved. He had himself drawn up a similar paper, but accepted General Robinson's as a substitute.

When the negotiations closed, the citizens gathered in front of the hotel to learn the result. From the speeches made by Governor Shannon and others, a suspicion was awakened that something had been conceded by the free state leaders which would imply a recognition of the Territorial laws. Old John Brown, who had come to the defense of Lawrence, with his five sons and a quantity of arms, rose to speak. Although an attempt was made by some to prevent his being heard, he persisted, and demanded that the terms of the treaty be made known; that rather than recognize the Border Ruffian usurpers as rulers, they would die fighting in the trenches, or on the prairies. General Robinson then gave them to understand that no such a concession had been made, but that the same principles they had always professed, were yet maintained. With these assurances all were satisfied and retired. The feeling of the soldiers against the Governor was very intense. While speaking one man raised his gun to shoot him, but was prevented by others more prudent and discreet.

The treaty, as it has been called, between Governor Shannon and the people of Lawrence, reads as follows:

"WHEREAS, There is a MISUNDERSTANDING between the people of Kansas, or a portion of them, and the Governor thereof, arising out of the rescue at Hickory Point of a citizen under arrest and other matters; AND WHEREAS, A strong apprehension exists that said misunderstanding may lead to civil strife and bloodshed; AND WHEREAS, As it is desired by both Governor Shannon and the citizens of Lawrence and its vicinity to avoid a calamity so disastrous to the interests of the Territory and the Union, and to place all parties in a correct position before the world; Now, therefore, it is agreed by the said Governor Shannon and the undersigned citizens of the said Territory in Lawrence now assembled that the matter is settled as follows, to wit:

"We, the said citizens of said Territory protest that the said rescue was made without our knowledge or consent, but that if any of our citizens in said Territory were engaged in said rescue, we pledge ourselves to aid in the execution of any legal process against them; *that we have no knowledge of the previous, present or prospective existence f any organization in the said Territory for the resistance of the laws;* and we have not designed, and do not design to resist the execution of any legal service of any criminal process therein, but pledge ourselves to aid in the execution of the laws when called upon by the *proper authority* in the town of Lawrence, and that we will use our influence in preserving order therein, and declare that we are now, as we have ever been, ready to aid the Governor in securing a posse in the execution of such a process, *provided*, that any person thus arrested in Lawrence and its vicinity while a foreign foe shall remain in the Territory, shall be only examined before a United States District Judge of said Territory in said town, and admitted to bail; and *provided further*, that all citizens arrested without legal process shall be set at liberty; and *provided further*, that Governor Shannon agrees to use his influence to secure to the citizens of Kansas Territory, remuneration for any damage suffered in any unlawful depredations, if any such have been committed by the Sheriff's posse in Douglas County; and further, Governor Shannon states that he has not called upon persons, residents of any other States, to aid in the execution of the laws, that such as are here, are here of their own choice, and that he does not consider that he has any authority to do so, and that he will not call upon any citizens of any other State who may be here.

"We wish it understood that we do not herein express any opinion as to the validity of the enactments of the Territorial Legislature.

"Wilson Shannon,
"Charles Robinson,
"J. H. Lane.

"Done in Lawrence, K. T., Dec. 8, 1855."

At the solicitation of Governor Shannon, General Robinson and Colonel Lane accompanied him to the Wakarusa Camp that evening. Here they counciled with thirteen pro-slavery leaders. The Governor, Colonel Lane and General Robinson made speeches setting forth their views. It was finally agreed by the Missouri chiefs to assist Mr. Shannon in carrying out his plan to quietly and peaceably withdraw and disperse the Sheriff's posse.

The night setting in proved most tempestuous, dark and fearful. Generals Robinson and Lane start for Lawrence at 7 o'clock. A guard had been promised them, but only one man made his appearance for that purpose. He, after going with them about one hundred yards, bade them "good night," and turned back. Alone, amid the storm and darkness, the two free state leaders were left to make their way home. From the fact that three armed men were seized near Lawrence that night, who could not give a satisfactory account of themselves, it was thought that there had been a plot to assassinate Generals Robinson and Lane on their way back to Lawrence.

The following morning Governor Shannon issued his orders to the three commanders, Richardson, Strickler and Jones, for them to disband their forces. A reply to one will suffice:

"CAMP WAKARUSA, December 8, 1855.

"SIR: Being fully satisfied that there will be no further resistance to the execution of the laws of this Territory, or to the service of any legal process in the county of Douglas, you are hereby ordered to cross the Kansas River to the north side as near Lecompton as you may find it practical with your command, and disband the same at such time and place, and in such numbers as you think most convenient. Yours, with great respect,

"WILSON SHANNON.

"Major-General RICHARDSON."

Many of the pro-slavery men were disappointed and indignant at the conduct of the Governor. General Stringfellow informed his followers that "the thing is settled," "they are sold," "Shannon has turned traitor," "he has disgraced himself and the whole pro-slavery party." Sheriff Jones in conversation afterwards declared "if Shannon had not been a d—n fool, that place would never have been spared. He would have wiped out Lawrence." Ex-Senator Atchison exerted himself to prevent an attack. He said to his motly gang, that "they can not fight now. The position which the Lawrence people have taken is such that it would not do to make an attack upon them; it would ruin the Democratic cause, too. But, boys, we will fight sometime by G—d!" Through the active exertions of the Border Ruffian chiefs, the opposing elements of darkness, cold and storm, and the want of whisky, no attack took place that night. But, it is thought, had the weather been pleasant and clear, the result would have been different. The invading army chiefly left the following morning, but some remained for several days.

On the evening of the 9th of December, there was a "social" in the Free State Hotel at Lawrence, and Governor Shannon was there. Every body seemed in a good humor. The Governor, who had taken a few quaffs to enliven his feelings, declared "it was the happiest time of his life." While "all went merry as a marriage bell," a messenger brought word that "there was a large irregular force near the town of Lawrence, who were threatening an attack." At this juncture General Robinson solicited authority from Governor Shannon to defend the city in case of an attack, which was given in in the following words:

"*To* C. ROBINSON *and* J. H. LANE, *commanders of the enrolled citizens of Kansas:*

"You are hereby authorized and directed to take such measures, and use the enrolled forces under your command in such a manner for the preservation of the peace and the protection of the persons and property of the people in Lawrence and its vicinity, as in your judgment will best secure that end. WILSON SHANNON.

"LAWRENCE, December 9, 1855."

It is but justice to the Governor to say that he never designed the authority conveyed in this document to legalize the proceedings of the previous conduct of the free state men, or to have any reference to the future, but simply appertained to the threatened attack that night.

Several prisoners had been taken during the campaign on both sides. Every person that attempted to make egress from, or ingress into, Lawrence, had been almost invariably seized and detained a prisoner. George F. Warren and Dr. A. G. Cutler were taken at Atchison and carried to Lecompton and kept in confinement during the disturbances, subject to many indignities. The former lived at Leavenworth, and had been to Doniphan to take Dr. Cutler home, who was sick. On his return he was seized by a mob at Atchison, who demanded his papers. Refusing to hand them over, they began to search him, whereupon he pulled them out and began tearing and chewing them up. They then sent for Dr. Cutler, and conveyed them both as prisoners to Lecompton. Here Kelley, approaching the camp where the latter was confined, cried out, "I want blood; I am bloodthirsty; I want to take the God d—d abolitionist out and hang him." Dr. Cutler was very sick all the while during his imprisonment—at times delirious. E. C. K. Garvey, of Topeka, came near being hung, and would have been, had not the officers interposed. Mr. Parrott, of Leavenworth, was seized while passing from that place to Lawrence, and conveyed to camp at Lecompton. William Phillips, correspondent of the New York "Tribune," had many interesting adventures among the Border Ruffian camps, but always managed his escape. Several others were seized and held prisoners by the pro-slavery mob; but when the *treaty* was effected they were all released.

On Monday evening, December 10, the peace party was held in the Free State Hotel. Soldiers of both parties, ladies and officers were there; a burdened table of eatables afforded a repast; conversation, speeches, flirtation, &c., afforded amusements. But the most remarkable of all was that Sheriff Jones was there "an invited guest." He was treated with civility; but some who had received wrongs which their charity could not forgive, nor magnanimity cover up, watched their opportunity to take his life, and were only prevented by the prudence and vigilance of others, who acted from the sacred obligation of a host.

On the following day the free state forces were reviewed, addressed by their officers and then disbanded. Eleven companies had fifty-five men each enrolled. Besides these there were the artillery and cavalry forces, and men ready to join the ranks whenever the emergency demanded it. Each soldier received a certificate that he had served gallantly and faithfully so many days in defense of Lawrence.

We should not close the history of this invasion without rendering "honor to whom honor is due." The heroic conduct of women gilds the pages of history. The heroism of the ladies of Lawrence shines with the splendor and beauty that immortalized those of Sparta and the American Revolution. While pro-slavery women fled to Missouri to escape the rabble that professed to be their friends, the free state women of Lawrence refused to desert their husbands and brothers in the hour of danger. Nor did they remain with idle hands and timorous minds, but performed a useful part in the defense of their homes. They not only cheered and inspired the soldiers, but threw open their houses for those who had hurried to the assistance of the town, and ministered to their wants. They met together, moulded bullets, made cartridges and laid plans for the comfort of the soldiers. As we have noticed, at one time they went into the country through the enemies pickets, and procured ammunition, which feat no man could have accomplished. Indeed it was the blustering boast of the debauched invaders, that they intended to kill all the men of Lawrence and keep the women for something worse. With these threats before them, it was the determination of the ladies of Lawrence, should the Missourians have raised the black flag and rushed upon their devoted town, to seize the weapons of their fallen friends and take their places in the line of battle. For this purpose they had practiced with fire arms, and had the necessity demanded it, there would have been a display of heroism unparalleled in history.

The women of Lawrence in that day were the most inteligent and refined. They had recently come from the cities of the East, where they had only read of wars and dangers. With all the feminine graces and accomplishments of refined society, they were not of that class who recognize labor a disgrace, and fear a virtue. While they possessed all the embellishments of education and good breeding, they regulated their conduct by common sense. Never upon the frontiers was there a community with women of such acquirements and genuine worth; never upon the frontiers did women perform such acts of valor and greatness as distinguished the ladies of Lawrence—not through this war only, but through many a subsequent and bloodier assault. *Surely, if women should be entitled to vote anywhere, it is in Kansas.*

CHAPTER XXIII.

ROBINSON AND LANE.

Governor Charles Robinson was born on the 21st of July, 1818, at Hardwick, Worcester County, Massachusetts. His parents belonged to the class of respectable poor, who labored to rear their children up in habits of industry and morality. At the age of eighteen Charles entered upon a regular collegiate course of study in Amherst College, to which he assiduously and enthusiastically applied himself. But at the end of two years he was suddenly seized with inflammation of the eyes, from which cause he was reluctantly compelled to abandon school.

When his eyes had sufficiently recovered, he began the study of medicine. He attended lectures at Pittsfield, Massachusetts, and Woodstock, Vermont, and graduated at the former place with distinguished honor. In 1843 he began the practice of medicine at Belchertown. While there, he first publicly exhibited that hatred for tyranny and oppression which has characterized his life. There was a religious sect, called "Perfectionists," in that vicinity, who were loudly abused and vilely slandered by others of different persuasions. Dr. Robinson, though holding no sympathy for their tenets, admiring the purity of their lives and witnessing the unprovoked attacks upon their character and religion, took a public stand in their defense. He held a debate with a preacher of another denomination, in which he eloquently and ably defended the despised sect, and fully vindicated the reasonableness of their views and the purity of their conduct. He began his contest with system-bound doctors, who refused to countenance any man of their profession unless he followed the beaten and time-worn path of a certain school, for which reason he himself was denominated by them a "quack." He believed that professional worth should be acknowledged and respected wherever found. In 1845 he went to Springfield to look after a store which he had secured in payment of a debt, and there continued the practice of his profession. While there, he became noted for his success in the treatment of chronic diseases with the galvanic battery, and was joined in partnership by Dr. Holland, *alias* Timothy Titcomb, who had been his class-mate in the medical school. The following year he went to Fittsburg, Massachusetts, and engaged in the practice of medicine.

In 1849, soon after the gold excitement broke out, he started, as surgeon of a party, for California. On his way thither he passed through Kansas, was struck with its loveliness and fertility, and marked the site of Lawrence as a beautiful location for a city. Upon arriving in California, he worked in the mines a short time, then went to Sacramento and opened an eating house. He was not there long before a difficulty arose between the squatters and a class of speculators. The former had entered upon their lands by pre-emption—a title universally respected in a new country. But, the town improving rapidly, and giving promise of greatness, a class of speculators came in and secured a quitclaim title to a vast tract of country in that vicinity, including the town site, from Mr. Sutter, who held a Spanish title to 99,000 square miles in California. These speculators strengthened themselves by selling or giving lots to new comers, and soon warned those who held lots by preemption to leave the premises. Upon the latter's refusing to observe this demand, the matter was placed in the hands of the Sheriff. In vain the squatters sought to stay any violent action by offering to give bonds for the safe keeping and use of the premises until the title was legally decided in the courts. They, therefore, determined to defend their homes, and prepared for resistance. For thus putting themselves in the attitude of self-defense, the authorities first sought to arrest them; but they agreed to avoid arrests until the opening of the courts, by secreting themselves in various places. While thus absent from their homes the Sheriff took possession of several of their houses, whereupon the squatters collected and marched to retake them.

Dr. Robinson, from the first, had warmly espoused the cause of the squatters, and was their recognized leader, planning and shaping his policy with that prudence and sagacity which characterized him in Kansas.

The squatters, some fifteen in number, upon reaching the houses, said to be held by the Sheriff, found no one there and started to return to their respective abodes. As they retired a rencounter took place between them and a crowd headed by the Sheriff and Mayor. The latter fired, which was promptly returned by the squatters, whereupon the mob scattered and fled. One was killed on each side, and the Mayor and Dr. Robinson fell badly wounded. The doctor crept into an old house, where he remained some time, when he was taken on board a prison ship and detained for ten weeks. While there he was elected to the first Legislature, which he attended, and was highly respected and esteemed by the members for his heroic and noble stand in defense of right and justice. He contributed to the election of General Fremont to the United States Senate. He afterwards published a daily paper for a short period at Sacramento.

On the 1st of July, 1851, he sailed for home. The steamer upon which he took passage was wrecked on the Mexican coast, but the passengers narrowly escaped from a watery grave to the land, and were compelled to travel on foot forty miles before they could again take passage on a boat.

From Panama to Cuba the doctor was employed as surgeon aboard a boat filled with sick workmen, who had been engaged in the construction of the railroad across the Isthmus.

Dr. Robinson, upon reaching his native State, settled in Pittsburg and resumed the practice of medicine. About the time when Kansas first engaged the attention of the public, he published several letters relative to it, founded upon his observation in passing through the Territory to California. The attention of the Emigrant Aid Society was attracted by these letters, which at once, upon learning of his character and experience, employed him as its agent to visit the Territory. The important and conspicuous part he performed in the critical times of our Territorial difficulties, we leave the reader to note for himself.

Governor Robinson has always been very radical in his views—always favored universal suffrage and opposed slavery, or partial legislation of any description. Though he did not endorse the higher law doctrine, still he was always a constitutional abolitionist, and believed in using every legal remedy for the removal of slavery. He was pre-eminently fitted as leader of the free state movements. With inflexible principles, great prudence, caution and sagacity, he combined unflinching courage. Never swerving from his principles in his whole life, he seldom miscalculated in shaping his plan and policy. He preserved the utmost confidence of the free state men until late in our Territorial history, when the Free State party broke up in a general scramble for office.

General James H. Lane was born, June 22, 1814, on the banks of the Ohio, in Boone County, Kentucky. His father, Amos Lane, cousin of Joseph Lane, of Oregon, was an eminent lawyer and a member of Congress. James' mother, who was a woman of superior intellectual and moral qualifications, superintended his early education. Always restive and unable to confine himself to his books, he attained but the rudiments of school learning, even under the excellent tutorship of his mother.

James first began an independent struggle of life in Lawrenceburg, Indiana, as a merchant and pork-packer. He followed this business until 1843, when he married and began the study of law. When the Mexican war broke out in 1846, he raised a company of men, and, having volunteered as a private, was elected captain. With his men, he rendezvoused at New Albany, where he was appointed Colonel of the 3d Regiment. In this capacity he served with distinguished honor throughout General Taylor's campaign. After the expiration of their term of service, he returned with his regiment in June, 1847. He was immediately authorized to reorganize the 3d, which he did, and it was mustered in as the 5th Regiment of Indiana Volunteers. With it he returned to Mexico, where he remained until peace was declared.

Upon his return from the war, he was elected Lieutenant Governor of Indiana in 1849, and, before his term of office expired, was chosen a member of Congress from the 4th Congressional District, and shortly aftewards elector for the State at large for Franklin Pierce as President. He was in Congress at the time of the Kansas-Nebraska agitation, and voted for the repeal of the Missouri Compromise.

In April, 1855, Colonel Lane removed to Kansas, settling on a claim adjoining Lawrence, where he afterwards made his home, and where his widow still lives. He came to the Territory a strong Democrat, and an administration man, and remained conservative in his speeches, until he saw that it was more popular to be radical, then changed to be the most radical man in the West. From his bluster and buncombe speeches, he soon became a terror to the Border Ruffians, and, as such, was useful to the free state cause. The free state men never had any confidence in his courage, his qualifications as a leader, or his character as a man. Though his public life was shifting and stormy, still he managed his political barque so skillfully that he always rode the popular wave, and attained the highest position to which the State could elevate him.

He was elected United States Senator by the first State Legislature in 1861, and during the same year took an active part in recruiting and organizing volunteers. He formed his brigade and commanded it as Brigadier-General, though he held no commission until the following year. In 1863, he was appointed Recruiting Commissioner for the Department of Kansas, and under this authority raised five regiments of infantry, one of which was a colored regiment. In the winter of 1864-5 he was re-elected United States Senator for the term commencing on the 4th of the following March. Upon taking his seat in Congress he endorsed Johnson in his opposition to the Freedmen's Bureau and the Civil Rights bill, for which, on his return to Kansas, most all of his old friends refused to recognize him or tender him any courtesies.

Feeling thus rejected by his fellow statesmen, and fearing, it was thought, an investigation and divulgence of certain Indian frauds, he became partially deranged at St. Louis. He returned from that place to Kansas. On the following morning after his arrival at Leavenworth, as he was going out to the government farm, in company with others, he shot himself, discharging a pistol in his mouth, the ball passing through his brain to the top of his cranium. He lingered, unconscious, for several days, then died on the 10th of July, 1866. Thus ended the career of this wonderful man. Over his faults and vices let the silence of the grave forever rest. Though not a *real* man, yet, in many respects, he was a *great* man. As a politician he has no equal in the nineteenth century, and has left his impress upon the political elements of Kansas, which it will require years to remove. Let the youths of this State practice his untiring energy and unfaltering perseverance, but let them flee from the way of the ungodly, which perisheth.

Such is a brief sketch of the lives of these two great rivals in Kansas politics, Hon. Charles Robinson and Hon. James H. Lane. Neither without his faults, neither without his virtues, both have been too much praised and too much censured. Robinson never swerved from principle from beginning to end; Lane, when he broke off from the Democratic party, shaped his action entirely by the signs of the times. The former was cautious, prudent and brave; the latter reckless, rash and cowardly; the first discreet in council, true in judgment and firm in danger, was well suited as a leader of the free state movement; the other, impetuous, blustering and dashing, happily offset the conduct of the Border Ruffians. Robinson, gored and wounded by abuse, grew petulent and refractory; Lane, strengthened and encouraged by it, grew sublime and magnanimous in his brightening prospect of success.

General Robinson, commander-in-chief, delivered this parting address to the forces assembled for the rescue of Lawrence:

"FELLOW SOLDIERS:—In consequence of a 'misunderstanding' on the part of the Executive of this Territory, the people of this vicinity have been menaced by a foreign foe, and our lives and property threatened with destruction. The citizens, guilty of no crime, rallied for the defense of their families, their property and their lives, and from all parts of the Territory the true patriots came up resolved to perish in the defense of their most sacred rights, rather than submit to foreign dictation. Lawrence and her citizens were the first to be sacrificed, and most nobly have her neighbors come to her rescue. The moral strength of our position was such that even the 'gates of hell' could not have prevailed against us, much less a foreign mob, and we gained a bloodless victory. Literally may it be said of our citizens, 'They came, they saw, they conquered.'

"Selected as your commander, it becomes my cheerful duty to tender to you, fellow soldiers, the meed of praise so justly your due. Never did true men unite in a holier cause, and never did true bravery appear more conspicuous, than in the ranks of our little army—death before dishonor was visible in every countenance, and felt in every heart. Bloodless, though, the contest has been, there are not wanting instances of heroism worthy of a more chivalric age. To the experience, skill and perseverance of gallant General Lane, all credit is due for the thorough discipline of our forces, and the complete and extensive preparation for defense. His services can not be overrated, and long may he live to wear the laurels so bravely won. Others are worthy of special praise for distinguished services, and all, both officers and privates, are entitled to the deepest gratitude of the people. In behalf of the citizens of Lawrence, in behalf of the ladies of Lawrence, in behalf of the children of Lawrence, in behalf of you, fellow soldiers, of Lawrence, and in my own behalf, I thank you, of the neighboring settlements, for your prompt and manly response to our call for aid, and pledge you alike response for your signals of distress. The citizens who have left their homes to come to our assistance have suffered great privations and many discomforts and exposures, while citizens of Lawrence have incurred heavy expense; but all has been submitted to without a murmur, and in a spirit of a people engaged in a high and holy cause."

On the 16th of December, Sheriff Jones arrested S. F. Tappan and S. C. Smith, without any resistance, and took them to Lecompton. It will be recollected that they were not with the party of rescuers when they first intercepted Jones, but came up during the parley. The Sheriff had appealed to their patriotism, and fears to induce them to comply with his demands, saying that he did not think that such men as they were would be participants in such work, and that unless they surrendered his prisoner, he would bring a myriad of men from Missouri and destroy Lawrence.

On the day following their arrest these two gentlemen were examined before Mr. Shepherd, a Justice of the Peace, so appointed by the Shawnee Legislature. The only witness that appeared against them was Sheriff Jones, who testified in regard to the part they took in the rescue.

They did not introduce any rebutting testimony, nor did they give bail, but insisted upon an immediate trial. The Court, however, which should have been in session at that time, had adjourned over, in consequence of the indisposition and absence of Chief-Justice Lecompte. The two prisoners were held until the 22d of December, when they were released on a parole of honor for three months.

Hugh Hutchingson, Paul Jones, and two others of the rescuers were arrested, underwent a preliminary trial, and held over to the next term of Court on $500 bail. At the following term of Court all the prisoners appeared for trial before Lecompte, but their cases were deferred to the next sitting of the Court. This was the end of the Wakarusa war.

The term "Border Ruffian" was early applied to those individuals on the western border of Missouri, who sought by illegal and violent means, to determine the domestic institutions of the Territory. And never was a name more appropriately applied, nor ever a name more gloried in by those upon whom it was bestowed. There was a large number at the towns on the border, who spent their time in loafing, drinking, gambling, and carousing, that were genuine ruffians long before the troubles in Kansas arose, who readily lent themselves as willing tools of designing politicians to harrass and oppress the free state men. This work just suited them, and perhaps the mass of the people of Western Missouri never had as much happiness in their lives as they enjoyed during the difficulties in this Territory. In the more general invasions of Kansas, these ruffians were joined or led by the more respectable men of the Border, who at such times vied with the vilest in debauchery, crime and the grossness of their conduct. In this way men of eminent ability, who had occupied high and responsible positions of public trust and profit, would pass over into the Territory, and unmindful of dignity and honor, would throw off all restraint, and imitate, in appearance, character and actions the real *ruffian*.

Nor was this at all an unpopular appellation among the border gentry. They gloried in it as much as Cicero or Socrates did in that of *Philosopher*, or the soldiers of the Seven-hilled-city that of *Roman*. Boats on the Missouri river took to themselves the name; hacks, omnibuses, hotels, "*doggeries*," horses, dogs, and were not unfrequently adorned by the title "Border Ruffian." And woman—beautiful, fair and intelligent woman—so far became blinded to the pure and virtuous, as to take unto herself the name of BORDER RUFFIAN, and admire and praise those of that character.

I have given in another place a description of the Missourians, and a dark picture of humanity it is, though I sought to draw it with a pen of truth. The contest in Kansas afforded a happy field for them to display their natural qualities, and certainly they did so to good advantage. No other people would or could have done the dirty work for slavery that the Missourians did with ready hands and willing hearts. They were pre-eminently adapted to the "nasty job," and most *nastily* they performed it. Go into a saloon or hotel, and you would most likely be accosted by some long, gangling, red-eyed, blurred faced specimen of humanity with slouched hat and butternut clothes, thus: "Stranwhar ure from? No d—d Yankee I guess? Wall, I'm none of yer city raised down easters; I'm a Border Ruffian, by G—d. I can draw my bead at forty rod, and am bound to shoot center any how. If the crowd wish I dont care if we have a hand fight before this here bar; I'm dreadful easy to whip—yes sir'ee, dreadful easy—so just jump me up, stranger, and we'll smash in all createdly. Wall, I 'spect you think I'm a d—d cuss, so come up here and liquor."

CHAPTER XXIV.

VARIOUS EVENTS OF THE WINTER.

The termination of the Wakarusa war was by no means satisfactory to the Achilles of the Border. It only served to scatter the clouds of the tempest that they might re-gather and break with greater violence. The Border Ruffian chiefs immediately plotted for the utter overthrow and destruction of free state men. But let us notice events as near as we can in chronological order.

The election on the adoption of the Topeka Constitution was held on the 15th of December. Amid the excitement which had recently prevailed in the Territory, the settlers had partly lost sight of the free state movement. The public speakers failed to meet their appointments, consequently the subject was not agitated and discussed before the people to a great extent. Copies of the Constitution had been freely circulated, and notices of the election posted up, but in a few places even this was not done. The election in all Border towns was not allowed to be held. These facts were supposed to account for the vote being no larger. At Atchison no election was attempted.

The result of the election was as follows: In favor of the Constitution, 1,731; against it, 46; for the general banking law, 1,120: opposed to it, 564; for the exclusion of negroes and mulattoes, 1,287; against exclusion, 453; total number of votes cast, 1,778.

By the order of General Eastin, the militia of his command was required to meet for muster at Leavenworth on the day of the election, and receive their discharge, which entitled them to pay from the United States for their military services. Early in the morning these ruffians, whom the General termed "Kansas Militia," began crossing the Missouri River from Platte County. About noon this motley crew, several hundred in number, led by Colonel Payne, a member of the bogus Legislature, and Judge of Leavenworth County, so appointed by that body, and another man by the name of Dunn, a grocery keeper, and consequently a man of great influence among the Border Ruffians, attacked the house where the polls were held. Two of the men in the house escaped without injury, but the third, by the name of Wetherill, throwing the ballot-box under the counter, rushed into the street. He had scarcely reached it, before he was knocked down by clubs, seriously beaten and trampled in the mud by the crowd. He would probably have been killed had not a pro-slavery man, and two free state men by the names of Anthony and Brown, interposed and rescued him. The ruffians, having obtained possession of the ballot-boxes, paraded them through the streets, yelling and shrieking like barbarians.

The office of the "Territorial Register" was loudly threatened, but no attack was made upon it. On the afternoon these rag-a-muffins were mustered, addressed and complimented by General Eastin for their faithful and patriotic services.

On the following Saturday night a mob, calling themselves Platte County Regulators, destroyed the printing press of the "Territorial Register," by throwing it and the type into the river. They were organized at Kickapoo, and marched down under command of Captain Dunn, G. W. Perkins, Dr. Royal and James Tyler. Mr. Delahay, the editor, who was absent at the time, was the most conservative among the free state men. A personal friend of

Stephen A. Douglas, an enthusiastic admirer of squatter sovereignty, notwithstanding the border ruffian invasions, a national Democrat, he had always advised obedience to the laws of the Territorial Legislature. But he had identified himself with the Free State party in their lawful and constitutional measures to make Kansas a free State. He had refused assistance to Lawrence, when calling loudly for help, and repeatedly declared in the Free State meetings, "I had as lief buy a negro as a mule." The hight of his offense was that he favored a free State.

Mr. Delahay has been a true friend to Kansas, taking an active part in public affairs. He has many friends, and could wield a wonderful influence, were he a little more temperate in his habits. He has for some time occupied the position of United States District Judge in this State, and still makes his home at Leavenworth.

As quick as the result of the election was announced, an election was called for State officers. A convention met at Lawrence on the 22d day of December for the purpose of nominating candidates. There was but little harmony and unanimity between its members. The feelings of the minority were that if conservative men were elected, the conservative administration and Congress of the United States would be more ready to recognize them and favor the free state movement. They accordingly *bolted* from the regular nominations of the convention and formed a "Free State Anti-Abolition Ticket." This movement did not meet with general favor, even among the conservative elements. In the nomination of the convention both Radicals and Conservatives were about equally represented.

By the election which took place on the 15th of January, 1856, the regular nominees were duly elected with large majorities. The following are the first State officers regularly chosen by the people of Kansas: Dr. C. Robinson, Governor; W. Y. Roberts, Lieutenant Governor; P. C. Schuyler, Secretary of State; G. A. Cutler, Auditor; J. A. Wakefield, Treasurer; H. Miles Moore, Attorney-General; M. Hunt, S. N. Latta and M. F. Conway, Supreme Judges; S. B. McKenzie, Reporter, and S. B. Floyd, Clerk of the Supreme Court; John Speer, State Printer; M. W. Delahay, Representative in Congress.

The free state Mayor of Leavenworth, intimidated by the demonstrations at the December election, and from the hopeless prospect of being able to perform his duty in the future, resigned. The pro-slavery Mayor elected to fill his place, at the solicitation of the business men of the city, who feared a riot, issued a proclamation forbidding an election to be held in that town on the 15th of January. The election, however, was held in an informal way, by carrying the ballot-box around and getting individual votes. In this way about two hundred votes were polled, and returned to the Executive Committee, a majority of whom, after some contention, agreed to issue certificates to members thus elected. When, however, these members presented themselves at the Legislature the following March, claiming seats, they were, after considerable discussion, refused admission by that body.

At Eastin, about twelve miles north-west of Leavenworth, and in the same county, the election was deferred two days after the time fixed by the Executive Committee, on account of the threats of the Kickapoo Rangers and pro-slavery men in the neighborhood, that the polls should be seized and the election broken up, as had been done previously at Leavenworth. The election was held at the house of Mr. Minard, about a half mile from the village. In the morning a company of eight persons went out from Leavenworth in a wagon where the election was held, among whom was Captain E. P. Brown. Men generally went armed to the polls, in consequence of the violent threats that had been made. About seventy-two voted, and every thing passed off quietly during the day.

About 6 o'clock in the evening a company of thirty horsemen made an advance upon the house where the polls were kept. A party of free state men rushed out and confronted them, with arms in their hands. The leader of the assaulting party ordered a charge several times, but his men refused to obey. In a few moments they wheeled and retreated to the village. Shortly after this, messages were sent to Minard, by the Ruffians, that they wished the ballot-box given up, and unless it was, they would come and take it. No disturbance, however, occurred for some time, though persons of both parties passed to and fro from the village and the house of Mr. Minard.

About 2 o'clock that night a report reached the free state men that one of their number, Stephen Sparks, on his way home, had been taken prisoner by the Ruffians at Eastin, and was still held as such by them. Captain Brown, with fifteen men, immediately set out to rescue him. They passed down to the village, and found Sparks and his son in the fence corner, surrounded by a mob, like a wolf at bay by a gang of hounds. They demanded the delivery of Sparks, and as quick as the mob perceived the strength of the free state men, they let the prisoner go with threats that he would be speedily recaptured.

The two parties had not separated far before the pro-slavery men began hallooing and the firing of guns. The free state men returned it. The firing was kept up for about ten minutes, when the latter returned to Mr. Minard's. One pro-slavery man was killed, and two free state men slightly wounded, in the affray.

In the morning, about eight or nine o'clock, the Leavenworth party set out for home. Having proceeded about six miles, they were met by two wagons—one with four horses—both filled with armed men. They hurried down the hill, passed the free state men, stopped and called upon them to halt. Scarcely had the Leavenworth party time to check their horses before they beheld another party approaching from the top of the hill—two wagons and thirty horsemen. They were armed with hatchets, bowie knives, guns and revolvers. They rejoiced at seeing Brown in their power. The free state men, on being assured that they would be treated kindly as prisoners, gave up their arms, seeing they could do nothing against such odds. The ruffians seemed mad with excitement and whisky. Mr. Taylor came near losing his life from a violent stroke of a hatchet.

The prisoners were then conveyed back to Eastin. The mob grounded their action upon a report that a pro-slavery man had been killed at Eastin the night previous, and they wished all to go back to investigate it, and have the murderer brought to punishment. They were the Kickapoo Rangers, led by J. W. Martin. They had been sent for soon after the disburbance the evening previous.

On their arrival at Eastin they were placed in a small room of Dawson's store house, and closely guarded. In a short time two or three more prisoners were brought in from the surrounding country. In a half hour Captain Brown was called out and taken into Dr. Motter's office, to undergo his trial. Not more than a half hour elapsed before Captain Martin returned to the prisoners and informed them that it would be impossible to save Brown, and perhaps them too, unless they could effect their escape. The guard agreed to let them go, and conducted them a short distance. They all effected their escape.

But alas, sad was the fate of poor Brown. He was kept locked up in a room during his trial to prevent the mob from interfering. On being told by Captain Martin that they had concluded to take Brown to Leavenworth to await his trial according to the laws, the mob cried out, "no, he'll escape like McCrea," and that they intended to punish Brown themselves. The Captain did all he could to prevent the rashness of the mob, but finding himself unable to control them, left. They broke open the door and rushed in upon Brown with hatchets and knives. He offered to fight any one of them, but they gave him no chance for his life. He was taken out of doors, dragged, chased and pulled around, stabbed and chopped until literally hacked from head to foot. He was finally thrown into a wagon and jolted ten miles over frozen ground to his home, and handed over to his terror-stricken wife. To the inquiries about his fate, he replied, "I have been murdered by a gang of cowards in cold blood, without any cause," then laid his head back and breathed his last.

Mr. Brown was a prominent member of the Free State party; had taken part in the defense of Lawrence, and was a member elect of the Legislature. He left a young and accomplished wife and one child. The first Legislature, convened on the 4th of March, passed the following:

"WHEREAS, R. P. Brown, Esq., a member of this House, was inhumanly murdered at Eastin, on the 18th of January last, by a body of armed men from Missouri and the city of Kickapoo; and, whereas, justice to ourselves as well as respect to the memory of the deceased, requires a tribute at our hands; therefore,

"*Resolved*, That in the cold blooded murder of R. P. Brown, by the hand of a mob of mercenaries and desperadoes, from a neighboring State, we have sustained an irreparable loss, the State has been deprived of the services of a man of intelligence, integrity, honor, patriotism and true courage, and his family of a kind husband and father.

"*Resolved*, That we extend to the bereaved widow our heartfelt condolence on account of the afflicting calamity, and assure her that the whole country joins with her in her grief.

"*Resolved*, That while we condole with her in her afflictions, we feel that Providence will overrule for good. Mr. Brown has joined the host of Martyrs, whose blood has watered the tree of liberty. His name, with Dow and Barber, will survive and adorn the brightest page in the future history of Kansas, while those who were the instruments of this outrage, like the perpetrators of other foul crimes, will be remembered as a monster in the catalogue of human depravity.

"*Resolved*, That we recommend to the lovers of freedom and justice to erect a monument to the memory of the deceased, with suitable inscriptions, and that the State make liberal contributions in aid of such an enterprise.

"*Resolved*, That we wear the badge of mourning for thirty days in commendation of the heroic conduct of our deceased friend and co-laborer in the cause of freedom.

"*Resolved*, That copies of these resolutions be furnished the several papers in Kansas, and that they be requested to copy the same, and that copies be forwarded to the widow of the deceased."

The pro-slavery men not satisfied with the death of Brown, determined to drive out the Free State men from Eastin. They accordingly notified them to leave, by leaving notices at their houses, signed by some fifteen or twenty persons. The Free State men fortified, and gathered their forces to protect themselves, and sent for aid to Topeka and Lawrence. A company from these two places went up to their rescue, but the Missourians hearing of their advent, hurried back to their native State.

This winter was one of unusual frigidity. Storms, hail, snow and ice rendered it exceedingly disagreeable. The settlers were much exposed to the cold and sleety blasts, having in many instances only open shakes for houses. But it was not the natural elements that caused the most suffering and privation. Settlers were frequently compelled to leave their families upon the lone prairies, to flee either to the rescue of their friends or to make their own escape from the threatened violence. I shall have occasion to speak in the following chapter of the dangers which filled the land, of the gathering hosts of invaders, not from Missouri only, but from the whole South.

CHAPTER XXV.

EXTERMINATION.

The President, in his special message to Congress on the 24th of January, took the position that the enactments of the Territorial Legislature were valid and binding, and, hence, must be enforced. He denounced the free state movement as a party one, and not that of the people. Speaking of it he said:

"No principle of public law, no practice or precedent under the Constitution of the United States, no rule of reason, right or common sense, confers any such power as that now claimed by a mere party in the Territory. In fact, what has been done is of a revolutionary character. It is avowedly so in motive and in aim as respects the local law of the Territory. It will become treasonable insurrection if it reach the length of organized resistance by force to the fundamental, or any other, law, and to the authority of the general Government."

Again he said:

"Entertaining these views, it will be my imperative duty to support public order in the Territory; to vindicate its laws, whether federal or local, against all attempts of organized resistance; and to protect its people in the establishment of their own institutions, undisturbed by encroachments from without, and in the full enjoyment of the rights of self-government assured to them by the Constitution and the organic act of Congress."

He recommended to Congress as a means to quell the troubles and adjust the difficulties, to pass a bill authorizing the people of Kansas to frame a constitution with a view to admission into the Union.

Here was a distinct assurance that not only were the Missourians to be allowed to overrun Kansas and trample upon the rights of its people, but all the power of the federal Government would be applied to compel a recognition of these bogus laws.

The Missourians began their preparations for again invading Kansas in earnest and determination. They keenly felt that they had been the losers in the recent campaign in the Territory, notwithstanding their number and boasting. They saw, too, that the conquest of Kansas was not so easy, that the free state men were not only prepared with superior arms, but possessed courage and skill. They knew, too, that unless their designs in the conquest of Kansas could be effected the coming year, that it would be lost to slavery. They, therefore, determined upon exterminating the free state men by fire and sword.

The Border Ruffians very well knew that the free state men never intended to recognize the Shawnee Legislature as legitimate, as the treaty with Governor Shannon clearly showed. To preserve the cloak of law and order around their infamous designs, Sheriff Jones addressed the following note to the free state commanders:

"LAWRENCE, K. T., January 15, 1856.

"GENERALS ROBINSON AND LANE:

"GENTLEMEN: Did you or did you not pledge yourselves, at a council held in Franklin on the — day of December, to assist me, as Sheriff, in the arrest of any person in Lawrence against whom I might have a writ, and to furnish me with a posse to enable me to do so?

"SAMUEL J. JONES,
"Sheriff Douglas County, K. T."

To which the following reply was made:

"SAMUEL J. JONES, ESQ., SIR: In reference to your note of yesterday, we state that at the time and place mentioned, we may have said that we would assist any proper officer, in the service of any legal process in this city, and also no further resistance to the arrest by you of one of the rescuers of Branson would be made, as we desired to test the validity of the enactments of the body that met at the Mission, calling themselves the Kansas Legislature, by an appeal to the Supreme Court of the United States.

"Yours, Respectfully, "C. ROBINSON,
"J. H. LANE."

It will be seen by this correspondence, that though the free state leaders had agreed to submit to the arrest of the rescuers, it was with the view of testing the legality of the Shawnee Legislature before the highest court in the land. Though they had agreed to assist any *proper* officer in the service of any *legal* process, they still retained the privilege of determining who is a *proper* officer and what is a *legal* process. The treaty no longer covered the breach between the two parties, but it yawned open wider than before.

Early in the winter tumultuous preparations for subduing Kansas began. They sounded like the mutterings of a gathering storm, and echoed far down in the Southern States. Kansas matters were discussed in the weekly sessions of the Blue Lodges, plans were concocted by the leaders and approved by public meetings. Mounted horsemen in companies of fifty each were suggested as effective guerrilla parties for scouring the Territory, harrassing the settlers and preventing them from putting in their crops. Finding that their legislative enactments did not punish free state men sufficiently, they urged the necessity of calling an extra session of the Legislature to make more stringent and penal laws for free state men. After showing the legal difficulties that embarrassed the pro-slavery leaders during the seige of Lawrence, the squatter sovereign suggested that these be removed as soon as possible. In an article of two columns it says: "We say if the abolitionists are able to whip us, and overturn the Government that has been set up here, the sooner it is known the better; and we want to see it settled. We want to see it determined whether honest men or rogues are to rule here." Dr. Stringfellow proposed to sell shares in several towns to procure arms "for the volunteers and militia of Atchison County when in service." He heads his article upon the subject thus:

"WAR! WAR!!

"It seems now to be certain that we shall have to give the abolitionists at least one good thrashing before political matters are settled in this Territory. To do so we must have arms; we have the men. I propose to raise funds to furnish Colt's revolvers and other arms for those who are without them."

The Kansas "Pioneer," on the morning after the disturbances at Eastin, sounded the war cry thus:

"Rally! Rally! * * * * * Forbearance has now ceased to be a virtue. Therefore we call upon every pro-slavery man in this land to rally to the rescue. Kansas must be immediately rescued from the tyrannical dogs. The Kickapoo Rangers are at this moment beating to arms. A large number of the pro-slavery men will leave this place for Eastin in twenty minutes. The war has again commenced, and the abolitionists have again commenced it. Pro-slavery men, law and order men, strike for your altars! strike for your firesides! strike for your rights! Avenge the blood of your brethren who have been cowardly assailed, but who have bravely fallen in the defense of southern institutions. Sound the bugle of war over the length and breadth of the land, and leave not an abolitionist in the Territory to relate their treacherous and contaminating deeds. Strike your piercing rifle balls and your glittering steel to their black and poisonous hearts! Let the war cry never cease in Kansas again until our Territory is wrested from the last vestige of abolitionism."

The following is taken from a speech delivered in Platte City, Missouri, February 4, by General D. R. Atchison:

"I was a prominent agent in repealing the Missouri Compromise, and opening the Territory for settlement. The abolition orators drummed up their forces and whistled them on to the cars and whistled them off again at Kansas City; some of them had '*Kansas* and *Liberty*' on their hats. I saw this with my own eyes. These men came with the avowed purpose of driving or expelling you from the Territory. What did I advise you to do? Why to meet them at their own game. When the first election came off I told you to go over and vote. You did so, and beat them. Well, what next? Why an election of members of the Legislature to organize the Territory, must be held. What did I advise you to do then? Why meet them on their own ground, and at their own game again; and cold and inclement as the weather was, I went over with a company of men. The abolitionists of the North said and published it abroad that *Atchison was there with bowie knives, and by G—d it was true. I never did go into that Territory—I never intend to go into that Territory without being prepared for all such kinds of cattle.*

"They have held an election on the 15th of last month, and they intend to put the machinery of a State in motion on the 4th of March. Now, you are entitled to my advice, and you shall have it. I say prepare yourselves. Go over there. Send your young men and if they attempt to drive you out, then, damn them, drive them out. Fifty of you, with your shot guns, are worth two hundred and fifty of them with their Sharp's rifles. Get ready—arm yourselves, for if they abolitionize Kansas you lose $100,000,000 of your property. I am satisfied I can justify every act of yours before God and a jury."

The Border chiefs did not forget to keep themselves right with the administration at Washington. That was an object of great concern with them. They sent a special messenger to represent Kansas matters to the President and his cabinet. In order to retain the sympathy of the Democrats North and South, they denied that any outrages had been committed by them in Kansas; they declared that pro-slavery men were being driven from the country or shot down on their claims, and that the "invasion," of which the abolition presses were saying so much about, was but the rush of a few Missourians to the rescue of their friends, and to give a helping hand to the Governor in upholding the laws. They represented free state men as factious and attempting to set up a government in opposition to the legally constituted one already established, and that in carrying out their undertaking they were assisted by money and arms from the East. In this way did they attempt to cover up their foul crimes and dark deeds. Nor were they unsuccessful, as an extract from the "Washington Star," a semi-official organ of the President, will show:

> "The latest troubles in Kansas grew wholly out of the fact that the free state men have already violated the terms of their recent agreement at Lawrence, in essaying to open the polls under the pretense of taking the sense of the people on their pretended State Constitution. The people opposed to them refused to put up quietly with their flagrant disregard of their solemn pledges, and at Leavenworth and elsewhere smashed their ballot-boxes and made their voting places too hot for them. That's all. Had they kept their faith there would have been no disturbance whatever."

The South, which stood abashed at the high-handed acts of injustice first committed by the Border Ruffians, at length was led to participate in the struggle. In the latter part of November, Jefferson Buford published his card, calling for three hundred young men capable of bearing arms, to go with him to Kansas. He promised to pay their passage there and furnish them the first year's support after their arrival, and guaranteed them a homestead of forty acres of land. He proposed to contribute $20,000 of his own funds towards the object, and solicited donations from others, whom he promised to remunerate in land. The

"Eufaula Spirit of the South," alluding to this movement shortly afterwards said:

"We are gratified to see that the proposed expedition of our friend, Major Buford, to Kansas, is beginning to attract the attention it so eminently deserves. Of late there has been an almost unmistakable stirring of the waters, and the South begins to move like the strong man in his sleep. From Virginia and Tennessee, from South Carolina, Georgia and Mississippi, every mail brings tidings of gallant young men buckling on their armor for the struggle that is to give Kansas to the South or surrender her to the vagabond creatures of the Emigrant Aid Society of Massachusetts. Warm, true hearts all over the South yearn towards the fearless champion of our rights who nobly perils every thing in the cause. Meetings of the citizens in Montgomery and Columbus have recognized him as a leader worthy of the enterprise and the occasion, and have tendered him not only their sympathy, but material aid. At the former meeting, Colonel Gayle, of Dallas, pledged the people of his county for not less than $5,000. Truly the work goes bravely on."

The Legislature of Alabama appropriated $25,000 towards equipping and transporting emigrants to Kansas. At a meeting in Gainsville, Mississippi, the following resolutions were passed:

"*Resolved*, That we regard the abolitionists as our dire and mortal foes, and denounce them as traitors to their God, who, in his beneficent wisdom, ordained the institution of slavery—as traitors to the laws of our common country, which acknowledge and sanction it, and as traitors to ourselves, whose injury and destruction they wantonly seek.

"*Resolved*, That we form ourselves into a society to be called 'The Kansas Emigration Society,' and that we solicit the junction of every friend of Southern Rights in the country.

"*Resolved*, That each member, upon admission, pay one dollar, and that the money so raised, and by voluntary contributions, be devoted to defraying the expenses of the above named emigrants to Kansas.

"*Resolved*, That those patriotic Missourians who extended counsel and assistance to their fellow citizens of Kansas, are entitled to the warmest gratitude of the whole South.

"*Resolved*, That, in the opinion of this meeting, the Legislature of Mississippi should place $25,000, subject to the order of the Governor of this State, to be employed when deemed expedient, in aid of the people of Kansas in defense of their legal and constitutional rights."

Similar meetings were held in various Southern States with similar results. The Legislatures contributed in accordance with these petitions. Emigrant Aid Societies were formed to induce young men to go to Kansas by paying their expenses, and furnishing them with arms. They sent out men to *vote* and to *fight*. Accordingly Colonel Buford, of South Carolina; Colonel Titus, of Florida; Colonel Wilkes, of Virginia; Captain Hampton, of Kentucky, and Colonel Treadwell, of South Carolina, all organized companies and arrived in Kansas early in the Spring. The following notices are copied from the Missouri papers:

"Southern Sharp Shooters! Twelve young men, emigrants to Kansas, from South Carolina, arrived at St. Louis on Friday. They were armed with rifles, and determined to extend the 'area of slavery!'"

"A large body of Tennesseans arrived at St. Louis on Saturday, on their way to Kansas. About fifty of the party carried rifles, and were amply supplied with munitions of war."

The people of the border sent speakers into the Southern States "to fire the Southern heart," and solicit funds and emigrants. Silas Woodson, General B. F. Stringfellow, and others, were sent upon a mission of this kind. In January, a letter, of which the following is an extract, went the rounds of the Southern press:

* * * * "We are in a constant state of excitement here (Platte City.) The 'Border Ruffians' have access to my rooms day and night. The very air is full of

rumors. We wish to keep ourselves right before the world, and we are provoked and aggravated beyond sufferance. Our persons and property are not for a moment safe, and yet we are forced by the respect we owe our friends elsewhere, by respect for the cause in which we are engaged, to forbear. This state of things can not last. You are authorized to publish the whole or part of what I have written. But if Georgia intends to do any thing, or can do any thing for us, let it be done speedily.

"Let your young men come forth to Missouri and Kansas. Let them come well armed, with money enough to support them for twelve months, and determined to see this thing out. One hundred true men would be an acquisition; the more the better. I do not see how we are to avoid civil war; come it will. Twelve months will not elapse before war—civil war of the fiercest kind—will be upon us. We are arming and preparing for it. Indeed, we of the border counties are prepared. We must have the support of the South. We are fighting the battles of the South. Our institutions are at stake. You far Southern men are now out of the nave of the war; but if we fail it will reach your own doors, perhaps your hearths. We want men—armed men. We want money—not for ourselves, but to support our friends when they come from a distance. I have now in this house two gallant young men from Charleston, South Carolina. They are citizens of Kansas, and will remain so until her destiny is fixed.

"Let your young men come in squads as fast as they can be raised, well armed. We want none but true men.

"Yours, truly, D. R. Atchison.

"P. S. I would not be astonished if this day laid the ground work for a guerrilla war in Kansas. I have heard of rumors of strife and battle at Leavenworth, seven miles from this place; but the ice is running in the Missouri River and I have nothing definite. I was a peace-maker in the difficulty lately settled by Governor Shannon. I counseled the ruffians to forbearance; but I will never again counsel peace. D. R. A."

CHAPTER XXVI.

FREE STATE PREPARATIONS AND PROCLAMATION OF THE PRESIDENT.

Not a week passed after the Wakarusa war that the free state men at Lawrence did not stand in constant apprehension of an attack from Border Ruffians. Rumors would reach them of some deep laid plan being perfected on the Border for the destruction of Lawrence, but its character was not fully known. Pro-slavery leaders would ride into town, consult members of their own party, and in a short time be in another settlement. Then the border presses were constantly teeming with invectives—threats and inflammatory appeals. It was evident that something was brewing secretly, but the more to be dreaded from the fact that it was secret.

Messengers would bring reports of military stores being collected on the Border, and companies of men organizing; and "that they were only awaiting a favorable change in the weather to commence an attack." "It is supposed," says the "Herald of Freedom," "they premeditate an attack on horseback—probably after night—of two or three hundred persons, meeting simultaneously from different points, and that they propose an arrest of several of our principal citizens, and then flee as they came, to make another attack after they shall have tortured and finally killed their victims, as was the case with the martyred Brown."

"We understand that an attack is also expected at Topeka, and that our friends there are also preparing for defense." "The friends of freedom in the East may be prepared at any time to hear of the blow being struck. When the war shall be opened in Kansas it will be under different auspices than on former occasions. It will be a struggle in earnest, and we appeal to our friends in the north and the east to hold themselves in readiness to march at a moment's notice to our rescue. They may rest assured that the people of Kansas will stand upon the right, and that they will die before they will surrender."

From all that the free state men could see the signs of the times augered trouble, war and extermination. They knew that if the attack was not made in the winter, the difficulties would be renewed in the spring, not by Border Ruffians alone, but also by ruffians and scrapings of Southern cities. Dark and gloomy was the prospect of the scattered freemen of Kansas. Far removed from friends and aid; with a large and inimical State intervening to cut off succor in the hour of trial, with no chance of subsistence only from what they raised from their fields and little hope of being able to till them; with a dark clond ready to burst upon their heads, which was still more dark and portentious towards the horizon—they did not despair, but resolved to prepare, as best they could, for the worst.

Lawrence strengthened her fortifications. The largest earthwork stood at the foot of Massachusetts Street, to guard the approach from the river. It was one hundred feet in diameter, five feet high, and four feet wide on the top. Upon this the sentinel made his constant beat. Inside was a cabin for the comforts of soldiers, with arms and ammunition.

Companies were armed, equipped and mustered into service. The most noted of these was Company "A," called "Stubbs," from their stubby appearance. Couriers were dispatched through the Territory to give warning to free state men of the expected attack, and to hold themselves in readiness to come to the rescue. Arms, ammunition and provisions were collected from the vicinity and stored in the city. The Free State Hotel was a barrack for soldiers; pistols and guns lay on the mantle pieces, stood in the chimney corners; officers slept in their council rooms.

On the 4th of January the Executive Committee appointed a deputation, consisting of Messrs. Lane, Emery, Hunt, Goodin, Dickey and Holliday, to visit all the principal towns of the free States "to plead the cause of the people of Kansas, and convey and lay before Congress the Constitution of the State recently adopted." The Governors of the free States were addressed by the same committee and appealed to for aid. Governor Wright, of Indiana, responded at length, refusing any such assistance, on the ground that it would be derogatory to the principles of non-intervention, and that if the people of the Territory were aggrieved it was the duty of the President of the United States to redress them. But letters of sympathy and promises of aid came in abundance from other quarters. The protection of the general Government was invoked by the following letter to the President:

"LAWRENCE, K. T., January 21, 1856.

"HON. FRANKLIN PIERCE, *President of the United States:*

"SIR: We have authentic information that an overwhelming force of the citizens of Missouri are organized on the Border, amply supplied with artillery, for the avowed purpose of invading the Territory, demolishing our towns and butchering our unoffending free state citizens. We respectfully demand, on behalf of the citizens of Kansas, that the commandant of the United States troops in this vicinity, be instructed to interfere to prevent such an inhuman outrage. Respectfully, "J. H. LANE,

"Chairman of Executive Committe, Kansas Territory.

"C. ROBINSON, Chairman Executive Committee of Safety.

"J. K. GOODIN,

"Secretary of Executive Committee, Kansas Territory.

"GEORGE W. DEITZLER, Secretary of Committee of Safety."

In two days afterwards they addressed another letter to the same official, requesting him to issue his proclamation forbidding an invasion. The President, whose ear had already listened to other representations, numbered the free state men among the disturbers of the peace, and equally as guilty as the Border Ruffians, in the following proclamation:

"WHEREAS, Indications exist that public tranquillity and the supremacy of law in the Territory of Kansas, are endangered by the reprehensible acts, or purposes of persons, both within and without the same, who propose to control and direct its political organizations by force; it appearing that combinations have been formed therein to resist the execution of the Territorial laws, and thus, in effect, subvert by violence all present constitutional and legal authority; it also appearing that persons residing without this Territory, but near its borders, contemplate armed intervention in the affairs thereof; it also appearing that other persons, inhabitants of remote States, are collecting money and providing arms for the same purpose; and it further appearing that combinations in the Territory are endeavoring, by the agencies of emissaries and otherwise, to induce individual States of the Union to interfere in the affairs thereof in violation of the Constitution of the United States; and, whereas, all such plans for the determination of the future institutions of the Territory, if carried into action from or within the same, will constitute the fact of insurrection, and from without that of invasive aggression, and will in either case justify and require the forcible interposition of the whole power of the General Government, as well to maintain the laws of the Territory as those of the Union.

"Now, therefore, I, Franklin Pierce, President of the United States, do issue this my proclamation, to command all persons engaged in unlawful combinations against the constituted authority of the Territory of Kansas, or of the United States, to disperse and retire peaceably to their respective abodes, and to warn all such persons that an attempted insurrection in said Territory, or aggressive intrusion into the same, will be resisted, not only by the employment of the local militia, but also by that of any available forces of the United States; to the end of assuring immunity from violence and full protection to the persons, property and civil rights of all peaceful and law abiding inhabitants of the Territory.

"If in any part of the Union the fury of faction or fanaticism, inflamed into disregard of the great principles of Popular Sovereignty, which, under the Constitution, are fundamental in the whole structure of our institutions, is to bring on the country the dire calamity of an arbitrament of arms in that Territory, it shall be between lawless violence on one side and conservative force on the other, wielded by legal authority of the General Government.

"I call on the citizens, both of adjoining and of distant States, to abstain from unauthorized intermeddling in the local concerns of the Territory, admonishing them that its organic law, is to be executed with impartial justice; that all individual acts of illegal interference, will incur condign punishment, and that any endeavor to interfere by organized force, will be firmly withstood.

"I invoke all good citizens to promote order by rendering obedience to the law; to seek remedy for temporary evils by peaceful means; to discountenance and repulse the counsels and the instigations of agitators and disorganizers; and to testify their attachment to their pride in its greatness, their appreciation of the blessings they enjoy, and their determination that republican institutions shall not fail in their hands, by co-operating to uphold the majesty of the laws and to vindicate the sanctity of the Constitution.

"In testimony whereof, I have hereunto set my hand and caused the seal of the United States to be affixed to these presents.

"Done at the City of Washington, eleventh day of February, in the year of our Lord, one thousand eight hundred and fifty-six, and of the Independence of the United States the eightieth.

"By the President. FRANKLIN PIERCE.

"W. L. MARCY, *Secretary of State.*"

This proclamation was evidently aimed at the free state men, and only tended to render their condition more helpless. While it arrayed their movements in disowning the Shawnee Legislature and refusing to observe its enactments directly against the power of the United States, it in no way restrained the violence of the Border Ruffians, who claimed to be acting under the laws and officers of their own making. This proclamation was received with general satisfaction among the pro-slavery men, except in one particular, viz: that they were engaged in open resistance to the laws of the Territory. At a meeting in Independence, Missouri, called to consider the proclamation, they passed resolutions denying that the people of the Border had in any way sought to resist the laws of the Territory, and proffering their assistance to the President to aid in the execution of said laws. Surely this was cool. Why should Missourians resist the laws? They made them and could change them whenever they wished. Said one of their spokesmen in the Wakarusa war. "We made them—Missouri made them—sir, and she has a right to enforce them; and if she don't who will?" Then this proclamation added "the whole force of the Government" to that of Missouri, in upholding the "bogus laws" of the Territory.

On the 16th of February, by a letter from Secretary Marcy, Governor Shannon was authorized "to make requisition upon the officers commanding the United States military forces at Fort Leavenworth and Fort Riley, for such assistance as may be needed" "for the suppression of insurrectionary combinations, or armed resistance to the execution of the laws."

CHAPTER XXVII.

STATE LEGISLATURE.

The winter passed by without any attack from the Missourians. It was the opinion of many that if the assault should be deferred, it would take place on the 4th of March, when the State Government should go into operation. "Senator Atchison, in his speech in Platte City," some time in February, "told his friends to hold themselves in readiness against the 4th of March, when they should be called upon to march into the Territory." A notice likewise appeared in the Independence "Dispatch," "for the militia of the border counties of Missouri to rendezvous at Fort Scott" on the 29th of February. These militia consisted of mounted riflemen, who could sweep through the Territory without opposition.

It was confidently asserted by the pro-slavery men after the President had issued his proclamation, that the assembling and organization of the free state Legislature, by its members taking the oath of office, would render them guilty of treason. President Pierce, in his message to Congress, had denounced the free state movement as revolutionary in character, and that if it should reach an organized resistance to the Territorial laws, it should be suppressed by the power of the General Government, and denominated it "treasonable insurrection." It was, therefore, feared by the friends of the free state movement that the members of the Legislature, on taking the oath of office, together with the state officers, would render themselves liable to arrest, on which account many advised against this step.

Nevertheless, the Legislature convened on the 4th of March, at Topeka, and likewise the officers of the State Government, agreeable to the call of the chairman of the Executive Committee. The House was called to order by Colonel J. H. Lane, the oath of office administered, and the roll called by the Secretary *pro tem.* Thirty-two men responded to their names as called. T. Minard, of Eastin, was elected Speaker; Joel K. Goodin, of Blanton, Clerk; Samuel Tappan, of Lawrence, assistant Clerk; J. Snodgrass and J. K. Goodin transcribing Clerks, and J. Mitchell Sergeant-at-Arms. The Senate having organized, both Houses went into joint session, to witness the installation of State officers. They all took the oath of office, which was administered by John Curtis, President *pro tempore* of the Senate. The Governor then delivered his inaugural address, of which one thousand copies were ordered to be printed.

The following day the Governor's message was received by both branches of the Assembly. It was a straight forward and high toned document. After referring to the difficulties in the way of forming a new state government, and calling attention to many subjects of importance that should engage their consideration, he referred to the relation of the new State government to that of the Territorial government, in the following discreet manner:

"It will be remembered that a skeleton of a government still exists in our midst, under the Territorial form, and although this was but the foreshadowing of a new and better covenant, collision with it should be carefully guarded against. A Territorial Government should be transient in its nature, only writing the action of the people to form one of their own. This action has been taken by the people of Kansas, and it only remains for the general Government to suspend its Territorial appropriations, recall its officers, and admit Kansas into the Union as a sovereign State.

"The reasons why the Territorial Government should be suspended and Kansas admitted into the Union as a State, are various, In the first place it is not the government of the people. The executive and judicial officers have been imposed upon the people by a distant power, and the officers thus imposed are foreign to our soil, and are accountable not to the people, but to the Executive 2,000 miles distant."

* * * * * * * * *

"Again; Governments are instituted for the good and protection of the governed, but the Territorial Government of Kansas has been, and still is, an instrument of oppres- and tyranny, unequalled in the history of our Republic. The only officers that attempted to administer the laws impartially, have been removed, and persons substituted who have aided in our subjugation."

* * * * * * * * *

"The Territorial Government should be withdrawn, because it is inoperative. The officers of the law permitted all manner of outrages and crime to be perpetrated by the invaders and their friends with impunity, while citizens proper are naturally law abiding, and order loving, disposed rather to suffer than do wrong. Several of the most aggravated murders on record have been committed, but as long as the murderers are on the side of the oppressors no notice is taken of them. Not one of the whole number has been brought to justice, and not one will be by the Territorial officers. While the mauraders are thus in open violation of all law, nine-tenths of the people scorn to recognize as law the enactments of a foreign body of men, and would sooner lose their right arm than bring an action in one of their misnamed courts. Americans can suffer death, but not dishonor, and sooner than the people will consent to recognize the edicts of the lawless as laws, their blood will mingle with the waters of the Kansas, and this Union will be rolled together in civil strife."

He then proceeded to review the late Legislature and the conduct of the President of the United States with reference to it, and likewise with reference to the free state movement.

Three Commissioners were appointed by joint ballot of both Houses to codify the laws for the State of Kansas. J. H. Lane and A. H. Reeder were elected United States Senators, to take their seats when the State should be admitted. Rules and regulations to govern the deliberations of the Legislature were reported and adopted. Several bills of too little importance to note were passed. Salaries and duties of State officers were fixed, and a bill for the encouragement of agriculture was passed. A memorial for Congress, in a Conference Committee of both bodies of the Legislature, was prepared and passed, asking the admission of Kansas to the Union as a State, under the Topeka Constitution. Without taking any steps that would necessarily bring the two governments in the Territory in conflict, the Legislature on the 15th of March adjourned until the 4th of July, 1856. They were not interrupted in their deliberations by attempts at arrest or interference of any kind. Sheriff Jones, however, attended the sessions, taking notes and recording the names of members and officers in a memorandum book.

The Executive Committee of Kansas Territory made its report to the Legislature and closed its existence. Its duties, powers, privileges and responsibilities, passed into the Executive Department of the new government. The workings of this committee, which exercised the functions of the primitive free state government, and directed the movement, which resulted in a free state organization, demands a more extended notice. The following is clipped from the "Herald of Freedom," and no doubt perfectly reliable :

" The committee held a meeting in Lawrence to decide upon a plan of action. Colonel Lane was appointed chairman and J. K. Goodin Secretary. They opened an office, and were almost constantly in session. Without money or any means, save such as was furnished by themselves, or the script which they issued, they organized the entire Territory into election districts, and held the election of October 9, 1855, for Delegates to the Charleston Convention. The expenses of that convention were defrayed by scrip, as were all the incidental expenses of sending agents through the Territory with election documents, holding elections and making returns at the adoption of the Constitution on the 15th of December, as well as the election of officers under it, on the 15th of January following.

"It is difficult to convey to the reader an idea of the vast amount of unrequited labor, which was performed on that occasion, and by that Committee. Judge Schuyler was commissioned, in December of 1855, to visit the East, and solicit funds for the Committee; but instead of appropriating the funds raised by him to enable the Committee to go on with their onerous duties, they were employed to pay the expenses of defending Lawrence against the invasion from Missouri, indorsed by Governor Shannon.

"Mr. Parrot also visited the East, his object being more specifically to make the acquaintance of members of Congress, and interest them in the affairs of Kansas, and in favor of the new constitution. It so happened that Mr. Holliday was compelled to be absent most of the time from the Executive sessions; hence, on the four remaining members of the Committee devolved the principal burden. Colonel Lane and Judge Smith were actively employed continually, while Mr. Goodin, as Secretary, found hardly time to repose. Their office was shifted from place to place to accommodate the necessities of the occasion, and during the winter it was with the greatest difficulty, at times, they could get up sufficient warmth to keep their hands in a condition for writing.

"The Committee, through their chairman, after having organized a State Legislature, submitted to that body a full report of their action, from which it appears that the whole cost of organizing, and perfecting the State Government to that date was but a trifle over eleven thousand dollars. They rendered to that body their books and papers, and thus completed their labor. Whether beneficial or otherwise, they accomplished with fidelity the duties they were commissioned to perform; and completed, in the brief period of less than six months, all the necessary work of projecting and setting in motion a State Government, and that in the face of difficulties, which ordinary men under like circumstances would have abandoned as impracticable.

"Complaints were made at the time because the constitution was not earlier submitted to Congress after its adoption by the people. The Committee vindicated themselves against this charge, and amply sustained their position before the country for the delay. They claimed that it was inexpedient to submit it to Congress until that body was fully organized, which was prevented by divisions there until near the close of January; then the difficulties at Eastin followed, which delayed action until about the time the State Legislature were to convene, when it was thought best to accompany it with a memorial from the State Legislature."

The writer has looked over the records of the Treasurer of the Executive Committee, and ascertained therefrom that the total amount of scrip issued by that body was $15,265.90. The Topeka Constitution required the first Legislature to make provisions for the redemption of this script, which it did; but as the Legislature itself never had any practical existence, its legislation was of no avail. This scrip at first was bought and sold in market, a considerable amount negotiated in the East to the friends of Kansas, and those who had faith in the Topeka Government. Much of it was employed in carrying on the Wakarusa war. When it became apparent that the Topeka Government would not succeed, it lost its value, and finally became worthless when that government was abandoned.

The following were the members of the first free state Legislature:

SENATORS.

Adams, J. M. Cole, J. Curtis, J. Daily, — Dunn, L. Fish, P. Fuller, J. C. Green, B. Harding, G. S. Hillyer, H. M. Hook, J. M. Irvin, D. E. Jones, S. B. McKenzie, B. W. Miller, J. H. Pillsbury, J. R. Rhaum, T. G. Thornton, W. W. Updegraff.

REPRESENTATIVES.

S. N. Hartwell, J. B. Abbott, John Hutchingson, H. F. Saunders, James Blood, C. Hornsbury, E. B. Purdam, J.

McGee, M. C. Dickey, W. R. Frost, W. A. Sumnerwell, S. McWhinney, S. T. Shores, S. R. Baldwin, David Rees, D. W. Cannon, Isaac Landers, J. M. Arthur, H. H. Williams, H. W. Labor, A. B. Marshall, J. D. Adams, T. W. Platt, Rees Furby, B. H. Brock, John Landis, E. R. Zimmerman, W. T. Burnett, L. P. Patty, F. A. Minard, Isaac Cady, Thomas Bowman, J. Brown, jr., Henry Todd, J. Hornby, Abraham Barre, Richard Murphy, William Hicks, B. R. Martin, William Bayliss, J. W. Stevens, J. K. Edsaul, S. J. Campbell, S. Goslin, H. B. Strandiford, Isaac B. Higgins, T. J. Addis, D. Toothman, William McClure, J. B. Wetson, William B. Wade, A. Jameson, A. D. Jones, William Crosby, S. Sparks, R. P. Brown, A. Fisher.

CHAPTER XXVIII.

CONGRESS—INVESTIGATING COMMITTEE.

The thirty-fourth Congress assembled on the 3d day of December, 1855. In the House neither party had a majority; the Senate was strongly pro-slavery. Congress partook of the excitement in which Kansas was involved, and which affected the whole country. Nine weeks were consumed in repeated efforts by the House to elect its Speaker. Finally a majority voted that the plurality rule should be applied to end the contest, whereupon Mr. N. P. Banks was elected. This was regarded as an anti-slavery triumph.

On the 4th of February Mr. Whitfield appeared as the duly elected delegate from Kansas Territory, was sworn in and took his seat in the House of Representatives. Mr. Reeder then came forward and gave notice that he would contest the seat of Mr. Whitfield, as the duly elected delegate from Kansas Territory. The latter claimed his seat because elected according to law, the former, because elected by the settlers of Kansas Territory.

The House, which had the power to determine the qualification of its members, chose not to trust to conflicting rumors in regard to Kansas affairs, but appointed a committee on the 19th of March to proceed to the scene of difficulties and take depositions in regard to them. The following are the resolutions of the House providing for the committee:

"March 19, 1856.

"*Resolved*, That a committee of three of the members of this House, to be appointed by the Speaker, shall proceed to inquire into and collect evidence in regard to the troubles in Kansas generally, and particularly in regard to any fraud or force attempted or practiced, in reference to any elections which have taken place in said Territory, either under the law organizing said Territory, or under any pretended law which may be alleged to have taken effect therein since. That they shall fully investigate and take proof of all violent and tumultuous proceedings in said Territory at any time since the passage of the Kansas-Nebraska act, whether engaged in by residents of said Territory, or by any person or persons from elsewhere, going into said Territory, and doing or encouraging others to do any act of violence or public disturbance against the laws of the United States, or the rights, peace and safety of the residents of said Territory, and for that purpose said committee shall have full power to send for and examine and take copies of all such papers, public records and proceedings as in their judgment shall be useful in the premises; and, also, to send for persons and examine them on oath or affirmation as to matters within their knowledge touching the matters of said investigation; and said committee, by their chairman, shall have power to administer all necessary oaths or affirmations connected with their aforesaid duties.

"*Resolved, further*, That said committee may hold their investigations at such places and times as to them may seem advisable, and that they have leave of absence from the duties of this House until they shall have completed such investigation. That they be authorized to employ one or more clerks and one or more assistant sergeants-at-arms to aid them in their investigations; and may administer to them an oath or affirmation faithfully to perform the duties assigned to them respectfully, and to keep secret all matters that may come to their knowledge, touching such investigation as said committee shall direct, until the report of the same shall be submitted to this House; and said committee may discharge any such clerk or assistant sergeant-at-arms, for neglect of duty or disregard of instructions in the premises, and employ others under like regulations.

"*Resolved, further*, That if any person shall in any manner obstruct or hinder said committee, or attempt to do so in their said investigation, or shall refuse to attend on said committee, and to give evidence when summoned for that purpose, or shall refuse to produce any paper, book, public record, or other proceeding in their possession or control, to said committee when so required, or shall make any disturbance where said committee are holding their sittings, the said committee may, if they see fit, cause any and every such person to be arrested by said assistant sergeant-at-arms and brought before this House, to be dealt with as for contempt.

"*Resolved, further*, That, for the purpose of defraying the expenses of said commission, there be and hereby is appropriated the sum of ten thousand dollars ($10,000) to be paid out of the contingent fund of this House.

"*Resolved, further*, That the President of the United States be and is hereby requested to furnish to said committee, should they be met with any serious opposition by bodies of lawless men, in the discharge of their duties aforesaid, such aid from any military force as may at the time be convenient to them, as may be necessary to remove such opposition, and enable said committee, without molestation, to proceed with their labors.

"*Resolved, further*, That when said committee shall have completed said investigation, they report all the evidence so collected to this House."

The following gentlemen were appointed members of this committee by the Speaker: Messrs. John Sherman, of Ohio; William A. Howard, of Michigan, and Mordecai Oliver, of Missouri. The committee, with four clerks, one reporter, and three sergeants-at-arms, arrived at Lecompton on the 18th of April, and immediately entered upon their work. Messrs. Reeder and Whitfield were requested to be present at the examination of witnesses, and to subpœna such witnesses as they chose. Many public papers and documents at Lecompton were authorized to be copied by the Committee. On the 23d of that month they met at Lawrence, where they began taking depositions. After taking sixty-four they adjourned successively to the following places, and continued their examinations: Tecumseh, Lawrence, Leavenworth City, Westport, steam boat "Polar Star," Detroit, New York and Washington. They were absent four months, and took three hundred and twenty-three depositions, and gathered a mass of various documents, all tending to throw light upon the affairs of Kansas. Their report was published in full, making a large octavo volume of twelve hundred and six pages, and containing an exposition of the most flagrant crimes and wanton outrages ever perpetrated in America. The committee reported "the following facts and conclusions as established by the testimony:"

"*First*, That each election in the Territory, held under the organic or alleged Territorial law, has been carried by organized invasion from the State of Missouri, by which the people of the Territory have been prevented from exercising the rights secured to them by the organic law.

"*Second*, That the alleged Territorial Legislature was an illegally constituted body, and had no power to pass valid laws, and their enactments are therefore null and void.

"*Third*, That these alleged laws have not, as a general thing, been used to protect persons and property and to punish wrong, but for unlawful purposes.

"*Fourth*. At the election under which the sitting delegate, John W. Whitfield, holds his seat, was not held in pursuance of any valid law, and that it should be regarded only as the expression of the choice of those resident citizens who voted for him.

"*Fifth*. That the election under which the contestant delegate, Andrew H. Reeder, claims his seat, was not held in pursuance to law, and that it should be regarded only as the choice of the resident citizens who voted for him.

"*Sixth*. That Andrew H. Reeder received a greater number of votes of resident citizens than John W. Whitfield for delegate.

"*Seventh*. That in the present condition of the Territory a fair election can not be held without a new census, a stringent and well guarded election law, the selection of impartial judges, and the presence of the United States troops at every place of election.

"*Eighth.* That the various elections held by the people of the Territory, preliminary to the formation of the State government, have been as regular as the disturbed condition of the Territory would allow; and that the Constitution passed by the convention held in pursuance of such elections embodies the will of the majority of the people."

The appointment of this committee was the work of the anti-slavery sentiment in the House, supported by those who desired the development of truth. Many of the people of the North imagined that the Kansas difficulties grew in an equal measure out of the distinct factions of settlers, pro-slavery and free state men, each aided and abetted by societies in the States. Others were disposed to regard accounts of invasion and outrages by Border Ruffians as greatly exaggerated. The appointment of this Committee was hailed with feelings of satisfaction in the North, as being the means of exhibiting the true status of affairs in the Territory of Kansas, and shaping the action of Congress in accordance with the wishes of the actual settlers.

On the other hand, the appointment of this Committee was bitterly opposed by pro-slavery men. Ninety-three voted against it in the House of Representatives, and one hundred and one for it. They had no desire to have matters settled in Kansas equitable and just to both parties interested. They fully knew the character of the proceedings of the Missourians, and had been advisory to them all. From the very beginning of the Kansas controversy, they had resolved that Kansas should be made a slave State, regardless of the means employed. They, therefore, desired no peaceable settlement of the question, unless it should be by surrendering Kansas up to slavery without a struggle.

Stung to madness by the prospect of having their black designs and vicious conduct exposed to the world, and the cause of justice vindicated, the Border Ruffians plunged into greater excesses of oppression and wickedness. Contempt for the General Government was openly declared, that Kansas should be made a slave State at every hazard, and in case of any interference on the part of Congress, the Union should be shivered into fragments.

They immediately began to carry out their previous and oft-repeated threats of war and extermination. The idea of blockading the Missouri was first announced in the "Squatter Sovereign," in these words:

"We suggest the propriety of the 'Border Ruffians' establishing a Quarantine, some where between St. Louis and Kansas City, where all steam boats may be searched, and the infectious political papers be prevented from tainting the air of Kansas Territory with their presence. We see no impropriety in, and should they not do it, they will have to bear the name of having so done. Have they not been branded as 'Ruffians,' 'Cut-throats,' 'Robbers' and 'Traitors'—if they are to bear such names, let them do something, we say, that will entitle them to the 'honor.' We are opposed to receiving something for nothing. We suggest Lexington as a suitable place for the establishment of a Political Quarantine."

This suggestion, which seemed ridiculous at first, was subsequently practically carried out. On the 9th of March the steamer "Arabia" was detained at Lexington, and a lot of Sharp's rifles, in the care of Mr. Hoyt, designed for the free state men, were taken off and retained by a mob. Henceforth we shall repeatedly notice the searching of boats, the indignities heaped upon free state passengers, and their frequent arrest and detention, until we shall see the Missouri River entirely blockaded against free state emigrants.

The Rev. Pardee Butler, as he was passing through Atchison, on the 30th of March, was again seized by a mob and subjected to gross indignities. The Ruffians, principally Southerners, headed by Robert S. Kelly, gave him a mock trial, first sentenced him to be hung, but afterwards changed it. They stripped him of his clothing to the waist, then applied tar and "cotton wool" to his body. Placing him in his buggy they conducted him to the suburbs of the city, and sent him home to his family on Stranger Creek, with the emphatic assurance that if they should catch him in Atchison again, they would certainly hang him.

The Investigating Committee made their report on the 1st of July to the House. The Committee on Contested Elections soon after introduced a resolution to oust Mr. Whitfield and admit Mr. Reeder, which was lost by 196 nays to 3 yeas. The question was divided and the resolution ousting Mr. Whitfield was passed, August 4, by 110 yeas to 92 nays; while the resolution admitting Mr. Reeder was defeated by 113 nays to 88 yeas.

CHAPTER XXIX.

THE LEADING FREE STATE MEN ARRESTED, OR DRIVEN FROM THE TERRITORY.

In April emigration from the different States in the Union began pouring into the Territory. In consequence of the threatening prospect of Kansas, a general interest and sympathy was felt for her free state settlers. Public meetings were held, speeches made, and exhortations given, for men to go to the rescue of the overpowered free state men in Kansas. Though many came to find homes in the Territory, yet others came more especially on account of the anticipated conflict. They came armed, prepared for, and expecting, a battle.

Among those who had gone East to lecture on Kansas difficulties, was Mr. S. N. Wood. He had left Kansas soon after the Wakarusa war to escape arrest by Sheriff Jones. He returned in April with a party of about one hundred from Ohio. Mr. Wood was identified with the free state movement from the beginning, and contributed much to its success. He is a genius in his way; extremely radical, always in politics and always elected. He is as aspiring, scheming and ambitious as Lane was, but a better man in principle and morals. He is now a Kansas Judge, and resides at Cotton Wood Falls.

Emigration likewise poured in from the South in great numbers. They were chiefly young men, of vicious and reckless characters. They were a mercenary set of rogues, who had been hired to come out and subdue Kansas. Their expenses were paid, a year's support guaranteed, and a promise of a homestead given. We have already noticed the preparation of the South to send out men to maintain slavery in Kansas. They came armed, as we have seen, and desired and expected a fight.

The chief band of Southern emigrants that came into the Territory this spring was led by Colonel Buford. They were a desperate class of young men, composed chiefly of thieves and robbers from Southern cities. They robbed their leader of a considerable sum of money on their way up the Missouri River, and soon fell into disrepute with the Missourians. On arriving at Kansas City, they were drawn up in military array and called upon to sign a pledge, and in the most sacrilegious manner, upon their bended knees, gave an oath that they would not leave Kansas until it was made a slave State; that they would be ready to fight for "Southern rights whenever called upon; that they would never vote anything but the pro-slavery ticket, and should be subject to the direction of their leaders," &c. A business contract was likewise promulgated, which created dissatisfaction, because the Southern youths declared it different from that which had been presented on their setting out. They were quartered for some time along the Border, and supported by contributions from the South and levies upon the Border towns. We shall narrate some of the flagrant acts and brutal outrages committed by these Southern gentry during the following summer.

Not all of these Southern emigrants were rogues. Some were high minded and honorable young men, many of whom soon became disgusted with the whole pro-slavery proceedings in Kansas and returned home.

The persecutions were commenced by attempts on the part of Territorial authorities to arrest free state men for old or trivial offenses. On the 19th of April Sheriff Jones made his appearance in Lawrence, and proceeded to arrest S. N. Wood, who had just returned, upon the stale charge of rescuing Branson. He obtained possession of his person, but a crowd gathering around, by a kind of sportive mockery and ridiculous interference, diverted the Sheriff's attention, slipped his pistol from him, and permitted the prisoner to quietly walk away. Jones thus baffled in the discharge of his functions as bogus Sheriff, left the town in rage and repaired to Lecompton. There he gathered a posse of four men, and returned to Lawrence on the following day—Sunday—with additional warrants against those who had indirectly aided Wood's escape. The citizens were quietly and peaceably assembling for church when he entered the town. He summoned some of those with whom he met to assist him in his arrests, but they passed on and paid no attention to him. He searched for Wood, but was unable to find him. Seeing Tappan, one of Branson's rescuers, in the crowd, which by this time had gathered to witness the pompous display of legal authority, the Sheriff pounced upon him with great violence. It will be remembered that this individual had been arrested before, and was anxious for trial in order to test the Territorial laws in the Supreme Court; but he could not get a hearing before the Territorial Courts. Jones having seized him so roughly, he struck the official. This was indignity and contempt enough. The Sheriff left in rage, declaring "he would bring in the troops, and the arrests should be made. He had now some forty names on his paper, against whom warrants should be served."

This was no empty threat; for the execution of it would afford a pretext for what the Sheriff had long plotted to accomplished—the destruction of Lawrence. On returning to Lecompton he addressed the Governor, stating the above facts, and that he had been resisted in his attempts at arrests, his prisoners rescued and violence offered himself, and called upon the Governor for a military force to enable him to execute his warrants.

Governor Shannon immediately wrote to Colonel Sumner, requesting an officer and six men from the Federal forces, to act as a posse for the Sheriff in executing his warrants. Colonel Sumner, who at once complied by sending a detachment of ten men, under Lieutenant McIntosh, sent the following letter to Lawrence:

"HEADQUARTERS 1ST CAVALRY,
"FORT LEAVENWORTH, April 22, 1856.

"SIR: A small detachment proceeds to Lecompton this morning on the requisition of the Governor, under orders of the President, to assist the Sheriff of Douglas County in executing several writs, in which he says he has been resisted. I know nothing of the merits of the case and have nothing to do with them. But I would respectfully impress upon you and others in authority, the necessity of yielding obedience to the proclamation and orders of the General Government. Ours is emphatically a government of laws, and if they are set at naught there is an end of all order. I feel assured that on reflection you will not compel me to resort to violence in carrying out the orders of the Government. I am, sir, very respectfully, your obedient servant, E. V. SUMNER,
"Colonel 1st Cavalry, Commanding.

"To the Mayor of Lawrence."

Mr. Jones, arriving at Lawrence on the 23d of April, with his United States *posse comitatus*, arrested six respectable citizens on the charge of contempt, for not responding to his call for help a few days previous. These prisoners were lodged in a small room under the guard of dragoons, instead of being brought before a Squire and admitted to bail. In thus treating them as felons, it was evidently the design to exasperate the feelings of their friends and provoke a rescue. The quasi-Sheriff had obtained another warrant to arrest Mr. S. N. Wood, from the United States

Marshal, upon the charge of larceny, but was unable to find him.

That evening Mr. Jones remained with Lieutenant McIntosh in his tent. About 10 o'clock at night he was fired upon three times from the darkness, the third shot taking effect in his spine between his shoulders. He fell apparently dead, and was quickly carried to the hotel, the surgical aid of Dr. Stringfellow called in, and every attention and care was bestowed upon the wounded man.

At this tragical occurrence all was excitement and confusion in town. No one knew who the assassin could be, and no traces of him could be discovered. The people of Lawrence were as ignorant and innocent in regard to the attempted murder as the friends of Jones. And the author is not aware that it is known to this day who committed the offense. On the next morning the citizens who deprecated the unfortunate event, met and passed resolutions declaring the act "unexpected and unlooked for by the community, and unsustained by any portion of them;" that "it was an atrocious outrage upon Mr. Jones, and an insult and injury to the public sentiment and reputation of our town, and a crime deserving condign punishment;" that "we deeply sympathize with the wounded man, and will afford him all the aid and comfort in our power;" "that a committee of five be appointed, whose duty it shall be to investigate the circumstances connected with this deplorable occurrence, and, if possible, to ferret out the guilty agent." No sympathy was manifested for the murderous act, and a reward of $500 was offered by George W. Dietzler, as Secretary of the Committee of Safety, for the apprehension of the assassin.

Sam. Salters, an ignorant brute, was immediately constituted deputy Sheriff, in consequence of the disability of Jones. He, with deputy Marshal Fain, a South Carolinian, continued the harass of free state men. They had writs for the arrest of the rescuers of Branson, and many who had treated with indifference Mr. Jones' call for assistance. These men, unwilling to be dragged away from home and cast into prison, or to recognize the bogus authority by giving bail; not wishing to come into conflict with the United States troops, which, by order of the President, were now brought to bear upon them, they determined to elude the search of the Territorial officials and thus escape arrests. This they did most effectually for several days. Some would secrete themselves in brush or ravines during the day and visit their homes at night; others whose homes were more constantly watched, dared not even do this, but would repose at night wherever they found it safest. Free state families left their doors unlocked that fugitives might find shelter beneath their roofs. All the while Salters and Fain, with a United States posse trooping at their heels, continued incessantly their search, visiting the homes of free state men, pursuing the fleeing fugitives. Many laughable and exciting incidents could be related about this hunting for free men; but our space will not allow us.

Meantime Lawrence, the doomed city, the Ilium of Kansas, had been environed by armed men, and all egress precluded by bands of patrols. Two days before Jones was shot a company of Ruffians had encamped in the Delaware reserve, opposite Lawrence. Great excitement prevailed in the town. General Whitfield, who had been attending the meetings of the Investigating Committee, declared it unsafe for himself and witnesses to remain there, and requested the Committee to adjourn to some other place. Mr. Oliver made a motion to that effect, but it was lost, and the Committee continued its work at Lawrence.

Colonel Sumner, who had received a dispatch from Lieutenant McIntosh in regard to the Lawrence difficulties, immediately set out with his command for Lecompton. He reported himself to the Governor, who informed him that no more arrests could be made in Lawrence, as the persons against whom writs were held had fled the country, and that a small posse would answer the purposes of the deputy Sheriff. The Colonel returned to Fort Leavenworth soon afterwards.

Colonel Sumner, while in camp near Lawrence, wrote a note to Governor Robinson advising non-resistance to legal processes, and thus avoid a conflict with the United States forces under his command, and that the people of Lawrence should take measures for the arrest of Jones' assassin. Governor Robinson replied that the citizens of Lawrence condemned the shooting of Mr. Jones; that they were without any municipal government, and hence had no one to speak officially for them; that he believed they were loyal to the Government and ready to do all in their power to maintain the laws. He likewise sent a copy of the resolutions passed at the meeting of the citizens relative to the attack upon Mr. Jones.

Mr. Reeder having failed to obey a subpœna to appear before the Grand Jury of Douglas County, a writ of attachment was issued for contempt of court. This was placed in the hands of deputy Marshal Fain, who, on the 7th of May, proceeded to execute it. He found Mr. Reeder in the room with the Investigating Committee at Lawrence. Mr. Reeder had been indefatigable in his efforts to elicit truth before the Committee by introducing witnesses and cross-examining others. The object of his subpœna and arrest, it was thought, was to deprive him from serving the Committee. From the deep hatred with which the pro-slavery party regarded him on account of his impartiality as Executive of the Territory, and his final alliance with the free state party, it was apprehended that his person would be greatly endangered among the ruffians at Lecompton. When the writ was placed in his hands, he appealed to the Committee for protection as privileged from arrest as a member of Congress, and because having been cited to appear with them to take part in the investigation. The Committee, after consultation, decided that "the privilege from arrest given by the laws to the members of this Committee and the sitting and contesting delegates was not a matter for them to enforce, and declined to make any decision whatever, or take any action upon the application thus made."

Mr. Reeder, on hearing this decision of the Committee, rose to his feet, and, looking the Marshal steadily in the face, said: "As the Committee have refused to protect me, I fall back upon my natural rights, and any man who lays hands upon me, whether as an officer or otherwise, does so at his peril." The timid Marshal quailed before this stern language, left the room, and retired to Franklin to consult his Southern friends who had gathered there.

Indictments and writs were made out against all the leading free state men in the Territory. Some were indicted for high treason and usurpation of office; others for perjury, contempt of court, larceny, &c. Agreeable to the instructions of Chief Justice Lecompte, the Grand Jury of Douglas County indicted for treason, Andrew H. Reeder, Charles Robinson, James H. Lane, George W. Brown, George W. Deitzler, George W. Smith, S. N. Wood and Gaius Jenkins.

The following day the Committee adjourned and proceeded to Tecumseh in company with several free state men. While there it was ascertained through Mr. Legate, a member of the Grand Jury then sitting at Lecompton, that indictments would be issued by that body against all the leading free state men of Douglas County, and writs for their arrest. In consequence of the representations of Mr. Legate, to whom the pro-slavery men had revealed their plans, it was apparent that the design of this movement on the part of the Territorial authorities, was to arrest and hold in custody all the State officers and members of the Legislature, and thus prevent the Topeka Government from going into practical operation. To thwart that design it was decided, at a conference between Messrs. Sherman and

Howard, of the Committee, and Messrs. Roberts and Robinson, that the free state officers residing in Douglas County should avoid arrest, and that the Lieutenant Governor, who resided in Shawnee County, should call a meeting of the Legislature on the 15th of June, before the opening of the session of the Grand Jury in that county, which it was known would immediately issue indictments, not only against the State officers residing within their jurisdiction, but also against every member of the Legislature, which had previously assembled at Topeka. The Legislature thus assembled in advance of the Grand Jury in that county, should immediately enact a militia law for the organization and equipment of the State forces, with a view to sustain and uphold the State Government. Then should the Territorial authorities seek to arrest any of the members of the Legislature or of the State Government, they should be resisted by force. In this way it was the design of the free state men to put themselves in the attitude of defending their State Government instead of their individual persons in opposing the arrests.

The free state officers against whom it was known writs were to be issued by the Grand Jury for their apprehension, and who should succeed in eluding all efforts for their arrest, were to meet with the other officers and members of the Legislature at Topeka, and all unite in opposition to interference with the discharge ot their official functions. But, as we shall see, this whole plan was entirely frustrated by the failure of these men to escape arrest.

With a view to enable him to avoid this anticipated arrest, Governor Robinson was selected to visit the free States, ascertain their feelings and secure their support in the coming conflict in the Territory ; to convey a portion of the testimony taken by the Congressional Committee to Washington to prevent its being destroyed by a mob, as was feared. He designed to return by the time the Legislature should meet. He had proceeded down the Missouri River as far as

Lexington, when he was taken from the boat on the pretext that he was fleeing from an indictment. Notwithstanding he assured those who arrested him, that he was not aware of any indictment having been found against him, that he had not at any time attempted to conceal himself, that the Marshal in the Territory could have arrested him at any hour while there, and that if he had been desiring to escape he would certainly have avoided Lexington, they persisted in their demands. Mrs. Robinson, who had charge of the official documents, was permitted to pass on the next day. She visited several of the States and performed the object for which her husband had set out.

Governor Robinson was thus seized without the least show of authority. The indictment for treason was issued a week subsequently. But evidently the citizens of Lexington understood that it was to be issued. He was detained more than a week at this place, until Governor Shannon made requisition upon the Governor of Missouri for his return to the Territory. He was conveyed first to Independence, thence to Westport, thence to Franklin in a carriage, in charge of Colonel Preston and Captain Donaldson. At the latter place orders were received by the Marshal from Governor Shannon to return to Kansas City and proceed to Lecompton by way of Leavenworth, lest their prisoner should be forcibly taken from them by Ruffians, who had sacked Lawrence the day before, and who still lingered in that vicinity, and by them suffer violence and, perhaps, death. Arriving at Leavenworth on the 24th of May, the prisoner was placed under the guard of Captain Martin, of the Kickapoo Rangers, and three other men. Here he was detained during the reign of terror in that city, of which we shall speak in another place. Captain Martin faithfully guarded him, although many attempts were made at his destruction. Judge Lecompte slept by the door of the room in which Governor Robinson was kept, and General Richardson slept in the same bed with

Gov. Reeder's escape down the Missouri River in a Skiff

him, to shield him in case of an attack. On the 1st of June he was conveyed to Lecompton and placed in camp with seven other prisoners like himself.

Governor Reeder on the day that Marshal Fain attempted to arrest him finding it unsafe to remain longer with the Investigating Committee, retired to a friend's house in the vicinity of Lawrence. After remaining there a few days, seeing all the powers of the Government arrayed against him, and threatened by lawless ruffians, he determined to leave the Territory. But his enemies not finding him at Lawrence, had sent messengers to all the border towns to intercept his exit from the Territory. Guards were stationed along the roads and at the steamboat landings, up and down the Missouri for some distance. With the assistance of Mr. Jenkins, he eluded the vigilance of his enemies and arrived safe at Kansas City. Here Mr. Eldridge took charge of him and secreted him in the American Hotel. His concealment becoming more unsafe every day, and there being no other mode of escape, he disguised himself in the dress of an Irish laborer, cut off his whiskers and moustache, with an ax on his shoulder, a budget in his hand and a pipe in his mouth sauntered around unnoticed. As soon as it was dark, in company with Mr. Edward Eldridge, he entered a skiff on the river and rowed during that night twenty-eight miles, to Liberty Landing. Here they waited until a boat came along, when Mr. Reeder went aboard, took deck passage with the hands, and descended to St. Charles. Disembarking at this place he made his way across the country to Illinois in safety.

Mr. G. W. Brown, editor of "The Herald of Freedom," returning to Kansas City on the 14th of May, after an absence from the Territory of several weeks, soon found himself watched by a mob. This was at the same time Mr. Reeder was there. About two o'clock the following morning, it having been announced that the coast was clear, in company with Mr. Jenkins, he set out on horseback for

Lawrence. They had proceeded but a short distance before they were arrested and taken to Milt. McGee's house, one mile south of the city. The next morning they were conveyed to Westport where they were detained for some time and joined by their wives. They were subsequently conveyed, by a circuitous route, south of Lawrence, to Lecompton, and placed under guard. Mr. Jenkins was soon released, but, as we shall see, soon recaptured. Their affectionate wives clung tenaciously and tenderly to them, sheltered them from many indignities and, perhaps, murder.

The following is a copy of the indictment against the leading free state men on the charge of treason:

"UNITED STATES OF AMERICA,
"Territory of Kansas, County of Douglas. }

"*In the District Court of the First Judicial District of the Territory of Kansas. April Term, A. D.* 1856.

"The Grand Jurors of the United States of America within and for the First Judicial District, Douglas County, Territory of Kansas, sworn to inquire upon their oath, present, that Andrew H. Reeder, Charles Robinson, James H. Lane, George W. Brown, George W. Deitzler, George W. Smith, Samuel N. Wood, Gaius Jenkins, late of the County of Douglas, First Judicial District of the Territory of Kansas, owing allegiance to the United States of America, wickedly devising and intending, the peace and tranquillity of the said United States, to disturb and to prevent the execution of the law thereof within the same, to wit: 'the law of the said United States, entitled an act to organize the Territories of Nebraska and Kansas, approved May 30, 1854, on the first day of May, in the year of our Lord one thousand eight hundred and fifty-six, in the County, District and Territory aforesaid, and within the jurisdiction of this court, wickedly and traitorously did intend to levy war against the said United States within the same, and to fulfill and to bring to effect the said traitorous intention of him the said [names], afterwards, that is to say on the 17th day of May in the year of our Lord one thousand eight hundred and fifty-six, in the said Territory, District and County aforesaid, and within the jurisdiction of this court, with a great multitude of persons, whose names to the Grand Jurors are unknown to a great number, to wit: the number of one hundred persons and upwards, armed and arrayed in warlike manner, that is to say, with guns, swords, artillery, and other warlike weapons, as well offensive as defensive, being then and there unlawfully and traitorously assembled, did traitorously assemble and combine against the said United States, and then and there, with force and arms, wickedly and traitorously, and with the wicked and traitorous intention, to oppose and prevent by means of intimidation and violence, the execution of said law of the said United States within the same, and array and dispose themselves in a warlike and hostile manner against the said United States, and then and there with force, and in pursuance of such traitorous intention, they, the said [names], with the said persons so, as aforesaid, traitorously assembled, armed and arrayed in the manner aforesaid, wickedly and traitorously did levy war against the said United States, and further, to fulfill and bring to effect the said traitorous intention of him, the said [names], and in pursuance and in execution of said wicked intention and traitorous combination, to oppose, resist and prevent the said law of the United States from being carried into execution in the Territory and District aforesaid, they, the said [names], afterwards, to wit: on the 17th day of May, A. D. 1856, in the Territory, District and County aforesaid, and within the jurisdiction of this court, with the said persons whose names to the said Grand Jurors aforesaid are unknown, did wickedly and traitorously assemble against said United States, with the avowed intention by force of arms and intimidation to prevent the execution ot the said law of the United States, within the same, and with the intention then and there and thereby to subvert the Government of the said United States, in the same Territory of Kansas, and in pursuance and in the execution of said wicked and traitorous combination and intention, they, the said, [names], then and there, with force, with the said persons to a great number, to wit: the number of one hundred persons and upwards, armed and arrayed in a warlike manner, that is to say, with guns, pistols, swords, artillery, and other warlike weapons, as well offensive as defensive, did then and there unlawfully and traitorously assemble for the purpose and design of overthrowing and subverting, by force and violence, the Government of the said United States, in the Territory of Kansas aforesaid, contrary to the form of the statute in such case made and provided, and also against the peace and dignity of the United States.

"A. I. ISAACS,
"United States District Attorney of Kansas Territory."

CHAPTER XXX.

THE SIEGE OF LAWRENCE.

From the time Sheriff Jones first failed in his arrests at Lawrence and called upon the Governor for a posse, Border Ruffians began to congregate in the vicinity of that town. The Southerners, who had assumed nomadic habits, on coming into the Territory, were the first to encompass the devoted city.

The attempt upon the life of Mr. Jones was a happy pretext for the assembling of all the Border Ruffian forces. The "Squatter Sovereign" declared, "*His death must be avenged. His murder shall be avenged if at the sacrifice of every abolitionist in the Territory.*" "We are now in favor of leveling Lawrence and chastising the traitors there congregated, should it result in the total destruction of the Union." It censured the Governor for calling upon the United States troops without first calling out the militia, to whom the duty properly belonged. In the next number the editors suggested as the motto of the Border Ruffians in all future difficulties with the abolitionists, "war to the knife, and knife to the hilt; neither asking quarters nor granting them."

When Deputy Marshal Fain failed to arrest Reeder, instead of reporting to the Governor and applying to him for aid, he consulted with Marshal Donaldson, who issued the following proclamation that was circulated only along the Border:

"PROCLAMATION.

"*To the People of Kansas Territory:*

"*Whereas*, Certain judicial arrests have been directed to me by the First District Court of the United States, etc., to be executed within the county of Douglas, and whereas an attempt to execute them by the United States Deputy Marshal was evidently resisted by a large number of the people of Lawrence, and as there is every reason to believe that any attempt to execute these writs will be resisted by a large body of armed men; now, therefore, the law abiding citizens of the Territory are commanded to be and appear at Lecompton, as soon as practicable, and in numbers sufficient for the execution of the law.

"Given under my hand this 11th day of May, 1856.

J. B. DONALDSON,

"United States Marshal for the Territory of Kansas."

"P. S. No liability for expenses will be incurred by the United States until its consent is obtained."

Meantime the people of Lawrence, becoming alarmed at the hostile demonstrations of the bands of Southerners around them, committing depredations, stopping loaded wagons and confiscating the contents, detaining travelers, robbing houses and stealing cattle and horses, addressed the following letter:

"LAWRENCE CITY, May 11, 1856.

"*To His Excellency*, WILSON SHANNON, *Governor of Kansas Territory:*

"DEAR SIR: The undersigned are charged with the duty of communicating to your Excellency the following preamble and resolution, adopted at a public meeting of the citizens of this place, at 7 o'clock last evening, viz:

"WHEREAS, We have the most reliable information from various parts of the Territory, and the adjoining State of Missouri, of the organization of gurilla bands, who threaten the destruction of our town and its citizens; therefore,

"*Resolved*, That Messrs. Topliff, Hutchingson and Roberts, constitute a committee to inform his Excellency of these facts, and to call upon him in the name of the people of Lawrence, for protection against such bands, by the United States troops at his disposal.

"All of which is very respectfully submitted, &c.,

"C. W. Topliff,
"W. Y. Roberts,
"John Hutchingson."

To this, Governor Shannon, who was now surrounded by Border Ruffians, made the following reply:

"Executive Office, May 12, 1856.

"Gentlemen: Your note of the 11th inst. is received, and in reply I have to state that there is no force around or approaching Lawrence, except the largely constituted posse of the United States Marshal and Sheriff of Douglas County, each of whom, I am informed, have a number of writs in their hands for execution against persons in Lawrence. I shall in no way interfere with either of these officers in the discharge of their official duties.

"If the citizens of Lawrence submit themselves to the Territorial laws, and aid and assist the Marshal and Sheriff in the execution of processes in their hands, as all good citizens are bound to do when called upon, they, or all such, will entitle themselves to the protection of the law. But, so long as they keep up a military or armed organization to resist the Territorial laws and the officers charged with their execution, I shall not interpose to save them from the legitimate consequences of their illegal acts.

"I have the honor to be yours with great respect.

"Wilson Shannon.

"Messrs. C. W. Topliff, John Hutchingson, W. Y. Roberts."

By a public meeting held in Lawrence on the 13th of May, it was resolved that the allegations and charges against them in the Marshal's proclamation "are wholly untrue in fact and the considerations which are drawn from them;" that they will acquiesce in the service upon them of any judicial writs against them "by the United States Marshal for Kansas Territory, and will furnish him a posse for that purpose, if so requested; but that" they "are ready to resist, if need be, unto death, the ravages and desolations of an invading mob."

The leaders of the free state men had all left the Territory. Robinson, Reeder and Lane were absent. The people were without a leader, and hence confused, divided, yet filled with apprehensions; the evils of danger that environed the city, thickened and tightened, the more alarmed they became—the more anarchy and dissension prevailed in their midst.

There was a remnant of the old Committee of Safety that had rendered itself equal to a similar emergency, but its chief men, those in whom the people had confidence, were gone. This remnant met, and decided upon its policy. It favored submission and non-resistance—was opposed to military organization and preparation. This did not satisfy a large class of the citizens and the Committee resigned.

A meeting of the citizens was immediately called and a new Committee of Safety elected, composed of the following persons: W. Y. Roberts, G. W. Deitzler, Lyman Allen, John A. Perry, C. W. Babcock, S. B. Prentise, A. H. Mallory, and Joel Grover. In a day or two, S. C. Pomeroy arrived from the East, and was constituted chairman by acclamation. This Committee endorsed the action of the old Committee. The reasons for this decision are here given by a gentleman present at the time, and a friend of the Committee:

"The ground distinctly assumed was that in this first movement of the Federal authority to espouse the cause of the Southern Ruffians, they should have a clear field to show their hands. In Congress it had been confidently asserted by Douglas and others, that the people of the Territory were in open resistance to the Federal authority—rebels and traitors. They would at the first opportunity verify the slanderous charge. If they should proceed, as we felt confident they would, to commit outrages, the *United* States Government should be responsible."

It will be seen that the circumstances now were not exactly similar to those last winter when the town was threatened. Then the Ruffians were alone, excepting the Territorial authorities; now they led the United States forces and carried the sanction of the General Government in their assaults upon Lawrence. It was the Federal troops that created the embarrassment; for no one wished to resist or fight them.

The decision of the Committee was not satisfactory; murmers were loud, and discontent manifest. Some held that the Marshal should be permitted to enter the town, but his posse should be kept out. Others were for arming themselves with nothing but revolvers, proceeding to Franklin and offering themselves to the Marshal as a part of his posse, and thus get hold of the United States arms. The Committee offered to resign, but the majority of the citizens refused to accept their resignation, there being no men then in Lawrence in whom they had more confidence.

When the policy of non-resistance was definitely determined upon, many left the place and sought shelter and safety in the country and surrounding towns. Word was sent to the military companies in various parts of the Territory, who were then marching, or preparing to march, to the rescue, that their services were not needed. Those who had thus set out for Lawrence returned home, except the Wakarusa Company, which remained prepared for action during the entire period.

Marshal Donaldson's proclamation had the designed effect of gathering the Southern chivalry and Border Ruffians around Lawrence. On the same day it was issued a company of one hundred, under the command of Dr. Stringfellow and Kelley, editors of the "Squatter Sovereign," left Atchison for Lecompton. Generals Atchison and Stringfellow mustered the Platte County riflemen, and marched across the Delaware Reserve. The South Carolinians, Georgians, Alabamians, Floridians and Mississippians, who were encamped at Franklin, were increased by Missourians from Westport, Kansas City, and Independence. As the numbers around Lawrence multiplied, their depredations increased. Provisions were taken from farm houses, horses "pressed into the service," private arms seized and travelers molested.

On the 13th of May, Mr. A. J. Weaver, assistant sergeant-at-arms of the Congressional Committee, who was on his way to Lawrence with a witness, was stopped, taken into custody by the self-styled militia, and carried to Lecompton. After considerable delay he was permitted to proceed with the following pass:

"LECOMPTON, Kansas, May 13, 1856.

"*To all whom it may concern*:

"This is to certify that I have examined the papers of Mr. A. J. Weaver, in company with General Cramer, and I am satisfied that he is acting under the authority of the United States House of Representatives and should pass unmolested.
WARREN D. WILKES,
"Of South Carolina."

On the 16th, Mr. Stowell, coming from Kansas City, was stopped at Franklin and fifty old fashioned muskets taken from his wagon, that were designed for Lawrence. A wagon load of flour was likewise seized.

Dr. Root and Mr. Mitchell returning from Lawrence to Wabansee on the 14th of May, on passing the camp of Marshal Donaldson, were taken prisoners; two gentlemen, a little in advance of Messrs. Root and Mitchell were accosted, but escaped by the fleetness of their horses amid a shower of bullets. At the same time Judge Conway and Hon. P. C. Schuyler returning to the Territory from a tour in the States, were taken from a boat at Parkville and detained by a mob, but were soon released through the interference of the more respectable class of citizens.

On the 13th of May Mr. Cox, a pro-slavery man of Lawrence, was deputed to visit Marshal Donaldson to see if some arrangements might not be made to remove the necessity for bringing his posse into the town. Mr. Donaldson replied: "The three following demands must be complied with before I shall consent not to enter Lawrence with all my force: First, That every man, against whom a warrant is issued, shall be surrendered up. Second, All munitions of war in Lawrence, shall be delivered up. Third, That the citizens of Lawrence pledge themselves implicitly to obey the present enactments of Kansas—test oaths, taxes and all."

On the reception of this answer, the people of Lawrence assembled in council, which gave rise to the following letter:

"LAWRENCE, May 14, 1856.

"J. B. DONALDSON, *United States Marshal, for Kansas Territory:*

"DEAR SIR: We have seen a proclamation issued by yourself, dated 11th of May, inst., and also have reliable information this morning, that large bodies of armed men, in pursuance of your proclamation, have assembled in the vicinity of Lawrence.

"That there may be no misunderstanding, we beg leave to ask respectfully, that we may be reliably informed what are the demands against us. We desire to state most truthfully and earnestly, that no opposition will now or at any future time, be offered to the execution of any legal process by yourself or any person acting for you. We also pledge ourselves to assist you, if called upon, in the execution of any legal process.

"We declare ourselves to be order-loving and law-abiding citizens, and only await an opportunity to test our fidelity to the laws of the country, the Constitution and the Union.

"We are informed also, that these men collecting about Lawrence openly declare that their intention is to destroy the town, and drive off the citizens. Of course we do not believe that you would give any countenance to such threats, but, in view of the excited state of the public mind, we ask protection of the constituted authorities of the Government, declaring ourselves in readiness to co-operate with them for the maintenance of the peace, order and quiet of the community in which we live. Very respectfully,

"ROBERT MORROW,
"LYMAN ALLEN,
"JOHN HUTCHINGSON."

Mr. Cox delivered this letter and brought back the following reply:

"OFFICE OF THE U. S. MARSHAL,
"LECOMPTON, K. T., May 15, 1856.

"*Messrs.* G. W. DEITZLER *and* J. H. GREEN, *Lawrence, Kansas Territory:*

"On yesterday I received a communication addressed to me, signed by one of you as President, and the other as Secretary, purporting to have been adopted by a meeting of the citizens of Lawrence, held on yesterday morning. After speaking of a proclamation issued by myself, you state, 'That there may be no misunderstanding, we beg leave to ask respectfully, that we may be reliably informed what are the demands against us. We desire most truthfully and earnestly to declare that no opposition whatever will now, or at any future time, be offered to the execution of any legal process by yourself or any person acting for you. We also pledge ourselves to assist you if called upon, in the execution of any legal process, etc.'

"From your professed ignorance of the demands against you, I must conclude that you are STRANGERS and not CITIZENS of Lawrence, or of recent date, or been absent for some time; more particularly when an attempt was made by my deputy to execute the process of the First District Court of the United States for Kansas Territory, against ex-Governor Reeder, when he made a speech in the room and in the presence of the Congressional Committee, and denied the power and authority of said court, and threatened the life of said deputy, if he attempted to execute said process, which speech and defiant threats were loudly applauded by some one or two hundred of the citizens of Lawrence, who had assembled at the room on learning the business of the Marshal, and made such hostile demonstrations that the deputy thought he and his small posse would endanger their lives in executing said process.

"Your declaration that you will truthfully and earnestly offer now, or at any future time, no opposition to the execution of any legal process, &c., is indeed difficult to understand. May I ask, gentlemen, what has produced this wonderful change in the minds of the people of Lawrence? Have their eyes been suddenly opened, so that they are now able to see that there are laws in Kansas Territory which should be obeyed? Or is it that just now, those for whom I have writs have sought refuge elsewhere? Or it may possibly be that you now, as heretofore, expect to screen yourselves behind the word 'legal,' so significantly used by you. How am I to rely on your pledges when I am well aware that the whole population of Lawrence is armed and drilled, and the town fortified—when, too, I recollect, the meetings and resolutions adopted in Lawrence and elsewhere in the Territory, openly defying the laws and the officers thereof, and threatening to resist the same to a bloody issue, as recently verified in the attempted assassination of Sheriff Jones, while in the discharge of his official duties in Lawrence. Are you strangers to all these things? Surely you must be strangers at Lawrence. If no outrages have been committed by the citizens of Lawrence against the laws of the land, they need not fear any posse of mine. But I must take the liberty of executing all processes in my hands as the United States Marshal, in my own time and manner, and shall only use such power as is authorized by law. You say you call upon the constituted authorities of the Government for protection. This, indeed, sounds strange, coming from a large body of men, armed with Sharp's rifles, and other implements of war, bound together by oaths and pledges, to resist the laws of the Government they call on for protection. All persons in Kansas Territory, without regard to location, who honestly submit to the constituted authorities, will ever find me ready to aid in protecting them; and who seek to resist the laws of the land and turn traitors to their country, will find me aiding in enforcing the laws, if not as an officer, as a citizen.

"Respectfully yours,

"J. B. Donaldson,

"U. S. Marshal, Kansas Territory."

Again the citizens of Lawrence sent a letter to the Marshal, calling his attention to the depredations committed by his men in the vicinity of their city, to which no reply was given. Every thing was done to avert the calamity, of which peaceable measures would admit. Deputation after deputation visited the Governor, and invoked his influence and authority to stay the madness and lawlessness of the mob; they visited the Marshal also, and plead with him the cause of humanity and justice; but they were met only with rebuke, and were frequently taken prisoners, robbed, tried, and otherwise mistreated. Messengers passed between Lawrence and Leavenworth night and day, endeavoring to secure the interposition or protection of the United States troops. The influence of the Congressional Committee was invoked and the humane feelings of Colonel Sumner touched; but in vain, the troops could not move without orders.

One effort seemed to furnish for a season a prospect of success. On the 18th ot May Messrs. S. W. and T. B. Eldridge undertook the embassy to the encampment of the sons of the South. They had just removed from Kansas City to Lawrence, and opened their nicely finished and richly furnished hotel. They were not, therefore, personally obnoxious to pro-slavery men, and on this account were chosen for this work. They carried a letter from the Committee proffering that if Governor Shannon would order Colonel Sumner with his force to encamp in the vicinity of Lawrence, the arms in the town should be given up and deposited with him for safe keeping, while the Marshal should come in and make his arrests, the arms to be returned when the troops left. This proposition, supported by the influence of the two gentlemen, seemed to meet with favor, and they were invited to return the following day, when it was thought every thing could be satisfactorily adjusted.

But the hopes thus inspired were doomed to disappointment. They returned to Lecompton the next day after being detained as prisoners in Colonel Stringfellow's camp for some time. Governor Shannon now informed them that the only thing which will satisfy the South Carolinians is for the arms to be given up to him or the Marshal, instead of Colonel Sumner. The Governor was told that the people of Lawrence would never submit to this, but would fight first, whereupon he exclaimed, "War, then, by G—d," and left the room.

On the same day that these negotiations closed, a young man by the name of Jones, returning home a few miles south of Lawrence, with a bag of meal for his widowed mother, was shot in cold blood. A band from the Marshal's posse rode suddenly upon him near Blanton's Bridge, and one of them discharged his gun at the inoffensive youth, when he exclaimed, "O, God, I am shot," and fell dead. When the affair was announced at Lawrence a few resolute young men, but mere boys, started for the place where the murder happened. When they had proceeded about a mile, they were met by two men from the camp at Franklin. They were accosted, insulted, and finally fired upon by the Ruffians, and one of the number, Stewart, was killed. His comrades carried him back to Lawrence. The announcement of these two unprovoked murders and the bleeding corpse of Stewart which had been brought in, filled the town with indignation and excitement. A company was formed, composed chiefly of boys, for the fighting men had left, which set out for Franklin to attack the invaders, but was recalled by the Committee of Safety.

A proposition was made to have about four or five hundred men stationed at a convenient distance from Lawrence so that when the posse should attempt any outrage on the town they could be prepared for the rescue. But the Committee feared that this would taint their spotless policy of non-resistance and rejected it.

Another and a final attempt was made to avert the impending destruction of the city. It had been reported that Colonel Sumner had said, "in case of actual collision, he should not wait for orders, but would take the responsibility of separating the combatants." A most earnest appeal was drawn up. It was represented that actual collision and bloodshed had taken place, and his presence as a peace-maker was again invited. The messenger, who had just made a trip to the Fort and back, mounted a fresh horse and bore this dispatch to Leavenworth. But it was all unavailing; Colonel Sumner's sense of the strict duty of a soldier forbade him to interfere without orders.

CHAPTER XXXI.

THE SACK OF LAWRENCE.

On the 20th of May the invaders prepared to attack Lawrence on the following day. General Atchison, with his Platte County Riflemen and two pieces of artillery; the Kickapoo Rangers, under Captain Dunn, reinforced by recruits from Leavenworth and Weston; General and Doctor Stringfellows, Bob Kelley and Peter Abell, at the head of forces from Atchison and vicinity; Colonel Wilkes, of South Carolina, and Colonel Titus, of Florida, with a number of their fellow statesmen, were all in camp between Lecompton and Lawrence. At Franklin, Colonel Boone, of Westport, and Colonel Buford, of South Carolina, with several prominent men from Liberty and Independence, Missouri, headed a large force of Southerners and Missourians. Both camps could muster eight hundred men, a part of whom were mounted and a part on foot. They were all supplied with United States arms by the Territorial authorities, and, besides Atchison's cannon, they had two more pieces of artillery.

Before the day spring streaked the clear eastern sky, on the twenty-first, the camp near Lawrence broke up and marched towards that place. At sunrise the inhabitants of that town, "just shaking off their slumbers," beheld two hundred horsemen, armed with rifles, revolvers and bowie knives, drawn up on Mount Oread that overlooks the place.

A red war flag, with "Southern Rights" inscribed upon it, floated over them. With what consternation and despair must they have gazed at the sight! They were defenseless. The faithful picket was not there to warn them of the enemy's approach. The alarming drum and shrill noted fife called no stalwart arms and brave hearts to the trenches and the line of battle. Alas, a different counsel had prevailed; the cannon lie buried in the ground as "silent as the grave," and the Sharp's rifles were concealed in the garret, or were far away upon the prairies. The few brave men left in the city, and the brave women wept when they beheld the advance of the invaders, that they could not die in defense of their homes, rather than see them demolished and themselves stricken down, or insulted like dogs, by a remorseless and arrogant foe.

At 7 o'clock the advance guard on the hill moved forward to its brow nearest the town, and took possession of Governor Robinson's house further down, which they used for headquarters. This was long musket range from the town, but good range for breech-loading rifles. Here they planted a cannon so as to overlook the town, which they directed towards it. In about one hour the infantry force from the western camp arrived and took position on the summit of the hill.

During the forenoon they sent runners into town who reported back, "All quiet in Lawrence; the few men there are busy about their employments." At eleven o'clock Deputy Marshal Fain, who had been in Lawrence the evening previous and made two arrests without opposition, rode into town with a guard of ten men without guns. They went directly to the hotel and were respectfully received. The Deputy then summoned Dr. Garvin, D. A. Perry, C. W. Topliff, Wm. Jones, S. W. Eldridge and T. B. Eldridge to assist him in making arrests. These readily complied and G. W. Deitzler, G. W. Smith and Gaius Jenkins were arrested without any difficulty. The Marshal took his dinner at the hotel; left without paying his bill and returned to the posse on the hill, which had now been increased by the arrival of Col. Buford's men. He then dismissed them, saying "he had no further use for them, but Sheriff Jones has writs to execute and they were at liberty to organize as his posse."

Sheriff Jones, "who once was dead, but now is alive again," rode forward and solicited the aid of the forces amid loud and prolonged cheers.

While Deputy Marshal Fain was in town the Committee of Safety, who had shown every respect to this officer, penned and signed the following document:

"LAWRENCE, K. T., May 21, 1856.

"J. B. DONALDSON, *United States Marshal, Kansas Territory:*

"We, the Committee of Public Safety, for the citizens of Lawrence, make this statement and declaration to you, as Marshal of Kansas Territory:

"That we represent the citizens of the United States and of Kansas, who acknowledge the constituted authorities of the Government; that we make no resistance to the execution of the law, national or territorial, and claim it as law-abiding American citizens.

"For the private property already taken by your posse we ask indemnification; and what remains to us and our citizens we throw upon you for protection, trusting that under the flag of the Union, and within the folds of the Constitution, we may obtain safety.

"SAMUEL C. POMEROY, C. W. BABCOCK,
"W. Y. ROBERTS, S. B. PRENTISE,
"LYMAN ALLEN, A. H. MALLORY,
"JOHN PERRY, JOEL GROVER."

It is due to the four last mentioned gentlemen to say that they repudiated the letter and declared that they never signed it. But this avowed recognition of the Territorial laws by the committee—laws which the people of Kansas had, time and again, in convention assembled pledged themselves, their lives, fortunes and sacred honors, "never to recognize as valid"—did not turn aside the wrath of the invaders. About three o'clock in the afternoon Sheriff Jones rode into town at the head of twenty armed men, halted in front of the Free State Hotel and called for General Pomeroy. This gentleman soon appeared and shook hands with Jones, when the latter said:

"General Pomeroy, I recognize you as one of the leading citizens here and as one who can act for the people of Lawrence. I demand that all the arms of Lawrence be given up or we shall bombard the town. (Taking out his watch.) I give you five minutes to decide upon this proposition and a half hour to stack the arms in the streets. I am authorized to make this demand by the First District Court of the United States."

General Pomeroy rushed up stairs and communicated this intelligence to the Committee of Safety, there sitting like the Roman Fathers when the Barbarians entered the imperial city. In a few moments he returned and said "the cannon will be delivered up, but the rifles are private property and will be retained." Jones replied, "very well, give up the cannon." The General, with other members of the Committee, accompanied the Sheriff to the spot where the twelve pounder brass howitzer and four other small cannons were buried under the foundation of a house, dug them up and surrendered them to Jones. A few Sharp's rifles were also obtained.

While this scene was being witnessed in town, the posse, numbering from five to eight hundred men, had marched down to the foot of the hill, formed in a hollow square, to whom General Atchison was making a speech, which was cheered by tremendous yells and whoops.

"'Boys, to-day I'm a Kickapoo Ranger, by G—d. This day we have entered Lawrence, and the abolitionists have not dared to fire a gun.' Various reports of this speech have been published, but all more or less incorrect. It was an odd mixture of drunken enthusiasm, restraining forbearance, partisan ferocity and profanity. He declared that the Free State Hotel must be destroyed and the printing offices demolished; but told them they must deport themselves as Southern gentlemen and 'law and order men.' He said they must not forget to be gallant and must respect ladies, but added, 'if you find a woman armed as a soldier, and thus putting off the garb of her sex, trample her under foot as you would a snake.' He said the people of Lawrence seemed determined not to resist, and that, therefore, it would not do to attack them; but said, if there was the least appearance of resistance, no quarters should be shown. He alluded to the distance the young Southerners had to come to aid them in the defense of 'Southern rights,' and complimented them on their zeal and courage. He commenced speaking on his horse, and then dismounted and got on a brass cannon, from which he spoke. He was interrupted by the arrival of Jones, who, after the guns had been delivered up, rode out of town. Jones told them that he had orders from the First District Court of the United States for Kansas to demolish the hotel and destroy the printing offices. Loud and enthusiastic cheers were then given for Jones. Atchison resumed his speech, telling them: 'And now we'll go in with our highly honorable Jones and test the strength of that d—d Free State Hotel.' He said something more urging them to bravery and good order, and finished by saying: 'If any man or woman stands in your way, blow them to h—ll with a chunk of cold lead.'"

The army of invaders then began their march into Lawrence with various banners and inscriptions upon them. There was one with a crimson star in the center and the words, "Southern Rights;" another with a tiger crouching ready to spring. One bore the inscription "South Carolina;" another, "The Supremacy of the White Race," &c. The Grand Jury which indicted several free state men for treason, also indicted several public buildings in Lawrence as nuisances, and as such ought to be abated. The following is a copy of their finding:

"The Grand Jury sitting for the adjourned term of the First District Court in and for the County of Douglas, beg leave to report to the Honorable Court that from the evidence laid before them showing them that the newspaper, known as the 'Herald of Freedom,' published at Lawrence, has from time to time issued publications of the most inflammatory and seditious character, denying the legality of the Territorial authorities, addressing and commanding forcible resistance to the same; demoralizing the popular mind and rendering life and property unsafe, even to the extent of advising assassination as a last resort.

"Also, that the paper known as the 'Kansas Free State,' has been similarly engaged, and has recently reported the resolutions of a meeting in Johnson County in this Territory, in which resistance to the Territorial laws, even unto blood, has been agreed upon, and we respectfully recommend their abatement as a nuisance. Also, that we are satisfied that the building, known as the Free State Hotel, in Lawrence, has been constructed with the view to military occupation and defense, regularly parapetted and port-holed, for the use of cannon and small arms, and could only have been designed as a stronghold of resistance to law, thereby endangering the public safety and encouraging rebellion and sedition in this country, and respectfully recommend that steps be taken whereby this nuisance may be removed.

"OWEN C. STEWART, Foreman."

Jones first halted in front of the Free State Hotel, and notified Colonel Eldridge to remove his furniture by five o'clock. The proprietor told him he could not remove it in so short a time, and that he would not try. About fifty or a hundred then proceeded to the building, in which was the office of the "Kansas Free State," under the leadership of G. W. Clark. They entered it cautiously, for fear of secret mines. They then assailed the press with axes, broke it in several places so as to render it useless, and smashed the type in pieces. They then carried both press and fragments of type to the river and threw them into the water. Three hundred volumes of books, fifty files of papers, a large quantity of exchanges, and paper stock, were torn up, scattered in the streets, set on fire and burnt up or carried off. The total loss sustained by the firm was about $10,275.

In a few moments after the office of the "Free State" was assailed, another party entered the building occupied by the "Herald of Freedom." They, too, were fearful of mines and infernal machines; in order to test the safety of the ascent to the printing office, they drove two or three free state men up before them. Soon the same work of demolition was begun here; the press hammered and bruised, the type broken into fragments, were both conveyed to the river. Growing weary in carrying type, they cast a portion out of the window. Papers, books, &c., were destroyed, making a loss to the firm of nearly $17,000. A blood red flag was first hoisted above the building, with a lone star in its centre, but in fifteen minutes was removed to the hotel. The building was fired several times, but the fire was as often extinguished.

Meantime preparations had been made to destroy the hotel. The ruffians had removed a portion of the furniture which they had dashed into the streets. Four cannon were planted within a few yards from the building. General Atchison sighted the first shot. As he swaggered over the gun giving directions he stammered out, "A little higher, boys, a little lower—a little higher. That's it, boys; let her rip." Bang went the gun, the ball passing clear over the building. It was duly lowered and fired with better effect. The other cannon opened their blasts upon the house, but only two of them would send a ball through its walls. Some fifty rounds were thus fired without affecting the building much. Finding this slow work, they next attempted to blow it up by exploding a couple of kegs of powder in the cellar. This did not have the desired effect, and fire was applied, by which in a short time the whole house was filled with flames.

The hotel was a beautiful three story structure, with solid stone walls. It was seventy feet long by fifty wide, with an addition twenty-four by forty-five feet and contained seventy-five rooms. It was built by the New England Emigrant Aid Society at a cost of $20,000, and had been in course of erection from the spring of '55 until May, 1856. Messrs. Eldridge & Bro. had rented the building in the fall of '55 at $5,000 per year, and purchased their furniture and provisions, expecting to enter it immediately; but the Waka-

DESTRUCTION OF THE FREE STATE HOTEL.

rusa war breaking out prevented the completion of the house so that they did not get it ready for the public until May following. It was very neatly and richly furnished and the cellar was well stored with luxuries. The proprietors estimated their loss by the delay in the completion and by the destruction of the hotel at $60,717.

While the flames were hissing and crackling in and over the hotel, Jones, with the complacency of a monster, sat on his horse and witnessed the sight. At one time he turned to his companions and said: "Gentlemen, this is the happiest day of my life, I assure you. I determined to make the fanatics bow before me in the dust and kiss the territorial laws." When the walls of the burning building had fallen in, he exclaimed, "I have done it, by G—d, I have done it." Turning to his men he said, "You are dismissed, the writs have been executed."

This was the signal for a general plunder. Private houses, whose inmates had fled, were burst open, entered and ransacked. Money, clothing and guns were taken or destroyed. Stores were rummaged and robbed. Dr. Stringfellow secured two boxes of cigars and quietly walked off, saying, "Well, boys, I guess this is all the booty I want." The invaders arrayed themselves with a new suit of clothes, ribbons and tassels; many were loaded down with books, provisions, goods, guns, etc., etc. They conveyed their spoils out of town to the wagons they had prudently brought up for the purpose, and thus secured them. They began leaving about seven o'clock, and by nine all was quiet. As the rear guard departed, they fired Governor Robinson's house at the foot of Mt. Oread; the flames soon lit up the darkness of the night. In this way the Governor lost some fifteen or twenty thousand dollars. During the sacking only one man was killed. He was one of the pillagers—killed by the falling of a brick, swept off the Hotel by the South Carolina flag. Another one of the gang fell from his horse and broke his leg, while in pursuit of a fugitive whom he supposed to be Reeder.

It is scarcely possible to estimate the amount of property destroyed or taken during this campaign against Lawrence. The invaders not only gathered subsistance from the settlers, but distroyed houses, carried off clothing, stole more than two hundred horses, and robbed persons and dwellings of a vast amount of money and arms. The camps at Franklin and Lecompton were filled with plunder, resembling that of a victorious clan of savages, or those of the Goths and Vandals. Some of them rode through the streets of Westport and Kansas City the next day, their horses adorned with cords and tassels, and their persons with sashes, taken from the windows of the Free State Hotel.

CHAPTER XXXII.

DIFFICULTIES AT LEAVENWORTH.

The posse dispersed the day after the sacking of Lawrence and retired towards the border. Some of the Southerners, disgusted with what they witnessed, returned home; others rejoicing in robbery, rapine and murder, lingered in the Territory and on the Border committing depredations. As some of them retired from Franklin they robbed Fish's grocery, ransacked his house, tore down his fences and took some of his horses. The day following the destruction of Lawrence General Atchison with his company of Platte County riflemen, rode through the place, dragging one piece of artillery, and crossed the Kansas River at the north side of town. He had previously obtained permission to pass through from the citizens.

The Westport paper delivered a war appeal simply because some boys had remarked to a pro-slavery man in Lawrence that it was not safe for him to remain there. It called upon the Missourians and Southerners to stay in the Territory, and not only finish the demolition of Lawrence, but level "every other abolition settlement in Kansas with the ground." In response to this appeal Captain Pate, with a company of Westport gentry, which were denominated as "Shannon's Sharp Shooters," and Coleman, the murderer of Dow, remained between Lawrence and Westport, south of the Kaw, where they would stop travellers and rob them, search the United States mail, plunder loaded wagons, steal or take horses and provision from the settlers, and commit depredations generally.

The free state men scattered and disorganized, driven in many instances to madness, began at this time to form guerrilla companies for retaliation and self-defense. The leading free state men had no part in the organizations. They were composed of youths deprived of their situations and little worldly possessions by the destruction of Lawrence, and of men of reckless character, who rejoiced in the opportunity to destroy, rob and pillage. They confined their operations chiefly against pro-slavery men, who had taken an active part in the troubles, and against similar bands of Border Ruffians. At one time they stole three horses from Captain Pate's company; again a party of eight secreted themselves in a ravine and fired upon eighteen Southerners as they rode by. They killed several, put the rest to flight, and captured horses and arms. A squad of free state guerrillas robbed and trespassed upon a pro-slavery man by the name of Bernhardt, in the same way that Pate's company treated the Shawnee Indian Fish.

Thus the country was soon infested by roaming bands of guerrillas, vieing with each other in deeds of violence and wrong. Whenever opposite factions met there was a fight, and wherever they moved, oppression, robbery and bloodshed marked their course.

The people of Lecompton, quaking under a guilty conscience, with the plunder of Lawrence in their houses, became alarmed lest the free state men should attack the town. Governor Shannon, who had already lost two fine horses, shared in the feeling of the inhabitants. From this fact, and seeing the pro-slavery men generally worsted in guerrilla encounters, the Governor ordered the United States troops posted at Lecompton, Lawrence and Topeka, to preserve the peace, and "as the only way to prevent civil war between the two contending parties."

There was a brave and determined free state man by the

name of Captain Walker, who lived between Lecompton and Lawrence. He became Colonel in the war for the Union, in which he distinguished himself. He now lives at Lawrence. The pro-slavery men hated him intensely, and decreed his destruction. While in camp at Lecompton, Colonel Titus said "he would have his head on or off his shoulders, and for it would give any man five hundred dollars." A party from the pro-slavery camp resolved to make an attempt to secure this outlaw. Captain Walker having been informed of the intended attack, gathered some thirty of his neighbors together at his house. They posted themselves and awaited the attack. About midnight a party of twelve men rode up before the house, all armed with revolvers and bowie knives. Several of them dismounted and entered the yard. Just as they were preparing to march up to the house, Captain Walker and his men fired. One horse fell dead in the gate-way, and in the twinkling of an eye every one made a hasty retreat. Some dropped their knives and revolvers; one, in his hurried jump over the paling fence, left a portion of his coat-tail with a bottle of whisky in it, dangling in the air. As they skedaddled they rushed into another squad of Captain Walker's men, and two were captured. The prisoners were detained during the night, but liberated next morning, promising to amend in the future.

They, however, ungratefully repaid their liberators. They reported the names of those who had come to Captain Walker's defense, and writs were made out against them. The Captain was compelled to leave his house and find safety in ravines or thickets. Judge Wakefield, one engaged in the defense, on learning that a writ had been issued against him, set out to leave the Territory, with a view of gathering a company of men and returning, but was arrested at Leavenworth and brought back to Lecompton, where he was soon liberated.

About the same time an attack was made upon the house

of Mr. Storrs, who lived on a beautiful claim on Washington Creek. He, with five men, was in his cabin determined to defend it, while a party of Georgians were reconnoitering and planning an attack. A widow lady, on observing their demonstration and comprehending their nature, mounted a horse and galloped to Lawrence for help. Two dragoons and three free state men hurried to the rescue. As they approached, the Georgians, observing them, fled. When within two hundred yards, they were commanded by those in the cabin, who mistook them for their enemies, to "halt," but on they came at full gallop. Failing to regard the summons "halt," which was again shouted, the fire of a half a dozen rifles flashed from the cabin. "In a twinkling, both the foremost dragoons rolled over, horse and man; one with a bullet in his arm, and another in his leg; both horses were wounded, and though the other dragoon was not shot, he came down with an emphasis that left him stretched for a minute or two senseless. In his summersault his sabre flew out of its scabbard and the scabbard bent double." As the firing was kept up and the bullets whistled their piercing music, the company which had come to succor the free state men hurried away. They supposed that the house had been taken and occupied by the Southerners, and knew no better until the next day when the mutual mistake was discovered.

During all these troubles Governor Shannon at Lecompton was under the control of the South Carolinians. He was feasted and toasted by them until he entirely lost sight of his dignity and responsibility. The Southerners being generally worsted in guerrilla encounters, at their suggestion, the Governor not only had United States troops posted at Lecompton to protect the place against a general attack, but at the head of a squad began his memorable perigrinations through the Territory in search of Sharp's rifles. He went from house to house, ransacked household goods and wherever he could pick up a musket, shot-gun or rifle, he reckoned that he had weakened the insurrectionists so much. Many ridiculous incidents marked the tipsy Governor's search for arms.

The Committee of Investigation having completed their work at Lawrence soon after the troubles began, adjourned to Leavenworth City. They had evinced a determination to perform their mission impartially, to expose fraud and injustice, and the monstrous iniquities practiced upon the people of Kansas. On this account pro-slavery men desired its sittings broken up, the evidences it had accumulated against them destroyed, the Committee compelled to abandon their undertaking and retire from the Territory. To attain this object, it was thought, had given rise in some measure to the demonstrations upon Lawrence. After the sack of this place many of the dispersed posse repaired to Leavenworth and resumed their efforts to disturb the Committee.

The following notice was one morning found posted on the door of the Committee room:

"MAY 26.

"*Messrs.* HOWARD *and* SHERMAN:

"SIRS: With feelings of surprise and disgust we have been noticing the unjust manner in which you have been conducting this investigation, we wish to inform you can no longer sit in this place.

"We therefore request you to alter your obnoxious course, in order to avoid consequences which may otherwise follow.

"CAPTAIN HEMP,
"In behalf of the citizens.

"LEAVENWORTH CITY, 1856."

The ruffians from their first entrance into town daily grew more bold and warlike. All persons in any way affected with anti-slavery sympathies were either notified to leave the Territory or threatened with death by the rope or the rifle. On the morning of the 28th of May the "Leavenworth Herald" issued a reprint of the "war extra" from the Westport paper. The account of the Pottowattomie murders was published, which served to exasperate the ruffians. A pro-slavery meeting was immediately held in which Stringfellow and Richardson took a prominent part. They passed a resolution requiring all active free state men to leave the Territory and resolved themselves into a Vigilance Committee to enforce it. A list of the most obnoxious freesoilers was drawn up, presented to the officer of the day—Warren D. Wilkes, of South Carolina. This gentleman, at the head of a body of Southerners and Kickapoo Rangers, armed with United States muskets and bayonets, paraded the streets, and placed guards in various portions of the town to prevent the escape of fugitives. The mob then proceeded to make arrests. Mr. Sherman of the Congressional Committee seeing Mr. Conway, who had been acting as clerk for the same, among the persons thus held prisoners, inquired of Mr. Wilkes "if he had arrested one of the clerks of the Committee on any legal process." This official replied "he had not, but, at all hazards would arrest those whose names he had on his list." Thus they continued their work until they held thirty free state men prisoners. These were guarded in a frame building until dark, when many were permitted to escape on promising to leave the Territory. These violent demonstrations lasted for some time, and did not entirely subside until the last of October.

CHAPTER XXXIII.

"OLD BROWN'S" WARFARE.

It was at this stage of affairs that Captain John Brown, Sen., began to figure in the stirring events of the times. He was a man of characteristic ancestry, being sixth in descent from Peter Brown, one of the Puritans who fled from the intolerance of England in the Mayflower, and landed at Plymouth Rock on the 22d of December, 1620. His grandfather and namesake was Captain of the West Sunsbury train band, and as such joined the Continental army at New York in the spring of 1776. After two months' service he was seized with camp fever, and died in a barn a few miles north of the city.

Captain John Brown was born in Torrington, Connecticut, on the 9th of May, 1800. His mother was the daughter of Gideon Mills, who served in the Revolutionary war, and attained the rank of Lieutenant. His father, Owen Brown, when John was but five years old, emigrated to Hudson, Ohio, and during the war of 1812 furnished beef cattle to the American army. John, then fourteen years of age, accompanied his father as cattle driver. In this capacity he witnessed the movements of the army, and Hull's surrender at Detroit. He became so disgusted with what he saw of military life that when he attained a suitable age, he refused to take part in the militia drills, and either paid his fine or furnished a substitute.

In his early days he enjoyed few advantages for mental

acquirements, from which cause he knew little even of the primary branches of school education. At the age of eight, he suffered the loss of his mother, which he lamented for years afterwards. When sixteen years of age, he joined the Congregational Church, and from fifteen to twenty learned the tanner and currier's trade. At the age of twenty he went East, with a view of acquiring a liberal education in some good college, and preparing himself for the ministry. Having nearly fitted himself for college under the instructions of Rev. Moses Hallock, he was suddenly seized with the inflammation of the eyes, which compelled him to quit school. He returned to Ohio, where he married his first wife, by whom he had seven children. She, dying in 1832, he shortly afterwards married a second time, from which union were born thirteen children, of whom three sons were with him at Harper's Ferry, two of whom lost their lives and the third escaped.

From 1821 to 1826, he spent his time in Ohio at tanning and farming, and then moved to Crawford County, Pennsylvania, where he continued in the same vocation. In 1835 he returned to Ohio, Portage County, where, besides carrying on his trade, he speculated in real estate, which resulted in financial loss. In 1840 he engaged in the wool business, and in 1846 removed to Springfield, Massachusetts, where he sold wool extensively on commission for growers along the shore of Lake Erie. Here he undertook to dictate the prices of wool to the New England manufacturers, who, forming a league against him, forced him to send his wool to Europe for a market. He shipped two hundred thousand pounds to England, where he sold it for one-half its value, and returned bankrupt. In 1849 he removed to Essex County, New York, upon a piece of land given him by Gerret Smith. This was located among the Adirondack Mountains, rugged, cold and bleak. Here the same benevolent philanthropist had granted lands to negroes, who had formed a small settlement upon them. In 1851, Brown returned to Ohio and engaged in the wool traffic again, but in 1855, on starting to Kansas, he removed his family to their former home at North Elba, in New York, where they still reside, and where his grave was afterwards made.

As early as 1839 Brown conceived the design of liberating the slaves in the South, although from his boyhood he had been a "*determined abolitionist.*" The character of his reading, his travels in Europe, and his residence among the blacks in New York, all tended to fit and prepare him for the great object of his life. When Kansas was thrown open to settlement, his four elder sons determined to emigrate thither, which they did, and settled in the spring of 1855, about eight miles from Ossawattomie, on Pottowattomie Creek. They came with the view of assisting in making Kansas a free State, and of securing to themselves comfortable homes. Troubles soon breaking out in the Territory, and they themselves being harrassed and threatened, they wrote back to their father for arms, with which they might protect themselves. These the father procured through the generosity of his friends, and instead of sending, went with them to Kansas.

He came here, therefore, unlike free state men generally, not to settle and make a home, but to fight in the battles of freedom, and, when the conflict was over, to return. Still, while here, when not engaged with the enemy, he was industriously employed upon his claim, building a house, laying out his fields and attending to stock. The part which he took in the Kansas troubles will appear in connection with the events. In the fall of 1856, after the demonstration upon Lawrence, he left with his four sons for the East, by way of Nebraska. In November he appeared before the National Kansas Committee, soliciting aid, but without much success; in January he appeared before the Massachusetts Legislature, to whom he made a speech detailing his experience in Kansas. While East he contracted for the pikes which he afterwards used at Harper's Ferry, and labored to secure friends and further his designs generally against slavery. The celebrated Canada Conference was held, a constitution for a provisional government drawn up, and the whole scheme of liberating the Southern slaves, as afterwards developed, framed. It was the arrangement to have made the attack at Harper's Ferry sooner, but várious causes led him to defer the matter and make a strike in Kansas first. He accordingly labored to secure funds and arms with which to equip a company of one hundred men for demonstrations in South-eastern Kansas. Unsuccessful in a great measure in the accomplishment of the latter object, he returned, dissatisfied with his Eastern visit, in November, 1857, to this Territory, where, the following fall and winter, he co-operated with Montgomery against the Ruffians in Southern Kansas.

Old Brown, as he was familiarly called in Kansas, was no politician, and had taken no interest in politics since the first election of Jackson. He was decidedly a man of action and had no faith in the overthrow of iniquity and sin by moralizing and theorizing. His religious convictions were deep and settled; and it is only when we consider his unswerving and abiding *Faith that the overruling Providence would protect and give success to the Right*, that we are enabled to understand the reasons which actuated the man. He was a great lover of the Bible, and especially of the Old Testament, among whose characters Gideon was his favorite. He believed with the most unclouded Faith that the same Lord that strengthened Gideon, would strengthen him in his stroke for the oppressed. Viewed in any other light than that of Christian faith, his scheme for the liberation of the slaves is fanatical and absurd.

In January 1859, Brown left Kansas with a lot of slaves taken from Missouri. He proceeded to Canada, where the details of his subsequent raid in Virginia were arranged. He spent the spring and summer in preparing for the anticipated stampede. On the 16th of October he made his well known assault at Harper's Ferry, which cost him and two of his sons their lives.

Captain John Brown, Jr., upon hearing that Lawrence was menaced by a large body of invaders, set out with a company of sixty men to join in the defence of that place; but in consequence of the peace policy adopted, his services were never brought into requisition. After the sacking of the town he returned, disbanded his men and retired to work on his claim.

Pro-slavery men in the region of Osawattomie had for some time been very impudent, bold and threatening. The spirit of extermination which incited the destroyers of Lawrence and which had been breathing its threats along the Border all spring, at once seized the pro-slavery men of that section. To illustrate this fact, the case of Mr. Bell, who now lives near Baldwin City, will suffice. He had come from Missouri a short time before and settled in a pro-slavery neighborhood near where he still lives. He occupied a house belonging to a pro-slavery man and was kindly received by that party, they supposing, as he came from Missouri, that he was all "sound on the goose." But ascertaining his free state proclivities, they dropped him, and about the time that Lawrence was invaded, ordered him out of the house. In vain he entreated to be allowed to remain until his wife would recover from her sickness, and that he might be able to look around for another house. The order was imperative and with his afflicted family he moved into a rail pen for shelter. Leaving his family with only provision enough for two days he went to Missouri for a supply, but on his return, when within eight miles of home, was seized, taken back and held prisoner, though he earnestly importuned to be allowed to convey his provisions to his famishing wife and children.

While the men about Osawattomie were absent at Lawrence, their pro-slavery neighbors visited their defenseless, families, insulted and notified them to leave the country, and threatened, in case they did not observe this order to kill them all. A certain man who had a store was shockingly abused because he had furnished the free state men ammunition when they set out for Lawrence. It was then, and is yet, believed by the residents of that part of the country that a plan had been arranged for the destruction of all the free state men in the neighborhood the latter part of May and especially those of the Browns.

On the return of Captain John Brown, junior, and his company, and learning the deep laid plots of assassination, a

JOHN BROWN STARTING OUT TO BEGIN THE WAR.

council was held near Osawattomie, at which the question of taking the field and engaging in actual hostilities was discussed, of which Captain John Brown, senior, warmly advocated the affirmative. The majority of the company on its being put to vote, deciding against him, he stepped out from the ranks, and with sword upraised, called upon all who were willing to begin "the war in earnest" to follow him. About eight responded, and with them, he left the camp of his son, to begin his memorable career. Proceeding up the Maries Des Cygnes a short distance, he halted his men, and there, in the still and deep-tangled woods, held a council. Exactly what was said is not known. But Brown soon infused in his followers his own spirit of determination and hostility to slavery. At this council it was determined whenever any demonstration towards executing the plot to massacre free state men should be made that certain parties should be killed on the spot.

While Brown went North for aid, on the night of the 24th of May, Mr. Doyle and his two sons, Mr. Sherman and Mr. Wilkinson, were all taken from their houses and murdered. The act had been precipitated in consequence of certain outrages committed by the above mentioned parties the day before. Old Brown, who was absent at the time, fully sustained and approved of the deed.

Good people every where were shocked at the announcement of this seeming act of barbarity, so utterly at variance with the conduct and policy of free state men, many of whom strongly denounced it. But still, when men became familiar with the aggravating causes, the awful state of affairs in that section of the Territory, they viewed the matter in a different light. While all the reasons, which we have sought truthfully to state, that impelled the actors in this bloody drama, may not excuse their conduct, they tend in a great degree to palliate it. Perhaps it approaches nearer a cold blooded atrocity than any other which attaches itself to free state men in Kansas. While, therefore, we would not excuse, though we would not censure unjustly, an outraged and oppressed community, we can but deplore the occurrence, as partaking too much of the remorseless character of the Border Ruffians.

This occurrence, like the "murder of Jones," was used as a pretext for new outrages by Southerners and Missourians. The usual "war extras" were issued, S. G. Cato exerted himself to bring the murderers to justice, Shannon was petitioned for troops and arms, a messenger was dispatched to Fort Scott for aid, and every thing was hurry and confusion, as though an invading army was upon them.

Accordingly, Governor Shannon dispatched Captain Wood, then commanding at Lawrence, to the scene of difficulties. In a day afterwards, receiving word that armed bands were collecting on the Pottowattomie Creek, he sent Lieutenant Church with a small detachment to investigate the facts. This officer proceeded south of Lawrence about eighteen miles, where he met Captain Brown with a force of about eighty men, whom he commanded to disperse. Agreeable with this requisition, Captain Brown and his men repaired to their homes; the Lieutenant returned and reported that there were no men collecting for the purpose of invading the Territory.

For the purpose of capturing or destroying "Old Brown," Captain Pate, towards the last of May, set out for Osawattomie with his company of "Shannon's Sharp Shooters." He was a Virginian by birth, good looking and intelligent. Of some experience as a journalist, he made an excellent correspondent of the "Missouri Republican," in which he gave the pro-slavery version of Kansas matters. He took an active part with the Border Ruffians, and seemed to enjoy the invasions as the happy diversions of life. At the sacking of Lawrence he rode a fine horse, decorated with ribbons.

On arriving in the neighborhood of Osawattomie, he captured two of "Old Brown's" sons, John, a member of the State Legislature, and Jason, both of whom he found quietly working on their farms. They were charged with murder, kept in irons and treated with severity. Captain Pate proceeded to arrest other persons, and burn houses. Shortly Captain Wood arrived, when the prisoners were delivered over to him, by whom they were treated with the same inhumanity. Being unable to find Captain Brown, Sen., Pate, with his company and United States troops, set out, on the 31st of May, for the Sante Fe road. The troops, with the prisoners, encamped on Middle Ottowa Creek. They afterwards continued their journey to Lecompton, distant twenty miles. The prisoners were driven before the dragoons, in the hot sun, chained two and two. John Brown, Jr., who was of a sensitive nature, excited by the horrid stories told him about the murder of his father, became insane while in the camp at Leavenworth.

Captain Pate and his company advanced as far as Hickory Point, on the Santa Fe Road, and encamped on the head of a small branch called Black Jack. His camp was five miles south-east of Palmyra, and the same distance in an eastern direction from Prairie City, at the head of a ravine in the edge of the prairie. "The bottom of the ravine at Black Jack, besides the growing timber, had some deep water drains or ruts, round which was a thicket. There was also several bogs on the spot where the camp was."

That night Captain Pate's company plundered Palmyra, and took several prisoners—Dr. Graham, of Prairie City, who was out reconnoitering, and Father Moore, a Baptist Preacher. The latter was an old man, from Missouri, and known to some of his captors. They cruelly maltreated him by putting a funnel in his mouth and pouring whisky down his throat, in order, as they said, "to make the old preacher drunk." On the following morning they returned and completed the plundering of the place. In the afternoon they undertook to repeat the same thing on Prairie City. Six men started upon this expedition. It being Sunday, people of that village were assembled in the house of worship. But men went armed in those days, even to church, and when the watchman announced the approach of the Missourians, the congregation rushed out; the men threw themselves in front of the enemy and captured two of them and made strange music for the balance.

Meantime every effort had been made to discover Pate's encampment, with the design of attacking it and releasing the prisoners. Captain Brown was on the tramp all the time. "Like a wolf," says a contemporary writer, "robbed of its young, he stealthily but resolutely, watched for his foes, while he skirted through the thickets of the Maries Des Cygnes,* and Ottawa Creeks." Captain Shore, commander of the Prairie City company, was also diligent in the search.

On Monday morning two scouts brought tidings of the enemy's whereabouts. Immediately Captain Brown, with nine men, and Captain Shore, with nineteen men, left Prairie City and rode towards Black Jack. On arriving within one mile of this place, they dismounted, left their horses in charge of two guards and dispatched two messengers for help, one to Palmyra and the other to Captain Abbott's company on the Wakarusa. The remaining twenty-six men then marched towards the enemy.

Captain Pate had now about fifty men under his command. They had formed a kind of breast work by placing three or four wagons in a line on the prairie a few rods from the bottom of the ravine. They had pitched one of their tents immediately behind the wagons. When it was announced that the free state men were coming, Captain Pate drew up his men behind this rolling fortification and prepared for the attack.

"When they reached the enemy's position, Captain Brown wished Shore to go to the left and get into the ravine below them, while he with his force would get into the upper or prairie part of the ravine, in the bottom of which was long grass. As the ravine made a bend they would thus have got in range of the enemy on both sides, and had them in cross-fire, without being in their own. Captain Brown, with his nine men, accordingly went to the right. Captain Shore, with more bravery than military skill, approached the foe over the hill to the west of their camp, marching over the prairie, up within good range, fully exposed and with no means of shelter near them."

In a moment Captain Shore poured down upon the Missourians a volley of lead in the front while Captain Brown

*A French name, signifying "The Swamps of the Swans."

who had secreted his company in the tall grass, within the outer banks of the ravine, opened a galling fire upon their left flank. After the battle had lasted about five minutes the Missourians retreated from the wagons to the ravine, where they found secure lodgment. This left Captain Shore's men exposed to the fire of a concealed foe. They, therefore, retreated back until out of range, except the Captain and two or three of his men, who went down and joined Brown. The firing on both sides now continued with little effect. Captain Brown visited the boys on the hill, some of whom he found had gone after ammunition, others fixing their guns, and directed them to shoot at the horses of the enemy across the ravine.

The prisoners whom Pate held, were stationed in the tent by the wagons with a guard. When the firing began they lay flat upon the ground and, though in the most exposed place, the bullets whistled over them harmlessly. After this ineffectual fire had been kept up for some time, one of the Missourians in the ravine swore that "he would see to the prisoners." He rushed into the tent where they were confined and as he raised his pistol to shoot, Dr. Graham sprang up. The weapon went off and inflicted a flesh wound in the Doctor's arm. Graham rushed from the tent and his guards, and made his escape to the men on the hill. As he did so several shots were fired at him but only one took effect, wounding him in the hip.

The firing lasted about three hours. Two of the free state men and three pro-slavery men were wounded. At length a young Southerner and a prisoner were sent out to Brown's camp with a flag of truce. When they reached the free state men, Captain Brown demanded of the Southerner if he was the commander of the forces in the ravine. The reply having been given in the negative, Captain Brown said: "Then you stay here with me, and let Mr. Lyman, (the prisoner) go and bring him out. I will talk with him." In a short time Captain Pate made his appearance.

After some little parleying, in which the Missouri commander attempted to excuse himself by claiming to act under the authority of the United States Marshal, Captain Brown cut him off short by demanding his unconditional surrender. With only five men Brown entered the Missouri camp and received Pate's surrender. He thus captured twenty-one men besides the prisoners, twenty horses and mules, several wagons, provisions, camp equipage, and a vast amount of plunder which had been taken at Palmyra. In the course of an hour the free state forces were augmented by the addition of Captain Abbott's company of fifty men, and towards night by others from Lawrence. The wounded were carried to Prairie City and cared for; Captain Brown afterwards moved with his prisoners and strongly entrenched himself in the thick woods of Middle Ottawa Creek, immediately back of Prairie City, about a quarter of mile from where Dr. Coughill's house now stands.

As soon as the battle of Black Jack was announced, the various bands of opposing forces began to march in that direction. Franklin had not been entirely abandoned by the pro-slavery forces since the sack of Lawrence. On the night of the 14th of June there were a number of Buford's men and Missourians assembled at this place. They had a quantity of arms, ammunition, provisions, and a brass six pounder, all of which properly belonged to Lawrence. The plunder gathered from intercepted wagons, and from Lawrence had in large quantities been stored here, and the Border Ruffians went and come at this town whenever they chose. It had always been used as a pro-slavery rallying point and headquarters, in case of invasion from Missouri.

For the purpose of recapturing this stolen property, and breaking up this stronghold of the enemy, who would have Lawrence at their mercy when the free state forces should go below to relieve Brown, an attack was planned by the free state companies in the vicinity of Lawrence. But the details of the attack were poorly defined and there was little concert of action.

A party of sixteen left Lawrence on the night of the 4th of June for Franklin. Failing to find the Wakarusa company at the point agreed upon, they sallied into town amid the darknes, to the place where they understood the cannon was posted. But not finding it where they expected, they rambled about in town for an hour in search of it and to ascertain the position of the enemy.

The Missourians had received word of their coming and had taken the cannon into the guard house, where they had it loaded. They numbered twenty three, were well armed and fortified and were anxiously awaiting the attack. The Lawrence boys readily concluded that nothing could be effected without making an assault upon the guard house. So up to it they marched and demanded the surrender of its garrison. This demand was contemptuously refused and a volley of rifle shots soon lit up the darkness. This was returned by the free state men, when the six pounder howitzer was let off with an unearthly noise. It had been loaded with nails, horse-shoes and chains which went screaming through the darkness wildly but harmlessly. The firing was continued on both sides and the pro-slavery men from the other houses began to bang away at—they scarcely knew what. The free state party lay flat down in the streets and the balls whistled over them. Here they loaded and fired their Sharp's rifles with impunity.

The Wakarusa company, which had become bewildered, in the darkness and lost their way, guided by the firing, entered Franklin ; but not knowing the position of friends or foes, they were unable to take part in the engagement. They, however, burst open a storehouse full of plunder. They filled one wagon with powder, guns and provisions and hurried it away. Had they brought four or five wagons they could have filled them all. But as it was they ob-

43

tained many of the Sharp's rifles and old alligator guns which had been seized from the free state men.

At the break of day the guard house was abandoned by all except the wounded. The free state men fearing the approach of the United States troops who were in camp near Lawrence, were compelled to leave the town. Not having any horses they were unable to remove the cannon they had so bravely captured. By a better planned attack they might have secured all the powder, shot, caps, guns, flour, sugar, coffee, bacon, &c., that Buford had taken and stored away for his men. But one of the free state men was hurt in the rencounter, while four of the opposite party were badly wounded, two of whom subsequently died.

A large force of Missourians and Southerners was by this time assembled on Bull Creek, about twelve miles east of where Baldwin City now stands, under the command of General Whitfield, the Missouri-Kansas Delegate to Congress. He had a regular organized army of about three hundred men, properly officered and armed. Some of the noted men of the Border were with him; Captain Reed, of Independence, and a candidate for Congress, Milt. McGee, now a prominent stock holder in Kansas City, Coleman, the murderer, Captain Jenigen, who had been taken prisoner by Captain Walker, Captain Bell, and several prominent Southern officers from Buford's regiment. On the 5th of June they marched up and encamped a half mile to the south of Palmyra in a ravine.

Failing in his attempts at disarming the free state settlers of Kansas Territory, who still proved victorious in every conflict, the Governor issued his proclamation, immediately after the battle of Black Jack, for all armed bands to disperse and go home; the United States troops were empowered to carry out this order, and in case of companies reassembling, they were to be disarmed. To carry out this proclamation and to make further arrests, Colonel Sumner was ordered with his command and Deputy Marshal Fain, to proceed to the scene of disturbance.

This proclamation deterred and diminished the gathering of the free state forces. Nevertheless by June 5, there were encamped at Hickory Point, about one mile from Palmyra, one hundred and eleven free state men, composed of fifteen from Franklin, a few from Bloomington under Captain Walker, some from Lawrence under Captain Cracklin, and Captain Abbott's company. Captain Shore with forty men was encamped back of Prairie City; while a few miles further west was a regular guerrilla band of young free state men under Captain Lenhart, formerly a printer in Lawrence, twenty in all, with whom were Cooke* and Hopkins, who sometimes acted as Captains of guerrilla parties. The whole number of free state men then under arms in that vicinity was about two hundred.

Colonel Sumner, who had started on the 4th, arrived in Prairie City on the 5th of June. There were then in that vicinity, within a space of four miles square, three distinct forces numbering in all about seven hundred men. Learning the position of Captain Shore's company, Colonel Sumner first went and dispersed it. He would not likely have discovered Captain Brown's camp in the woods had not the latter heard that he wished to see him. He, therefore, dispatched a messenger to Colonel Sumner to inform him if such was the fact he would come out and have an interview. The Colonel sent back the messenger to tell him to come out. Captain Brown, thinking that Colonel Sumner wished only to hold a military conference, was some what surprised when he came in the presence of this official to find himself a prisoner. Yielding himself up without resistsnce he led Colonel Sumner and the Deputy Marshal to his camp. There lay twenty-seven prisoners guarded by fifteen of Brown's men. But Colonel Sumner afterwards remarked that Brown had so entrenched himself in the choice selec-

*Hung at Harper's Ferry.

tion of his company ground that a thousand men could not have taken him. When the Deputy Marshal, who was filled with trepidation at the thought that the surrounding forest was likely filled with armed free state men, replied that he had no writs to execute upon any person there, he was upbraided by Colonel Sumner for having told him the contrary.

The prisoners, who had been treated with marked kindness during their detention, were set at liberty. Their horses, baggage, arms and camp equipage, were restored to them. When Colonel Sumner saw the United States arms handed over to the prisoners, he administered a scathing rebuke to Captain Pate for thus employing United States property to such an unauthorized and dishonorable purpose. Brown's company was ordered to disperse. When the Captain reminded the Colonel that free state men could not disband and retire to their homes, while an invading army was in their midst destroying lives and property, the latter promised that he would at once visit Whitfield and disperse his force.

Colonel Sumner then proceeded to General Whitfield's camp, where he was received very courteously. They represented themselves as residents of the Territory, assembled in arms to release their neighbors who were held prisoners, and to protect the country from the outrages of a belligerent foe. Colonel Sumner, having accomplished this object partially, and assuring them he would fully, they promised, on their honor, to disperse and return to their homes.

Accordingly Sumner fell back towards Prairie City and encamped. The next day he returned to Fort Leavenworth. General Whitfield and his command removed to Black Jack and encamped that night on the spot where the battle had been fought. Captain Pate and his company were with him. On their way thither they captured a young free state settler by the name of Cantral, and plundered a house. Cantral was a Missourian and had participated with the free state party in the battle of Black Jack.

Early next morning Whitfield's army decamped and divided. About one hundred and seventy under Captain Reed, of Independence, Captains Pate, Bell and Jenigen, started for Osawattomie; twenty more started for Washington Creek, where they lived; the remainder, under Whitfield, left for Missouri, carrying with them the prisoners, of whom they had several. When the latter division had proceeded some fifteen miles in the direction of Westport, they encamped on Cedar Creek. Here they went through the farce of trying Cantral as a traitor to Missouri and found him guilty. He was then led away by four men, one of whom was Milt McGee, of Westport, into a ravine and shot. Cantral's body was afterwards found with three bullet holes in his breast and taken home to his afflicted widow. Several other prisoners were supposed to have been killed in the same way, as seven dead bodies were afterwards found in that vicinity. Mr. Bell, who now lives near Baldwin City, was one of the prisoners and witnessed the facts as above narrated.

When Cantral was first taken, efforts were made to get Colonel Sumner to effect his release but in vain. This officer relied too much upon the empty pledge of Whitfield.

When, however, the next day three pro-slavery guerrillas were seized and held prisoners by free state men, Colonel Sumner immediately sent a squad of dragoons to rescue them.

The division of invaders under Captain Reed encamped at Paola on the evening of the 5th of June. A messenger from Osawattomie came from the free state camp near Palmyra, informed them of the expected attack and solicited assistance. Efforts were made to get the United States troops to move to the protection of the town, but it was answered that a force under Major Sedgewick was encamped in the vicinity of that place which could preserve order and prevent injury. On the following morning Sedgewick with his forces, unaware of the attack to be made upon Osawattomie, moved several miles further up. But the settlers and those aware of the movements of the Border Ruffians did not believe that they designed to attack the place but merely to surround the town and cut off travelers and supplies on the road. The consequence was, there was no preparation made for defense.

Early on the morning of the sixth of June these Missouri forces decamped and marched for Osawattomie. They entered the town suddenly, startling the inhabitants by their presence. They began that wholesale pillage which characterized the sack of Lawrence. Stores were entered and their contents appropriated; private dwellings burst open and rummaged; horses, guns, clothes, liquors, etc., etc., were taken, while the air was rent with wildest profanity and deadly threats all over town. The printing press which had not yet been put up, was hunted for in vain by the destroyers. They took womens' apparel—petticoats, ear-rings, dresses, &c.; set fire to several houses which was put out by the inhabitants. When they had gathered all the plunder they could carry, they hastily retreated lest the abolitionists should come upon them, and retired to the Border, like hawks to the solitudes, to feast upon their booty.

CHAPTER XXXIV.

RELIEF FOR KANSAS AND THE DISPERSION OF THE LEGISLATURE.

It would be too tedious and painful to relate the many outrages that were committed during the summer. Guerrilla bands scoured the country; men were robbed on the highway; several hung in the forests, and many shot down on the prairies. Women were insulted and violated; families driven from their claims, their houses burnt, and fields laid waste. Few were the harvests reaped, and little was the provision stored away. All the evils of civil war filled the land.

Not content with oppressing and driving out the free state settlers of Kansas, the "law and order party" stopped emigrants, robbed and turned them back. Ten families, from Iowa and Illinois, with farming implements and household furniture, moving in wagons, were stopped near Platte City, by one hundred and fifty men, armed with United States muskets, bowie-knives, revolvers and shot guns. Their wagons were searched, a few gaming rifles taken, and the whole body of emigrants forbid entering the Territory. They were turned back, and finally found lodgement in some old houses, ten miles beyond Liberty, where they remained until the troubles were over. Seventeen other emigrants, from Illinois, were robbed and scattered by a mob at Leavenworth.

Boats containing passengers coming up the Missouri river were stopped and searched. Arms, clothing, money and other valuables, were thus taken, and free state men driven back. The Missouri River was completely blockaded to eastern shipment and travel. The provisions and clothing sent out by Eastern friends to the sufferers in Kansas were deliberately taken. The following is a notice of the arrest and turning back of Eastern emigrants:

"MORE ABOLITIONISTS TURNED BACK.

"The steamer Sultan. having on board contraband articles, was recently stopped at Leavenworth City and lightened of forty-four rifles, and a large quantity of pistols and bowie-knives, taken from a crowd of cowardly Yankees, shipped out from Massachusetts. The boat was permitted to go up as far as Weston, where a guard was placed over the prisoners, and none of them permitted to land. They were shipped back from Weston on the same boat without ever being insured by the shippers. We do not approve fully of sending these criminals back to the East to be re-shipped to Kansas—if not through Missouri, through Iowa and Nebraska. We think they should meet a traitor's death, and the world can not censure us if we, in self-protection, have to resort to such ultra measures. We are of the opinion if the citizens of Leavenworth City or Weston would hang one or two boat loads of abolitionists, it would do more towards establishing peace in Kansas than all the speeches that have been delivered in Congress during the present session. Let the experiment be tried."

In consequence of the excited condition of the Territory and the waste of property, the spring found the free state men in great want of the necessities of life. Appeals were made to the people of the free States for aid. Vast contributions were raised, and provisions and clothing were sent to the needy in Kansas. Much of these supplies were seized on their way up the river. The Boston Relief Committee raised and appropriated about $20,000. Collections were made by lecturers, and relief furnished from all sections of the free States by individual donations.

The people of the Northern States watched with solicitude the affairs in Kansas. And after the Congressional report was made public, those who were incredulous of the alleged outrages now believed the worst had never been told. They were connected with the majority of the settlers in Kansas, not only by the kindred ties of blood, but also by sympathy and interest. They regarded the emigrants here as fighting the battles of freedom against slavery, and in the cause of justice and right. When they asked for provision and clothing, the free States liberally responded. And, now, when the soil of Kansas was overrun by armed invaders, the settlers driven from their homes and many compelled to leave the Territory, when their towns were sacked or threatened with destruction; their leading men imprisoned or expatriated; when the natural course of travel and freighting was obstructed; goods seized and taken from boats; emigrants robbed and driven back, they were prepared to lend not only the means of sustenance, but of protection to the people of Kansas. This is what gave rise to the Kansas Aid Societies and meetings.

Early in the spring Kansas meetings were held at various towns, companies organized, and funds raised for Kansas. On the 1st of March such an one was held in Milwaukee, Wisconsin, at which $3,000 in money and a quantity of arms were contributed, and a plan set on foot to organize an Emigrant Aid Company, with Auxilliary Societies in each county.

About the middle of March Rev. Henry Ward Beecher lectured at New Haven, Connecticut, for the benefit of a colony of seventy emigrants that were about to start to Kansas. At this meeting money was secured, by contributions, to purchase fifty-two Sharp's rifles, the funds for twenty-five of which Mr. Beecher pledged his congregation to raise. The company arrived in the Territory about the middle of April, and settled at Wabaunsee. It was organized and conducted under the supervision and leadership of

C. B. Lines, now State Commissioner of Claims. Such was the character of some of the first Kansas Aid Meetings.

When the people of McLane County, Illinois, learned that a number of their fellow-citizens had been intercepted in their emigration to Kansas, robbed and driven back with violent threats, they held a meeting, raised money, arms and men for the purpose of removing the obstructions to the peaceful emigration of free state men to the Territory. W. F. Arny was the leader of this movement. In a few days an enthusiastic meeting was held at Chicago, which raised over $20,000 in one night for the relief of Kansas. To the committee appointed by this meeting Mr. Arny went, and a plan was arranged to co-operate together and extend their work over the State.

But about the first of July, at a general meeting of the friends of free Kansas in Buffalo, the Grand Kansas Aid Committee was organized, composed of one member from each of the Free States, except Illinois, which had three representatives. They appointed an Executive Committee to reside in Chicago, whose duty it was to receive, forward and distribute the contributions of the people, whether provisions, arms or clothing, to the needy in Kansas. Auxilliary Societies were formed in every free State except Massachusetts, and the committee previously at work in Illinois joined in and co-operated with the National Committee. The Executive Committee was composed of Mr. J. D. Webster, Chairman, Mr. George W. Dole, Treasurer, Mr. H. B. Hurd, Secretary. They received and distributed in money alone, about $120,000. Of this $10,000 was expended in arms. Besides this they received donations, in small and large quantities, of provision, clothing and arms. Two hundred Sharp's rifles and ammunition belonging to this committee, were seized at Waverly and Lexington, Missouri. The directors held their second and last meeting in New York during January 1857, before whom John Brown appeared and solicited aid.

The Boston Relief Committee was organized early in the spring, for the purpose of sending clothing, provisions and money to the free State settlers in Kansas. It collected in Boston, chiefly in small sums by a spasmodic effort, $20,000. In June the State Kansas Committee of Massachusetts was organized, and took the place of the Boston Relief. Geo. L. Stearns was chairman of the former committee. He had been laboring as agent for the latter, previously. This society extended its operations over the State, and collected in small sums from all classes. They would appoint a meeting in a locality, have a speaker to address the people, to tell the story of Kansas' wrongs and sufferings, and then take up a collection for the relief of the settlers. In this way they raised in money about $78,000, one-half of which Mr. Stearns was instrumental in securing himself. Until about the 1st of August they sent nothing but money, provisions and clothing; at that time the Missouri River was closed to emigration, and earnest entreaties were made for arms. Two hundred Sharp's rifles and ammunition were immediately sent by way of Iowa, to the Territory. They were detained at Mt. Tabor, Iowa, and never reached Kansas. They finally fell into the hands of John Brown, and were taken to Harper's Ferry. The Committee also assisted in the elections of 1857–8, in the Territory.

There were many things during this summer that tended to increase the interest which the North felt in the welfare and success of free state men in Kansas, and the odium with which they regarded the slave propagandists. The Presidential campaign had opened in full blast, and was characterized by a popular excitement, scarcely equalled in the history of our country. And the wrongs and outrages committed in Kansas were held up in public meetings before the world, the Border Ruffians were burlesqued by grotesque figures and mocked in their atrocious conduct. Many a time has the writer seen Generals Stringfellow and Atchison personified by an individual of blackened face and tangled hair, with a long tin sword, a lofty three-cornered hat and slouched military clothes, mounted upon a horse, as though leading a gang of ragamuffins into Kansas to vote. I well recollect the impression such scenes had upon my boyish mind. I then had no idea that those two gentlemen laid any claims to respectability.

To increase the popular flame, those individuals, driven from the Territory at the peril of their lives, attended many of the conventions and told the story of their wrongs, and of the atrocities they had witnessed. Emigrants robbed and driven back, returned to verify the statements of oppression and desperation on the Border. The Congressional Committee had hung up before the nation the gloomy and doleful picture of Kansas outrages.

On the other hand, similar proceedings were carried on throughout the South. Military companies armed and equipped, as we have seen, entered Kansas early in the spring, with no other object than to fight and to vote. Large sums of money were raised in the South for the support and pay of these men, by property tax, and voluntary contributions. Speakers from the Border visited the Southern cities, made speeches and collected money. The South liberally granted her funds towards the cause, with her characteristic want of system, keeping no account or record of what was done, or the manner of doing it. A long address represented as emanating from the "law and order" party in Kansas Territory, and signed by Atchison, Stringfellow, Buford and others, on the 21st of June, was sent to the South. It set forth that their party composed the majority of the settlers in the Territory, that they had beat the opposite faction fairly at the ballot-box, and now they had been called upon to enforce the laws against the rebellious and traitorous party; that the abolitionists were daily murdering and robbing pro-slavery men, and were receiving large reinforcements and assistance from abroad; that they were increasing in numbers so fast that the law and order party must be replenished or they would be overthrown; that Missouri had been heavily taxed to attend to her interests in the Territory for the past two years, and now they stand in special need of help. They earnestly implored aid in money and men. Companies and parties kept coming from the South all summer.

As the time neared for the reassembling of the Legislature, the subject attracted the attention of both parties. As the Missourians had threatened to assail and break up the Legislature, should it convene, the active and influential free state men thought proper to assemble as large a body of citizens at Topeka as possible on that occasion, in order to furnish protection to the Legislature. Accordingly a mass convention was announced to be held at Topeka, on the 3d of July, for the purpose of taking into consideration the condition of the Territory. It was the design by this movement to have had assembled, at the above mentioned time and place, at least two thousand men under arms. These could have continued in military parade on the 4th, as is customary in our country, so that they would have been in readiness and at hand to have furnished protection to the Legislature in case of an assault or violence, though in no way connected with the legislative body themselves.

But there were various obstacles to prevent a large concourse of settlers at Topeka, at that time. The principal free state presses having been destroyed, the chief source of communicating with the people at large, on short notice, was cut off. Guerrilla bands infested the roads and prairies, ready to rob or kill the traveler, or defenseless families, so that it was dangerous both for themselves and families to venture abroad. Besides these causes many free state men who thought it impolitic for the Legislature to meet, used their influence against the measure.

Despite the active exertions of a few citizens, there was not collected at the convention, besides the Legislature, more than eight hundred persons; and about one-half of these came unarmed. On the 2d of July the members of the popular convention began to assemble. Those who had been regarded as leaders of the free state men were not there; some were in prison, others were driven from the Territory. "Under these unfavorable circumstances a meeting was held by a few of the most influential men, and, as the difficulties were great, and the prospect threatening," the acting Governor of the State of Kansas, John Curtis, took the responsibility to issue a proclamation, calling both branches of the Legislature to convene on the third day of July, at 8 o'clock A. M., in extra session.

Governor Shannon, who started for St. Louis on the 23d of June, had left orders with Colonel Sumner if "this pretended legislative body should meet as proposed, you will disperse them, peacably if you can, forcibly if necessary. Should they reassemble at some other place, or at the same place, you will take care that they be again dispersed. The civil authorities will be instructed to co-operate with you if it is found necessary, in order to break this illegal body, and to institute proceedings against the several members under the above statute." The statute to which reference is here made, is the Territorial law.

The Missourians, therefore, understanding that the administration at Washington had determined to break up the free state movement by the United States troops, considered it useless for them to interfere.

Accordingly, before the day arrived for the meeting of the Legislature, Colonel Sumner, with several companies of dragoons encamped on the south side of Topeka, and four companies of dragoons from Fort Riley encamped on the north side in the Kaw bottom.

Secretary Woodson, then acting Governor, as Shannon was absent, received word, June 30, that Lane, with a large body of armed men, was marching from the north to invest Topeka and defend the Legislature. It was this rumor that created the above display of force. No doubt the acting Governor rejoiced in the prospect of a collision between the free state men and United States forces.

In accordance with the acting Governor's proclamation, the Legislature assembled, for special session, on the 3d of July, the adjournment having been to the 4th. The chief question which engaged their attention, and that of the convention which had also assembled, was what course would be the best to pursue in view of the circumstances surrounding them? Upon this subject there was a difference of opinion, and the discussion was animated and excited. Some did not wish the Legislature to meet at all, or if it met to adjourn immediately; the majority favored the assembling of the Legislature, pursuant to adjournment, and proceeding with its business until dispersed by the troops of the United States. A few enthusiastic ones favored putting the town in an attitude of defense, and resisting any attempts of the United States forces to interfere with their deliberations. The special session adjourned in the evening, without adopting any policy, except that of agreeing to reassemble at the time appointed for the opening of the regular session.

Meantime a committee of free state men had waited on Colonel Sumner, on the evening of the 2d, relative to the meaning of his war-like demonstrations. They received the following letter from him the next day:

"HEADQUARTERS 1ST CAVALRY,
"CAMP AT TOPEKA, K. T., July 3, 1856.

"GENTLEMEN: In relation to the assembling of the Topeka Legislature, (the subject of our conversation last night) the more I reflect on it the more I am convinced that the peace of the country will be greatly endangered by your persistence in this measure. Under these circumstances I would ask you and your friends to take the matter into good consideration. It will certainly be much better that you should act voluntarily in this matter, from a sense of prudence and patriotism, at this moment of high excitement throughout the country, than that the authority of the General Government should be compelled to use coercive measures to prevent the assemblage of that Legislature.

"I am, gentlemen, very respectfully, your obedient servant, E. V. SUMNER,
"Colonel 1st Cavalry Commanding."

Secretary Woodson, who was now acting Governor, with several other pro-slavery officials, had arrived at the camp of Colonel Sumner. In accordance with the programme, which they had arranged, United States Marshal Donaldson, with Judge Elmore, entered Topeka about 10 o'clock on the 4th. They went to the place where the popular convention was in session, and intimated to a few persons that they had something to communicate to that body. Having taken their places upon the platform at the invitation of some of the officers, the Marshal announced that he had several proclamations to read to them, but as he was no speaker, Judge Elmore would attend to it. The Judge then proceeded to read the President's proclamation of February, and several of Governor Shannon's, and finally the following one from Secretary Woodson:

"PROCLAMATION BY THE ACTING GOVERNOR OF KANSAS.

"WHEREAS, We have been reliably informed that a number of persons, claiming legislative power, are about to assemble in the town of Topeka, for the purpose of adopting a code of laws, or of executing other legislative functions, in violation of the act of Congress, organizing the Territory, and of the laws adopted in pursuance thereof; and it appears that a military organization exists in this Territory for the purpose of sustaining this unlawful legislative movement, and thus, in effect, to subvert by violence all present constitutional and legal authority; and,

"WHEREAS, The President of the United States, has, by proclamation bearing date, 11th of February, 1856, declared that any such plans for the determination of the future institutions of the Territory, if carried into action, will constitute insurrection and therein command all persons engaged in such unlawful combinations against the constituted authorities of the Territory of Kansas, or the United States, to disperse and retire to their respective places of abode; and,

"WHEREAS, Satisfactory evidence that said proclamation has been, and is about to be, disregarded, now, therefore,

"I, Daniel Woodson, acting Governor of the Territory of Kansas, by virtue of the authority vested in me by law, and in pursuance of the aforesaid proclamation of the President of the United States, and to the end of upholding the legal and constituted authorities of the Territory, and of preserving the peace and public tranquillity, do issue this, my proclamation forbidding all persons claiming legislative power and authority, as aforesaid, from assembling, organizing, or attempting to organize, or acting in any legislative capacity whatever, under the penalties attached to all unlawful violation of the law of the land, and the disturbers of the peace and tranquilllity of the country.

"In testimony whereof, I have hereunto subscribed my hand, and caused to be affixed the seal of the Territory, this 4th day of July, 1856, and of the independence of the United States, the eightieth.

[SEAL] "DANIEL WOODSON,
"Acting Governor of Kansas Territory."

"Proclamation of the President and the orders under it require me to sustain the Executive of the Territory in executing the laws and preserving the peace. I, therefore, hereby announce that I shall maintain the proclamation at all hazards. E. V. SUMNER,
"Colonel 1st Cavalry Commanding."

The convention quietly and respectfully listened to the reading of these various documents. When they were finished, the two Territorial officials, descended the platform and retired through the crowd. As they did so Marshal Donaldson halted, and asked if they had any communication to send to Colonel Sumner. He was then informed of his mistake—that this convention was not the Legislature to which the proclamation referred and hence could make no reply.

About noon Colonel Sumner, who seems to have been aware of the time the Legislature was to convene, approached the town with his companies of dragoons in battle array. At the centre of their front, the American Flag floated to the breeze, and a band was playing "Hail Columbia, Happy Land." They moved rapidly and impressively down Kansas Avenue and wheeled into line, facing Legislative Hall. It being the 4th of July, two companies of Topeka volunteers were drawn up near where the troops halted to receive a banner from the ladies, and the street was filled with men, women and children. Two cannon were also planted up the street a few hundred yards, loaded, the fuses smoking, and the cannoneers ready for the word "fire." The dragoons from the bottom approached the edge of town, on the north, and stood in readiness for a charge. Thus was the entrance, as though they expected armed resistance.

Colonel Sumner, having got his troops posted to suit him, dismounted and entered the Hall of the Legislature. The House was not yet called to order and the Speaker was absent. Colonel Sumner walked forward to the platform and was given a seat. The hour having arrived for calling the House to order, the First Clerk struck the gavel several times on the desk, and began calling the roll. No quorum answering to their names, the Sergeant-at-arms was requested to bring in absentees. The roll was called again and only seventeen responded, although twice that number of members were present. There evidently was a fear on the part of many, that thus answering to their names would subject them to arrest.

When the Clerk had finished calling the roll the second time Colonel Sumner arose and said:

"GENTLEMEN: I am called upon this day to perform the most painful duty of my whole life. Under authority of the President's proclamation, I am here to disperse this Legislature, and therefore inform you that you can not meet. I, therefore, order you to disperse. God knows that I have no party feeling in this matter, and will hold none so long as I occupy my present position in Kansas. I have just returned from the Borders, where I have been sending home companies of Missourians, and now I am ordered here to disperse you. Such are my orders, and you *must disperse*. I now command you to disperse. I repeat that this is the most painful duty of my whole life."

Judge Schuyler asked, "Colonel Sumner, are we to understand that the Legislature will be driven out at the point of the bayonet?"

Colonel Sumner—"I shall use all the forces at my command to carry out my orders."

The House dispersed according to orders, and Colonel Sumner repaired to the Senate. It was not yet called to order when he entered. He immediately proceeded to inform them of his orders, and that they must disperse. No one making any response, he asked:

"Well, gentlemen, do you consider yourselves dispersed?"

Mr. Thornton, President of the Senate, replied: "Colonel Sumner, the Senate is not in session, and can not make any reply to you; neither can any member of it."

On being asked if they might be permitted to convene so as to receive communications as a body, the Colonel replied: "No; my orders are that you must not be permitted to meet, and I can not allow you to do any business." After a threat of arrest by the Marshal, which was received with scorn, and a few more remarks by different individuals, Mr. Pillsbury said: "Colonel Sumner, we are in no condition to resist the United States troops; and if you order us to disperse, of course we must disperse." At the suggestion of Colonel Allen, this expression was assented to as the sentiment of all. Colonel Sumner then left the Hall and retired with his force to camp in disgust. He was mad when ordered to disperse the Legislature, and hurried through it as a dirty piece of business.

CHAPTER XXXV.

BOLD STROKES AND EXTERMINATION.

It would seem, indeed, that Colonel Sumner was harsh and severe in executing his orders against the free state men. But such was not the case; he executed them as mildly as the harsh and severe orders would permit. His sympathies were with the free state men; but he never expressed himself publicly, and most carefully concealed his feelings as a man; took no part whatever in politics, and only sought to do his duty as a military officer. He was, therefore, some times censured by one party and then by the other; but generally enjoyed the confidence and respect of free state men. The latter part of July this faithful officer was superseded in his command at Fort Leavenworth for no other reason, it was supposed, than the impartial discharge of his duty. He treated both parties alike, and on that account the President sent an officer to outrank him. He was a strict disciplinarian, respected by his soldiers, by whom he was termed "Old Bull of the Woods," on account of his gruffness. He remained at Fort Leavenworth for some time afterwards. He fought bravely in the late war for the Union, through several important battles in which he was known as Major-General Edwin V. Sumner, and finally died early in 1863, at Syracuse, New York.

General Percifer F. Smith superseded Colonel Sumner in command at Fort Leavenworth. He was born in Pennsylvania, but had spent much of his life in Louisiana, and was intensely pro-slavery in feeling and sentiment. His health had been failing for a long while, and he was confined to his room pretty much all the time he remained in Kansas, which was only until February, 1867. He had distinguished himself at the storming of Monterey.

About the 1st of August a road was opened through Iowa and Nebraska to Kansas, and emigration began to flow over it. This was the "advent of Lane's Northern army," of which a full account will hereafter be given. The first that came through was General J. H. Lane, who immediately became a terror to pro-slavery men. The mere mention of his name would cause them to quake, and news of his approach would create a stampede of the citizens in every pro-slavery town.

The free state guerrillas had in most instances retired from the field about the 1st of July, upon the assurances from Colonel Sumner that the Border Ruffians would be driven from the Territory. Although this officer had exerted himself in performing his duty, still the Ruffians would assemble in Indian reserves, and unfrequented places, and continue their depredations upon the surrounding country and passing travelers.

By the first of August the Ruffians had fortified themselves in various places, from which "strongholds they would sally forth, 'press' horses and cattle, intercept the mails, rob stores and dwellings, plunder travelers, burn houses and destroy crops." At the solicitation of the neighbors, on account of the outrages committed by this band, the fort near Osawattomie was attacked on the 5th of August by a company of free state men. The Georgians, who were in command of it, on learning that the free state men were approaching, abandoned the post and fled, leaving a large quantity of plunder. The Fort was taken and demolished.

The Georgians retreated to another Fort on Washington Creek, about twelve miles from Lawrence, where they renewed their plundering upon the settlers. The officers of the United States troops were earnestly importuned to disperse and drive them from the neighborhood; but they replied that they could not move without orders. On the 11th of August Major D. S. Hoyt, a peaceable and respected citizen, was sent by the people of Lawrence to the camp on Washington Creek, called Fort Saunders, to try and make some arrangements with Colonel Treadwell, the commander, for the suppression of these disturbances. On his return home he was brutally murdered, his body being riddled with bullets.

This occurrence so exasperated the free state men that they immediately attacked the pro-slavery headquarters at Franklin. The Ruffians were fortified in the same block house as on a former occasion, but it had been considerably strengthened since. They were asked to surrender before being fired upon. On their refusal the fight began and lasted about three hours. One man was killed and six wounded on the free state side; on the other side three were severely and one mortally wounded. The free state men at length pushed a wagon load of burning hay up to the building. Soon the cry for quarters was heard from within and the wagon was removed. The inmates then threw down their arms and fled. A vast amount of plunder, composed of provisions, guns, ammunition and a six pounder brass piece was secured by the victors.

The free state forces continued their assaults. On the 15th, Fort Saunders, on Washington Creek, at which the Ruffians from Franklin had congregated, was attacked and destroyed by a company under the leadership of Lane and Grover. The Georgians again fled at the approach of their opponents, leaving their plunder behind. Both here and at Franklin many articles were found which had been taken from Lawrence at the time it was sacked.

The next day's work demolished the last stronghold of pro-slavery men south of the Kaw. Colonel Titus had a fortified house near Lecompton, and constantly harbored guerrilla bands of pro-slavery men. Lecompton was the capital, and had been in constant fear of an attack for some time, The free state prisoners were held about two miles from the place in camp, and guarded by the United States troops. On the morning of the 16th, about four hundred free state men, composed of the Lawrence boys, Harvey's Chicago company, Dr. Cutter's* party, and others, marched up the California Road, and halted a little beyond Titus' house, which was north of the road about one mile and a half. Here they divided, one-half going to the left of the ridge, under command of Joel Grover, the other to the right, under the command of Captain Walker—both brave and determined men. About sunrise they made a simultaneous attack upon the house, sheltered by the ridge upon which, in front of the house, a cannon was posted, and opened a fearful fire. The gun was loaded with lead slugs, manufactured from the type of the "Herald of Freedom," which had been picked up from the streets and fished out of the river. As the gun first went off the engineer exclaimed: "This is the second edition of the 'Herald of Freedom.'" The fight lasted about a half an hour, and resulted in the capture of Colonel Titus and Captain William Donaldson, who had rendered themselves notorious at the sacking of Lawrence—and eighteen others. Five prisoners held by "these law and order men" were released, one of whom had been sentenced to be shot that same morning. Titus was found hid in the loft of the house, wounded in the shoulder and hand. When called out from his hiding place, he begged most piteously for his life. One of his party was killed and several hurt. Captain Shombre, of the free state men, a brave and highly esteemed gentleman from Indiana, was mortally wounded and died the next day. Walker and Grover, with their men and prisoners, hurried back to Lawrence.

*Author of Cutter's Physiology.

The people of Lecompton, filled with consternation at the firing of the first gun, made a general stampede. Many rushed to the river and sought to cross; others fled to the woods or camp of United States troops for safety.

When the firing first began Major Sedgewick* in command of the Government forces two miles from Lecompton, sent a company of dragoons to the town to ascertain the cause of this warlike demonstration. When the troops arrived there the Territorial officials could not be found. At length they were directed to the river, where they found the Governor on the eve of stepping into a scow to cross over. To the inquiry of the troops "what were his orders" he replied, "I don't think I will have any thing done with them, but we will go and see if they have disturbed Major Clark." On going to this gentleman's residence, they found it deserted, with many evidences that the inmates left in great haste. Clark, who, it will be remembered, was the accredited murderer of Barber, had ever since suffered fearful apprehensions for his own safety. At one time he had fired upon and wounded his friend, having mistaken him for a foe.

On the following day, Governor Shannon, in company with Major Sedgewick and others, visited Lawrence. Here he made his second treaty with the people of this city, the stipulations of which were that he should set at liberty the five free state men arrested since the attack upon Franklin; that no more arrests should be made under the Territorial laws; that the howitzer taken by Jones from Lawrence should be surrendered up; that Titus and his band should be set at liberty. Such was the treaty, more humiliating than the first. The Governor solemnized this treaty by a speech to the citizens, saying, "and the few days I remain in office shall be devoted, so help me Heaven, in carrying

*This officer was open and communicative to the free state men, and was their steadfast friend, He rose to distinction in the late war, and fell in an important engagement.

out faithfully my part of the agreement, and in preserving order."

On the 19th of August, a ruffian at Leavenworth made a bet of six dollars against a pair of boots that in less than two hours he would have an abolitionist's scalp. He accordingly sallied out as upon a gaming frolic, shot a young man by the name of Hops, returned with the scalp and claimed the stakes. A German expressing his abhorrence of the deed, was shot on the spot. A few days afterwards, a young lady of Bloomington was taken from her home one mile and a half by four ruffians; with her tongue drawn out and tied with a cord, her arms pinioned behind her, her person was violated.

Governor Shannon, after repeated solicitations, and having, it was thought, for some time contemplated it, at length resigned. On the same day of his resignation, the 21st of August, the papers containing his removal were received. Thus ended Mr. Shannon's career as Governor of Kansas. He had, in most instances, faithfully served the party which appointed him, and had generally enjoyed their confidence and praise. He allowed himself to be used as a pliant tool by the Border chiefs; he would heedlessly permit all the elements of war to gather, and only awake from his lethargy when they were about to break upon each other in bloody violence. He should be censured more for what he permitted and omitted than for what he committed. His fault lay not in the wickedness of his heart, but in the inactivity and pliability of his character. He was finally rejected by his friends, and left without protection from the robbers and assassins who had been his counsellors, and finally escaped from them out of the Territory at the hazard of his life.

Secretary Woodson exercised the functions of Executive until the arrival of the new Governor. The reason for urging Mr. Shannon to resign, was to get Woodson in as acting Governor, with the view of calling out the militia to begin their old work of extermination. As Mr. Shannon refused to make this call, they sought to prevail upon him to resign, that they might effect their object through Mr. Woodson.

Many of the pro-slavery men, terrified by a guilty conscience, and fear of retribution, left the Territory with their families, while others asked the protection of United States troops. A most pitiful and importunate appeal went up from the overthrown strongholds of pro-slavery men south of the Kaw. "FRANKLIN IS TAKEN BY THE ABOLITIONISTS AND BURNT TO THE GROUND? LECOMPTON IS SURROUNDED BY EIGHT HUNDRED MEN! COL. TITUS KILLED! LAW AND ORDER PARTY BEING MURDERED BY THE NORTHERN ARMY." "FAMILIES ARE FLEEING FROM BURNING HOMES." So ran the bulletin of the border. The old cry of "TO ARMS! TO ARMS!" with the usual threats and denunciations, was made.

The following are the closing lines of a circular issued on the 16th of August, by the chieftains of the Border to the ruffians.

"We give you no more rumors, but simple statements of undoubted facts. We say to you that war, organized and matured, is now being waged by the abolitionists, and we call on all who are not prepared to see their friends butchered, to be themselves driven from their homes, to rally instantly to the rescue!

"The abolitionists proclaim that 'no quarter will be given.' 'Every pro-slavery man must be exterminated.' What will be your reply?

"D. R. ATCHISON,
"W. H. RUSSEL,
"A. G. BOONE,
"B. F. STRINGFELLOW."

The following are extracts from the appeal of the law and order party at Lecompton:

"*To all true pro-slavery men in Missouri.*—We call upon our friends in Missouri, in the name of humanity, to come to the rescue, with men and provisions to support them. We have determined to clean the territory or fall in the attempt. We send expresses to-night to St. Joseph, Liberty, Platte City and to Westport. TO ARMS, AT ONCE, *and come to the rescue.* We are all under arms here to-night, and wil be ready to-morrow.

"E. C. McCarty,
"Pres. Law and Order Party."

On the 25th, Secretary Woodson, who had come into power, issued his proclamation declaring the territory in a state of insurrection, and calling out the militia. This was just what the border men desired. It rendered the Secretary's popularity still greater. The pro-slavery press resounded his praise, as it promulgated his call. Men were exhorted, in the spirit of desperation, to rush into a savage warfare of extermination.

General Richardson wrote to the Governor on the 20th, that having received information of Lane's coming into the Territory with his "northern army," he had called out the militia of his division to intercept him. The Secretary replied, approving the measure, and at the same time wrote to General Coffey, of Southern District of Kansas militia, to take the field with his command.

Under an article headed "Third and Last Time," the "Squatter Sovereign" says:

"Our friends have been collecting on the Border during the past week, and in a few days will have a well organized force in the field, equal to any emergency. We again reiterate, a crisis has arrived in the affairs of Kansas, and another week will tell a tale that will have an important bearing on the future fate of Kansas. It behooves every citizen to shoulder arms without any further delay. We have been slow to believe that any thing like serious fighting would occur; but we are now fully convinced that a deadly struggle must ensue, and one or more hard battles transpire, before the abolitionists can be subdued. * * * * * * Already the smouldering ruins of numerous dwellings, and the reeking blood of many a victim, cries aloud for vengeance. The cry is heard and will be answered with tenfold retaliation. If there is one breast still unpenetrated by this call, we urge that it instantly become alive to the importance of the emergency. The want of a few men may turn the fortunes of war against us. Then let every man who can bear arms 'be off to the wars again.' Let it be the 'third and last time.' Let the watchword be 'extermination, total and complete.'"

Atchison's forces assembled at Little Santa Fe to the number of four hundred and fifty. A party of them first made a descent upon the Quaker Mission on the Shawnee Reserve. They robbed it of horses and valuables, and treated the occupants with cruelty. On the 25th a company of Missourians, one hundred and fifty in number, under the command of Captain John E. Brown, encamped on Mound or Middle Creek, about nine miles south-west of Osawattomie. Companies of eighteen, forty and sixty men, under Captains Cline, Anderson and Shore, encamped the same evening in that neighborhood. On the following day the free state men marched within one mile of the enemy's camp, which they reached by 8 o'clock, and sent out scouts who brought in four prisoners. From these they learned that fifty of Brown's men were absent from camp, whereupon they determined to make an attack. About noon Captain Anderson passed around so as to come up below the enemy and cut off his retreat, while the other two companies advanced upon him from another direction. The latter first came upon eight of the Missourians, five of whom they captured. They had with them a free state man whom they declared "they would hang." He made his escape. As soon as Cline's men, who were in advance, came in sight of the camp of the Missourians, they opened fire upon them, which was promptly returned. The firing lasted about ten minutes. When Captain Shore's company arrived the Missourians fled, leaving their camp baggage, most of their horses, wagons, guns, boots, coats, vests, hats, &c., &c., and the best of all a good dinner prepared, which the free state men fell upon with devouring appetites. Lieutenant Cline, of Fort Scott, was badly wounded, and afterwards died. This was the only injury that happened to any person. Eleven prisoners were taken by the free state men, all of whom were liberated on the following day, upon their promise never to take up arms against the rights of the settlers. These free state forces were a portion of John Brown's command.

On the 29th of August four hundred Missourians, under Captain John W. Reed, aided by Rev. Martin White, left the head waters of Bull Creek for Osawattomie. It was their design to reach the latter place about midnight; but they were compelled to make a circuitous route to avoid a guarded ford, on which account they did not get there until about sunrise. As they approached they killed Frederick Brown, son of John Brown, senior, and William Garrison, who had offered no resistance, but whom they found peaceably engaged at work. They entered the town from the north-west.

The people of Osawatomie had been expecting an attack for some time. But still no particular arrangements were made for its defense. On the night previous no unusual watch was kept up, only the customary patrols having been sent out. Captain Brown commanded the free state forces; besides his own company, numbering seventeen men, there were Captain Updegraff with ten, and Captain Cline with fourteen men. When it was known that the enemy was approaching, these men sallied out and took position in the woods about a half mile from town. Captain Brown occupied the left, Captain Cline the right and Captain Updegraff the center. As the Border Ruffians approached they fired three guns, signalling for the free state men to surrender. Thereupon the latter, who had been commanded not to fire until orders had been given, impatient, returned the fire without orders. The enemy were then about six hundred yards distant. After firing a few rounds on both sides, the Missourians, who became somewhat confused by the murderous fire from the timber, wheeled the cannon into position upon the right of the free state men, at a distance of about four hundred yards, and opened fire. At each successive discharge they moved the gun about six rods to the east so as to scour the timber. They fired six shots without effect. All the time the free state men were pouring into the enemy a murderous fire, and moving to the east likewise, thus escaping the vollies from the artillery. The Missourians then dismounted and made an infantry charge upon the front and right wing of Brown's party. The latter, overpowered and without orders, retreated in confusion across the river, some swimming it, others passing over in a skiff. Two were killed while attempting to cross on horseback. After taking five prisoners the Missourians proceeded to demolish the town.

Osawatomie was a village of about two hundred inhabitants, owned principally by O. C. Brown, who was its founder. It was laid out in the spring of 1855, assisted by the New England Emigrant Aid Society, which located a mill there. It derives its name from the union of the two words Osage and Pottowatomie. Brown was a pro-slavery man, but lost his property when the town was destroyed. The women had generally left the village a few days previous to the attack. The Missourians first plundered the dwelling houses and stores. They filled the wagons which they had with them, and others which they procured in the town, with goods and other valuables. When they had thus secured their booty, they set fire to the dwellings and stores, and in a short time only four houses were standing on the town site.

With their loaded wagons, prisoners, a vast number of horses and cattle which they had collected from the town and surrounding country, they left for Westport. They had five wagons, which they kept a little distant from the others, and would not permit the prisoners to approach, but guarded them constantly. On this account they were supposed to contain the bodies of the dead. Of the prisoners they captured, Mr. W. Williams, a Missourian, was led to the edge of the town and shot. On September 1st, Charley Keiser, who had been kindly assisting them in driving cattle, in order to preserve their good will, was taken out a short distance from the camp on Cedar Creek, and shot by a guard of Kickapoo Rangers. He had been concerned in the battle of Black Jack—an unpardonable offence, and the same for which Cantral died. Messrs. R. Reynolds and H. K. Thomas were taken on to Kansas City, put aboard a boat, and sent down the river, with the warning that if caught again in the territory during the troubles, the penalty would be hanging. Beyond what has been mentioned above, the free state men suffered no loss, either in killed or wounded.

Captain Brown was last seen after the battle, slowly ascending the north bank of the Maries des Cygnes, with his sword thrown over his shoulder and a revolver in the other hand. All supposed that he was killed, until about a week afterwards, when Lawrence was in danger, he came riding into that town, to the astonishment of the people. He appeared like an appointed deliverer, and joy lit up the countenances of the inhabitants, as they gazed upon the hero of the Maries des Cygnes. He immediatety took command.

Rev. Martin White, for the service of killing Frederick Brown, was elected a member of the Lecompton Legislature. At its session, in a speech, he gave a glowing description of this wonderful and praiseworthy feat. When the assembly adjourned, he started home, but never reached it. His body was afterwards found upon the prairies, with a ball through his heart.

Word having reached Lawrence or Topeka concerning the demonstrations of Reed, General Lane, with about three hundred men, set out to intercept his retreat back to Missouri. Arriving in the neighborhood of Prairie City, he learned that the invaders had encamped on the head waters of Bull Creek. He marched his men on double quick, every one in high expectation of a fight. The cavalry, about thirty in number, approached the enemy first, and halted for the infantry to come up. The Missourians had formed in line of battle, in front of their camp, with four pieces of artillery planted and loaded.

As soon as the infantry arrived, General Lane ordered the whole command to fall back eight miles and encamp; the reason for which, as he afterwards explained, was, that it was too near dark to begin a battle. The men disappointed, dejected, in many instances, on the retreat, sank exhausted on the prairie, and a general murmur was heard throughout the lines. They had run over a rough country, beneath a broiling sun, without food, for twenty-five miles, in high hopes of a fight, and, at the moment they had an opportunity to pounce upon the enemy, were ordered back. Early on the following morning, Reed and his command decamped, and hurriedly marched for Westport. Lane, learning from his scouts that the enemy had left, returned with his command to Lawrence.

Meanwhile the pro-slavery forces at Lecompton were committing all manner of outrages, burning houses, taking property, seizing deputations that were sent to remonstrate against such flagrant conduct, and holding them prisoners. The county officials at the head of the United States troops were busy making arrests and insulting unprotected families. The Topeka boys, as they returned home, beheld the smoking ruins of six dwellings.

On the 30th of August General Richardson and command was ordered between Leavenworth and Lawrence to prevent Lane's escape. The following day Secretary Woodson, who did not fancy the idea of the Topeka boys in going down to operate against General Whitfield, ordered Colonel Cook, with his command, "to proceed, at the earliest moment, to invest the town of Topeka, disarm the insurrectionists, or aggressive invaders against the organized Government of the Territory, to be found at or near that point, leveling with the ground their breastworks, forts and fortifications, keep the head men or leaders in close confinement, and all persons found in arms against the Government as prisoners, subject to the orders of the Marshal." He wrote, "It is very desirable to intercept the invaders on the road known as 'Lane's Trail,' 'leading from Nebraska to Topeka.'" With credit to Colonel Cook, we have it to record that he refused to obey this order.

The Topeka boys responded to Colonel Lane's call for men, reaching Lawrence the same day they started, in time to join his command there in their march to Bull Creek. After a severe tramp of fifty miles, under a broiling sun and over rough roads, with spirits dejected and disappointed, they had sunk to rest in the grass upon the prairie. Next morning word reached them that Topeka was menaced with destruction, and their homes exposed to the attack of an unscrupulous and remorseless foe. This announcement shot like electricity from heart to heart, banishing weariness and dejection, and infusing the strength of a giant in every man. Quickly they began their homeward march. Unconscious of thirst or heat, with spirits too strong for nerves and muscles, they strode over hills and across hollows. As they passed opposite Lecompton, they witnessed the smoking ruins of six free state dwellings, and beheld the lonely wife and helpless children grieving by the ashy remains. Wild with rage, and urged on by the most intense solicitude, they pressed forward. Arriving at Big Springs, they received a dispatch that Topeka was unharmed and no enemy near. Assured that their homes were safe, their anxiety relieved, many sank exhausted along the roadside. But few reached Topeka that night; the others scattered from Big Springs to within a mile of their homes, slumbered in the grass along the highway, some of whom did not reach Topeka for several days.

On account of the offenses above enumerated it was determined by the free state men to make a demonstration upon Lecompton, and liberate the prisoners held by the bogus officials. On the evening of the 3d of September the forces left Lawrence in two divisions, one under the command of Colonel Harvey to the north of the Kaw, the other under Colonel Lane to the south of that river, with the design of making a simultaneous attack early the following morning. Colonel Harvey proceeded with his men and took position immediately north of Lecompton, so as to prevent the escape of fugitives. After waiting all night and next day, in a cold rain, and Lane not appearing, he presumed that the attack had been abandoned.

He made an assault in a different quarter. Learning that there was a company of Ruffians encamped on Slough Creek, about fifteen miles from Lecompton, who had been plundering and stealing, he resolved to attack them. Before the Ruffians were aware of their presence, Harvey's men had them surrounded. One of the members of the pro-slavery camp discharged his gun at the free state men, which brought upon the Ruffians a fearful volley of rifle balls, whereupon the latter immediately surrendered. They were disarmed, relieved of their plunder, of which they had a large quantity, and permitted to go their way. Several of them were badly wounded.

General Lane, who had, from some cause, delayed his march, did not reach Lecompton until the afternoon of the fourth. About four o'clock, he suddenly made his appearance on Capitol Hill, overlooking the village, and planted his cannon upon its frowning brow. A deputation was sent into town to demand of the commanding officer "the unconditional and immediate surrender of all the free state prisoners now in Lecompton." This deputation, on entering town, were informed that the militia were disbanded and the prisoners released that morning, and were to be escorted to Lawrence next day. Meantime the troops, in camp a short distance off, having received word of the attack, hurried to the rescue, and reached Lane's forces before the return of the embassadors from town. Colonel

Cook, commanding the United States forces, rather chided the free state men for their mistake in thus appearing after the militia were disbanded and prisoners released. Mr. Parrott replied, "Colonel Cook, when we send a man, or two men, or a dozen men, to speak with the Territorial authorities, they are arrested and held like felons. How then are we to know what is going on in Lecompton? Why, we have come here with an army to find out what is going on. How else could we know?" The prisoners were released according to promise, but that afternoon was the first intimation to any free state man that the militia had been disbanded or that the prisoners were to be released.

While these events were transpiring, horrid scenes were being enacted at Leavenworth. Teams sent to that city for supplies of provisions and goods were seized, and the drivers held "prisoners of war." "The roads," said Governor Shannon, "were literally strewn with dead bodies." Thirteen mutilated corpses were found in one place. These murderers and desperadoes were Missourians and Southerners; the former crossed over from Platte county. They were under command of Captain Emory, a mail agent, called themselves "The Regulators," and declared all free state men who did not leave would be killed.

On the 1st of September an election was held, at which Mr. Murphy was elected Mayor. They then proceeded to expel every free state man from the town. To this end they broke open stores and private houses, and drove the occupants into the roads, irrespective of age or sex. Under the pretext of searching for arms, they forcibly entered the house of Wm. Phillips, the same gentleman who had previously been tarred and feathered. Presuming that he was to be subjected to a similar outrage to that he had suffered before, he determined to defend himself. As they rushed upon him, he fired and killed two of them; in an instant his body was pierced by a dozen bullets, and he fell dead in the presence of his wife and another lady. Fifty of the inhabitants were that day driven on board the Polar Star, the captain of which was ordered not to leave without permission.

On the following day Captain Emory paraded the streets with eight hundred armed men. He drove one hundred more men, women and children aboard the boat, and with an escort started them for St. Louis. Others had fled to the woods and the fort to find protection. The reign of anarchy was complete. The commander of the fort refused protection to the refugees, and posted bills requiring them to leave the premises. Many of these sufferers, "among whom were men of the highest respectability, and women and children, were compelled, some of them without money or suitable clothing, to take to the prairies, exposed at every step to the danger of being murdered by scouting or marauding parties, or at the risk of their lives effect their escape upon the downward bound boats. Some of these were shot upon the river banks while making the attempt, whilst others were seized at Kansas City, and other Missouri towns, brought back as prisoners, and disposed of in such a manner as will only be made known in that great day when all human mysteries will be revealed. There is many an unhappy wife and mother in the States, looking anxiously, and hoping against hope, for the return of an adventurous husband or son, whose bones are bleaching upon the prairies or mouldering beneath their sod."

Darkness overshadowed the land. Heaven never looked down upon a sadder picture of human folly and corruption; angels, if they witness earthly scenes, must have wept as they gazed upon the innocent victims of rapine and violence. O, the depths of human depravity! The greatest enemy of mankind is man. While the men were absent, committing injury to their fellow-men, their homes would be visited by members of the opposite faction, their families driven out from their burning houses, and frequently, while their wives and daughters writhed in the foul embrace of the destroyer, the air was filled with their wild shrieks and piteous wails. Armed bands from Missouri, or gangs of Southerners, were constantly scouring the country, but all moving towards and gathering around Lawrence, in response to Secretary Woodson's proclamation, by which they legalized their proceedings. On the other hand, free state men were not idle. We have noticed the bold strokes and determined movements of an outraged and brave people. But aside from these, there were instances of pro-slavery neighborhoods and families being visited, robbed and otherwise abused, sometimes in retaliation for similar offenses received, more frequently by desperate and reckless characters, to satisfy their love of plunder and crime.

At the opening of the fall term of court, the State prisoners at Lecompton reported themselves ready for trial. But the Government was not ready, witnesses were not to be had, &c., and Judge Lecompte then discharged them upon bail for their appearance at the next term of court. The bonds ranged from five hundred to five thousand dollars. On the 10th of September, just four months after their arrest, they were set at liberty, and returned to the "treasonable city" of Lawrence.

At the spring term of court the prisoners again appeared for trial. The prosecuting attorney entered his *nolle prosequi* in all cases of treason. Governor Robinson was tried for usurpation of office, but was acquitted, the testimony showing that he was sworn in as Governor of the State of Kansas before there was such a State, and there was no such an office at that time known to the law.

CHAPTER XXXVI.

GOVERNOR GEARY.

Colonel John W. Geary was appointed by President Buchanan to supersede Mr. Shannon as Governor of Kansas. He was born in Westmoreland county, Pennsylvania, and was, at the time young men generally receive the most help from parents, thrown upon the world with the patrimony of a debt and the support of a widowed mother. He soon relieved himself of the former, contributed to the latter by teaching, and at the same time devoted himself assiduously to study. He graduated at Jefferson College, Pennsylvania, and, not liking the vocation of a teacher, first became a surveyor in Kentucky, and then in several other States. He afterwards filled all the offices, from clerk to superintendent, in the Alleghany Portage Railroad Company. On the breaking out of the Mexican war, he volunteered his services as a soldier, was first made Lieutenant Colonel of the Second Pennsylvania Regiment, and afterwards, upon the death of the Colonel, became his successor. He rendered valuable service in the war, for which, on the 22d of January, 1849, President Polk appointed him to the office of postmaster at San Francisco. On Mr. Taylor's coming into power, he was superseded; but was immediately unanimously elected by the citizens first alcalde of that city. The following year, under the first city charter, he was chosen mayor. All these various positions he filled with ability and general satisfaction to the public. In 1852 he left the Golden Gate, on a six months leave of absence, to visit his family and friends in Pennsylvania. Soon after his return home, his wife and several near relatives died, on account of which affliction he abandoned the idea of going back to California.

He was appointed Governor of Kansas in the latter part of July, and immediately prepared to start to the scene of his new labors and responsibilities. He reached Jefferson city on the 5th of September, where he held a conference with Governor Price, whom he engaged to remove the obstructions to free state travel on the Missouri. Soon afterwards, the navigation of this river was open and free to all the citizens of the Union. As the Governor ascended the Missouri, he witnessed the wild commotion of the citizens along its banks. At Glasgow, Capt. Jackson embarked a company of "Kansas Militia," and a cannon, on the same boat, and the new Governor had the pleasure of their company as far as Kansas City, where he beheld, in wildest confusion, a genuine display of Border Ruffianism.

The appointment of Gov. Geary was not at all satisfactory to the Border chiefs. They knew that he would not favor their nefarious designs, and hence desired a man selected from their number. The following is a portion of an address sent forth to their pro-slavery allies.

"We have asked the appointment of a successor, who was acquainted with our condition; who, a citizen of the Territory, identified with its history, would not be prejudiced or misled by falsehoods which have been so systematically fabricated against us; one who heretofore is a resident, as he is a native, of a non-slaveholding State, yet not a slaveholder, but has the capacity to appreciate, and the boldness and integrity requisite, to discharge his duty, regardless of the possible effect it might have upon some petty politician in a distant State.

"In his stead we have one appointed who is ignorant of our condition, a stranger to our people, who, we have cause to fear, will, if no worse, prove no more efficient to protect us than his predecessors.

"With, then, a Governor which has proved imbecile—has failed to enforce the laws for our protection—with an army of lawless banditti overrunning our country—what shall we do?

"Though we have full confidence in the integrity and fidelity of Mr. Woodson, now acting as Governor, we know not at what moment his authority will be superseded. We cannot await the occasion of the incoming of our newly appointed Governor. We can not hazard a second edition of imbecility or corruption.

"We must act at once effectively. These traitors, robbers and assassins must be punished; must now be taught a lesson they will remember.

"This is no mere local quarrel; no mere riot; but it is war; a war waged by an army; a war professedly for our extermination. It is no mere resistance to the laws, no simple rebellion of our citizens, but a war of invasion—the army, a foreign army—properly named the 'Army of the North.'

"It is not only the right, but the duty of all good citizens of Missouri, and every other State, to come to our assistance, and enable us to expel these invaders.

"Mr. Woodson, since the resignation of Governor Shannon, in the absence of Governor Geary, has fearlessly met the responsibilities of the trust imposed upon him, has proclaimed the existence of rebellion, and called on the militia of the Territory to assemble for its suppression.

"We call on you to come! to furnish us assistance in men, provisions and munitions, that we may drive out the 'Army of the North,' who would subvert our government and expel us from our homes."

These extracts will give an idea of the address thus sent forth to the Missourians. We have seen how they promptly responded. But we have also seen, they dearly purchased their plundering success. Still they were not satisfied. They wished the war to continue. Their strength was daily increasing; the provisions of the people of Lawrence and other free state towns were well nigh exhausted, and hence they were confident of success. They closely guarded the roads to Kansas City and Leavenworth, and seized every load of provision designed for the opposite party. When protection was asked of Secretary Woodson against these robberies, he answered, "submit to the Territorial laws and I will protect you."

In consequence of being cut off from supplies, and their scanty provisions at home being exhausted, free state men were frequently led by the first law of nature to make raids upon pro-slavery neighborhoods, and gather forage therefrom. For this purpose the Topeka boys visited the settlements at Burlington, Osawkee and Tecumseh, and farms adjoining their town. There was no other resource to obtain food for themselves and friends. Other free state men and towns were in some instances compelled to do likewise.

It was the design of the Border chiefs to delay in some way the arrival of Governor Geary until they had accomplished their purpose in inflicting summary punishment upon the settlers of Kansas. They wished to utterly destroy Lawrence and other free state towns, expel Lane and his force from the Territory, and intimidate all others. It was this scheme which created the commotion along the Missouri river, the mustering and shipment of troops two hundred miles from the Border. Governor Geary, on taking passage in the boat at Jefferson City, was warned by an armed ruffian that if he attempted to interfere with the arrangements of the pro-slavery party in the Territory, he would be assassinated.

But the Missourians, from some cause, failed to delay Governor Geary's approach, and he arrived in the Territory just in time to quash their movements. He reached Fort Leavenworth on the 9th of September. He had not been there but a few hours before a United States sergeant came in with a sad report to General Smith. He had been detailed as safe-guard to conduct Samuel Sutherland, E. B. Whitman and Abraham Wilder from Lawrence to Fort Leavenworth. When within a few miles of the latter place, Emory and his party seized the three men named, and with their wagons, horses and property, forcibly conveyed them to Leavenworth City. A detachment of United States troops was at once sent to the city to arrest the guilty parties. In a few hours the free state prisoners, Emory and his men, were brought in; after a slight rebuke administered to the insolent offenders they were set at liberty.

The following day Governor Geary addressed a note to Colonel Clarkson, who had command of the Territorial militia, stationed at Leavenworth City, urging him to guard against such occurrences, and take steps to restore the property of the men thus seized. On the same day he set out for Lecompton, where he arrived on the 12th of September. He found the people of that place in a state of great excitement in consequence of the recent visit of Lane. He immediately issued his address to the people of the Territory, setting forth his policy, and urging upon them to drop past differences and leave the result to a peaceable settlement at the ballot box. Subjoined are a few extracts:

"Is there no remedy for these evils? Can not the wounds of Kansas be healed, and peace restored to all her borders?

"Men of the North—men of the South—of the East, and of the West, *in Kansas*, you, and you alone, have the remedy in your hands. Will you suspend fratricidal strife? Will you not cease to regard each other as enemies, and look upon one another as children of a common mother, and come and reason together?

"In my official action here, I will do justice at all hazards. Influenced by no other consideration than the welfare of the whole people of this Territory, I desire to know no party, no section, no North, no South, no East, no West, nothing but Kansas and my country.

"Let us all begin anew. Let the past be buried in oblivion. Let all strife and bitterness cease."

At the same time he issued orders requiring the commandants of the militia to disband their forces, giving as his reason that he had at his command a sufficient number of United States soldiers to suppress all disorders. But the real object was to get rid of the armed invaders that were mustered under the specious title of "Territorial Militia." At the same time he issued a proclamation, requiring all free male citizens to enrol themselves as militia, to organize into companies, regiments and brigades, and to hold themselves in readiness for any emergency. He forwarded orders to the commanders of the militia to at once disband their forces.

The Governor was all this time unaware of the designs of the Missourians. He knew not that they meditated war, and were mustering in such large numbers.

On the morning of the 13th, he received a note from Wm. A. Heiskill, Brigadier General of Southern Division of Kansas Militia, stating that in response to the call of Secretary Woodson, he had eight hundred men in the field, armed, "ready for duty and impatient to act." The Governor immediately dispatched orders for their disbandment and return to their homes. Through his special agent which he had sent to Lawrence, he ascertained that a large military force of twenty-five hundred men, under the command of J. W. Reed, Atchison, Stringfellow and others, were threatening the town; that his proclamations had not yet been distributed, that the free state men were willing to disband as soon as these invaders should retire.

Governor Geary immediately set out for Lawrence, in company with Colonel Cook and three hundred dragoons. He found the city well fortified, but only about three hundred men in it, and the dangers surrounding it not so great as he expected. He was cordially received, made a speech to the inhabitants urging forbearance, and then returned to Lecompton.

Here he found the people stricken with a panic and filled with terror, which the mere mention of Lane's presence would always occasion. A few persons had come in from the neighborhood of Osawkee, with the sad and startling intelligence that Lane and his men were in their vicinity, laying waste the country, robbing, killing and driving off pro-slavery men. The facts in the case are as follows:

Upon the arrival of Governor Geary in the Territory, General Lane determined to retire from it. He left by way of Topeka. Here he started out on the 11th of August, with about thirty men, and, on arriving at Osawkee, learned that there was an armed body of Ruffians in the neighborhood of Hickory Point, about five miles distant, who had been committing depredations for some time in that neighborhood, and had that day entered Grasshopper Falls and robbed its stores. At the earnest solicitation of the citizens, he decided to attack them. He sent back messengers to Topeka for reinforcements. About dusk that evening, a company of fifty men, under command of Captain Whipple,* left Topeka on foot, who reached Osawkee about daylight, and joined Lane's command. The free state forces then marched to Hickory Point, where they arrived about eleven o'clock, and found the enemy strongly fortified in three houses, one of which was log, under the command of Captains Lowe and Robertson. They formed a line of battle,

---

*Captain Whipple has rather a singular history. He was born in Lisbon, Conn., in 1830. He was a bold, fearless boy, but kind-hearted and agreeable. At the age of fifteen he left home as a volunteer for the Mexican war. He was so shifted about from one command to another as to be in most all the hard fought battles, and distinguished himself as a soldier of undaunted courage. After the hostilities were over his command started for home across the plains. They had not proceeded far when a superior officer most grossly abused a private soldier. Whipple, who witnessed the brutal outrage for a short time, unable to restrain his indignation, pounced upon the officer and chastised him within an inch of his life. For this offense he was placed under guard, and when the troops arrived at Fort Leavenworth, was tried and sentenced to be shot. But, in consequence of his meritorious services as a soldier in the war, this sentence was commuted to three years of hard labor in the guard-house and shops, with a ball and chain attached to his ankle. He was thus serving out his time, when he effected his escape in January, 1856. After remaining for some time concealed in the wilds of the Delaware Reserve, he made his appearance at Topeka. Here he soon became familiar with the boys, was elected their Captain, and served with them during the troubles of that year. From his military knowledge and experience he was a great acquisition to the free state men. From the time of his escape from Fort Leavenworth, he went under the assumed name of Whipple, whereas his real name was Aaron Dwight Stephens.

He was with John Brown during the troubles in Lower Kansas, accompanied him to Harper's Ferry, took part in the raid, and perished on the gallows.

challenged the pro-slavery forces to an open field conflict, which was declined. Being unable to dislodge the enemy without artillery, Lane dispatched a runner to Lawrence for reinforcements and artillery, with instructions for them to come by way of Topeka and Osawkee. Retiring to the latter place himself, he encamped with his command. He there received the Governor's proclamation, ordering all armed forces to disband, and concluded to observe it. He sent word to Topeka to notify the Lawrence company of his determination, and for them to return. His command divided, the Topeka boys returned home, while he continued his journey North.

The Lawrence boys, instead of obeying the directions of General Lane, marched directly across the prairie to Hickory Point, where they arrived about ten o'clock on the following day, and commenced bombarding the houses with a twelve pounder. which had been taken by Colonel Doniphan, at Sacramento, and which the free state men had secured in the last engagement at Franklin. The contest lasted six hours, during which one or two were killed and several wounded. The party in the houses were allowed to capitulate upon the most honorable terms, and retire to their homes.

Rumors becoming more rife of difficulties in the vicinity of Osawkee and Hickory Point, the Governor on the following day, September 14, dispatched Colonel Cook an order to send a company of troops to that place. Accordingly about sunset eighty-one dragoons crossed the Kaw River, and proceeded to the scene of disturbances. About 11 o'clock that night they came suddenly upon a party of Colonel Harvey's command, consisting of twenty-five men and three wagons, whom they arrested. Continuing their journey, when within about four miles of Hickory Point they discovered the encampment of the main body of Harvey's men, whom they surprised and captured. They then returned with "one hundred and one prisoners, one brass field piece, seven wagons, thirty-eight United States muskets, forty-seven Sharp's rifles, six hunting rifles, two shot guns, twenty revolving pistols, fourteen bowie-knives, four swords, and a large supply of ammunition for artillery and small arms."

These prisoners were conducted to the camp of the United States troops and furnished inhospitable quarters. Their examination, after much delay, came off before Judge Cato, which was partial in its character. The Prosecuting Attorney was Joseph C. Anderson, author of the Kansas Black Laws, a notorious Ruffian from Lexington, Missouri. The whole party were re-committed to custody for trial on the charge of murder in the first degree. No bail would be allowed, though the murderers of Barber, Dow, Brown, Jones, and others were either never arrested at all or set at liberty upon straw bail. They were soon afterwards removed from the United States encampment, General Smith refusing to retain them any longer, were placed in a dilapidated old house, guarded by a company of militia, under the command of Colonel Titus, and fed by Dr. J. N. O. P. Wood. They fared miserably for the want of proper shelter and food.

The prisoners received their trial in October; some were acquitted, others convicted of various degrees of manslaughter, and sentenced to confinement for terms varying from five to ten years, at hard labor with the ball and chain. The latter part of the sentence was remitted by the Governor. Upon the disbanding of the militia, in December, the prisoners—thirty-one of whom had escaped—were placed in the charge of Captain Hampton, a just and humane man. He treated them with great lenity, and allowed them many privileges, for which he was bitterly denounced by the pro-slavery party, and came near losing his seat in its Convention and the confirmation of his appointment by the Legislature. On the 2nd of March, 1857, only seventeen prisoners remained in charge of the master of convicts.

They were all pardoned by the Governor, agreeably with petitions from all parts of the Territory, after having been in confinement nearly six months.

While these events were transpiring, messengers were constantly arriving, bringing intelligence of the threatening state of affairs around Lawrence. The Governor, on the 14th, sent Secretary Woodson, by whose orders these forces were assembled, and Brigadier General Strickler, with an escort of United States troops, to the pro-slavery camp on the Wakarusa, with instructions to disband the militia. These gentlemen arrived at Franklin, assembled the Border chiefs, and sought to prevail upon them to obey the orders of the Governor. But they would pay no attention to the orders, utterly refused to recognize his authority, to listen to the Governor's proclamation, denounced and threatened Geary and declared they were not going to return until Lawrence and every free state town in the Territory were leveled with the ground. Their designs were blood and plunder; they had entered upon the work of extermination for the "third and last time," and did not believe in abandoning their purpose so soon.

In the afternoon of the same day, the Governor ordered Colonel Cook, with all his command, to hasten to Lawrence, and accompanied them himself. He found the dangers as threatening as had been described. Twenty-seven hundred armed men were in camp at Franklin, under the command of Generals Heiskill, Reid, Atchison, Richardson and Stringfellow, raving to attack Lawrence. But three hundred men were in arms in the city. These, unlike on the previous occasion, had determined to defend their firesides or perish in the attempt. Old John Brown, who had surprisingly appeared in their midst, was in command. There was no fear nor sickly effiminacy there; brave hearts beat in every breast, strong arms held every rifle. They were strongly fortified, well armed, and commanded by a leader in whom they had the utmost confidence. They were fighting at their own door steps, in defence of their own firesides, and with the assurance that surrender would gain no more than defeat. Had there been an attack, and the free state men overpowered, the battle would have marked a Thermopylæ on the pages of history.

When the Governor addressed the citizens of Lawrence, he told them that the troops had come to protect them, and would do it. They offered to deposit their arms at his feet, and retire to their respective homes, but he bid them carry their arms with them, and use them, in the last resort, to protect their city and their lives.

Early on the following morning, the Governor started alone for the camp at Franklin. He met the advance party of three hundred about three miles out, preparing to make the assault. Already skirmishers and pickets had commenced firing. When he met them, he inquired who they were and what were their objects. They replied that they were the territorial militia, and were going up "to wipe out Lawrence, and every d——d abolitionist in the country." He informed them that he was the Governor of Kansas, and the commander-in-chief of the Territorial forces, and as such, ordered them to countermarch, and convey him to the center of the main line.

He at once summoned the officers together, and appealed to them in an earnest and feeling address, "setting forth the disastrous consequence of such a demonstration as was contemplated, and the absolute necessity of more lawful and conciliatory measures to restore peace, tranquillity and prosperity to the country," and directed their attention to his proclamations. The more prudent among them favored obeying at once his instructions, but such men as Jones, Clark and Maclean were loud in their denunciations of the Governor, and favored effecting their purpose, even if they had to fight the United States troops. They, however, disbanded and "retired, not as good and law-loving citizens, but as bands of plunderers and destroyers, leaving in their wake ruined fortunes, weeping eyes, and sorrowing hearts." Some left by way of Lecompton for Atchison, Doniphan and Northern Missouri; others took an opposite direction, proceeding to Fort Scott, Westport, and all the towns along the Border south of the Kaw, to return no more as invaders until they mustered in the cause of the Confederacy. It proved to be the "third and last time," indeed, but not for Lawrence, which continued to stand, grow and prosper until burnt and her people massacred by Quantrel.

CHAPTER XXXVII.

THE COURTS.

Governor Geary next sought to awaken and infuse new life and virtue into the Judiciary of the Territory. Notwithstanding for the past two years, robberies, murders and thefts were of daily occurance, but few, if any, offenders had been brought to justice. The Judges, like other United States officers in the Territory, had entirely lost sight of their official duties, in their blind devotion to party. We have seen the partiality employed in admitting pro-slavery criminals to bail upon worthless security, and refusing the same to free state men for mitigated crimes, though the best of vouchers were presented. They had eagerly declared the enactments of the bogus Legislature valid before any case arose under them; they had sought more to compel the free state men to recognize them as such than to punish an infraction of them. Their terms of court only lasted from five to nine days, twice a year in each county, and, in many instances, the Judges themselves were not present.

When Governor Geary visited the pro-slavery camp on the Wakarusa, he found Judge Cato performing the part of a soldier. This same official was among the ruffian invaders during the siege of Lawrence, in the fall of '55, and was with the party that killed Barber. When the five murders occurred on the Pottowatomie, he exerted himself wonderfully to bring the guilty to retribution. He wrote to Governor Shannon, "I shall do every-thing in my power to have the matter investigated," and the guilty parties brought to justice. But when Frederick Brown, William Garrison, Williams, Cantral and others were murdered by Reed's army, not a word was said about investigating the matter and administering justice.

The Governor induced Judge Cato to accompany him to Lecompton. On their road thither a most shocking spectacle met their view. As the northern division of the Territorial militia, under the command of Colonel Clarkson, calling themselves Kickapoo Rangers, and numbering about three hundred, retired home by way of Lecompton, when within a few miles of that place, six of these men "halted by a field where a poor unoffensive lame man, named David C. Buffum, was at work. They entered the field, and after robbing him of his horse, shot him in the abdomen, from which he soon after died." The Governor and the Judge arrived just in time to witness the writhing agony, and to receive the testimony of the dying man.

The Governor took immediate steps to have the murderer brought to justice. A warrant was drawn up and placed in the hands of the United States Marshal, a reward of five hundred dollars was offered for the arrest of the criminal, and secret agents were dispatched to Atchison and vicinity. Though the Marshal and his deputies were exceedingly active in arresting and bringing in all free state men for whom they had warrants, still they made but little effort to arrest this pro-slavery murderer. After almost two months elapsed the Governor finally succeeded in identifying and securing the person of tho guilty one, named C. Hays. On examination, he was committed for trial on the charge of murder in the first degree. Scarcely had this been accomplished when Judge Lecompte admitted the prisoner to bail, with the worthless man Jones for security. This was thought to be a strange and irreconcilable proceeding. The same Judge had refused bail to free state men charged with only manslaughter, even before any thing like a proper investigation of the matter took place, and would not entertain any evidence that would palliate their conduct.

The Governor was determined not to be baffled. He immediately issued an order to the Marshal requiring him to re-arrest Hays and to hold him until discharged by a Jury. This order was obeyed and the murderer again placed in safe custody. But before Governor Geary, who happened to be absent a few days, returned to Lecompton, the Chief Justice caused the prisoner to be brought before him on a writ of *habeas corpus*, and discharged him. Governor Geary pursued the matter no further, but attempted in vain to effect the removal of the Chief Justice.

As Judge Lecompte presided over the most populous district and became somewhat noted during the Territorial troubles, a short account of his life and character is here given.

Samuel Dexter Lecompte was born in Dorchester County, Maryland, December 13, 1814. At the age of sixteen he entered Kenyan College, Ohio, where he remained two years. Thence he went to Jefferson College, Pennsylvania, and graduated in 1834 with honor. He was diligent in school and enjoyed the respect and confidence of his instructors. At a contest exhibition between two literary societies, he represented one as debator and was awarded the honor by a committee of gentlemen selected for that purpose.

Leaving his alma mater, he entered the law office of Henry Page, a distinguished lawyer of Maryland. In 1837 he commenced practice in Carrol county, of his native State, and in 1840 was elected to the Legislature. In 1843, he returned to Dorchester county, Maryland, and continued the practice of his profession. He was a candidate for elector for General Cass, and also a candidate for Congress in 1850; but he, being a Democrat, and his district largely Whig, was defeated. Having removed to Baltimore city in

1854, he was soon afterwards appointed Chief Justice of the Supreme Court of Kansas Territory.

He is a man of some ability, and possessed the mental qualifications to have performed the functions of his office with credit. He is not the hard-hearted monster that he was sometimes represented to be, who placed no value on human life, nor had any respect for the right of property; on the other hand, he possessed tender and sympathetic feelings, and has ever been regarded, by those who knew him best, as an inoffensive and peaceable man. He frequently interposed to prevent the destruction of life and property. On two different occasions he was thought to have saved the lives of Governors Robinson and Geary.

But blindly devoted to party, and intensely pro-slavery in principle and policy, he was utterly disqualified for the impartial discharge of his duties. Like other men of respectability and talent, whose conduct during the troubles in Kansas stands out as anomalies in their lives, Judge Lecompte prostituted himself and his office to the interests of slavery; the blood of free state men, the tears and wails of widows and orphans over the pallid form of a murdered husband and father, the sufferings and privations occcasioned by the destruction of property, cried aloud unto him in vain for redress. It seemed that pro-slavery men of the highest grade and type lost sight of their manhood, and all the edvils of pandemonium took possession of them, goading them on to deeds of violence and bloodshed, or induced a tacit sanction of them.

The Judge said to the writer, not long since, that "he claimed to have discharged his duty with the most perfect impartiality, and to have been entirely free, in the performance of his duty, from partiality and prejudice. He knows that he never designedly departed from this path, and does not believe he ever did so undesignedly. He simply performed his duties of administering and expounding the laws as they were." "I am satisfied that on more than one occasion I saved the lives of men who are now living, to say nothing of property.

Judge Lecompte, after his removal in the spring of 1857, retired to his little farm not far from Leavenworth, where he has ever since continued the peaceful pursuit of agriculture. He is not wealthy, as he has been represented, but possesses only a comfortable share of this world's goods. Since the troubles of the Territory are over, he has enjoyed the respect and esteem of all his neighbors and acquaintances. He was elected a member of the State Legislature in 1866 and took an honorable part in the deliberations of that body.

When the Governor arrived at Lecompton in company with Judge Cato, he met Judge Lecompte, who had come at the request which Mr. Geary had previously sent him. Governor Geary sought to impress the Judges with the importance of holding regular terms of court, of laboring to bring criminals to justice. At this time persons from all parts of the Territory were constantly appearing before the Governor, with complaints of wrongs that they had suffered. It was clearly the duty of the Judges to hear these complaints and provide for the redress of their grievances. The next day the Governor went to Topeka with some United States troops to make arrests. During his absence, Lecompte, instead of examining the hundred and one free state prisoners there in custody, left the town, with directions to have them conveyed to Leavenworth in three weeks, to undergo preliminary examination. His excuse for so doing, as afterwards given, was that in consequence of the excitement then prevailing in Lecompton, all the "law and order" men had left, so that it was impossible to procure a competent jury. The Governor wrote to Judge Cato to get him to come and examine the prisoners, which he finally did, as has been before narrated. Governor Geary then addressed notes to all the Territorial officers relative to what they had done, remarking that much complaint had come to his ears of alleged neglect of duty on their parts. This communication called forth wordy and pithy replies from these officials, denying his right to question them in regard to the performance of their duty, but showing that they had done little or nothing in the strict requirements of their office.

The Governor labored very diligently to restore order and quiet in the Territory, and to stimulate the officers to the discharge of their duties. But the Marshal improved his opportunity in making requisitions upon the Governor for troops, with which to arrest free state men, while at the same time he disregarded warrants which he held against pro-slavery men. His deputies, (for he seldom went himself,) at the head of the United States troops, would enter towns, and under color of authority, commit offenses against the decency and quiet of the citizens more reprehensible than that of those for whom they were in search. The Governor finally declined to make any such requisitions, as peace was restored and no more opposition to the execution of the law offered. The people, therefore, to their joy and satisfaction, were rid of the annoyance occasioned by Deputy Marshals and Sheriffs trooping over the country with a squad of dragoons at their heels to defend them in their insolence and outrage.

CHAPTER XXXVIII.

LANE'S NORTHERN ARMY.

When it was announced in the free States that the Missourians had forbidden the passage of emigrants to Kansas, and had driven many back, those desiring to come to the Territory set out by the way of Iowa and Nebraska. Accordingly, about the latter part of May, companies of emigrants began to move towards the south-western corner of Iowa. By the 1st of August there were congregated in the neighborhood of Nebraska City, preparatory to entering Kansas, five hundred persons and sixty wagons. These were truly emigrants, who had, without any preconcerted action, from their common destination and purpose, met at a point in their journey where dangers and trials became common. It is true, the advanced portion of the party, on learning that others were coming, halted until the latter arrived, that they might have a larger force to open the road and repel any aggressions.

These emigrants came here to settle and make themselves homes. They were not an organized army, as was represented, coming here purposely to fight, but were mechanics, farmers, artisans, and some professional men, who came to follow their vocations. They had agricultural and mechanical implements, stock, and those things emigrants generally convey to a new country. They had from common purpose, destination and interest, congregated as peaceful emigrants.

That they had arms, might be expected, for few persons out West in those days were without them.

The first company that passed through was General J. H. Lane and six others, on horseback. They came disguised, in advance of the rest about one week, and had no connection whatever with them.

Three hundred of the first emigrant train stopped three miles south of the northern boundary of the Territory, laid out and established the town of Plymouth; fifteen miles further south seventy-five others laid out the village of Lexington, and about thirty miles south of this Holton was founded by thirty persons. This train opened the road, bridged the bad places, and established the stopping points above mentioned. The remnant of the train reached Topeka on the 13th of August, having traversed the whole length of the new route of one hundred and forty miles, led by C. M. Dickey, who superintended the train. Dr. J. P. Root and A. A. and S. V. Jamison were the committee to locate the route.

Such was the advance of Lane's "northern army" that, created so much talk and fear among the pro-slavery men. They were soon followed by other and numerous trains, and thus the tide of emigration, with its former channel closed, rushed around the obstacle, and found a new channel of its own. We shall now notice the efforts to stop this wonderful invasion. Armed bodies of Missourians could come over, lay waste fields, sack and burn towns, rob and kill the settlers, without any interference on the part of the United States troops; but let it be reported that Northern men are going to do the same thing, and the policy towards them is exactly the reverse.

Let it be remembered, let it go down in history, that Lane's "northern army," which Secretary Woodson telegraphed to the President numbered 1,000 armed men, and which was so reported over the world, consisted only of six men, in disguise.

Governor Geary, the latter part of September, having received reliable information that a large force, numbering one thousand men, with several pieces of artillery, were about to enter the Territory from the north, dispatched a detachment of United States troops, under Deputy Marshal Preston, to the northern frontier, with orders to arrest any illegally armed body that might be found within the limits of Kansas. Scarcely had they reached there, before one hundred and thirty men, armed, equipped, (as reported by the officers,) and under the leadership of James Redpath, entered the Territory. They were immediately arrested by the United States troops, and conducted into the neighborhood of Lecompton. Here they had an interview with the Governor, who, being satisfied that they were a company of peaceable immigrants, permitted them to go their way.

It was soon reported that Redpath's party was but the advance guard of the main body of Lane's men, and seven hundred more, with three cannon and small arms, were about to cross the river at Nebraska City. The Governor immediately dispatched Colonels Cook and Johnson, with three hundred dragoons, to intercept their march.

On the 1st of October a deputation, consisting of Major Morrow, Colonel Winchel, William Hutchingson and Colonel J. Jenkins, called upon the Governor, stating that they were sent by Colonel Eldridge, General Pomeroy, Colonel Perry and others, who were escorting three hundred immigrants into the Territory by way of Nebraska; that they did not come for warlike purposes, nor disturbers of the peace, but as *bona fide* settlers, with agricultural implements, and some guns to protect themselves and shoot game for their families, &c.; and that in the present disturbed state of affairs, they did not wish to enter the Territory under any circumstances of suspicion, without notice to the Governor. On their denying that they had any connection with Lane's "army of the north," the Governor told them he would welcome them as peaceable citizens, but that he would prevent all armed invaders from entering the Territory, to disturb and trouble the affairs therein. He gave them a letter, stating that they had called upon him with regard to their purpose, and commanding all military authorities to give the party under Colonel Eldridge and others, a safe escort into the Territory, in case the immigrants proved to be what they represented themselves.

That which followed is here given in the conflicting statements of Governor Geary and the leaders of the party, so that the reader can draw his own conclusions as to which was correct:

"Colonel William J. Preston, a Deputy United States Marshal, who had accompanied Colonel P. St. George Cooke and his command to the northern frontier to look after a large party of proposed immigrants, who were reported to be about invading the Territory in that quarter, in warlike array, and for hostile purposes, returned to Lecompton on the 12th inst.

"He informed me that he had caused to be arrested an organized band, consisting of about two hundred and forty persons, among whom were a very few women and children, comprising some seven families.

"This party was regularly formed in military order, and were under the command of General Pomeroy, Cols. Eldridge, Perry and others. They had with them twenty wagons, in which were a supply of new arms, mostly muskets, with bayonets and sabres, and a lot of saddles, &c., sufficient to equip a battalion, consisting one-fourth of cavalry and the remainder infantry.

"Besides these arms, which were evidently intended for military purposes, and none other, which were in the wagons, a search of which was strongly objected to, the immigrants were provided with shot-guns, rifles, pistols, knives, &c., sufficient for the ordinary uses of persons traveling in Kansas as any other of the Western Territories.

"From the reports of the officers, I learn that they had with them neither oxen, household furniture, mechanics' tools, agricultural implements, nor any of the necessary appurtenances of peaceful settlers.

"These persons entered the Territory on the morning of the 10th inst., and met Colonel Cooke's command a few miles south of the Territorial line. Here the Deputy Marshal questioned them as to their intentions, the contents of their wagons, and such other matters as he considered necessary in the exercise of his official duties. Not satisfied with their answers, and being refused the privilege of searching their effects, he felt justified in considering them a party organized and armed in opposition to my proclamation of the 11th of September. After consultation with Colonel Cooke and other officers of the army, who agreed with him in regard to the character of the emigrants, he directed the search to be made, which resulted in the discovery of the arms already mentioned.

"An escort was then offered them to Lecompton, in order that I might examine them in person, and decide as to their intentions, which they refused to accept. Their superfluous arms were then taken in charge of the troops, and the entire party put under arrest, the families, and all others, individually, being permitted to retire from the organization if so disposed. Few, however, availed themselves of this privilege. But little delay and less annoyance were occasioned them by these proceedings. Every-thing that circumstances required, or permitted, was done for the comfort and convenience of the prisoners. Their journey was facilitated rather than retarded. They were accompanied by a squadron of United States dragoons, in command of Major H. H. Sibley. One day's rations were dealt out to them, and they were allowed to pursue the route they themselves had chosen.

"Being apprised of the time at which they would probably arrive at Topeka, I forwarded orders for their deten tion on the northern side of the river, near that place, where, as I promised, I met them upon the morning of the 14th instant.

"I found them precisely as they had been represented to me in official reports; and while I felt disposed and anxious to extend to them all the leniency I could, consistent with propriety, duty and justice, and determined, at the same to enforce in their case, as well as that of every similar organization, the spirit and intent of my proclamation of the 11th ultimo, which commands 'all bodies of men, combined, armed and equipped with munitions of war, without the authority of the Government, instantly to disband or quit the Territory, as they will answer the contrary at their peril.' This I had done but a short time previous with a smaller body, who entered Kansas as this had done, from an entirely different quarter, and who, upon learning my purposes, not only submitted willingly to be searched, but by my order, without a murmur, and even with cheerfulness, disbanded and dispersed.

"I addressed these people in their encampment, in regard to the present condition of the Territory, the suspicious position they occupied, and the reprehensible attitude they had assumed. I reminded them that there was no possible necessity or excuse for the existence of large armed organizations at present in the Territory. Everything was quiet and peaceful, and the very appearance of such an unauthorized and injudicious array as they presented, while it could do no possible good, was calculated, if not intended, to spread anew distrust and consternation through the Territory, and rekindle the fires of discord and strife that had swept over the land, ravaging and desolating everything that lay in their destructive path.

"Their apology for this evident and undeniable disregard of my proclamation, though somewhat plausible, was far from being satisfactory. They had made their arrangements, they said, to emigrate to Kansas at a time when the Territory was not only disturbed by antagonistic political parties, armed for each other's destruction, but when numerous bands of marauders, whose business was plunder and assassination, infested all the highways, rendering travel extremely hazardous, even though every possible means for self-protection were employed.

"This excuse loses all its pertinency when it is understood that before the party crossed the Territorial line they were apprised, through a deputation that had visited me, that the condition of things above described had ceased to exist, and that such was the true state of affairs that any person could travel the route they proposed taking, without molestation or the slightest cause for apprehension. I informed them, through their messengers, that I heartily welcomed all immigrants, from every section of the Union, who came with peaceful attitude and apparently good intentions; and that to all such I would afford ample protection. While, on the other hand, I assured them that I would positively enforce my proclamation, and suffer no party of men, no matter whence they come, or what their political bias, to enter and travel through the Territory with hostile or warlike appearance, to the terror of peaceable citizens, and the dangers of renewing the disgraceful and alarming scenes through which we had so recently passed. It was quite evident that this party did thus enter the Territory, in defiance, not only of my proclamation, but my own verbal cautions; and I therefore fully approve of the action taken by Colonel Cooke, Major Sibley, and Deputy Marshal Preston, as well as all the officers of the army who assisted in their detention, search and guard.

After showing the necessity of so doing, I insisted upon the immediate disbandment of this combination, which was agreed to with great alacrity. The majority of the men were evidently gratified to learn that they had been deceived in relation to Kansas affairs, and that peace and quiet, instead of strife and contention, were reigning here. My remarks were received with frequent demonstrations of approbation, and at their close the organization was broken up, its members dispersing in various directions. After they had been dismissed from custody, and the fact was announced to them by Major Sibley, their thankfulness for his kind treatment towards them during the time he held them under arrest, was expressed by giving him three hearty and enthusiastic cheers.

"In concluding this hastily written letter, I must express my sincere regrets that societies exist in some of the States, whose object is to fit out such parties as the one herein described, and send them to this Territory, to their own injury and the destruction of the general welfare of the country Very many persons are induced to come out here under flattering promises, which are never fulfilled; and having neither money to purchase food and clothing, nor trades or occupations at which to earn an honest livelihood, are driven to the necessity of becoming either paupers or thieves; and such are the unfortunate men who have aided materially in filling up the measure of crimes that have so seriously affected the prosperity of Kansas. It is high time that this fact should be clearly and generally understood. This Territory, at the present season of the year, and especially under existing circumstances, offers no inducements for the immigration of the poor tradesman or laborer. The country is overrun with hundreds who are unable to obtain employment, who live upon charity, and who are exposed to all the evils of privation, destitution and want.

* * * * * * * * * *

"JOHN W. GEARY,
"Governor of Kansas Territory.

"W. L. MARCY, Secretary of State."

"KANSAS TERRITORY,
"TOPEKA, October 15, 1856.

"SIR:—We, the undersigned, conductors of an emigrant train, who entered the Territory on the 10th instant, beg leave to make the following statement of facts, which, if required, we will attest upon our oaths.

"1. Our party numbered from 200 to 300 persons, in two separate companies, the rear company (which has not yet arrived) being principally composed of families with children, who left Mount Pleasant, Iowa, three days after this train which has arrived to-day.

"2. We are all actual, *bona fide* settlers, intending; as far as we know, to become permanent inhabitants.

"3. The blockading of the Missouri river to free state emigrants, and the reports which reached us in the early part of September, to the effect that armed men were infesting and marauding the northern portions of Kansas, were the sole reasons why we came in a company and were armed.

"4. We were stopped near the northern line of the Territory by the United States troops, acting, as we understood, under the orders of one Preston, Deputy United States Marshal; and after stating to the officers who we were and what we had, they commenced searching our wagons—in some instances breaking open trunks and throwing out wearing apparel upon the ground in the rain—taking arms from the wagons, wresting some private arms from the hands of men, carrying away a lot of sabres belonging to a gentleman in the Territory, as also one and a half kegs of powder, percussion caps, and some cartridges; in consequence of which we were detained about two-thirds of a day, taken prisoners, and are now presented to you.

"All that we have to say is that our mission to this Territory is entirely peaceful. We have no organization, save a police organization, for our own regulations and defense on the way. And coming in that spirit to this Territory, we claim the rights of American citizens to bear arms, and to be exempt from unlawful search or seizure.

"Trusting to your integrity or impartiality, we have confidence to believe that our property will be returned to us, and that all that has been wrong will be righted.

"We have subscribed ourselves, cordially and truly, your friends and fellow-citizens.

"S. W. ELDRIDGE, Conductor.
"SAMUEL C. POMEROY,
"JOHN A. PERRY,
"ROBERT MARROW,
"EDWARD DANIELS,
"RICHARD REALF.

"*To His Excellency*, JOHN W. GEARY, *Governor of Kansas Territory*.

The above letter of Governor Geary clearly shows his prejudices and partialities at that time. It is a querry when he alludes to "a smaller body which had entered Kansas as this has done, from an entirely different quarter, and who on hearing my purposes to disband armed bodies, not only submitted willingly to be searched, but by my orders, without a murmur, with cheerfulness disbanded and dispersed," whether he alludes to the Border Ruffians who thronged the country around Lawrence, burnt Osawattomie, killed Frederick Brown, Williamson, Garrison, Keiser, Buffum, &c., who would not read his proclamation, pay any attention to his agents, disowned his authority, and whom he himself by persuasion and the display of United States troops prevailed upon with difficulty to abandon their deadly purposes. If he did not allude to this circumstance, he at least failed to mention it in his letter to the Secretary. The vain Governor vainly imagined that he could restore peace and tranquillity to Kansas, and save the credit of the Democratic party. He had to learn that Border Ruffians and the administration at Washington did not care a fig for him nor the Democratic party.

CHAPTER XXXIX.

PEACE—ARREST OF THE FREE STATE LEGISLATURE.

On the last day of September Governor Geary wrote to the Secretary of State, at Washington: "Peace now reigns in Kansas. Confidence is being gradually restored. Settlers are returning to their claims. Citizens are resuming their ordinary pursuits, and a general gladness pervades the community."

The guerrilla bands had been broken up and had disappeared; houses were no longer robbed and burnt; women could safely traverse the highways, and the citizens had begun to resume their peaceful labors. Prosperity and quiet once again dawned upon the distracted country. In various localities disturbances yet existed, and numerous complaints reached the Governor respecting them. He cited them to the local authorities for a redress of their grievances, and urged upon these officers prompt and efficient action. These were encouraged by the assurance that they should be backed by the power of the United States troops in the discharge of their duties, and soon the jarring and disturbing elements in every locality were removed through the proper exertion of the municipal authorities. United States troops protected loaded wagons from Westport, Leavenworth and Kansas City to all the towns in the Territory, and secured them against any danger of being robbed.

The Governor almost daily received complaints of the

continued outrages at Leavenworth, and he accordingly, on the 1st of October, wrote to the Mayor as follows:

"I regret to inform you that since the receipt of your last letter I have received numerous complaints from persons claiming to be your citizens. It is said there exists in your city an irresponsible body of persons, unknown to the law, calling themselves "Regulators;" that these persons prowl about your streets at night and warn peaceable citizens 'to leave the Territory, never to return, or they may be removed when least expected.'

"*This thing*, Mr. Mayor, *will never do, and cannot be tolerated for a single moment.* These 'regulators' *must disband* and leave the government of the city to yourself and the authorities known to the law."

Accordingly, the mayor of this city immediately issued his proclamation, declaring that he would rigidly enforce the law against these regulators, unless they desisted from their course of conduct. The consequence was, the decided action of the mayor soon checked the wild career of these desperadoes.

The Governor mustered into the United States service, three companies of militia, two of which he stationed at Lecompton and one at Lawrence, for protective purposes. They remained in service until the first of December, when it appearing there was no more need of them, as order and quiet were restored, they were discharged. Individuals from different parts of the Territory had, previous to the organization of these companies, solicited the privilege from the Governor, to organize military companies for home defence, but were invariably refused.

"By proclamation of the Governor, an election for members of the House of Representatives of the Territory and a delegate to Congress was held on the 6th of October. The free state people declined to take any part in the election, and in consequence but a small vote was polled. Whitfield, who was chosen delegate to Congress, came into the Territory from Westport, at the head of a party of such notoriously bad repute, that he declared himself ashamed to be seen in their company. They came up to Lecompton, voted for Whitfield, and returned to Missouri."

The Governor next made a tour of observation, passing through Lawrence, Paola, Osawattomie, head waters of the Neosho and Fort Riley. Finding all peace and order throughout his travels, he, on the 6th of November, issued his proclamation, appointing the 20th day of November for "thanksgiving and praise to Almighty God, for the blessings vouchsafed to us as a people." This was the first thanksgiving day that had been appointed in the Territory, except that by J. H. Lane, as chairman of the Executive Committee.

Marauders continued to infest the south-eastern portion of the Territory. To ferret them out and bring them to justice, Edward Hoagland, United States Commissioner, and John A. W. Jones, United States Deputy Marshal, with a squadron of troops, were dispatched to that section. They discovered considerable stolen property, and restored it to the owners; arrested five of the guilty parties, when the commander of the troops was ordered with his men into winter quarters at Fort Leavenworth. The Commissioners not being able to effect anything without the military, returned. Though little was accomplished, still the moral effect of the expedition was beneficial.

The Vermont Legislature, on learing that great suffering was being experienced by the settlers of Kansas on account of not being able to cultivate their crops the summer previous, generously voted $20,000 towards their relief. The Governor of that State so notified Governor Geary, who replied that he was not aware of such a state of things, but that the people generally had a sufficiency, that wages were good so that the industrious would not want, and with thanks for their kind offer, assured him that if cases of suffering came to his notice he would feel at liberty to make the application suggested. The Governor evidently was in a different mood when he wrote to Secretary Marcy upon another subject, "The country is overrun with hundreds who are unable to obtain employment, who live upon charity, and who are exposed to all the evils of privation, destitution and want."

In November Mr. Thadyus Hyatt, of New York, took a company of ninety young men, tools, farming implements, &c., down on the south branch of the Pottowattomie, and there founded the town of Hyattville. Hr. Hyatt was President of the Kansas Aid Committee, and projected this plan to secure employment for these youths, who otherwise were likely to be a charge to the neighborhood in which they lived.

Governor Geary's administration thus far had not met with endorsement by either party. He evidently designed to do right and administer the laws impartially; but he went to Kansas with the notion that the Border Ruffians were to blame some and free state men much more. To the latter, therefore, he was at first haughty and reserved, as though fearful that he might be contaminated by their association or entangled by their advice. The pro-slavery men from the first were prejudiced against him, and he sought not to gain their favor. He would favor neither the free state cause nor the "single issue," and would be nothing else but Governor. He came to the Territory, not to be one of the people, to uphold any local party or interest, but as an administration man, hoping to secure favor with the Democratic party by settling the difficulties in Kansas upon the principles of justice and equity. He sought not to please the inhabitants of the Territory, but to *govern* them, and for accomplishing this object he expected to be backed by the whole force of the General Government. He, therefore, sought to profoundly impress the people with the fact that he was Governor of Kansas Territory, and was fully capable and able to enforce the laws and restore order.

Peace and tranquillity were the leading objects of his administration, and he sought in his own way to attain them and coveted the glory.

But to administer justice in Kansas was to favor free state men and oppose pro-slavery men; because one only asked their rights, the other were the aggressors. From the first, therefore, though not desired on his part, Governor Geary grew more and more in favor with the free state men, and in dispute with the Border Ruffians. As a Democrat, his sympathies and feelings were with the latter, and for the sake of the Democratic party he would screen, though not justify, them in his reports.

Many of both parties feeling that the Governor was sincerely laboring to restore order, an effort was made to unite all such on a peace platform reposing upon confidence in the Governor, but as this movement declared some of the enactments of the Shawnee Legislature obnoxious, and at the same time that it was obligatory upon all persons to temporarily submit to them, thus involving a recognition of their validity, the effort was a failure.

The free state Legislature assembled on the 6th of January, 1857, but a quorum not being present, no organization was effected. They held an informal meeting and adopted a memorial to Congress. It was thinly attended from various reasons. An unusual desire for peace pervaded the people; they were heartily sick of war, contention and strife. Governor Geary had done much to allay the excitement in the Territory, was evidently laboring to do all he could in that direction, and made many good promises. Many thought that the meeting of this Legislature would be but the renewal of strife, with little prospect of accomplishing much good.

Governor Robinson, relying much on the numerous pledges of Governor Geary, and believing that the Topeka Constitution would be again submitted to the people, and fearing that as Governor of the State, on account of his well known radicalism, might embarass and endanger the success of the movement, determined to resign. He accordingly, on receiving assurances from Lieutenant-Governor Roberts that he would attend the session of the Legislature, handed over to this gentleman his note of resignation, to be delivered to that body. He repaired to Washington to labor for the furtherance of the free state cause, in hope that as a private citizen, divested of all show of selfishness, he would be more instrumental.

But when the Legislature assembled, neither Governor or Lieutenant-Governor was present, and no word of explanation from either to account for their absence. The members that assembled, and free state men generally, felt considerably provoked at this action on the part of these two officers, and especially the Governor, and rumors were afloat that he had abandoned the movement, and sold himself to the administration party. But a letter from Governor Robinson, which he wrote from Washington as soon as he saw the proceedings of the Legislature, fully explained the whole matter to the satisfaction of all who were disposed to be satisfied.

Governor Geary, trusting to the assurances of the leading free state men, did not apprehend any difficulty from the assembling of the Legislature. He, however, had his confidential agent on hand to report its proceedings, and had prepared himself for any emergency. Sheriff Jones, not willing to trust the control of so important a matter to a doubtful Governor, was accordingly on hand himself. Going before Judge Cato, he obtained, on his oath, a writ for the arrest of the Topeka legislators, with the view of getting up another "war." He expected that the members would resist his arrests, and hence would occasion the use of force, which would result in bloody strife. But in this attempt at mischief-making he was doomed to disappointment.

The writs were placed in the hands of Deputy Marshal

Pardee, Jones accompanying him, to prevent any mistake in carrying out his programme. But, contrary to the expectation of this official, the members of the Legislature quietly yielded themselves up as prisoners, and were conveyed to Tecumseh. Here, on the following day, they obtained a hearing before Judge Cato, and were severally discharged, on five hundred dollars of their own recognizance, for their appearance at the first term of court. Like that of all other State prisoners, their trial never came off, the district attorney always entering his *nolle prosequi* to every motion to proceed with it.

CHAPTER XL.

TERRITORIAL LEGISLATURE.

The Territorial Legislature assembled at Lecompton on the 12th of January. The Senate organized under the following officers: Thomas Johnson, President; Richard R. Rees, President *pro tem.*, Thos. C. Hughes, Chief Clerk; C. H. Grover, Assistant Clerk, and D. Scott Boyle, Engrossing Clerk. The House organized by electing Wm. G. Mathias Speaker, W. H. Tebbs, Speaker *pro tem.*, and Robert C. Bishop, Chief Clerk. A joint committee was appointed to wait on the Governor and receive any communication he had to give. His message was accordingly sent to both houses, read, referred to committees, and six thousand five hundred copies ordered to be printed. This document was not very palatable to rabid pro-slavery men, as it classed the action of the Territorial militia with that of Lane's men and those at Hickory Point. It urged them to abolish certain obnoxious laws, to be quiet on slavery, to correct the mis-print of the Organic Act in the copy of the statutes, and declared the Governor determined to act impartially.

At the first of the session, a secret caucus was held by the members of the Legislature, in which it was agreed to pass all the bills that the Governor might reject over his veto by a two-thirds vote. Pursuant to this resolution they passed several very objectionable acts. They authorized the District Court, or any Judge in vacation, to admit to bail any prisoner on charge, or under indictment for any "crime or offense whatever, whether such crime or offense shall have been heretofore bailable or not." This was designed to endorse Judge Lecompte and condemn Governor Geary in the murder case of Hays. The Governor sent in his objections to it, whereupon both Houses, without considering them, passed the bill with but one dissenting vote. The day after this bill became a law, "Geo. W. Clark, the murderer of Barber, Dr. J. H. Stringfellow, Captain William Martin and other pro-slavery men, against whom unserved warrants had been in the hands of the marshal for months, appeared voluntarily before Judge Cato, offered bail and were discharged." Another act vetoed by the Governor provided for the taking of the census, preparatory to an election of delegates to a convention to frame a constitution, which will be examined more fully when the occasion for which it was framed shall be described.

From the commencement of the session, the members of the Legislature were disposed to provoke a quarrel with the Governor. As we have seen, they resurrected the difficulty between him and Judge Lecompte; they next proceeded to involve him in trouble with the most excitable and irritable character in the Territory. The county commissioners had appointed Wm. T. Sherrard Sheriff of Douglas County, in the place of Samuel J. Jones, who had resigned. He was a Virginian, of respectable parents, but a drunken, quarrelsome scamp, who had openly declared, that if he could get to be sheriff, he would involve the Territory in war before a week expired. Soon after Sherrard obtained his appointment, he called upon the Governor, and somewhat insolently demanded his commission. The blanks being in the possession of the Secretary of the Territory, who was absent at the time, and as his signature and seal were necessary to legalize the document, the Governor so stated to Mr. Sherrard, and requested him to wait a few days, until the Secretary's return. "Soon after, Sherrard called again at the Executive office, and on this occasion his conduct was so exceedingly offensive and insulting, as to elicit from the Governor the inquiry why he (Sherrard) should be so inimical to him. Such were his defiances and threats, that even had the Secretary been present, the commission would not have been issued. Next day Sherrard wrote a note to the Governor, informing him that if the commission was not received within a certain time, a mandamus would be obtained to compel him to render it."

In the meantime, the members of the county board, who had made the appointment, had severally visited the Governor, requesting him to withhold the commission until they could hold a regular meeting for the purpose of revoking the appointment, which had hastily been made at the instance of Sheriff Jones, and without a proper knowledge of the character of the applicant, who, they were now convinced, was utterly unfit for the office, in consequence of the violence of his disposition, his being almost daily engaged in street and tavern broils, and his threats to disturb the general peace as soon as the commission was obtained. Numerous petitions to the same effect were also obtained from respectable citizens of the county.

The House of Representatives passed a resolution on the 19th of January, requesting the Governor to furnish their body a statement of his reasons for not commissioning Wm. T. Sherrard as Sheriff of Douglas County. The Governor replied, giving as his reasons the petitions he had received, the general character and daily conduct of the applicant, which they themselves knew to be that of a seditious, drunken and unscrupulous loafer.

The reply of the Governor greatly enraged the Legislators. The very reasons assigned for not commissioning Sherrard were to them strong arguments that he ought to be commissioned. They had lauded and eulogized Sheriff Jones, and now desired a man to fill his place, which no honorable and worthy man could do. They wanted one to stir up trouble, pursue free state men, insult ladies and attack defenseless villages, and consequently, Sherrard possessed strong recommendations in their estimation. Some of the Legislators fumed and vaporized, declaring that Geary was a d—d despot, assuming arbitrary power from which an autocrat of Europe would have shrunk dismayed; another thought he ought to be censured; while a third declared he was a "usurper, a monster, and a tyrant," more atrocious and cruel in his conduct than Nero or Caligula, in not commissioning Sherrard. And thus the speakers from little to greater vied with each other in their denunciation and abuse of the Governor. When they had freely vented themselves in words they unanimously passed a resolution legalizing the acts of Sherrard and commissioning him Sheriff of Douglas County. But the Council failed to concur in this resolution, and consequently their labor was in vain. It was not out of any respect to the Governor that the Council thus decided, for they declared that "they can not sustain the reasons of the Governor for his action in the premises," that he had no right to pass judgment upon the qualifications of an appointee, and that "he had no discretion left to him" than to commission Sherrard.

Sherrard thus sustained by the Legislature became extremely insolent and venomous towards the Governor, his appointees, and free state men. At one time he assailed John A. W. Jones, a member of the Governor's household, a man of weak and slight physical frame and wholly unarmed, by striking him without a shadow of provocation. Again, he, after failing to provoke a quarrel with the Governor's private Secretary, struck him on the cheek, and seizing the handle of his pistol dared him to resent the insult.

Sherrard next assaulted the Governor himself. On the 9th of February, as the latter was retiring from the chamber in which the members of the House held their session, he was confronted by Sherrard, who accosted him, "You have treated me, sir, like a d——d scoundrel." The Governor, affecting not to notice him, passed on, and the person of Mr. McAllster interposed between him and his assailant. Sherrard followed, spitting after the Governor, at the same time uttering oaths and threats of defiance, his right hand firmly grasping one of the pistols in his belt. Failing to provoke the Governor to a difficulty in which he might have some pretense and nerve for shooting him, Sherrard finally abandoned the undertaking, and retired to boast of the insults he had heaped upon Mr. Geary's head.

A resolution, in the afternoon of the same day, was introduced in the House, highly condemning the conduct of Sherrard, instructing the Sergeant-at-Arms to bring him before the bar of the House to answer for the offense, and excluding him from the privileges of that body.

This created a perfect *furore* among the members. Joseph C. Anderson, from Missouri, declared "the Governor had no business in the halls of the Legislature, and that he should confine himself to his Executive office." Mr. Johnson said he knew the assault was to be made, but did not think it proper to interfere, it being none of his business. Such was the apparent opposition to the resolution, that the mover withdrew it. A milk-and-water resolution was finally passed, for mere effect, "to express the disapproval and maintain the dignity of the House," by a vote of 17 ayes to 11 nays. The Council took similar action.

Judge Cato, having come by request to the Governor's office for consultation in regard to Sherrard's conduct, appeared indifferent about the matter, and thought "such outrages beyond the pale of the law, there being no statute by which they could be punished." A warrant, however, was obtained for the arrest of Sherrard, and after remaining unobserved for two days a messenger was dispatched to Judge Cato, urging him to have it executed at once. This official was found in company with Sherrard and Jones, and when his attention was called to the matter, remarked that the Marshal was absent, and that it could not then be served.

The Governor, observing the indisposition to have the warrant executed, obtained and destroyed it.

The free state men, and the better class of pro-slavery men, were highly indignant at the conduct of Sherrard and those who upheld him. Meetings were held in various parts of the Territory, denouncing these indignities toward the Governor, and extending sympathy and assurances of co-operation in his laudable efforts to restore peace and tranquillity.

A meeting of this character was held at Lecompton on the 18th of February. Many threats had been made that it should never be held, and efforts were employed to prevail on the Governor to prevent its assembling. But the Governor replied that he knew not what would be the sentiments of the meeting, whether they would endorse or censure his actions, and that it would be highly reprehensible to prevent the people from peaceably assembling and passing judgment upon the action of their officers.

Nearly four hundred persons were in attendance, and the malcontents were there in the majority. A pro-slavery Chairman was elected and a pro-slavery Speaker took the stand, who in drunken gesticulations, denounced Governor Geary. The Committee soon presented a majority report of resolutions, in accordance with the pro-slavery sentiments of the meeting, but a minority of the Committee reported resolutions highly complimentary to the Governor, fully endorsing his conduct and extending to him their aid and sympathy, "in view of the recent personal assault upon our worthy Executive, for an act done in his official capacity, and fully justified by all the circumstances."

As quick as the reading of the latter series of resolutions was finished, Sherrard sprang upon a pile of boards and declared in a loud voice: "Any man who will dare to endorse these resolutions is a liar, a scoundrel and a coward." Mr. Shepherd, who stood in the midst of the crowd, remarked: "I endorse them, and am neither a liar, a scoundrel, nor a coward!" "Whereupon Sherrard immediately drew his revolver, and fired all the loads as rapidly as he could pull the trigger, aiming at Shepherd, though endangering the lives of others. Three balls took effect on Shepherd, and a fourth slightly wounded another person. As soon as Sherrard commenced firing Shepherd pulled off his gloves and attempted to return the shots; but his caps being wet they burst without discharging the loads; and seeing that Sherrard was about drawing his other pistol, he dubbed his revolver, rushed toward Sherrard and struck at him with the butt, Sherrard not having an opportunity to fire, returning his blows in a similar manner. They were separated, and Shepherd was removed, severely, and it was supposed, mortally wounded."

"No sooner was Shepherd taken off than Sherrard seized his other pistol and advanced, with his finger on the trigger, towards John A. W. Jones, the young man whom he had assaulted a few days before, when Jones, perceiving his danger, also drew his revolver. Several shots were simultaneously fired, and Sherrard fell mortally wounded." Though it was difficult to tell who fired the fatal shot, "a hue and cry was raised to hang young Jones; but his friends were too numerous, and an attempt to have done so would have been attended with rather serious consequences."

"The fall of Sherrard put an end to the riot. The rioters had lost their leader, and there was no one left among them sufficiently bold and desperate to take his place; and to this fact they attributed the defeat of a well contrived scheme to again involve the community in destructive strife. This matter had long been in agitation, and Sherrard was the chosen instrument to accomplish the mischievous purpose. His fall put an end to the plot, and saved many a valuable life. He died early on the following Saturday morning, and his remains were removed to Winchester, Virginia." Jones, who killed Sherrard, was constantly threatened with being lynched, and a reward of five hundred dollars was offered for his assassination. He appeared for examination before Judge Cato, who pronounced judgment against him before the first witness had finished his testimony, gave bail in the sum of five thousand dollars, and escaped from the Territory through Nebraska and Iowa.

On the same day the Legislature convened, a convention, first called to be held at Leavenworth but afterwards changed to Lecompton, assembled at the latter place, which is distinguished for having changed the name of the pro-slavery party from the "Law and Order" to the "National Democratic Party of Kansas Territory." At the former session of the Legislature it was declared that such a step was fraught with more danger than any that had yet been agitated, and that they should "know but *one* issue—SLAVERY." When a primary convention at Tecumseh, which favored mutual conciliation, appointed delegates to this convention, and stated the object to be "to consult upon and propose a policy upon which the citizens of Kansas, without distinction of party, may unite for the preservation of peace and general conciliation," the "Squatter Sovereign," in commenting upon this subject, said: "We advise our Shawnee friends to hold 'another meeting' and appoint delegates to the pro-slavery convention, or their credentials may be rejected."

When the convention assembled, the first question that engaged its attention was by what name should it be called, as there was none given in the notice convening it. The cognomen "Law and Order" was first proposed, but was overruled by Dr. Stringfellow, who proposed that it be called the "Pro-slavery Convocation," and "offered a resolution which was almost unanimously carried, denying a seat in the meeting to any man who was not known to be absolutely in favor of making Kansas a slave State." Mr. L. J. Hampton came near being excluded from the convention by this resolution, from the fact that he had treated the free state prisoners with some humanity.

But imagine the surprise of the uninitiated when they heard Dr. Stringfellow, on the following day, make a motion that they call themselves the "National Democratic party, of Kansas Territory." He had not long since said that he would not labor for any measure unless it would embrace the interest of the pro-slavery party. But the matter was explained. The whole thing had doubtless been arranged at Washington before hand, and the plan had just been communicated. In no other way can the sudden change of this partisan be accounted for. They had certain objects to attain—certain requests to make of the administration, and while it might refuse them as the pro-slavery party, it dare not as the Democratic party. They had an "ax to grind," so they changed their name. The Cincinnati Platform was adopted and a committee appointed to prepare an address to the people of the United States.

The death of William P. Richardson occurred during the session of the Legislature. Respectful resolutions were passed, his seat draped in mourning, and the members agreed to wear a badge thirty days. He was Major-General of the northern division of Kansas militia, and took a prominent part in the affairs of the Territory. He introduced the resolution strongly censuring Sherrard for his conduct towards the Governor.

The Legislature refused to repeal or alter the slave laws, and became highly indignant at the Governor for suggesting such a thing. A great many paper towns, and many of the free state towns, as Lawrence and Topeka were chartered. Numerous roads were authorized to be laid out, and railroad companies incorporated.

The report of the Treasurer will show that $1,811.88 were received, and $1,809.50 expended during the year. The only source of revenue was poll tax. By the Auditor's report it will be seen that the indebtedness of the Territory amounted to $4,039.92.

The Lecompton Legislature clearly revealed to Governor

Geary the relation in which he stood to the pro-slavery party; that they were not merely political opponents, but his enemies, not because he would not do right, but because he would not be their tool. He saw that they cared nothing for the Administration, Democratic party, himself, justice or right, beyond using all these for the "single issue," and whenever either stood in the way of its interest, they would seek to sacrifice it. He discovered that they were enemies, hostile and deadly.

Governor Geary had never sought to conciliate them. He had always aimed to act independent of them, for he was not so particular about their favor as that of the Administration and the Northern Democracy, and hence, when he found that they were his irreconcilable enemies, he still trusted to the strong, far-extending arm of the General Government and the moral support of Democracy for success.

Though Mr. Geary clung to the throne, still "there was a power behind the throne more powerful than the throne itself." This was slavery. Whatever may have been the real desires of Mr. Pierce's or Mr. Buchanan's heart, and no matter what policy either would prefer, to the demands of slavery they were always bound to submit. This fact Governor Geary next learned. Immediately after the insult offered to him and others by Sherrard, in consequence of the danger which seemed to menace him, he wrote to General Smith, at Fort Leavrnworth, for two additional companies of troops, to be sent to Lecompton to preserve the peace. In a few days this officer replied that there were no laws for the employment of the troops for the purpose above mentioned, and that "all the forces had just been designated by the Secretary of War, and are under orders for other services more distant." This was the first intimation that he was to be stripped of all power to suppress disturbances and for his own protection. He was assured, on the position being tendered him, that all the force he might desire would be at his command.

But the matter is easily explained. Meantime Emory, Calhoun, Clark and other pro-slavery demagogues had gone to Washington, obtained the ear of the President through Jefferson Davis, and prepossessed his mind with false representations concerning Governor Geary, and had importuned his removal. There were no good grounds to sustain such an act before the country, so it was determined to drive him to a resignation. The troops were denied him; the payment of money, which Mr. Geary had taken out of his own private funds, was disallowed for the reason that all the appropriations of Congress for the Territory were exhausted; while rumors reached Lecompton that he had been removed and his successor named. "During all this time his dispatches to the outgoing and the incoming administrations, defining the true condition of affairs, and asking information and instruction, were unanswered, and apparently unnoticed." To cap the climax, the Governor was, in the next place, called upon by Secretary Marcy to explain certain discrepancies between his account of the Hay's case and that of Judge Lecompte's; to which Mr. Geary, who was now pretty well enlightened, replied: "What I have written, I have written, and have nothing to add, alter or amend on the subject."

Governor Geary, seeing that he was abandoned by the Administration, all military and pecuniary support withdrawn, his way hedged up by pro-slavery men, and his life in imminent peril, forwarded his resignation, on the 4th of March, to take effect on the 20th of that month. Before another day he was compelled to leave Lecompton, to escape an attack from the Ruffians. Under the generous cover of night he hastily left the capital, armed with two revolvers, and wended his lonely way to the residence of Captain Walker, a free state man, where he appeared pale with fright, and besought protection and conveyance out of the Territory. Ere the morning light fell upon the prairies, he was in Kansas City; taking a boat at this place, he issued his farewell address to the people of Kansas. Thus ended Governor Geary's career in the Territory, abandoned and forsaken by those whose reputation he had hoped to save. He never understood what the pro-slavery men of Kansas and the Administration at Washington wanted and *would have*, until compelled to leave the Territory, which, had he known upon the position being tendered him, doubtless he would never have accepted it, or acted, in many instances, very differently in the performance of his executive functions. Mr. Geary has since continued to rise to distinction, as Governor of Pennsylvania.

Governor Geary's career and experience in Kansas are similar to Reeder's. Both came from the same State, honest and devoted Democrats, and based their policy upon the same principles of impartiality and justice; both leaned, at first, towards the pro-slavery men, and winked at some of their outrages, because they were the pets of the Administration. Neither understood the character of the Democracy in Kansas nor at Washington, and the political predilections and prejudices of both were against free state men. But both were honest, and assiduously labored for the good of the Territory. Both were opposed and defied by the Legislature, their lives threatened; both were abandoned by the Administration that appointed them, simply because they wished to do right, instead of doing all they could for slavery. Reeder was removed, and Geary doubtless would have been, had he not resigned when he did. Both left the Territory in peril of their lives, under the friendly shade of night.

On the 10th of April, Mr. Buchanan appointed Hon. Robert J. Walker, Governor, and Hon. Frederick P. Stanton, Secretary, of Kansas Territory. Daniel Woodson, former Secretary, was promoted to the office of Receiver of the Delaware Land District.

CHAPTER XLI.

QUESTION OF VOTING FOR DELEGATES TO THE LECOMPTON CONSTITUTIONAL CONVENTION.

Hon. Robert J. Walker was the son of Judge Walker, one of the Judges of the Supreme Court of the United States, and was born in Pennsylvania, not far from the home of Mr. Buchanan. He studied law under his father, and practiced his profession at Pittsburg, where he married the daughter of Franklin Bache, of Philadelphia, and granddaughter of Benjamin Franklin. He made the first nomination of Mr. Jackson for the Presidency. He early emigrated to Mississippi, where he took an active part in politics; favored the independence of Texas and its annexation to the United States; but opposed Mr. Calhoun's project of making it all slave territory, taking about the same stand that he did in reference to Kansas that the character of labor in the different States of the Union was determined by climate and not by legislation. He conducted a famous canvass in Mississippi against Poindexter for the United States Senate, upon the issue of nullification. He bitterly denounced disunion in that early day as treason, set forth in the clearest light the relation of a State to the Federal Government, and proudly triumphed over his powerful competitor. This canvass has no parallel in the history of our country, considering the momentous issue at stake, the talented champions who conducted it, and the universal attention it attracted, unless it be the famous contest in Illinois between Hon. Stephen A. Douglas and Hon. Abraham Lincoln. Mr. Walker occupied a seat in Mr. Polk's Cabinet as Secretary of the Treasury, in which position he distinguished himself for his financial ability, by drawing up and establishing a system of revenue, that reduced duties more than one-half, while it produced upwards of $29,000,000 the first year.

Governor Walker is undoubtedly the greatest and most distinguished man that was ever appointed to any position in Kansas by the General Government. He stood firmly and devotedly by the Union in the recent great national conflict; an intimate friend and adviser of President Lincoln; contributing able articles to the "Continental Review" upon the subject of currency and the war; planning and carrying out in a great measure the wonderful policy of finance adopted by the General Government. He reluctantly and hesitatingly accepted the appointment of Kansas Territory at the repeated and earnest solicitations of President Buchanan and Stephen A. Douglas, but not until after a full understanding and perfect concurrence of opinion were had between himself and the President with reference to the policy which he afterwards pursued.

About the time of Mr. Walker's appointment, it was thought by the Administration, and the real friends of the Democratic party, that civil war was on the eve of breaking out in Kansas, which threatened to involve the whole Union. The Topeka Legislature had determined to put its government into practical operation, which would evidently bring on a collision between it and the Territorial authorities; each party would be supported by the different States, and thus war was inevitably the consequence. The policy therefore determined upon by Mr. Buchanan and Mr. Walker, in order to avert this calamity, was to sustain the dignity of the Territorial Legislature by compelling obedience to its enactments, and suspend action on the part of the State Legislature, by giving every assurance and guarantee that the election of delegates to the Constitutional Convention should be fairly conducted, and the constitution framed by them should be submitted to a fair and full vote for ratification or rejection by the people. Mr. Walker was urged to accept the appointment, in view of the dangers menaced, and on the grounds that he was best qualified for the work in being a northern man by birth and a southern man by long residence.

Hon. Frederick P. Stanton, who was appointed successor of Mr. Woodson as Secretary of the Territory, was born at Alexandria, D. C., on the 22nd of December, 1814, and consequently does not claim to be a native of Virginia, but always to have been under the flag of the Union, and to owe allegiance to it alone.

He obtained his education chiefly in the very excellent and well-known school of Benjamin Hallowell, of Alexandria, in which he became an assistant tutor at the age of eighteen. He graduated and obtained a diploma at the Columbia College, near Washington, D. C. His first employment after graduation was teaching, first in a village school in Occoquan, Va., and afterwards as an assistant teacher in an academy at Portsmouth, of the same State. At the age of nineteen he was elected principal of an academy at Elizabeth City, N. C., where, after spending two years, he was admitted to the bar of his native town, Alexandria, and immediately removed to the Western District of Tennessee. Here he engaged in his profession at the age of twenty-one, and for one or two years also conducted the editorial department of the "Gazette," published at Memphis. In 1845 he was elected to Congress from the Memphis District, which he represented for ten consecutive years. He was first chairman of the Committee on Naval Affairs, and then of the Committee on the Judiciary, took a prominent and decided part in the proceedings of the House, always supporting measures because he thought them right, rather than consult the interest of party, though a Democrat in politics.

In 1855 he voluntarily retired from Congress and began the practice of his profession at Washington, where, after an absence of several years in this Territory, he returned and still resides. He was a warm friend of the Union during the great rebellion, employing all his powers in the interest of his country, furnishing many valuable articles for the "Continental Review," to which he was a regular contributor for two years.

Mr. Stanton arrived at Lecompton on the 15th of April, in advance of Governor Walker several days, and took charge of the Executive affairs of the Territory. He came here strongly prejudiced against the free state men, a pro-slavery man himself, and with all his sympathies in that direction. He was somewhat bold and defiant in his demeanor towards them, declaring in a public speech at Lawrence that the Territorial laws should be obeyed, and the taxes, assessed under its authority, collected, and in case of resistance there would be "war to the knife, and knife to the hilt." In a few days after his arrival he issued his address defining the policy that had been agreed upon by the administration, and shortly published an apportionment of delegates to the Constitutional Convention.

Governor Walker arrived at Lecompton on the 27th of May, where he immediately issued his inaugural, to which we will again advert, after examining the provisions for calling the Constitutional Convention.

The Shawnee Legislature passed an act for submitting the question of "the expediency of calling a convention to form a State Constitution," to the determination of the people of the Territory, at the election in October, 1856. At this election 2,670 voted in favor of calling the Convention and only a few against it, while at the same time the total number of votes cast for Delegate were 4,276, and the number of legal voters in the Territory, as shown by the imperfect census returned were 9,251. But little interest was manifested in the matter, even among the pro-slavery men, whereas the free state men took no part whatever in the election.

On the 19th of February, 1857, the Legislature at Lecompton passed an act for taking the census, the apportionment of delegates, and calling a convention to frame a constitution. The census was to be taken between the first day of March and the first day of April following, by the Sheriffs of the respective counties, who owed their appointment, through the County Commissioners, to the Legislature. The provisions for taking the census were not at all objectionable, but eminently just and equitable, if properly carried out.

After the returns were completed the Governor was authorized to make an apportionment of sixty delegates among the districts into which the thirty-four counties were divided, and announce it by proclamation. The election of these delegates was to take place on the third Monday in June, 1857, and no one was to be allowed to vote whose name did not appear upon the numeration list. The delegates thus elected should meet at Lecompton on the first Monday of September following, and enter upon their work. No provision was made for submitting the Constitution when framed to ratification or rejection by a vote of the people.

The census was partially and incorrectly taken in fifteen counties, which were thus reported to have 9,251 legal voters. From Johnson county, which was then the Shawnee reserve, and excluded from settlement, and consequently no white person could have a legal residence upon it, 496 voters were returned. Doniphan county, was returned with about the same number as Douglas, though containing no more than one-half as many voters. But in nineteen of the counties no attempt was made to take the census, and no returns were received.

In some instances, doubtless, the free state men refused to give in their names; but it is not known that any violence or threats were offered to the census takers.

But the officers did not conform to the law where they pretended to take the census. They were required to make out a full and complete list of all legal voters, place them on file in the office ot the Probate Judge, who was required to keep the record open for inspection for several weeks, and allow people to make any corrections or amends. Similar lists were to be posted up and distributed among the voters. In many instances these provisions were wholly disregarded.

The plain intent of the law was, that no apportionment of delegates to the convention should be made, until the census should be completed, and the returns of such complete census made. But Secretary Stanton, ignorant of the Territory and its population, giving too much credit to the reports of pro-slavery men, with whom he was really in sympathy, after waiting some length of time, and no more returns coming in, made the apportionment of sixty delegates among the fifteen counties from which returns had been received; thus virtually disfranchising the other nine-counties, in which the enumeration had not been taken, though not the fault of the inhabitants.

In this way the border counties were entitled to most of the delegates, and about one-half the inhabited territory entirely disfranchised. Mr. Stanton was under no obligation to base the apportionment upon these returns, until they were completed; indeed, he had no right to, according to the act from which he derived his authority to make the apportionment at all.

Mr. Stanton acted sincerely according to the light he then had. He soon perceived his error, and was frank enough to admit it. In a speech at New York shortly afterwards, he said: "If I had then known what I have since ascertained, and what I now believe and know to be true, I should have hesitated before I would have made an apportionment which should have brought about the state of things which now exist. I should have suffered the whole law to fail. But, under the circumstances, supposing as I did then, that the people who had refused to go into this election, or to go into the process of registration, were in a measure factious, and not justified in what they were doing, and not knowing the character of the population in the other counties, or whether they had any population at all, or any considerable population, and being under the necessity of acting by a particular time—for the returns were to be made in my office on the 1st of May, and the election to take place on the 15th of June—I say, under the pressure of these circumstances, I could do nothing but what I did."

But there can be no question that Messrs. Walker and Stanton came here with the design and express understanding, of giving a fair and full opportunity to the people of the Territory to decide their difficulties at the ballot-box, by voting for delegates to the Constitutional Convention, and then by voting upon the adoption of the Constitution itself. Upon this understanding with Mr. Buchanan, they accepted the positions tendered them, and with the design of faithfully carrying it out, they came to the Territory and entered upon and conducted their work.

Governor Walker first sought to impress the people with the object of his mission, and the policy he intended to follow. In his inaugural, delivered at Lecompton on the 27th of May, he says:

"The mode of adjustment is provided in the act organizing your Territory—namely, by the people of Kansas, who, by a majority of their own votes, must decide this question for themselves in forming their State Constitution.

"Under our practice the preliminary act of framing a State Constitution is uniformly performed through the instrumentality of a convention of delegates chosen by the people themselves. That convention is now about to be elected by you under the call of the Territorial Legislature, created and still recognized by the authority of Congress, and clothed by it, in the comprehensive language of the Organic Law, with full power to make such an enactment. The Territorial Legislature then, in assembling this convention, were fully sustained by the act of Congress, and the authority of the convention is distinctly recognized in my instructions from the President of the United States. Those who oppose this course can not aver the irregularity of the Territorial Legislature, whose laws, in town and city elections, incorporate franchises and on all subjects but slavery, they acknowledge by votes and acquiescence. If that Legislature was invalid, then are we without law or order in Kansas, without town, city or county organization, all legal and judicial transactions are void, all titles null, and anarchy reigns throughout our border.

"It is my duty, in seeing that all constitutional laws are fairly executed, to take care, as far as practicable, that this election of delegates to the convention shall be free from fraud or violence, and that they shall be protected in their deliberations.

"The people of Kansas, then, are invited, by the highest authority known to the Constitution, to participate freely and fairly in the election of delegates to frame a constitution and State government. The law has performed its entire appropriate function, when it extends to people the right of suffrage, but it cannot compel the performance of that duty. Throughout our whole Union, however, and wherever free government prevails, those who abstain from the right of suffrage, authorize those who do vote to act for them in that contingency, and the absentees are as much bound under the law and constitution, where there is no fraud or violence, by the act of the majority of those who do vote, as though all had participated in the election. Otherwise, as voting must be voluntary, self-government would be impracticable, and monarchy or despotism would remain as the only alternative.

"You should not console yourselves, my fellow-citizens, with the reflection that you may, by a subsequent vote, defeat the ratification of the constitution. Although most anxious to secure to you the exercise of that great constitutional right, and believing that the convention is the servant, and not the master of the people, yet I have no power to dictate the proceedings of that body. I cannot doubt, however, the course they will adopt on this subject. But why incur the hazard of the preliminary formation of a constitution by a minority, as alleged by you, when a majority, by their votes, could control the forming of that instrument?

"But it is said that the convention is not legally called, and that the election will not be freely and fairly conducted. The Territorial Legislature is the power ordained for this purpose, by the Congress of the United States; and, in opposing it, you resist the authority of the Federal Government. That Legislature was called into being by the Congress of 1854, and is recognized in the very latest Congressional legislation. It is recognized by the present Chief Magistrate of the Union, just chosen by the American people, and many of its acts are now in operation here by universal consent. As the Governor of the Territory of Kansas, I must support the laws and the Constitution; and I have no other alternative, under my oath, but to see that all constitutional laws are fully and fairly executed.

"I see in this act, calling the convention, no improper or unconstitutional restrictions upon the rights of suffrage. I see in it no test oaths, or other similar provisions objected to in relation to previous laws, but clearly repealed as repugnant to the provisions of this act, so far as regards the election of delegates to this convention. It is said that a fair and full vote will not be taken. Who can safely predict such a result? Nor is it just for a majority, as they allege, to throw the power into the hands of the minority, from a mere apprehension—I trust entirely unfounded—that they will not be permitted to exercise the right of suffrage. If, by fraud or violence, a majority should not be permitted to vote, there is a remedy, it is hoped, in the wisdom and justice of the convention itself, acting under obligations of an oath and the proper responsibility to the tribunal of public opinion. There is a remedy, also, if such facts can be demonstrated, in the refusal of Congress to admit a State into the Union under a constitution imposed by a minority upon the majority by fraud or violence. Indeed, I can not doubt that the convention, after having framed a State constitution, will submit it for ratification or rejection, by a majority of the then actual *bona fide* resident settlers of Kansas.

"*With these views well known to the President and Cabinet, and approved by them, I accepted the appointment as Governor of Kansas. My instructions from the President, through the Secretary of State, under the date of 30th of March last, sustain 'the regular Legislature of the Territory' in 'assembling a convention to form a constitution,' and they express the opinion of the President that 'when such a constitution shall be submitted to the people of the Territory, they must be protected in the exercise of their right of voting for or against that instrument; and the fair expression of the popular will must not be interrupted by fraud or violence.'*

"I repeat, then, as my clear conviction, that unless the convention submit the constitution to the vote of all the actual resident settlers of Kansas, and the election be fairly and justly contested, the constitution will be, and ought to be rejected by Congress."

He took the position that there was an agency more powerful than human legislation which would determine the local institutions of the Territory. It was the same which Daniel Webster assumed in regard to the Territory of New Mexico. The isothermal line defined the limits of slavery and that to attempt to extend it beyond that line would be like an effort to change the laws of God. He urged them to cease from trying to effect a thing which had already been settled by the unalterable prohibition of Nature. This argument broke the strength of the pro-slavery party. Many of them already desirous of peace began to abandon the struggle. Governor Walker was highly censured by the more rabid pro-slavery men, and by their press all over the Union, for what was generally called his "isothermal argument."

The Governor labored faithfully and earnestly to prevail upon the free state men to take part in the election by assuring them that they should be protected from fraud and violence, and setting forth the practical and happy results in thus terminating existing difficulties in the Territory. Though the propositions of Governor Walker seemed fair and candid, still there were many reasons which made the free state men loth, and finally to refuse to contest the election.

It was not from any fear that they were numerically weaker than the opposite party that caused them to decline the contest, for it was generally conceded by pro-slavery men that their opponents surpassed them in numbers. Even the famous "Squatter Sovereign" paper gave up the struggle and closed its existence. There was no more threatening, no more raids, no more "wiping out of Lawrence," no more war appeals, or din and clang along the Border. The only hope of pro-slavery men lay in the election of a pro-slavery convention to form a constitution through the advantages which their own legislation had given them.

In the first place, free state men were strongly attached to the Topeka State organization, for it was a work of their own; whereas the calling of a Constitutional Convention was made by a body whose authority originated in fraud and oppression, an authority they had always repudiated. It seemed to them humiliating and degrading, after having so long protested against the validity of the Territorial Legislature, to turn around and so far recognize it as to vote under its appointment, and thus really supersede an illegally constituted body and derive their authority from it. Such was not a material objection, but it had its influence among the masses.

But the chief objection was the apprehension that there would be little fairness and justice in the elective contest. Although Governor Walker made every assurance that these fears would not be realized, yet he was a stranger to them, a Southern man in views and interest. Had Governor Walker been among the people long enough to have secured their confidence, as Reeder and Geary, who likewise at first were regarded with suspicion, and justly, the case would have been very different. Already, by the registration and apportionment, a monstrous fraud had been perpetrated, and how could they expect better treatment in the future.

With the unfair apportionment, it was doubtful whether they could elect a majority of the delegates, and as the act providing for the convention did not prescribe that the constitution, when framed, should be submitted to the people for ratification or rejection, there was no guarantee that the convention would likely do it. In case they did, the free state men could then go in and defeat it, so there could be nothing lost by not taking part in the convention. Though Governor Walker assured them that it should be so submitted, and in case it was not, Congress would and ought to reject it, still pro-slavery presses declared differently, and censured Governor Walker for raising the question of its submission. Says a Richmond paper:

"Upon the new plan which Governor Walker submits for the settlement of the Kansas difficulty, we cannot venture an opinion before we scrutinize it in detail. There is one point, however, upon which we can give an instant and emphatic decision; and that is, the proposition to submit the constitution of Kansas to a popular vote. In respect of general policy, such a step would inevitably involve very disastrous consequences. In the first place, it would inflame and prolong the controversy, and would ultimately throw Kansas into the arms of the abolitionists. But any discussion of the measure in regard to expediency is unnecessary and irrelevant, since a convention, which is to frame a State constitution for Kansas, is endowed with no authority to submit this their work to the popular vote. The act by which the convention assembles, ascertains and limits its powers, and in that act there is not one word about submitting the constitution to the people. The convention can do nothing for which there is not an express authority in the law; and as there is neither an express nor implied authority in the law to submit the constitution of Kansas to a vote of the inhabitants of the Territory, the step would be an illegal, an invalid usurpation of power. The proposition is too plain to allow of controversy. Submit it to any lawyer in the land, from Chief Justice Taney or Reverdy Johnson, to the poorest pettifogger in the most obscure country village, and the answer will be, that the convention in Kansas has no right to submit the constitution to a popular vote. The journals of the North concede the point, and declaim against the law calling the convention, on the ground that it makes no provision for a popular vote on the constitution. Why then does Governor Walker raise the question? It is especially surprising that he should assume an undeniably untenable position."

Governor Walker's policy for the adjustment of Kansas difficulties instead of being endorsed was received with distrust by both parties—one fearing it would not, the other that it would, secure a fair expression of the public will upon the constitution about to be formed. The South was enraged at his isothermal argument.

From these considerations the free state men resolved at a delegate convention held at Topeka on the 9th of June, not to participate in the election of members for the Constitutional Convention. They reaffirmed their adherence to the Topeka State organization, and recommended its maintenance. They "disown as invalid and of no force or effect the authority of the Territorial Government," and declared that "their admission into the Union under the Constitution which they have already formed, is the only method of adjusting existing difficulties, to which they will assent." They not only resolved "to disregard and permit to pass without any participation therein," the coming election, but that any one who "consents to become a delegate to the Lecompton Convention, or a candidate to the same, is unworthy the confidence and fellowship of the free state men, and should be regarded with suspicion every-where." It provided for a convention to be held at Topeka, July 15, for the purpose of nominating State officers, and consulting upon subjects of public interests.

Upon the same day the State Legislature convened, and proceeded with its business without any interruption, though Governor Walker was in town. It passed an act authorizing and providing for the taking of the census, and one dividing* a portion of the Territory into counties by the following names: Allen, Adams, Abbott, Arny, Barber, Brown, Blood, Beckerton, Blimmerton, Collins, Currier, Cantral, Curtis, Conway, Concklin, Shombre, Dickey, Deitzler, Dow, Dana, Delehay, Jamison, Jordon, Geary, Hillyer, Hopps, Howe, Hoyt, Holliday, Harding, Hutchingson, Harvey, Jones, Keyser, Lane, Leavenworth, Parrott, Pillsbury, Partridge, Powers, Phillips, Roberts, Robinson, Reeder, Redpath, Smith, Sackett, Stewart, Schuyler, Thornton, Updegraff, Williams, Walker and Wakefield. It passed an act providing for an election of State officers, on the third Monday in August following, with suitable directions, and made Topeka the capital of the State. It was not in session long and only passed such laws as were necessary to preserve its organization, having determined to await the development of Walker's policy.

*This failed to pass—only introduced.

CHAPTER XLII.

QUESTION OF VOTING FOR MEMBERS OF THE LEGISLATURE.

The Delegate Convention assembled at Topeka July 15, reaffirmed its adherence to the State organization, and again repudiated the Territorial Legislature. State officers were nominated for the election in August, and the people were urged to interest themselves in it. They recommended a submission of the Topeka Constitution to a vote of the people at the same time. On account of reports that Missourians were preparing to interfere with the fall elections, General J. H. Lane was appointed to organize the people in the several districts to protect the ballot-box.

The question of contesting the October election engaged in a great measure the attention of the convention. That a diversity of views were held might be expected, and the discussion was warm and earnest. It was finally resolved, in view of certain declarations of Governor Walker, looking to fairness and justice, to call a mass convention of the citizens of Kansas, to be held at Grasshopper Falls on the last Wednesday in August, "to take into consideration all that may be necessary in regard to that election." A Delegate Convention was likewise called at the same time and place, to carry out the views of the mass convention, composed of twice as many delegates as there were free state Senators and Representatives. It is a noticeable feature that A. D. Richardson was the chief secretary of this Convention.

At the free state election, held on the 9th of August, the following is the official vote upon all State issues: Judges of Supreme Court—S. N. Latta, 7,200, and M. F. Conway, 7,178; Secretary of State—P. C. Schuyler, 7,167; Auditor—A. G. Cutler, 7,177; Reporter of Supreme Court—E. M. Thruston, 7,187; Clerk of Supreme Court—A. Patrick, 7,200; Representative to Congress—M. C. Parrott, 7,267. Vote for the Constitution, 7,267: against it, 34.

About the first of August, Governor Walker surrounded Lawrence with four or five hundred dragoons, for the purpose of suppressing the city government. The people of that town refused to accept the charter proffered by the Territorial Legislature, for which a few had petitioned, and had organized a municipal government of their own. It was never brought into practical effect, but was designed only to regulate and control the action of those who would acknowledge its authority, and to be in readiness to go into operation, the moment that free state men should get control of Territorial or State legislation. Governor Walker heard of it, and determined to break it up. He issued his proclamation, entreating the citizens to abandon their city organization, and warned them of the consequence. It seemed much like magnifying a mole-hill into a mountain, by the flurry and display the Governor made about the matter; for he had no more right to interfere with this association of individuals, than with a voluntary debating society, until they attempted to enforce their requirements.

he inhabitants of Lawrence paid but little regard to the Governor's display of troops, nor his pronunciamentos, and quietly pursued their vocations. The dragoons, numbering some four or five hundred, after being kept on the outskirts of Lawrence for several weeks, to end the folly, were removed by order of the President.

The question of participating in the October election for members of the Legislature and delegates to Congress, engaged the attention of free state men during the summer.

Governor Walker had said in his speech on the 9th of June, "*In October next, not under the act of the late Territorial Legislature, but under the laws of Congress, you, the whole people of Kansas, have the right to elect a delegate to Congress, and to elect a Territorial Legislature.*"

The notion of abandoning the State organization was at first rather unpopular; citizens could not bear the idea of so far recognizing the validity of the Territorial Legislature as to vote under its provisions. But the more the subject was discussed, and renewed assurances from Governor Walker given, that fairness should be shown in the election, the more the idea prevailed. Some gentlemen, more of a chivalrous or morbid, than practical, sense of honor, revolted at the suggestion, and bitterly fought the measure throughout. They were generally of that class who had reaped much pleasure and profit from writing to Eastern presses about Kansas troubles, and who were interested in their continuance. But the common sensed and practical minded readily discarded such nice distinctions of honor and felt it not at all disreputable "to stoop to conquer." What was the Topeka Constitution to them, if they could but obtain the blessings of peace and liberty by forsaking it, in order to hurl their oppressors from power?

But still there were practical difficulties in the way of success should they contest the election. The apportionment of members to the Council and House of Representatives was partial and unjust. It was Governor Walker's duty in the first place to have made this; but the printing of the acts of the previous Legislature being delayed, he did not see a copy of the election law until after the time had expired in which he could make the apportionment. The duty now devolved upon the President of the Council and Speaker of the House of Representatives to do the work, and accordingly Mr. Mathias and Mr. Johnson did it to the entire satisfaction of the pro-slavery party. The apportionment of Councilmen was as follows:

Leavenworth County, 3; Atchison, 1; Brown, Nemaha, Marshal, Pottawottomie and Riley, with all that part of the Territory which lies west of Marshal, Riley and Davis Counties, 2; Jefferson and Calhoun, 2; Douglas and Johnson, 3; Shawnee, Richardson,[1] Davis, Wise,[2] Breckenridge,[3] Bourbon, Godfrey, Wilson, Dorn, McGee, Butler, Hunter, Greenwood, Madison, Weller, Coffey, Woodson and Allen, 2; Anderson, Lykins, Linn and Franklin, with all the Territory lying west of Wise, Butler and Hunter, 1; making in all 13 Councilmen.

The apportiontment of members for the House of Representatives was equally unfair. Leavenworth County had 8, whereas Douglas and Johnson, together with all the vast country west of what is now Morris, Chase and Butler, only 8; Doniphan had 5, and Atchison 3, while thirteen other counties, among which were Anderson, Franklin Allen and Bourbon, had but 3; Linn and Lykins had 2 apiece; Jefferson County 2, and Shawnee 1.

This apportionment was decidedly against the free state men, and comprised their chief embarrassment. It darkened their prospect of success, though they were double in numerical strength to their opponents. "It showed an unquestionable determinatlon to introduce voters from abroad. Sixteen counties, strongly free state, containing nearly one-half the entire population of the Territory, are not allowed a single representative in either branch. Of the thirteen members of the Council, all but three, and of thirty-nine members of the House of Representatives, all but ten, are elected in districts bordering on the Missouri line. Topeka is connected with Fort Scott, and Lawrence is attached to Shawnee Mission, adjoining Westport. The Lawrence and Doniphan districts are also made to embrace an indefinite extent of country, having no geographical connection whatever with them, away in the region of the Rocky Mountains, occupied only by Indian trading posts, here and there,

(1) Waubansee, (2) Morris. (3) Lyons.

at which fictitious precincts may be made, and from which fictitious returns may be sent in, at anytime after the election, to overcome the free state vote. Besides these things, our enemies have complete possession of the machinery of the election. Establishing places for voting, appointing the judges, canvassing the returns, declaring the result of the election, and all other matters of detail, are in the hands of county commissioners, who were themselves elected by fraud and violence from Missouri. Mr. Abel, partner of Mr. Atchison, says that Kansas will not be given up, and General Atchison sounds the note of renewed preparation to South Carolina, and declares that 'with one more effort, the work is done.'"

The qualifications of an elector, it was feared, would disfranchise many free state men. A residence of six months in the Territory was required, which would cut off from voting the vast immigration that had come in from the free States during the spring and summer. Judge Cato had just decided that all voters would be required to pay the Territorial tax, though Governor Walker held to the contrary.

But the Federal Government had recognized the Territorial Legislature as legitimate, which tended greatly to preclude the success of the Topeka Constitution. Should the free state men be victorious in the coming election they would have obtained all they sought by the State organization. Should they be defeated, they would stand the same chance of triumph under the Topeka government. They had, therefore, little to loose and much to gain by going into an election. With nothing but the oft repeated pledges of Governor Walker, for fairness and justice, to insure their success, they hesitatingly fell in with the idea of contesting the election.

The Mass and Delegate Conventions assembled at Grasshopper Falls on the 26th of August, "in a grove near the village." It was an important assemblage, and was a crisis in the history of the Territory. G. W. Smith was chairman of the Mass Convention, and W. Y. Roberts of the Delegate Convention. Spirited discussions were awakened by the proposition to contest the October election. Conway, Phillips and Redpath were the principal opponents; while Robinson, Lane, Pomeroy, Holliday, Smith, and others, favored it. Governor Robinson held that "the Territorial form of government was legitimate, and that although our present form of government was the offspring of fraud, yet it was recognized by the Federal Government, and before the United States Courts it was useless to contest—that there was no way of getting rid of it so effectually as by the ballot-box—and that in the measure contemplated, so far from abandoning the State government, we are actually forwarding it by preparing, in a legal and legitimate manner, to put its opponent out of the way."

"Mr. Phillips was opposed to the resolution, representing that a requirement of six months' residence, the registration, and the territorial tax, together with an irruption of previously registered voters from Missouri, rendered utterly impossible any prospect of success." He concluded by offering a resolution, that, should the free state men gain possession of the legislative powers of the Territory at the coming election, they should use them to destroy the old Territorial Government, and to establish that under the Topeka constitution.

The following are the resolutions passed by the Mass Convention:

"WHEREAS, It is of the most vital importance to the people of Kansas, that the Territorial government should be controlled by the *bona fide* citizens thereof; and whereas, Governor Walker has repeatedly pledged himself that the people of Kansas should have a full and fair vote, before impartial judges, at the election to be held the first Monday in October, for Delegate to Congress, members of the Legislature, and other officers. Therefore

"*Resolved*, That we, the people of Kansas, in Mass Convention assembled, agree to participate in said election.

"*Resolved*, That in thus voting, we rely upon the faithful fulfillment of the pledge of Governor Walker; and that we, as heretofore, protest against the enactments forced upon us by the voters of Missouri.

"*Resolved*, That this mass meeting recommend the appointment of a committee to wait upon the Territorial authorities, and urgently insist upon a review and correction of the wicked apportionment endeavored to be forced upon the people of Kansas, for the selection of members of the Territorial Legislature.

"*Resolved*, That General J. H. Lane be authorized and empowered to tender to Governor Walker the force organized by him under the resolution passed by the convention held at Topeka on the 15th of July last, to be used for the protection of the ballot-box."

General Lane, with characteristic adroitness, lingered on the outskirts of the convention until he saw the direction which the current of public opinion would take, then mounted the platform and made a flaming speech in favor of contesting the election.

M. F. Conway, opposing the proposed contest, "argued at length upon the impracticability of the proposition to vote, that to enter into that contest would be virtually abandoning the State government and Topeka constitution, which had so long been the efficient rallying cry of the free state party; that in doing so we take a step backward in our political history, which he feared it impossible ever to retrace. As a matter of principle, he feared the free state party, by so doing, would stultify itself, and render itself ignominous in the eyes of the lovers of freedom. As a measure of policy, he could see but one issue, and that was defeat."

Judge Smith favored participating in the election, and remarked, although "under very unfair and unusual restrictions, he yet considered it their duty to go to the polls in October next and vote, and he was confident that with proper organization and exertion, there was no question as to their complete triumph." "That it was necessary to contest the election, in order to satisfy our friends in the free States, since we had represented to them that we were numerically greater than our opponents, and since Governor Walker gave every assurance of fairness and justice, which was all we had asked."

The Delegate Convention nominated M. J. Parrott as candidate for Delegate to Congress, appointed a Territorial Executive Committee of twenty members, to have their office at Lawrence, five of whom should constitute a quorum, for the transaction of business, and recommended to the citizens of each voting precinct to choose a committee of three persons, who should keep a record of all the votes cast, those refused and the reasons of refusal, and that citizens be present in sufficient numbers to sustain such a committee.

The free state men entered upon this contest little sanguine of success. In their addresses to the people of the country they said. "With the administration against us—with one-half of the six months voters virtually disfranchised; with an election law framed expressly to keep the newly arrived emigrants from the polls; with the hellish system of districting staring us in the face; with most of the officers of the election Border Ruffians of the deepest dye; with the slave party of Missouri boldly avowing, through General Atchison, their determination to invade us; with only the already half violated pledge of Governor Walker to rely on, we do not feel at liberty to cherish a very lively expecation of a fair election."

The election on the 5th of October, notwithstanding the obstacles, resulted in favor of the free state men. Many of them, disdaining to act under the direction of the Territorial Legisiature, or having no hope of success, refused to vote. There were nine free state men and four pro-slavery men elected to the Council, and twenty-five free state men and fourteen pro-slavery men elected to the House of Representatives. M. J. Parrott was chosen delegate over ex-Governor Ransom* by about 4,090 majority. There were in all 11,687 votes for delegates.

But the election proved that the fears of the free state men were not unfounded. At a little town called Oxford, in Shawnee County, near the Missouri line, the polls were kept open two days, and 1638 votes were polled, of which not more than seventy-five or a hundred were legal. This was designed to counterbalance the vote at Lawrence,which was in the same district. In a precinct in the south-eastern portion of the Territory, in what was then called McGee County, twelve hundred votes were polled, where only fourteen were cast at the election a short time previous for delegate to the Constitutional Convention. Governor Walker, true to his pledge to fairness and justice, set aside these returns for the *alleged* reason of defects in the papers transmitting them, but for the *real* reason that he believed them to be fraudulent. At Kickapoo, and other places, frauds were perpetrated, but not so egregious, and were passed by unobserved.

Governor Walker having refused certificates to several claiming election, upon the fraudulent votes cast in the two precincts above mentioned, Judge Cato issued his mandamus, requiring the Governor to grant the certificates, or show reason for withholding them, and placed it in the hands of the parties interested to execute. Governor Walker refused to observe the mandamus, and set forth his reasons at length; closed his reply by assuring the Judge, if he would push the matter so far as to seek to arrest and imprison him, he (the Governor) would yield himself without resistance, and if he (the Judge) apprehended any disturbance of the peace by the proceeding, that he (the Governor) would make a requisition for the United States

*Formerly Governor of Michigan, but then a broken down politician.

troops to prevent it. The whole affair was supremely ridiculous. Suffice it to say, that the Judge pursued the matter no farther.

While the Kansas Governors generally proved true to their honest convictions, other appointees of the Administration, in most instances, used all their influence to serve partisan purposes. Such seems to have been especially the case with the *Judiciary*. Judge Cato, of Alabama, was perhaps the most perverse and partial of all others; Judge Elmore was the most prompt to duty, strict and impartial in his judgments; Judge Lecompte, the most learned and pliant tool; Judge Williams said the most and did the least—as cowardly as he was dishonest—and Judge Pettit, of Indiana, the staggering embodiment of all vices and virtues.

CHAPTER XLIII.

LECOMPTON CONSTITUTION.

The delegates to the Constitutional Convention were elected by only 2,200 votes, on the third Monday in June. The free state men did not participate in the election. They assembled at Lecompton on the 7th of September, and proceeded to organize their body. John Calhoun was chosen Presibent. Delegates from Anderson and Franklin Counties presented themselves, claiming seats; but as there had been no census taken in those counties, in consequence of the want of the proper officers, and no apportionment made to them by the Secretary, they were rejected. The convention, after organizing, adjourned on the 11th of September to the 19th of October, in order to take part in the election of the Territorial Legislature.

The indignation of free state men towards this convention ran high, and reached its culminating point after the election of the Legislature. The Federal Government recognized it as a legally constituted body, and protected it with the United States troops. Threats were loud against it in buncombe speeches and letters for Eastern presses, that it should never hold its session in Kansas, with the view of intimidating and deterring the delegates from re-assembling. A free state convention was called and held at Lecompton on the same day that the Constitutional Convention convened the second time, and loudly protested against that body framing a constitution for the people, and calling upon it to abandon its purpose. Local conventions were held, speeches and threats made, excitement kept up at boiling heat, and the denunciations of this body of usurpers, who had presumed to frame a government for the people, and who were protected in their work by Federal bayonets, rose from all parts of the Territory.

It was several days after the re-assembling of the Constitutional Convention, before a quorum could be mustered for the transaction of business. There evidently was a disposition on the part of a large number of pro-slavery men, to let the matter go by default, after the results of the recent election showed them the relation in which they stood to an enraged and indignant people. A quorum finally was secured, and they proceeded to frame a constitution for the State of Kansas, without molestation. After a session of about two weeks, they completed their work, and forty-three members affixed their names to the document.

It seems to have been the original design of the delegates to submit the constitution to a popular vote. The question having been discussed in the canvass, before the election, and the free state men charging it upon them that they did not design to submit, it the delegates nominated in Douglas county, among whom was John Calhoun, met on the eve of the election, came out in a card bitterly denying such intentions, and pledging themselves to favor a submission of the constitution, for ratification or rejection by the people, and Governor Walker testified that Calhoun never intimated, in frequent conversations he had with him, that he did not favor total submission, until shortly before the convention assembled.

It was generally believed at that time, as the Covode investigation of 1860 clearly shows, that the Lecompton constitution was transmitted entire from Washington, or at least those parts affecting admission and slavery, to the convention for its formal endorsement. Though it is evident that as late as the 12th of July, Mr. Buchanan must have known nothing of this movement, and probably did not until after the action of the Convention. The whole design originated where all the other abominable measures of the administration towards Kansas had their origin, in the treasonable brain of Jefferson Davis. It was a movement of the rabid pro-slavery men to either fasten slavery on Kansas, or to inaugurate a war that would eventuate in a disruption of the Union.

The leading features of this constitution were, that the boundaries of the State should be the same as those of the Territory, by the organic act; that the Legislature should have no power to interfere with the right to slave property held by the present inhabitants or future emigrants, and that the constitution could not be amended, altered or changed, until after the year eighteen hundred and sixty-four; "that free negroes shall not be permitted to live in the State, under any circumstances." It provided for a general election of State officers, in January, 1858.

The provisions for submitting the constitution to the people for their ratification or rejection, amounted to nothing more than a farce. The president of the Convention was to have complete control of the election. He was to appoint county commissioners, who were to appoint judges in their respective precincts; was to receive the returns, examine them and declare the result. "All the white male inhabitants of the Territory of Kansas, in the said Territory" upon the day of election, were to be entitled to vote; "the judges of said election shall cause to be kept the poll books by two clerks, by them appointed. The ballots at said election shall be endorsed, 'constitution with slavery,' and 'constitution with no slavery.' One of the poll books shall be returned within eight days to the President of the Convention, and the other shall be retained by the judges of election, and kept open for inspection." If a majority of the votes cast should be "constitution with slavery," the President of the Convention was then to send the constitution to Congress. If a majority of votes cast should be "constitution with no slavery," then the clauses relating to slavery were to be stricken out, and slavery was not to exist in the State, except that the right of property in slaves in the Territory should not be interfered with, and the constitution was then to be transmitted to Congress.

Thus it will be seen that this process of submission afforded no opportunity to reject the constitution entire, nor any assurance that the election would be conducted without fraud and dishonesty. The whole matter was in the hands of John Calhoun, the President of the Convention. He was an intense partisan and void of moral honesty; Surveyor-General, in the employ of the United States, and thus not strictly a citizen of Kansas. Through his office he controlled a vast patronage in the Territory, and wielded his influence with the money of the Federal Government to make Kansas a slave State. The only qualification of an elector required, as to residence, was his presence in the Territory, on the day of the election, thus offering a fair and legitimate opportunity for the Missourians to indulge their passion in coming over to vote at Kansas elections. Besides, if the slavery clause should be rejected then all objections to the constitution would not be removed. In the first place the convention had its origin in fraud. The delegates who framed the constitution did not represent the people of the Territory, or at least only a very small portion of them, and as an evidence of the people's feelings towards them, the United States troops were required to protect the convention during its sitting, and the expression of popular indignation was loud and full against its members. Most of the counties had no show of representation, and even the delegates from those counties, whose election was not regular, though no fault of their own, were rejected seats in the convention. There were other objectionable features in the constitution than slavery. Free negroes were to be excluded contrary to the Constitution of the

United States, a person to be eligible to the office of Governor must have resided in the United States twenty years, the banking law was defective, were objections held by different individuals.

There being no chance for a full and fair expression of opinion, no guaranty that the election would be honestly conducted, the free state men refused to participate in the election upon the adoption or rejection of the constitution.

It was now plainly an unfortunate occurrence that the free state men did not contest the election on the 15th of June. Had they promptly and vigorously attended to the registration, seen that it was properly made, the list corrected as prescribed by law, and then mustered their forces at the election, they could have obtained control of the Constitutional Convention, prepared such a constitution as they desired, had it properly submitted to the people, forwarded it to Congress, and thus passed safely and smoothly into the Union, as a free and independent State. But we have noticed the reasons that controlled their action, which justify their course.

Their situation now was most alarming and critical. A constitution had been framed by a body having no connection with more than four-fifths of the legal voters in Kansas, which had excluded this portion from any fair, full and legal expression of opinion in regard to that instrument, and was about to be forwarded to Washington, where, in all probability, it would receive the sanction of Congress, and thus be made the foundation for a permanent government in the Territory. It was, indeed, a high-handed outrage and audacious oppression, under the assumed cloak of law and order, whereby slavery should stalk into the legislative halls of the nation, and place her darkened diadem in the crown of the infant State.

Never in the history of enlightened nations were the rights of a people more daringly invaded; never did a community more fully appreciate their wrongs nor oppression

57

provoke such fearful hostility. High-handed injustice and fraud, backed by the power of the United States, had openly seized and held the .legislative control of the Territory, and had marked their reign with untold misery and suffering. Now, the twin monsters, with brazen audacity, were in the presence of this outraged people, guarded by United States troops, deliberately shaping and framing a permanent State Government to saddle upon them, and thus forever bind them down by all the power of the Federal Government.

Let not posterity be startled then, when they read of the awful measures which some of the people of Kansas contemplated in order to rid themselves of oppression. They united together in secret order and then, like Hannibal on the walls of Carthage, swore eternal hostility to the Lecompton Constitution. They thus pledged themselves to oppose, by all the means which might afford a prospect of success, the effective operation of this State Government. Rather than see it go into effect, they were to muster their force and slay every one who sought to uphold it. And there was a deeply laid plot, should the State be admitted under the Lecompton Constitution, and the election declared in favor of pro-slavery men, to assassinate the Territorial and State officers, and thus leave the whole machinery of government powerless. This organization was not extensive, but it shows the spirit of the people who were a unit in their determination to resist by all the means in their power the active preparation of the Lecompton Government.

But the free state men had other reasons for alarm than those before mentioned. Never was there a more damnable and stupendous scheme of outrage and oppression originated in the minds of men than the Lecompton movement. After the election of State officers under it, and the election returns inspected by the Governor, Speaker of the House and President of the Council—Calhoun, the President of the convention, refused to declare the result on the plea of awaiting further returns, but with the evident view of awaiting the action of Congress. When the constitution should be received by Congress and the State admitted, he would have declared the result of the election in favor of pro-slavery officers, by allowing certain fraudulent returns. It was then the purpose of Missourians and their friends to uphold these officers in the exercise of their functions, at the point of the bayonet, and thus carry the Government into effect. Should free state men offer resistance, they were to be exterminated, overrun and trampled under foot, by an army of invaders from Missouri and the Southern States.

That the Lecompton swindle anticipated these measures, admits of little doubt. Spies from the secret societies of the Border reported these facts to the free state men—spies who had truthfully reported other hellish schemes of the Ruffians in advance of their execution—all of which was confirmed by the conduct of the convention of pro-slavery men, and of Calhoun in withholding an official announcement of the election returns.

About the middle of November, Governor Walker went to Washington, to consult the Administration in reference to the Constitutional Convention. On arriving there, he had many long and animated interviews with the President, but all conducted with the most friendly feeling. He told the President that he could not, consistently with the pledges he had given to the people of Kansas, agreeable with the instructions from his Excellency, favor the action of the Lecompton Convention. He gave a history of the wrongs and frauds that had been perpetrated upon the citizens of this Territory, explained his action in reference to the election frauds, declared that four-fifths of the legal voters in Kansas were opposed to the Lecompton Constitution, in whole or in part, that he could not, without personal dishonor and disgrace, favor the mode in which this document was submitted to the ratification or rejection of the people. It was a proud and sublime spectacle! Mr. Buchanan wavered, and feared the party which had put him in power. He acknowledged that he had no other idea than that the constitution would be fully and fairly submitted to the people, when he gave his instructions, but declared that he had no right to dictate to the convention a course of action. Governor Walker said he would plant himself firmly upon the principles of the Democratic party and Popular Sovereignty, and, with the Constitution of his country and the Organic Act of the Territory in his hands, would go before the world and make his defense. He affirmed that "to force this constitution upon the people of Kansas, without their voice being heard for or against it, would be followed by rebellion and bloody civil war."

The President, however, in the face of his clear and undenied instructions and assurances* to Governor Walker, that the Lecompton Constitution should be submitted to the action of the people by a fair and full election, unmarked by fraud or violence, favored the conduct of the convention which framed it, in his message to Congress. He took the ground that "the Kansas-Nebraska act did not require the submission of any portion of the constitution to an election, except that which relates to the domestic institution of slavery."

Governor Walker, therefore, tendered[1] his resignation, setting forth at length the reasons which impelled him to take

---

* The President, in his celebrated letter written on the 12th of July, 1857, to Governor Walker, said:

"On the question of submitting the constitution to the bona fide resident settlers of Kansas, I am willing to stand or fall. In sustaining such a principle, we cannot fall. It is the principle of the Kansas-Nebraska Bill; the principle of Popular Sovereignty, and the principle of all popular government. The more it is discussed, the stronger it will become. Should the convention of Kansas adopt this principle, all will be settled harmoniously, and with the blessing of Providence, you will return triumphantly from your arduous, important and responsible mission."

This letter was written in reply to one from Governor Walker, in which he declared that "without that (submission of the constitution) civil war would soon be raging in Kansas."

(1) December 5.

that course. He was unwilling to embarass the President by retaining his position, or to throw upon him the responsibility of his removal. He could not favor the action of the Lecompton Convention, because of his oath to support the Constitution of the United States, and the Organic Act, and the solemn pledges to the people of the Territory that he would oppose its action if the constitution was not properly submitted for ratification or rejection by them. In his letter accompanying his resignation, he says:

"Indeed, disguise it as we may to ourselves, under the influence of the present excitement, the facts will demonstrate that any attempt by Congress to force this constitution upon the people of Kansas will be an effort to substitute the will of a minority for that of an overwhelming majority of the people of Kansas; that it will not settle the Kansas question, or localize the issue; that it will, I fear, be attended by civil war, extending, perhaps, throughout the Union, thus bringing the question back again upon Congress and before the people in its most damaging and dangerous aspect.

"The President takes a different view of the subject in his message, and from the events occurring in Kansas, as well as here, it is evident that the question is passing from theories into practice, and that as Governor of Kansas, I should be compelled to carry out my new instructions, differing on a vital question from those received at the date of my appointment. Such instructions I could not execute consistently with my views of the Federal Government and of the Kansas-Nebraska bill, or with my pledges to the people of Kansas. Under these circumstances no alternative is left, but to resign the office of Governor of the Territory of Kansas."

Secretary Stanton, who was acting Governor after Governor Walker left, witnessing the almost universal feeling of disapprobation towards the Lecompton Constitution and the measures adopted to force it upon the people, as expressed in the resolutions of their numerous conventions, and in nearly every paper in the Territory, and strongly urged to the measure by most of the leading men in Kansas, issued his proclamation, (December 1), convening the Legislature in extra session on the 7th of December. His reasons were thus expressed in his message to that body: "From representatives of majorities of your own bodies, I have reasons to know that recent events have produced a profound agitation of the public mind, and that a sense of wrong and injustice, whether well or ill-founded, and an apprehension of great evils to be suffered therefrom, have aroused the people of the Territory to a condition of dangerous excitement. The proceedings of the late Constitutional Convention are the immediate cause of the existing trouble and alarm."

It was hoped, therefore, that a remedy for existing difficulties might be found in assembling the Legislature. But what was the proper course for it to pursue in order to relieve the people of the Territory from their present embarrassments was a question hard to determine. It could not interfere with the validity of the convention by repealing the act of the former legislation by which it was created; for already the convention had passed upon that act, and executed its work. It having completed its labors and adjourned, and having left the constitution in the hands ot Mr. Calhoun with proper instructions, was entirely beyond the reach of the Legislature. About the only remedy for the Legislature to apply, therefore, was to make provisions for a full and fair expression of the popular will in regard to the constitution.

The Legislature convened at the appointed time and place. C. W. Babcock was elected President of the Council and G. W. Deitzler Speaker of the House. Hon. F. P. Stanton, acting Governor, sent in his message, advising as the only available remedy for the existing difficulties, an act providing for the re-submission of the Lecompton Constitution *entire*, to a popular vote. Provision for investigating the election frauds in Leavenworth county was made and upon the report of the committee for that purpose, the members who had received seats on their certificates were ejected, and their contestants admitted to their places.

The Legislature repealed the act creating the Lecompton Constitutional Convention, and adopted a joint resolution, earnestly protesting against Congress receiving Kansas into the Union under the constitution thus formed. Provision was made for the submission of the constitution to a fair and full vote of the people. Residence of thirty days in the State, preceding the election, and ten days in the county where the elector offers his vote, was made a necessary qualification for a legal voter. Those voting for the constitution with slavery, were to mark their ballots, "For the Constitution framed at Lecompton with slavery." Those voting for the constitution and against slavery, were to mark their ballots, "For the Constitution framed at Lecompton, without slavery," and those voting against it entire, were to have their ballots marked, "Against the Constitution framed at Lecompton." Any person voting illegally at this election was to be deemed guilty of felony, and, upon conviction thereof, were to be fined not exceeding five hundred dollars, or imprisoned for a term not longer than one year. An act was likewise passed, providing for punishing election frauds; one to organize and regulate the militia of the Territory, and one repealing the act to punish rebellion. The Legislature, by joint resolution, memorialized Congress to admit Kansas into the Union under the Topeka Constitution, as being agreeable to the wishes of the chief part of the inhabitants of the Territory. After having thus provided, as far as it could, against the dangers threatening the rights of the people, the Legislature, on the 17th of December, adjourned.

Towards the latter part of the session, Secretary Stanton received notice of his removal, and General Denver, who was at Lecompton at the time, connected with Indian affairs, received his appointment as Secretary and acting

Governor of the Territory. The President, the moment he heard of Mr. Stanton's having called an extra session of the Legislature, determined upon his removal. It created great excitement at Lecompton on reception of the news, and much feeling was manifested against General Denver, whom many regarded as a kind of spy, or secret agent of Buchanan. But they were not long in getting acquainted with him. They found him kind, affable and easily approached. He at once, by his quiet and easy way, displaced all resentment by the feelings of respect and esteem. All felt that he was no tyrant, and at the same time no fool. Confidence at once animated the free state men, and they rallied around their new Governor to hold up his hands. A full account of his life will be given in the next chapter.

The election on the slavery cause in the Lecompton Constitution came off on the 21st of December. The vote, as announced by Mr. Calhoun, stood, "constitution with slavery," 6,226; "constitution with no slavery," 569. The Missourians came over in large numbers and voted at the precincts on the Border. According to the qualifications determined by the convention, their presence at the polls rendered them legal voters. By the report of the commissioners, appointed by the following Legislature to investigate the frauds practiced at this election, and that of the 4th of January, it was shown that the following illegal votes were cast: At Kickapoo, 700; at Delaware City, 145; at Oxford, 1,200; at Shawnee, 675, making a total of 2,720 illegal votes proven to have been cast; how many more were polled was never determined. Deducting the number of votes against the slavery clause and the number of illegal votes above mentioned, leaves a majority in favor of the "constitution with slavery" of 3,506 votes.

The Lecompton Constitution was legally and properly submitted on the 4th of January, according to the provisions of the recent Legislature. It was the first fair and full election in the Territory, so far as free state men were concerned. The radical pro-slavery men did not participate in it, but many of the more conservative voted against the Constitution. The returns show "against the Lecompton Constitution," 10,226; "for the Lecompton Constitution with slavery," 138; "for the Lecompton Constitution without slavery," 24.

This exhibits the feelings of all classes and parties towards the Constitution. Pro-slavery papers were in many instances opposed to this high-handed fraud, and all that loved honesty and justice denounced it. At a convention of the Democracy in Leavenworth, on the 24th of December resolutions were passed bitterly denouncing the action of the Constitutional Convention, sustaining Walker and Stanton, and resolutions highly conciliating to Northern Democrats. They likewise memorialized Congress not to admit Kansas into the Union under the Lecompton Constitution.

The Thirty-Fifth Congress convened on the 7th of December. The President in his message took grounds in favor of the action of the Constitutional Convention and recommending the admission of Kansas into the Union under the Lecompton Constitution. He based his argument in reference to the mode of submission upon the Organic Act, which he declared required no other part of that document submitted to the vote of the people than slavery.

The Kansas difficulties soon engaged the attention of Congress. A bill was early introduced in the Senate by Douglas, authorizing the people of Kansas to frame a State Constitution; but, pending its discussion on the 2d of February, President Buchanan transmitted to that body the Lecompton Constitution, accompanied by a message recommending its acceptance. He most bitterly denounced the free state movement and strongly supported the action of the Constitutional Convention. The message and constitutional documents were referred to the Committee on

Territories in the Senate, and in the House to a select Committee of fifteen.

Mr. Green, of Missouri, presented the majority report in the Senate, warmly recommending the admission of Kansas under the Lecompton Constitution. It was filled with falsehoods and misrepresentations, bitterly denouncing the free state men as a factious minority, and strongly sustaining the action of the Constitutional Convention which, it declared, was under no obligation to submit any portion of the constitution to the ratification or rejection of the people. Mr. Douglas, from the same Committee, offered a minority report, adverse to the Constitution, on the grounds that there was no satisfactory evidence that it was the act and deed of the people of Kansas, or that it embodied their will, and defended his position with great power and eloquence. He argued at length its opposition to the spirit and letter of the Kansas-Nebraska act. A minority report was also presented by Messrs. Collamer and Wade, opposing the acceptance of the Constitution by Congress and reviewing the systematic and oft-repeated frauds and wrongs inflicted upon the people of that Territory.

Hon. A. H. Stephens, from the Select Committee of Fifteen, presented the Majority report, which warmly favored the admission of Kansas under the Lecompton Constitution. This committee refused an investigation of facts by taking depositions and examining records, but accepted the representations of J. C. Calhoun, the president of the convention. A minority report, signed by seven members, was presented by Mr. Harris, condemning the action of the Committee for not investigating the facts and adverse to the Constitution. They presented the report of the Commissioners appointed by the Territorial Legislature, to investigate the election frauds, by which the constitution was adopted.

At the same time Mr. Green submitted his report, he introduced a bill providing for the admission of Kansas into the Union under the Lecompton Constitution, which elicited a warm debate. On the 23d of March Mr. Crittenden offered as a substitute, a bill admitting Kansas with the condition precedent, that the Lecompton Constitution be submitted to the people of the Territory and properly ratified by them; in case it should be rejected, then they were empowered to make one to suit themselves. This substitute was lost by 24 yeas to 34 nays, and upon the same day the original bill slightly amended was passed by 33 yeas to 25 nays. Upon going to the House this bill was amended by striking out all after the enacting clause and inserting the substitute of Mr. Crittenden, and passed by a vote of 120 yeas to 112 nays. The Senate refused to concur in this amendment, and called for a Committee of Conference with the House; to which the latter, after some parliamentary maneuvering, agreed. Upon this Committee the Senate appointed Messrs. Green, Hunter and Seward; the House, Messrs. English, Stephens and Howard. Their report, from which Seward and Howard dissented, recommended a substitute for the amendment of the House what was generally known as the English bill. Their recommendation was acquiesced, in April 30, 1858, by both branches of Congress, by a vote of 112 to 103 in the House, and 31 to 22 in the Senate—a clear pro-slavery majority.

The English bill provided for the admission of Kansas under the Lecompton Constitution, upon the condition precedent, that the said constitution, at a fair and full election, held for that purpose, should be ratified by the people of Kansas. In case of its ratification the President should so announce the fact and promulgate the admission of the State by proclamation; in case the constitution should be rejected by the people, it should "be deemed and held that the people of Kansas do not desire admission into the Union with said constitution and the conditions of said proposition; in which event the people of Kansas are empowered to form for themselves a Constitution and State Government, and may elect delegates for that purpose, whenever, and not before it is ascertained by a census, duly and legally taken, that the population of said Territory equals the ratio of representation required for a member of the House of Representatives, (93,560), and whenever thereafter such delegates shall assemble in convention, they shall first determine by a vote whether it is the wish of the proposed State to be admitted into the Union at that time, and if so, shall proceed to form a constitution."

This bill contained a proposition from Congress, in the way of large land grants in case the constitution should be accepted, which had all the appearance of a bribe to the people. Sections 16 and 36, of each township, seventy-two sections for a State University, ten sections to pay for public buildings, amounting in all to 5,500,000 acres of land, would be thus donated to the State. Besides this enormous bequest, the State should have all salt springs within her boundary, not exceeding twelve in number, and six sections of land for each, and five per cent. of proceeds arising from sales of public lands for the construction ot State roads.

This was a scandalous proposition to the people of Kansas. Having failed to force the constitution upon the new State by fraud, they attempted to secure its success by the offer of a magnificent bribe, and by rendering it almost impossible for the State to be otherwise speedily admitted.

Every means was employed in Congress to force the Lecompton Constitution through. Money and office were freely offered to induce members to favor it, while proscription from the Democratic ranks, and ousting from office, was threatened those who should oppose it. It had its birth-place at Washington, in corruption, and when it returned to the place of its nativity, was zealously cared for in a characteristic manner. The hideous corruption and foulness of the Lecompton Constitution, was frightfully revealed in the investigation ordered by Congress, in 1860, under Judge Covode. The following is the summary of the Committee's report, with reference to the Lecompton measure:

"Your committee first direct the attention of the House to that portion of the testimony which relates to the Kansas policy of the present Administration of the government. The patriot will mourn, the historian will pause with astonishment, over this shameless record. Accustomed as the American people are to the errors and crimes of those in power, they will read this exposure with feelings of unmingled indignation. The facts revealed by the testimony prove conclusively—

"1. The emphatic and unmistakable pledges of the President, as well before as after his election, and the pledges of all his cabinet to the doctrine of leaving the people of Kansas 'perfectly free to form and regulate their domestic institutions in their own way.'

"2. The deliberate violation of this pledge, and the attempt to convert Kansas into a slave State by means of forgeries, frauds and force.

"3. The removal of and the attempt to disgrace the sworn agents of the Administration, who refused to violate this pledge.

"4. The open employment of money in the passage of the Lecompton and English bills through the Congress of the United States.

"5. The admission of the parties engaged in the work of electioneering those schemes, that they received enormous sums for this purpose, and proof in the checks upon which they were paid by an agent of the Administration.

"6. The offer to purchase newspapers and newspaper editors by offers of extravagant sums of money.

"7. And finally, the proscription of Democrats of high standing, who would not support the Lecompton and English bills."

CHAPTER XLIV.

LEGISLATURES.

At the same time that the free state men voted upon the constitution, an election was held for State officers and members of the Legislature, preparatory to the admission of Kansas as a State, according to the provisions of the Lecompton Constitutional Convention.

The pro-slavery men, under the specious name of Democracy, assembled in convention at Lecompton on the 7th of December, for the purpose of nominating candidates to the State offices. Much confusion prevailed in their ranks and a large number withdrew from the convention. They adopted resolutions endorsing the Lecompton Constitutional Convention, denouncing Governor Walker and Secretary Stanton, lauding Buchanan and reaffirming their adherence to the platform laid down by their party in January, 1857. They declared "that prior to the advent of Walker and Stanton in our midst, the Democracy of the Territory were united and harmonizing;" that "since their arrival all their efforts have been directed to serving disunion in our ranks with a view to further their own ambitious schemes." The following ticket was nominated: Governor, F. J. Marshall, of Marshall County; Lieutenant Governor, William G. Mathias, of Leavenworth; Secretary of State, W. T. Spicely, of Douglas County; Auditor, Blake Little, ot Bourbon County; Treasurer, T. J. B. Cramer, of Douglas County; Congress, Joseph P. Carr, of Atchison.

It was a question of considerable discussion among the free state men, "Should they contest the election?" In case the Territory should be admitted into the Union as a State by Congress, it would leave the successful party at the election in control of the State Government for the next four years beyond all legal remedy. On the other hand it was extremely odious and humiliating to so far recognize the Lecompton swindle as to vote under its appointment and control.

A delegate convention, called and assembled at Lawrence, on the 2d of December, for the purpose of considering this question, declared, "this election a crime and a misdemeanor against the peace of the Territory and the will of the majority;" that they re-endorse the Topeka Constitutian and that after it receives the sanction of the people at an election appointed by the present Legislature, they "will maintain it against all opposition."

The design in calling this convention was to determine whether free state men should vote at the State election about to be held; but as the Governor had, between the calling and the assembling of the convention, issued his proclamation convening the Legislature in extra session, when the delegates met, they hoped that the Legislature might find a remedy. to relieve their present embarrassment and danger and, hence, they adjourned without taking any decisive action upon the subject. It was manifest, however, that a majority were opposed to voting at the January election.

But the Legislature having assembled and found itself utterly unable to remove the difficulties, at the call of the Chairman of the Territorial Executive Committee the free state convention again convened on the 23d of the same month and for the same purpose as on the former occasion. It remained in session two days, during which time the discussion was interesting and lively. The vote was taken on the second day in reference to participating in the coming election; forty-seven recording their votes in favor of it and forty-four against it. "But by an arrangement the vote was counted by districts, by which one or more persons cast the entire vote of his district. In this manner the result was declared sixty-four yeas, to seventy-five nays, and upon this report the convention refused to contest the election."

An incident occurred during this convention, that well illustrates the political tactics of General Lane. Those in favor of contesting the election, had been sanguine of carrying their point, and everything indicated that they would be successful, until shortly before the convention adjourned. The debate had been intensely earnest and exciting. General Lane readily saw that the non-contestants were defeated in debate. With a ready ingenuity, he contrived and dexterously executed a piece of strategy. Just before the convention took a final vote upon the question of contesting the election, a messenger, urging forward a jaded and foaming steed, came riding into town, and inquired in a hurried and excited manner for the convention. He soon stood upon the platform before that body, trembling, and apparently almost exhausted with fatigue, and related, in a seemingly very truthful manner, that the Border Ruffians had begun the war of extermination in south-eastern Kansas, that they had routed the free state forces with great slaughter, and were laying waste the country with fire and sword, and that he had ridden night and day to receive assistance at their hands. Then in the most dramatic style asked, "Will you stand here idly debating an election question, while your brethren, weakened and disorganized, with homes made desolate and families scattered, are calling for help?" After a speech from Lane, of the wildest sublimity, the convention, in some confusion and excitement, voted upon the main question, with the result as before shown.

Many were not satisfied with the result of the convention's deliberations, feeling that it had been imposed upon by political schemers. Immediately upon its adjournment, a few of this class met in G. W. Brown's cellar kitchen, in what they called "mass convention," but which their opponents denominated "Bolter's Convention." They resolved to participate in the election, and, in an address to the public, urged upon all opposed to the Lecompton Constitution, to unite with them in electing the candidates nominated by that convention. The following is their ticket of nominations: Governor, G. W. Smith; Lieutenant-Governor, W. Y. Roberts; Secretary of State, P. C. Schuyler; Treasurer, A. J. Mead; Auditor, J. K. Goodin; Congress, M. J. Parrott. These candidates pledged the Convention, that in case of their election and the admission of Kansas into the Union under the Lecompton Constitution, "to adopt and execute immediate measures for enabling the people, through a constitutional convention, to obtain such a constitution as the majority will approve." It was the distinct and explicit understanding, that if these candidates were elected, they should never act officially under the Lecompton government.

Seeing a desire and determination on the part of a large portion of the citizens to participate in the election, local conventions were held, and generally those not opposed to the October election united to help elect the ticket of the "Bolters."

This election, like that of October, resulted decidedly in favor of the free state men. They elected the State officers by the following majorities: Governor, 330; Lieutenant Governor, 501; Secretary of State, 301; Treasurer, 371; Auditor, 304; Representative in Congress, 696. For the Senate they elected 13 members, while the opposite party elected but 6; for the House they elected 29 members, pro-slavery men 15. The free state Governor received 6,875 votes, and his opponent 6,545, of which more than half were fraudulent. Says the President of the Council and Speaker of the House, who witnessed with Governor Denver the counting of the votes, in announcing the result, "This triumph was accomplished by a party greatly distracted on the subject of voting under a constitution that they hate, and loath, and abhor, to the centre of their hearts, with a short and imperfect notice that failed to reach many of the more distant districts. These causes together, it is safe to say, reduced the free state vote to the extent of 5,000 votes."

The State officers thus elected immediately prepared a memorial to Congress, urging upon that body not to admit Kansas into the Union under the Lecompton Constitution.

The free state Legislature assembled at Topeka on the 5th of January, and organized by electing Harris Stratton Speaker of the House and J. R. Root President of the Senate. Governor Robinson sent in his message in which he urged that the State organization should be preserved intact, ready for any emergency. The second day they adjourned to Lawrence, where they hoped to constrain the Territorial Legislature to remove all legal obstructions to the practical establishment of the State government. The design was to have the Missouri code of laws repealed, and a new one enacted by the Territorial Legislature, which the General Government recognized as legitimate, and for it then to give way to the active and practical application of those laws by the State organization, "thus making the former a stepping stone to the latter."

On arriving at Lawrence they presented the following communication, which had passed the House and Senate, to the Territorial Legislature:

"WHEREAS, The people of Kansas, in the absence of any legitimate government, originated at Topeka, on the 23d day of October, 1855, a State constitution, and, subsequently, elected officers under the same; and

"WHEREAS, The people have, on certain occasions, affirmed and re-affirmed said constitution and government, and have elected the present State officers and Legislature, in order to maintain said State organization as the government for the State of Kansas; therefore,

"*Resolved*, By the House of Representatives of the State

of Kansas, (the Senate concurring,) That we at once proceed to complete the organization of the State government under the constitution, and enact such laws as the necessities of the people seem to demand. And,

"*Resolved*, Now, as heretofore, the Federal authority represented in the Territorial laws and Territorial Legislature, is an obstacle to the successful execution of the will of the people through the State government, under the State constitution; therefore,

"*Resolved*, That we respectfully urge the General Assembly of the Territory of Kansas, now in session at Lawrence, to take immediate steps to remove the forms of a Territorial government, so that it shall not obstruct and embarrass the State Government.

"*Resolved*, That the Speaker of the House cause a copy of these preamble and resolutions, properly authenticated, to be laid before the Council and House of Representatives of the General Assembly of the Territory of Kansas; and we respectfully request them to give it their earliest consideration, and that they send a reply to the respective officers of the two branches of the State Legislature."

In the Council, Mr. Harding, Chairman of the Special Committee, to whom was referred the memorial of the State Legislature, submitted the following report:

"The committee, to whom was referred the memorial of the State Legislature, now in session in Lawrence, having had the subject matter therein contained under consideration, beg leave to submit the following report: That we will manifest our readiness to accede to their wishes, so far as we can do so consistently with the views which we entertain of our duty to our constituents and to our country, by adopting such measures, as soon as practicable, as, in our judgment, may meet with the hearty concurrence and support of the people of Kansas. But, under the embarrassing circumstances in which we are placed, by the complicated condition of political affairs in Kansas, and the relation in which we stand to the Federal Government; the uncertainty existing with regard to the policy indicated by the Congress of the United States towards us; in view of the understanding which we have of the wishes of our constituents, and regarding, as we do, the peace, well being and general welfare of Kansas, as of paramount importance; and in view of the fact that the Territorial Legislature is the only legal, law making power in Kansas acknowledged by the General Government, we can not consent to set aside the form of the Territorial Government until further development may seem to render it necessary.

"Submitted, B. HARDING,
"C. K. HOLLIDAY."

Mr. Mead, from the same committee, made the following minority report:

"The committee to whom was referred the petition in the form of concurrent resolutions, from the State Legislature, now in session in Lawrence, ask leave, respectfully, to state that they have had the same under consideration, and can not concur in the views of the petitions expressed, and said concurrent resolutions, respecting the position of the present Territorial Legislature, declaring it to be an obstruction to the successful execution of the will of the people; and, in view of the complex character of the various questions which are now before the people of this Territory, your committee feel that there is great necessity for wise and just legislation; and further state, that it is the opinion of your committee, any action at the present time favoring the policy embodied in said resolutions, would be unwise, and in conflict with the legitimate purposes of this Legislature.

"Respectfully submitted, ANDREW J. MEAD."

In the House, Mr. Cooper, chairman of the select committee, to whom was referred the concurrent resolutions of the Free State Legislature, submitted the following report:

"The select committee, to whom was referred the concurrent resolutions of the Free State Legislature, under the Topeka Constitution, would, in accordance with the instructions of the House, respectfully report the following resolution:

"*Resolved*, That we have every confidence in the wisdom, patriotism and prudence of the Free State Legislature; that we believe the movement it represents originated in a public necessity, and, that it is their province to take such action in their own capacity, as they may think legitimate and proper—they being responsible for their own action, and we not for them. And, as the Territorial Legislature is not, legitimately, in a position to dictate or concur in their acts, we have only respectfully to reiterate to them the course of action which we shall pursue, as clearly indicated in the resolution passed by this body, to the effect that we would proceed to the enactment of an entire code of laws, which shall supersede all laws or pretended laws passed prior to the special session of this present Legislature.

"S. S. COOPER,
"JOHN SPEER,
"W. P. BADGER,
"E. N. MORRILL,
"H. MILES MOORE."

The report was adopted, and ordered to be spread upon the journal,

The State Legislature, after remaining in session about ten days at Lawrence, and having received the above replies to their communication, adjourned. Several of its members were also members of the Territorial Legislature, and thus their duties in both branches conflicted.

On this account, and there being nothing for them to do until the Territorial Legislature should take favorable action on their request, they adjourned, with the understanding that, should measures be taken for the effective operation of the State government, they would meet in regular session on the 4th of March.

General James William Denver was born on the 23d day of October, 1817, in Frederick County, Virginia. His parents emigrated to Ohio in the year 1831, and located in Clinton County, in the spring of 1832. The family consisted of four sons and six daughters, all of whom lived to the age of man and womanhood, since which period two of the daughters died. His father was a farmer, and brought up his son on the farm, giving him the advantage of the neighborhood school, (being very fond of books himself,) of a much better library than is usually found in farm houses.

At the age of twenty-one James had a severe attack of rheumatism, caused by exposure and hard labor on the farm. This induced him to look around for some other means of making a livelihood. Having acquired a pretty thorough knowledge of civil engineering, theoretically and practically, he went to Missouri in the spring of 1841, to engage in that profession; but being unable to get a contract for surveying public lands, he took charge of a school in the north-western part of Clay County, in that State, at what was known as Hartsel's School-house, and while there boarded with Mr. John Eaton. Here he spent one of the happiest years of his life, and left it with sincere regret, his associations with parents and pupils being of the most agreeable cheracter. Having determined to enter the legal profession, he returned to Ohio in 1842, and commenced the study of law with Griffith Foos, Esq., ot Wilmington, Ohio, and graduated at the Cincinnati Law School in the spring of 1844. Soon after, in connection with R. H. Stone, now of Cincinnati, he opened an office at Xenia, Ohio. In the spring of the following year, he returned to Missouri, locating first at Plattsburg and subsequently at Platte City.

In the spring of 1847, he was appointed a captain in the 12th Regiment, U. S. Infantry, and served to the end of the war under General Scott in his campaign in Mexico. After its close he returned to Platte City and remained in Platte county until 1850, when he crossed the plains to California and located in Trinity County, in that State. In 1851 he was elected to the Senate of that State. In 1852 he was appointed by the Governor, a commissioner upon the part of the State to carry provisions across the Sierra Nevada Mountains, for the relief of the emigrants, who were found to be in great distress. In 1853, he was appointed Secretary of State of California, which office he held until November, 1855. In 1854, he was elected Representative to the Thirty-Fourth Congress, and took his seat, December

1855. Whilst there, he was appointed Chairman of the Special Committee on the Pacific Railroad, and prepared a bill which relieved it from the opposition it had met with before from the most prominent railroad men of the country and which was substantially the plan subsequently adopted.

At the close of the sessions of the Thirty-Fourth Congress he was appointed Commissioner of Indian Afiairs, and entered upon the duties of that office in April 1856. He made an important treaty with the Pawnees that year. Subsequently he was sent out to make treaties with the Indians in Kansas, but before he could conclude them, the President became dissatisfied with the administration of Hon. F. P. Stanton, Secretary, and acting Governor of Kansas, (Governor Walker being then in Washington) and removed him, appointing General Denver his successor.

In the Spring of 1858 Governor Walker resigned, and the General was appointed Governor—Hugh S. Walsh succeeding him as Secretary.

In October following he resigned, and returned to Washington, arriving in November. Upon his return to Washington the President again tendered to him the position of Commissioner of Indian Affairs which he accepted, but becoming dissatisfied, he resigned the office and returned to California in the spring of 1858.

He entered the canvass of 1860 very warmly in favor of Mr. Douglas, and was always opposed to secession.

In 1861, the Legislature of California appointed S. B. Smith, Esq., and General Denver, Commissioners on the part of the State, to settle and adjust certain claims arising out of the Indian difficulties in that State. In June, 1861, he left California, and on the 14th of August following, he was appointed by President Lincoln Brigadier-General of Volunteers, and was ordered to Kansas on duty in the following November. In January, 1862, he was ordered to West Virginia, and in March of the same year was ordered back to Kansas. In the following May, he was ordered to report to

Gen. Halleck, at Pittsburgh Landing, on the Tennessee river. He was there put on duty with General W. T. Sherman, on the extreme right wing of the army, in the advance on Corinth, Mississippi, commanding a brigade of Ohio troops, composed of the 70th, 72d, 53d and 48th regiments.

After the capture of Corinth, he went with General Sherman across to Memphis. On the way, he halted some time at Moscow; from there, marched down and captured Holly Springs. He was stationed at, and in command of Fort Pickering, Memphis, Tennessee, where he remained until November, 1862, when the army proposed to move on Vicksburg. It arrived below Oxford, Mississippi, from whence it was compelled to return, by the destruction of the railroad communications between that point and Vicksburg.

He remained at Lagrange, Tennessee, through the following winter, and resigned in the spring of 1862, to attend to his private business.

After the adjournment of Congress, on March 4th, 1865, he formed a copartnership with Hon. James Hughes, of Indiana, and Colonel A. J. Isacks, of Kansas, and shortly afterwards opened an office for the practice of his profession, in Washington, D. C. Colonel Isacks was in bad health, and died before being able to return from Leavenworth, Kansas.

The Territorial Legislature convened for regular session on the 4th of January, at Lecompton, and organized by electing the same President of the Council and Speaker of the House, as at the extra session. Secretary Denver's message was short, but replete with good sense and valuable suggestions. On the second day the Legislature adjourned to Lawrence and continued its deliberations until the 12th of February.

On the 21st of January an act was passed to provide a Board of Commissioners to investigate the frauds perpetratated at the last two elections, and empowering them to subpœna witnesses, employ clerks and other assistants. Henry J. Adams, E. L. Taylor, Thomas Ewing, J. B. Abbott, Ely Moore and Dillan Pickering, were appointed members of this board. They faithfully and fully performed the duties imposed upon them. They began their labors on the 19th of January, and closed them on the 15th of February. They examined seventy-four witnesses, fully and clearly established the frauds, a summary of whose report we have given.

Provisions were made for the election of delegates in March, to frame a State Constitution a full account of which will be given in the proper order of events.

An act was also passed, locating the seat of government at Minneola, then a paper town, a few miles south of Prairie City, and granted a charter to this embryo metropolis, enabling the town company to hold two thousand acres of land. The Governor vetoed the bill, and, though it was passed over his veto, he never recognized it as valid, nor did any succeeding Legislature. Corruption marked it in the face, and public opinion universally contemned it.

The Legislature was composed chiefly of men inexperienced in legislating, and hence they moved slowly and awkwardly. Most of their time was consumed upon local questions and laws.

They failed to repeal the Missouri code or remove many of its obnoxious features. Even the apportionment of members to the Legislature, which had occasioned so much complaint, was not remedied. They followed too closely the example of their predecessors, in enacting laws for their own pecuniary advantage. They failed to meet the expectations of the people, and were subject to much censure from all parties. But they had a difficult task in the way of legislation. The greater portion of the people had been without law since the organization of the Territory. Innumerable enactments had been passed by the former Legislatures, some good and some bad, and it was difficult for young and inexperienced legislators to determine how to proceed. They broke the ice, however, and opened the way for their successors. They set out with the design of enacting a new code of laws, but failed to complete the work laid out, for want of time.

CHAPTER XLV.

TROUBLES IN SOUTH-EASTERN KANSAS.

About the time General Denver was appointed Secretary, difficulties of an alarming character in Lynn and Bourbon counties began to attract attention. The origin of these disturbances is coeval with the settlement of that country. As in other portions of the Territory, the two antagonistical elements—slave-state and free-state—met together there to decide the question of supremacy. The Missourians, whose autocrats had declared, "Kansas is ours and we will have it; peaceably if we can, forceibly if we must," taking advantage of their proximity to the Territory, first passed over and took possession of the best claims the country afforded. Emigrants from the free States subsequently came in, either entered upon entirely new claims, or purchased those which had been previously occupied.

As Captain James Montgomery is the principal actor in the Territorial history of South-eastern Kansas, it is proper that a short account of his life and character should be given, He was born, December 22d, 1814, in Astabula county, Ohio, of highly respectable parentage, and is cousin of General Richard Montgomery, who fell at the storming of Quebec. Having received an excellent academical education, he emigrated to Kentucky in 1837, where he engaged in school teaching. Here he married his first wife, who, subsequently dying, he again, after the lapse of a considerable time, entered the matrimonial alliance. In 1852 he removed to Pike county, Missouri, where he remained one year and then came to Jackson county, preparatory to entering Kansas as soon as it should be open to settlement. Here he made the acquaintance of Dr. Thornton, a prominent citizen of that county, who, on learning his design, advised him not to go to Kansas, as he would certainly meet with trouble there; that the Missourians were determined that no free state man should be allowed to settle in the Territory; but, on the other hand, he urged him to go to Bates county, Missouri, where he could find better unoccupied land, which he could securely hold without molestation. Agreeable with this friendly admonition, he went to Bates county the latter part of July, 1854, where he spent a week in looking at the country. Not satisfied with what he saw there, and his high sense of honor stung by reflecting upon the reasons which had turned him from his plan of entering Kansas, he rose suddenly one morning from the breakfast table and, without a moments hesitation, made a straight march for the Territory, "From that moment henceforth," is his own expressive language, "I was a man."

The first place he halted was in the vicinity of Mound City, where he found many of the Missourians, dissatisfied with the country and growing weary in watching to keep out abolitionists, preparing to return to their native State,

He purchased a claim from a family of this class, on "Little Sugar," for $11.00—all the money he had with him, except a few cents. He moved his family upon his new possessions that fall but remained himself in Missouri, engaged in building a barn for Dr. Thornton. In this way he made $300, which he invested in cows and calves, and with them, in the spring, returned to Kansas, where he has continued to reside ever since.

Colonel Montgomery is a humane man, nothing fierce or savage in his character; a devout christian, and believes in the practical supremacy of the Higher Law. Although a resident of a slave State for a number of years, he has always been bitterly opposed to slavery extension, but never sought to interfere with it in slave States. He is about six feet high, slim and nimble as a deer, with intelligent features, high forehead, large nose and a most piercing and penetrating eye; a tenacious memory, sound logic, talks fluently with an agreeable voice, and in the best selected and arranged words. His courage is unquestioned; he is fearless yet wary; valorous in battle, yet generous in victory. When the war for the Union broke out he became Colonel of the 3d Kansas Regiment, and acting commander of a brigade. He was afterwards Colonel of the 2d South Carolina Negro Regiment, and distinguished himself in the army of the East. When the war was over he returned to his family on his beautiful farm near Mound City.

Thus far Montgomery had attracted little or no attention from the pro-slavery men, who knowing that he came from Missouri, supposed him all "sound on the goose." But it was not long before the opportunity presented itself for them to discover the sentiments and character of the man. Soon after his return from Missouri, in April, he happened to go down to Mound City, only five miles distant, and was surprised to find a convention in session for the purpose of nominating candidates for the Legislature. The question of making Kansas a slave or free State had never been raised by the settlers who had not yet been in an election, and had been intent upon the construction of their homes. It was the policy of the political aspirants of that day not to allow this "distracting issue" to arise, but to keep it out of the canvass, and thus secure votes from both parties. Such was the design of Colonel J. P. Fox, the prime mover in this convention. This gentleman had wiliy evaded the issue by telling the people that the time had not yet come to raise that question, and would not until a convention should be called to frame a State Constitution; that all the

Legislature had to do was to make wholesome laws for the Territory. But when in private conversation with pro-slavery men he was strongly in favor of making Kansas a slave State; on the other hand when endeavoring to secure the ballot of some free state man he was the representative of his principle.

In the organization of the Convention, Mr. Montgomery was elected secretary, and that body soon entered upon its work according to a prescribed programme. Names were submitted to the convention as candidates for nomination, and an immediate balloting urged. Mr. Montgomery readily comprehended their designs, and determined to disconcert their movements. He arose, and with that cool discretion which characterized him in council as well as in battle, called their attention to the fact that the Missourians had vowed that this should be a slave State, and that they were making extensive preparations to accomplish their purpose; that as the Organic Act guarantees them, as settlers, the right to determine the character of their own institutions, he was in favor of making Kansas a free State, on the principle of self-interest, as slavery was injurious to poor white men. He thought that the Legislature would have a wonderful controlling influence over the domestic affairs of the Territory, and that, therefore, in selecting candidates to represent them, they should know their views upon the vital issue of the day. His remarks, delivered in an earnest and persuasive manner, were the hearty response of most all settlers convened—one after another of whom arose and fully endorsed his sentiments.

Finally, Col. Cox, seeing that he could not get the nomination without committing himself, came out openly in favor of making Kansas a free State, and publicly pledged himself to labor for that end. Mr. Montgomery thereupon stated that, as few of the settlers were aware of the Convention, and few were present, he thought it better for them to adjourn to some future day; in the meantime the reassembling of the Convention could be published, the whole matter fully understood by the people, and a general turn-out secured. He accordingly made a motion to this effect, which was carried.

At the second meeting of the settlers, Colonel Coffey, an Indian agent, and other violent pro-slavery men, were present. Before the convention was called to order Col. Coffey mounted a goods box and began haranguing the crowd in favor of making Kansas a slave State, upon the grounds that the free negroes of Missouri would flock over here and become a pest and expense to Kansas in case she should be a free State, that the Missourians would ship all their worn out and worthless negroes in this Territory, and thus rid themselves of their support, that the negroes thus thrust upon them would become insolent, and would finally control the whites. That they would thus establish society upon the basis of negro equality, which he declared was the real meaning and aim of abolitionism, and triumphantly asked the question how they would like to see their daughters riding with big buck niggers? This piece of sophistry, so nicely prepared to suit the prejudices of the masses, caused the free state men to look discouraged. When Colonel Coffey had finished, Montgomery was called out, and all was breathless attention to hear how he would meet the preceding speaker. He told them that he had an abiding faith in the white people, that as long as they had six times the population of the blacks, and were so far in advance of the latter in intelligence and wealth, they could always continue in the political ascendency; that other free States bordered on slave States, and he had yet to learn of the trouble to which the former speaker adverted about free negroes becoming a pest and expense to the State. Colonel Coffey's question, "how would you like to see your daughter riding with a big buck negro," he could but consider a reflection upon the custom of slave States, where ladies, as a mark of quality, were attended in their rides by a *big buck nigger*, if they pleased, and he was sorry to have it to say that even in this domestic relation of the races, not unfrequently did an unwelcome mulatto make his appearance under the roof of the master. Surely then slavery did not provide against the evils to which the gentleman alluded. In a very masterly and happy manner Captain Montgomery replied to the remarks of Colonel Coffey, and his speech was frequently greeted by loud and prolonged applause. Before he had finished, Coffey and his associates retired from the field as won. J. P. Fox was nominated for Representative in the Territorial Legislature, though many desired Captain Montgomery. The latter declined, as he knew that the former would run any way, so it was better for the free state men to make him their candidate and hold him to his pledges.

At the election the Missourians came over in vast numbers with candidates and voters, and elected their own men. A few weeks before the Legislature met, a convention of free state men, held at Mound City, resolved not to recognize the enactments of that body, and pronounced it a creature of force and fraud.

Affairs in South-eastern Kansas remained comparatively tranquil until the fall of 1856. The first show of armed force in that section of the country was a company of pro-slavery men from Fort Scott, going up to join in the raid on Osawattomie. Montgomery, knowing their designs, went up also, but arrived only in time to behold the smoking ruins of the town. On returning, he kept himself close at home, so as not to excite the alarm of the free state men by communicating the startling intelligence of what was going on above, lest they should abandon the Territory. On the fourth day after his return he visited Mound City, where he found the people filled with consternation, they having just received the news, and could see an armed force then going into camp at Paris, only a few miles distant. Upon Montgomery's informing them of the order which he had heard the ruffians give an old gentleman near Osawattomie, that all free state men should be compelled to leave the Territory. Judge Cannon remarked, "gentlemen, you hear the order and we all know what it means." They immediately began preparations to leave. Many left that night, all in a few days, except Montgomery and one old blind man. The next day the pro-slavery men began their plundering, taking stock, robbing houses, pursuing the flying free state men, and seizing the little amount of property they sought to carry away, or compelling them, under duress, to sign a bill of sale for property left behind.

In about twenty days, many of the free state men who had thus stampeded, returned to their claims. Early one morning, Judge Cannon and others went to Montgomery's in great haste, informed him that the pro-slavery men had again appeared, and threatened to drive off the returned free state men and kill him. Montgomery, at their request, visited Governor Geary, to inform him of the state of affairs in southern Kansas, and solicit his protection. The Governor received Captain Montgomery with contempt, and treated his account of the troubles with distrust. He blamed the free state men for the course they had pursued, and was disposed to regard the present evils with which they were afflicted, as a just recompense for their conduct. Meeting with this rebuff from the Governor, he went to Lawrence, and there appeared before the Committee of Public Safety, to whom he related the grievances of the free state men in southern Kansas, and appealed for aid.

The people of northern Kansas were in no condition to lend assistance to their brethren in the south. Twenty-seven hundred armed men around their town, wildly clamoring to be allowed to "wipe out Lawrence," had just retired to the Border, and were liable to march back at any moment. The Committee, therefore, replied to Captain Montgomery, that they could not possibly leave their own firesides; that they had arms which they would give him, and with these he could return to his family and neighbors, and do as they were doing—defend their homes. Equipped with a Sharp's rifle and a Colt's revolver, Captain Montgomery set out for home, resolved to fight it out as best he could.

Behold him, as he wends his way over the trackless prairies to his unprotected family on Little Sugar! His neighbors, filled with alarm by the threats of armed bands, had fled; the few who had ventured to return, were again threatened by the presence of armed companies, that went about stealing and robbing. He himself had been singled out for death. At the request of his excited neighbors, he had visited the Governor, to lay their wrongs before him, and invoke his interposition: but he had met with insult where he sought justice. He went before those aggrieved like himself, and again told the story of his and his neighbor's wrongs. Here, hearts of sympathy received him; but their friendly hands could do no more than extend to him what they possessed—weapons of self-defence. Armed with these, this meek and humble christian was suddenly converted into a warrior. He was no visionary romancer; he felt that the danger which threatened him was a reality, and like a real man he determined to meet it, appealing to the God of Right to witness the justice of his course. While he thus pondered, firmly he clenched his weapon and quickened his homeward march.

Arriving at home, he found that his neighbors had again left, and that the enemy were in search of himself. Stopping with his family, who had been insulted in his absence, only sufficiently long to learn this intelligence, he set out after the enemy, single handed and alone. Like a tiger whose den had been invaded, he skirted Little and Big Sugar Creeks and the Osage, firing from the cover of brush or rocks, wherever he could get sight of the enemy. So swift, concealed and lucky were his movements, that he spread confusion and terror among the pro-slavery men, who began to imagine that every thicket and rock concealed a free state man.

Four days after his return six brave men from the north joined him. Three days afterwards they attacked the house of Davis, a violent pro-slavery man and a leader of the desperadoes. He was a Captain of a company of Territorial militia, who were armed with United States muskets. With the view of securing the Captain and what guns he might have at his house, they made the attack. But meantime Governor Geary appeared with three hundred troops; Davis and his men, seeing him, had taken to the brush. Montgomery and his party only found, therefore, at Davis' house, one man by the name of Brown, bogus Sheriff of Linn County. They secured him and a number of arms, and a quantity of ammunition. While they were engaged in concealing the arms, Brown managed to make his escape. It was their design to attack the pro-slavery men on Big Sugar, and disarm them; but Brown having made his escape, who would spread the alarm, they feared the troops and militia. To avoid the troops they made a circuitous tour of some twenty miles south, and on their return came in sight of some Texan Rangers, who immediately fled to Fort Scott, where they gave such an exaggerated report of the number of free state men in arms, marching upon the place that the inhabitants abandoned it in a panic.

Montgomery with seven men next set out to attack two points in Missouri, where pro-slavery men were in the habit of gathering, and from which they would sally out on plundering expeditions to Kansas, and to which they would return with their spoils. These men about three weeks previous had sought to waylay and kill Montgomery as he passed from that State into the Territory with provision for his family. When collected at those places, they would freely partake of their favorite beverage and loudly boast that one pro-slavery man could whip six free state men. On arriving in this neighborhood Montgomery and his men feigned to be Indians, in order to draw the pro-slavery men out, as the latter were in the habit of seizing Indians whenever they came into that vicinity to hunt, and flogging them. Failing to call the pro-slavery men out in this way, they entered Burnet's house, but found no one, except women and children, in it. They resolved to wait, knowing that the ruffians would soon gather as the presence of free state men in the neighborhood was known. Shortly the pro-slavery men began to drop in, one and two at a time, who were severally seized as they came, disarmed and placed under guard until twenty-one were thus held. At last Burnet appeared, who, first informed by a woman of what was going on, declared that he would fight rather than surrender. But on his approach a single man went out, disarmed and brought him in prisoner. They then broke the captured guns, took $250 in money, provided themselves with good horses, liberated their prisoners and returned.

Montgomery next marched upon some invaders, encamped on Bull Creek; but at his appearance they fled. Thence he, with ten men, crossed into Missouri after negroes, but their presence and mission being discovered, and being pursued, they were so closely pressed that they seized sixteen good horses, escaped to Kansas and visited Lawrence. Here, in accordance with the advice of prominent free state men, he determined to go home and keep quiet. On his way thither, when about one mile beyond the Wakarusa, he suddenly met two of Geary's United States militia, one of whom immediately seized his horse by the bridle. Montgomery, with the agility of a panther, leaped from his saddle upon the opposite side of the horse; snatched his revolver from the holster, and with his person shielded by the horse leveled it upon his assailant, who was in the act of raising his musket. The soldier, with his hand grasping his weapon, dared not level it, knowing that a ball would pierce his heart the moment he should make the at-

Montgomery and the Militia.

tempt. Thus they eyed each other for a moment, when, without saying a word, the militia turned, passed on and left Montgomery to pursue his journey unmolested.

During the winter of '56 and '57 the pro-slavery men held the claims and appropriated to their own use the stock that the free state men had left. They kept up their military organization and committed some depredations the ensuing spring.

Early in the summer of 1857 new free state immigrants began to pour into that section of the Territory, and many of those driven off the fall previous, began to return. Thus the free state element in that locality continued to increase all summer.

As might be expected, a conflict soon ensued between the two parties. The returned free state men first undertook to gather up their stock, which they had been compelled to abandon the fall previous; but those who now held it refused to give it up; whereupon the former, being the stronger, took it. They next banded themselves together for the repossession of their claims. The first difficulty of this kind was the restoration of Mr. Stone, who had been driven off the fall previous, to his claim, now occupied by Southwood, a Methodist preacher of the Church South. The free state men built Stone a little cabin near the one in which Southwood lived, and moved his family into it, that he might await the opening of the land office, when he could properly prosecute his right to the claim. A difficulty soon arose between the two families about a well of water, which led to an assault by Mrs. Southwood upon Mrs. Stone. The aggravating circumstances attending this attack, together with the conduct of the former's husband, exasperated the free state men of the neigborhood, insomuch that they gave Southwood orders to leave the premises by a named time. The pro-slavery men, notified of this order, prepared to remove Mr. Stone by an armed force of two hundred men the day before the time allowed Southwood. The free state men informed of this design, eight of them collected at Stone's cabin to defend the premises. That night they were attacked, but the ruffians, unable to dislodge the free state men in the log house, soon left for Fort Scott with the threat that they would return with re-inforcements and cannon the following evening, and if the premises were not vacated, would seize and hang every man found on them. The free state men increased their number the next day, to sixty, and prepared a warm reception for the enemy. But the latter returned only in small force the following night, and, on approaching the pickets of the free state men, retired. Southwood left before his allotted time expired, and Stone was moved into his former house. Here the free state men guarded him the first night, and the next day informed his pro-slavery neighbors that, as they could not guard him all the time, they would hold them responsible for his protection from disturbance. This the pro-slavery men carefully attended to; for they well knew that any wrong done Mr. Stone would be followed by fearful retaliation upon them.

A few weeks after this and similar occurrences, the United States court, under Judge Williams, opened at Fort Scott. The grand jury indicted most all the free state men in that vicinity for various offenses, some under the rebellion act, and others for theft or robbery. Upon an indictment under the rebellion act, Messrs. Davis, Bone and Hoffnagle were arrested and taken to Fort Scott, where they were thrust into prison, and treated with great indignity. Montgomery raised a party of men to rescue them. He first sent Dr. Kimberland, to ask the liberation of the prisoners on bail, who, upon making the request, was informed that the crime with which the prisoners were charged was of such magnitude, that personal security could not be taken, but the Court would require the deposit of $800, in hard cash, for the recognizance of each. Not willing to entrust so much money with the pro-slavery gentry at Fort Scott, the Doctor declined to make the deposit. Meantime, Montgomery had arrested a pro-slavery man, informed him of his project, and let him go. Knowing that in this way news of his design would soon be communicated to the Fort, Dr. Kimberland was again sent, with instructions to renew his application for bail, whenever he should be assured that the Court was informed of the intended attack. He waited in the court-room all day, and began to despair of the news having any effect, or of its being received at all. But later in the afternoon, as he was urging his application by alluding to the intended rescue in an allegorical way, a messenger entered the room, whispered something in the Judge's ear, and retired. In a moment all was changed. Judge Williams soon arose, delivered his opinion that it was unconstitutional and unheard of to refuse the prisoners bail, and thereupon discharged them upon their own recognizance. One was sent home on a horse that evening, and the other, who was sick, was conveyed home next morning in a carriage.

Indictment against free state men followed indictment, and arrest followed arrest; some for theft, because they sought to regain their own property; others for the usurpation of claims, because they sought to reinstate themselves in the homes from which they had been forcibly expelled. They were taken to Fort Scott, thrust into prison, and required to give $100 as a "backer," to some pro-slavery lawyer, to take charge of their case. When tried, the verdict would invariably be against their interest, and a heavy cost thrust upon them. In one instance, where a free state man shot a pro-slavery man in self-defence, before he even had a show of trial, his property and that of his father-in-law were seized by the sheriff and publicly sold at auction, in Fort Scott, to satisfy the widow of the deceased.

The war having subsided in Northern and Middle Kansas, and peace and order having been there restored, the Border Ruffians of the worst character had congregated at

Fort Scott. G. W. Clark, the Indian agent, and murderer of Barber, Brocket, who fled from Leavenworth to escape justice, Titus, who had rendered himself illustrious at the sacking of Lawrence, Hamilton, a Southerner, who was emulous of Border Ruffian fame, and others of similar character, had taken up their quarters in Southern Kansas. They would there drink, gamble and carouse; occasionally sally out, rob, insult, and plunder the free state settlers.

The latter, finding that there was no justice to be had from the United States Court at Fort Scott, but rather long, harrassing and costly trials, while they themselves were subject to indignities and abuse, determined to organize a court of their own as an offset to the one at the Fort, with a view of burlesqueing the United States Court, and at the same time administering impartial justice in the adjustment of difficulties. Dr. Gillpatrick, of Osawattomie, was constituted Judge under the cognomen of "John Brown," and the court had all the ordinary attendants of a judicial body. Its demeanor was very grave and procedure regular. It measured its fees and penalties by its contemporary at Fort Scott, but its decisions were more in accordance with justice than the latter. The Sheriff, Captain Abbott, from the Wakarusa, with a well selected posse, carried out its mandates and gave it a practical existence. In one instance a free state man by the name of Beason made complaint that some fellows were in the act of butchering his hogs. The court immediately ordered the arrest of the robbers, and for them and the stolen property to be brought before that body. In a very short time three criminals were introduced with the several hogs which they had butchered. Their trial was conducted in the most grave and solemn manner. The slaughtered swine were retained, to defray the expenses of the court, while the robbers were required to make ample restitution to the owners in money. This they first refused to do; but finding that the court would not be trifled with, one of them sold his claim, and with the money made the required restitution.

It was, in a short time, decreed by the court at Fort Scott that the Squatter Court should be arrested and broken up. Accordingly Marshal Little was dispatched upon this errand with seventy men. He halted the troops about one-fourth of a mile from the Court, while Little advanced until he met Montgomery and others, with whom he held a conversation. The object of the court was explained and its proceedings narrated. Little apparently sanctioned the conduct of the squatters and left, informing them, if he should return, he would advance under the show of a white flag.

In a few days, at the head of about two hundred troops, the Marshal again made his appearance, held a parley with the free state men, and haughtily demanded the surrender of the Court within thirty minutes, declaring that unless his demand was complied with he would fire upon them; to which the Court replied that they would accept the alternative of a fight, rather than surrender. Captain Abbott, commanding the free state forces, ordered ten men to go out some thirty yards from the log house in which the Court had taken shelter, and conceal themselves among the trees. As the troops under Little advanced, these men fired upon them and rushed towards them; whereupon the troops beat a hasty retreat. One man and a horse were wounded which was the only loss sustained.

Anticipating another attack, and rumors being rife to that effect, the free state men increased their defense and dispatched messengers for help. Colonel Wm. A Phillips, then Adjutant-General of the Territorial Militia, soon arrived and took command of the forces, now numbering about two hundred armed men. General Lane followed him next day. Colonel Phillips, at the head of his command, started to capture Fort Scott; but learning that a large force of United States troops from the north were there, he abandoned the movement and countermarched to Sugar Mound. General Lane organized a regiment ot troops, appointed Captain Shore, of Prairie City, Colonel, and Mr. Williams, of Osawattomie, Lieutenant-Colonel. On the evening of the same day he disbanded it, ordering all the men to return to their homes, except the companies of Captains Montgomery and Baynes, who were to keep the field, and protect the citizens. He organized, at the same time, a lodge of the secret society, whose object was the destruction of the Lecompton Constitutional measure. He returned to Lawrence and made a pompous report to the Legislature.

CHAPTER XLVI.

TROUBLES IN SOUTH-EASTERN KANSAS—CONTINUED.

The difficulties at Fort Scott continued during the winter. In February Johnson, who had suffered much from the Ruffians in that town, came to Montgomery for assistance. A writ was procured for the arrest of the offenders, and Montgomery, at the head of forty-three men, set out to execute it. Meantime some of the more timid free state men had sent a couple of messengers to the town to ask the authorities to voluntarily surrender up the culprits; this deputation Montgomery met when he reached the outskirts of the town, accompanied by some of the leading citizens of the place. To the demand of the persons of those for whom writs were held, they replied that if the prisoners would be retained at Fort Scott for trial they would be surrendered up; but otherwise they would not, and that they should fight, every man of them, before yielding to the latter demand. Montgomery replied, "then fight, that is what we want," and immediately put his men in motion towards the town. Crawford and other Fort Scott gentry hurried back into the village. By the time Montgomery reached the principal street Crawford and Judge Williams met them, and reported that all the mauraders had left, and tendered the free state men the hospitalities of the place. The latter partook of a hearty breakfast and received a pledge from Judge Williams that the goods taken from

Johnson and others should be deposited at Barnesville within a few days, subject to orders. Not being able to see any thing of those for whom they held writs, the free state men left the place. In a few days, when the troops under Captain Anderson arrived, the Fort Scott authorities, instead of restoring the property, sent word to the free state men, "Come on, we are ready to fight you."

Upon receiving this challenge, Montgomery sent to Lawrence for a howitzer, and Leonhardt, a Polander, who had seen much service in Europe, came down with it, accompanied by quite a number of others. Perceiving that they were unable to drive the Ruffians out of Fort Scott the free state men determined to change their tactics and drive them from the country into the Fort, and then starve them into submission by a siege. Pursuant to this arrangement, they first struck a pro-slavery settlement high up on the Little Osage. They attacked Zumkault, who had been the perpetrator of at least three free state murders. In attempting to enter his house they shot and badly wounded him, but left him properly cared for by the neighbors. From this place they visited the residences of other obnoxious pro-slavery men, who fled in terror at their approach. The pro-slavery men in that vicinity sent for the troops at the Fort, but Captain Anderson replied that if they wished protection they should all come to Fort Scott, as he was unable to afford them any security at their isolated homes. Filled with alarm by the bold strike of the free state men, and still more by guilty consciences, the pro-slavery men flocked, with their families, to Fort Scott.

After this occurrence, which was in February, Montgomery proposed to retire from the field, and attend to the improvement of his claim. He requested that the men be organized under Captain Stewart and Lieutenant Walker, who should be actively on the watch to keep the pro-slavery men in check. These, after performing a few praiseworthy deeds, began plundering, robbing and stealing, and running off the spoils to the north. They spread terror and ruin wherever they went, threatening pro-slavery men, many of whom fled the country with their families. They continued this dishonorable course, until they had brought disgrace upon their party, and aroused the whole country against them. Stewart was a Methodist preacher, commonly known in southern Kansas as "the fighting preacher," but he was better qualified for a spy, or daring and unscrupulous adventure, than anything else. He was in the employ of the government during the rebellion as secret agent, and did admirable service. He afterwards abandoned his family, and ran off with a strumpet to Canada.

The men having become so demoralized under Captain Stewart, and committed so many gross outrages, Montgomery resolved to take the field again as their leader. He first restored what stolen property he could, and sought to correct the morals of his command. A portion of them, under the leadership of Stewart, with their avarice excited by their recent plundering, separated from those under Montgomery, and started north on a thieving expedition. In this way they brought odium upon the free state party in south-eastern Kansas, and many good free state men censured them. Those that thus set out north, generally, were worsted in their unlawful and dishonorable attempts, and finally returned, the best of whom were reinstated in the original command.

But justice to Captain Montgomery requires us to say, that he never indulged in wholesale robbing and stealing. He took from pro-slavery men alone, and only from those who were deeply implicated in the troubles. He took their arms, their horses, (if he needed any), and provisions. He aimed to feed, clothe and supply his men with that which he took from the enemy. He never sold a horse thus taken, but either restored it when through with it, or gave it to some good free state man who had suffered loss. Wherever he obtained provision of peaceable citizens, he paid for it, as his neighbors will bear testimony. Though himself as poor as afflicted Job, he never bettered his condition by spoils taken from the enemy.

It should be observed that these parties who gave themselves up to plunder in Kansas, generally met, soon after, violent deaths. We have noticed Stewart's downfall; Lenhardt, a young printer, from Lawrence, who had been leader of a guerilla party since 1856, and who continued robbing and plundering long after peace was restored, finally was killed at Doniphan; Hamilton perished in the mountains; Titus wandered to Arizona, and no one knows what became of him, and so with others.

Those pro-slavery men who had been driven out by Stewart, soon began to return with reinforcements from Missouri. They retaliated upon the free state men, notifying them to leave, on pain of death. This again filled the country with alarm. Montgomery collected the threatened families at various places, and put them in an attitude of self-defence. While thus engaged, a party wearing United States uniform, came out from Fort Scott, killed Denton and Hedrick, and attempted to murder Davis. Old man Denton lived only sufficiently long after he was shot, to obtain a pledge from his sons that they would avenge his death. He called them to his bed side, and when they had solemnly obligated themselves to comply with their father's request, he seemingly died in peace. The boys faithfully fulfilled their vow, killing one of the murderers the next day, and three or four others subsequently.

This startling occurrence spread terror and confusion among the free state men, and it required the utmost exertions of Montgomery to prevent a stampede of the settlers. He wrote a letter to the northern counties, for their friends to hold themselves in readiness to come at a moment's warning to their assistance, but, as yet, they were able to take care of themselves, while he informed his neighbors, in order to quiet their fears, that he had really sent for help. He then went to the Neosho, where he organized the settlers in a lodge of a secret order, for the purpose of self-defense. Upon his return he found that the free state men had rallied their courage, had made an attack (April 1) upon a body of Ruffians assembled at Wasson's, killed one certain, and likely others. Their fears had fled and they talked no more of abandoning their homes.

It is proper to remark here, in order that the reader may understand the movements of Montgomery and his men, that they were always duly informed of the plans of the Ruffians in Missouri and at Fort Scott, in time to frustrate them. He had a spy in the Secret Lodge in Missouri, and one in the lodge at Fort Scott, who would report to him the intended movement of the Ruffians in advance. On these reports he would frequently make a bold stroke, when to the public there was no justifying cause. In this way he and his men received the title of "Jayhawkers," from the resemblance of their actions to that of a hawk, suddenly and unexpectedly pouncing upon a jay-bird. They knew the plans of the Ruffians, where they would assemble; without a moments warning, at the time the Ruffians would imagine themselves secure and safe, and Montgomery and his party remote, the latter would suddenly fill them with consternation and alarm by his unexpected presence.

Before the Maries Des Cygnes murders took place, Montgomery knew the designs of the Missourians through his faithful spy, who now lives, I believe, at Westport. The plan of Hamilton, which was never fully carried out, was as follows: He had prepared a list of free state men, numbering about sixty or seventy, whose death had been decreed. With a small squad of men he was to pass from the Border into the Territory, seize as many of these as he could, suddenly slay them and retire immediately to Missouri. After the lapse of a week, when the excitement should have subsided, he would repeat the stroke and return as before; wait a week and again strike. Thus he would continue until the proscription list was exhausted, which was reckoned would take four or five weeks, then with his clan he would flee to Arizona.

Perhaps a short account of this barbarous man and the scene of his operations will not be uninteresting to the reader. Captain Hamilton and his two brothers came to the Territory in 1855, and settled on claims about four miles from Chouteau's Trading Post, on the Marias Des Cygnes, where the Leavenworth and Ft. Scott road crosses it, and about forty miles north of the latter place. This point had been occupied as a post of traffic with the Indians many years before the Territory was organized, and contained a few log buildings of a rude and decayed character. Captain Hamilton was a violent pro-slavery man, at first wore the appearance of a gentleman, with all the swavity and politeness of a Southerner. He brought slaves with him to the Territory. But as the prospect of making Kansas a slave State grew gloomy, he grew frantic, threw off his assumed garb of refinement, converted his house into a fort, collected around him a band of desperadoes and became a terror to the community in which he lived. All the winter of '57 and '58 he had carried on a predatory warfare, robbing and stealing from free state men. He had frequent quarrels with his neighbors, in which he threatened them with murder or assassination.

"After the passage of the Lecompton Constitution, in some shape, was regarded as certain in Washington, and intelligence to that effect had been received in Western Missouri, Hamilton spent a great portion of his time at West Point and the border counties of Missouri, assisting to revive the secret societies that had gone down since '56, and making arrangements with leading citizens of Missouri for a general guerrilla warfare on the settlers of Kansas."

All spring Hamilton had been making his threats of extermination; but, having repeated them so often, the settlers came to disregard them. Montgomery, about the middle of April, learning that the troops at Fort Scott would be withdrawn, and fearing on this account that Hamilton, who was then in that vicinity committing depredations, would carry his murderous plot, as above given, into execution, sought to draw him out to battle by making a "drive" upon the pro-slavery men in the settlement where he had been operating. Taking with him sixteen men, he made a descent upon a neighborhood along the Marmaton, about twelve miles south-west of Fort Scott, among whom he spread terror and consternation. Hamilton, instead of giving battle, fled to the Fort, where he and Judge Williams prevailed upon Captain Anderson, with a squad of soldiers, to go out, for the purpose of arresting the free state men.

As Montgomery and his men were riding along the road, they unexpectedly came in sight of the United States troops. He instantly ordered a retreat, and fell back, at full speed, to the Yellow Paint, the troops in hot pursuit. Upon reaching this stream he formed his men in a narrow defile, up which only three horsemen could approach abreast. A portion of his men, who outran the others, had passed beyond the creek, and hence he was left with only about half of his command to resist an attack of fifty regulars. Captain Anderson, at the head of the troops, entered the narrow ravine, and approached within about twenty-five steps, when the free state men opened fire. The troops immediately retreated, being unable to withstand the murderous volley from a concealed foe. Anderson's horse fell dead, with his rider fast under him; his right hand man tumbled from his saddle mortally wounded, and several horses fell in the defile. Some of the troops, who had not descended into the hollow, fired on the free state men from the hill, and wounded one. The soldiers soon sent down a flag of truce, asking permission to release their fallen commander, and carry away the wounded. The request was granted, and Captain Anderson, who had boasted so much of destroying free state men, was pulled out from under his horse.

He was afterwards compelled to resign, or submit to be court-martialed for dishonorable conduct in the presence of the enemy, and making war upon citizens. He chose the former, left the service; when the rebellion broke out, he joined the rebel army, and rose to Brevet Lieutenant-General. Montgomery and his men retired to a circular thicket of woods, which the troops, augmented by reinforcements to two hundred and fifty, refused to penetrate. After parleying a short time, they abandoned the attempt to arrest the "jayhawkers," and repaired to the Fort.

This skirmish had the effect to divest the United States troops of the charm of invincibility, and taught them and the Ruffians that even they could not pursue and harass free state men with impunity. Pro-slavery men were in the habit, during all the Kansas troubles, whenever the free state men became aroused, and were marching to retaliate for wrongs suffered, to set the United States soldiers upon them, knowing that they dreaded an encounter with regular troops, both from the fear of defeat, and out of respect to the General Government. And the latter had become exceedingly insolent and boastful, especially when affected with pro-slavery proclivities, on account of the estimation in which they were held. But this rencounter with the "jayhawkers" disarmed them of their dreaded character, and taught them a lesson which they never sought to take again, that oppressed citizens would and could fight, while it encouraged and strengthened the free state men.

Captain Hamilton, after the troops returned to the Fort, left them, and proceeded to his log house, some distance north. Montgomery, well informed of his bloody designs, and even furnished with a list of the proscribed men, hung close upon his heels, resolved to slay him the first opportunity he could get, or at least prevent the massacre. On arriving at Hamilton's, he found that he could do nothing in the way of an attack upon the house with rifles alone; so he dispatched a squad of men to bring the howitzer.

Before its arrival, the United States troops, on their road to Leavenworth, were called to Hamilton's relief. Montgomery dispersed his men, with instructions to meet at Jones', eight miles above. Two of them lingered on the ground, and narrowly escaped the following morning, by jumping down a precipice, like General Putnam, over which their pursuers feared to follow.

Montgomery then went to the Sheriff, reported to him the designs of Hamilton, showed him the list of the proscribed, and obtained from this official assurances that the free state men should be protected from all harm.

Hamilton thus relieved of the Jayhawkers by the presence of the troops, set out for Missouri, full of wrath and venom, to prepare for the execution of his bloody plot, and the accomplishment of his long coveted object. During the subsequent ten or fifteen days he was occasionally seen prowling about the neighborhood in which he lived, spying around and holding secret meetings. On the 19th of May there was a large meeting at Thomas Jackson's, just across the line in Missouri, composed of Ruffians from Fort Scott and Missouri, at which the best policy to be pursued in invading Kansas, was the question of discussion. "Some were in favor of stealing from, and harrassing, the settlers until they would become wearied out, and for the sake of peace flee the Territory; while others of the genuine 'Border Ruffian' order advocated as strongly an indiscriminate slaughter of the abolitionists, until the last of the Yankee race was exterminated." Hamilton was in favor of the latter method, and warmly advocated his plan of striking a series of fearful and successive blows, and closed his remarks by calling upon all who were for blood to follow him into the Territory. Twenty-five men, eight from Fort Scott and seventeen from Missouri, responded to his call, with whom he immediately set out for Kansas.

The free state men had concluded that as Hamilton was quiet so long, he had abandoned his purpose, and were off their guard. Hamilton and his men appeared at Chouteau's Trading Post, about one o'clock, and began collecting prisoners until they had nineteen in custody. These were generally quiet and peaceable men who had taken little or no part in the Territorial troubles, but who were known to be free state men. Eight of them were soon afterwards liberated; the other eleven were taken a few miles away, drawn up in line in a ravine with the armed Ruffians opposite them. At the command given by Hamilton, "fire," they were shot. All fell, five dead, and five badly wounded, feigned to be dead; the remaining one, though not hurt, fell also. After rifling their pockets and shockingly abusing some of the bodies, they left them for lifeless. The killed were J. F. Campbell, William Stilwell, P. Ross, Colpetzer, and M. Robinson. After the commission of the murders, Hamilton and his gang hurried back to Missouri.

As might be expected, this tragical affair created a wonderful excitement among the settlers. They assembled in numbers, at the Trading Post from all parts of the surrounding country. In the evening, Montgomery, who had been on a "drive" in Johnson county, arrived with his fearless band of twenty or twenty-five men. The following morning the citizens, then numbering about two hundred, under the leadership of General McDaniel and Colonel R. M. Mitchell, with Montgomery and his men, set out for West Point, where it was believed that the offenders had fled. Upon arriving near the town, which was about ten miles distant, a council was held at which, against the remonstrance of Montgomery, it was agreed to send a deputation into town and ask the leading citizens to come out to a conference. While this deputation was delayed in the town, men were seen leaving on the opposite side, after whom Montgomery and his men gave chase. The leading citizens, after much delay, made their appearance and were demanded to join in the effort to ferret out and arrest the guilty parties. They pretended to deplore the affair, denied any knowledge of the murderers, and refused to assist in apprehending them. Montgomery returned with one rough looking chap, against whom they could bring no proof of guilt, and he was set at liberty. Every evidence showed that the murderers had returned from the Territory to that town, and had either left or concealed themselves at the approach of the free state men.

The settlers retired to the Border where they seperated into two divisions, one going north, the other south, to watch upon the line to prevent the re-entrance of Hamilton, according to his wicked arrangement. They thus guarded the Border until superseded by regular troops, under Captain Weaver.

The Border was guarded all summer and fall. Hamilton never again made his appearance, having abandoned his purpose in consequence of the prompt and efficient action of the free state men.

While watching along the line, Captain Montgomery intercepted a messenger bearing dispatches to General Denver, from Fort Scott, rerepresenting that the "Jayhawkers" were about to take the place, were driving off settlers, robbing and stealing indiscriminately, &c., and earnestly soliciting him to send troops to Fort Scott to protect them. Montgomery detained the courier over night, read his dispatches, and in the morning enclosed a note with them to the following effiect and sent him on with a pass: That the representations contained in these dispatches were unreliable, and he had better come down and investigate matters for himself; that if he would allow the Sheriff of Bourbon county to be elected by the settlers, withdraw the troops from Fort Scott and place the town under the free state men of Marmiton, he (Montgomery) and his men would surrender themselves up for trial.

About this time Captain Walker, Deputy Marshal, arrived, having been sent down by the Governor to arrest Montgomery, on the charge of murder and theft. Upon reaching the scene of disturbance, he found that the free state men all sustained Montgomery, who, they asserted operated only against the worst character of Ruffians, and without whom they would all long since have been expelled from the country; that the pro-slavery hatred of him was based on fear rather than the depredations he committed. Marshal Walker, who was a free state man, and who had himself been driven and hunted by the Ruffians, resolved not to make any attempt to arrest Montgomery, whom he gave to so understand through his friends, and also that Montgomery should keep out of his way or prevent a recognition of himself by the Marshal, so that there would be no legal occasion for the execution of the writ the latter held against him.

On consultation with Marshal Walker, and securing his consent to execute them, the free state men procured writs from a Justice of the Peace against some Ruffians at Fort Scott, who were implicated in the Maries Des Cygnes murders, and placed them in the hands of the above named officer.

Captain Walker, with a posse composed of free state men, among whom was Montgomery in disguise, proceeded to serve his warrants. He dispatched a few to the east of Fort Scott to prevent the escape of fugitives to Missouri. With the others he entered the town, where they scattered in squads, each of which hurried to perform the part assigned it. After some search the Marshal learned the whereabouts of G. W. Clark, the Indian agent. He immediately called upon the citizens for a posse of eight or ten men to assist in arresting this offender. None but free state men, of course, responded, among whom was Montgomery; with these the Marshal proceeded to Clark's residence. Arriving there the latter, after repeated calls, finally made his appearance on the portico, armed with a rifle and revolvers. The writ was handed him, and on reading it, he told them that he would not observe it, on the ground of there being no such Justice of the Peace in the county, and that he would resist its execution. After parleying some length of time, the Marshal growing impatient, said, "Colonel Clark, you know me, I have not time to trifle. Unless you lay down your arms and surrender up your person in five minutes, I will order my men to fire," and taking out his watch, noted the time.

When three of the five minutes had expired Clark was so notified, and the Marshal ordered his men to cock and level their pieces. An awful suspense followed. In the windows, hall and balcony of Clark's house, pro-slavery men stood with arms presented at the free state men, and all the time saying to Clark, "Don't give up, we will stand by you," while from the upper windows and doors of adjoining buildings, rifles and revolvers protruded, waiting the given signal. It was evident should the five minutes elapse, Clark would fall dead in an instant, and equally evident that not a moment would pass before every free state man would be pierced with as many balls. Four minutes expired, and still Clark stood firm and unmoved, constantly urged to stand by those in his rear. "But one-half minute more," says Marshal Walker, "and you are a dead man." Clark suddenly turned pale, began to tremble, lowered his gun, unbelted his revolvers and surrendered, amid the loud oaths and denunciations of his friends. Two other Ruffians, for whom he had writs, were arrested by the Marshal, and all the prisoners were placed in jail to await their trial.

The pro-slavery men, however, had recognized Montgomery in the Marshal's posse, and procured a writ for his arrest which they placed in Walker's hands. The latter was embarrassed, being bound to execute the writ, however much against his inclination; and he knew if Montgomery should resist he would be joined by all the free state men. But the matter was quickly settled when Montgomery learned what had occurred. He immediately went up to the Marshal, made himself known, laid down his arms and surrendered himself a prisoner. With him in custody, Captain Walker and his posse set out to retrace their steps. On reaching the outskirts of town, word was brought them that Clark and other prisoners, whom they had taken, had been released and were at large. Walker, incensed at such conduct, at once liberated Montgomery and restored him his arms.

Following the above events was the visit of Governor Denver, who, acting in accordance with the suggestion of Captain Montgomery, sent him in the pro-slavery dispatches, came in person to Fort Scott, where he arrived on the 14th of June. As he passed down he held consultations with the citizens of Moneka and Raysville, by whom he was fully informed in regard to the difficulties. At the latter place he made a speech to the assembled citizens, there he announced his policy for settling the troubles, which was substantially the same as he afterwards followed.

The following is a synopsis of the Governor's remarks at Raysville, to the people there assembled, as reported by a gentleman who heard them:

"Fellow-Citizens: I have come to southern Kansas at your earnest solicitation, to assist, by my presence, in removing existing difficulties in your midst. In the prosecution of my purpose, I shall treat the actual settlers without regard to past differences. I shall know no name and know no party. I do not propose to dig up or review the past. I believe both parties have been to blame for by-gone difficulties; but with that I have nothing to do. My mission is to secure peace for the future. I propose as a basis for an agreement, whereby to produce tranquillity throughout the Territory, the following conditions:

"1. The withdrawal of the troops from Fort Scott.

"2. The election of new county officers in Bourbon county by the citizens of the county, irrespective of party.

"3. The stationing of troops along the Missouri frontier, to protect the settlers of the Territory from future invasions.

"4. The suspension of the execution of old writs, until their legitimacy is authenticated before the proper tribnnal.

"5. The abandonment of the field by Montgomery and his men, and all other parties of armed men, whether free state or pro-slavery."

Scarcely had the Governor crossed the Maries des Cygnes, *en route* to Fort Scott, than Captain Montgomery and his men, who seemed ubiquitous, joined his train. At Moneka, the Captain solicited an interview with his Excellency, but the latter declined it, until after he should visit Fort Scott. Montgomery and his band accompanied the Governor's train, holding frequent conversations with his suit, and contributing to the agreeableness of the journey. No sooner had the Governor concluded his speech, than cries were made for Captain Montgomery, who came forward and spoke in substance as follows:

"FELLOW-CITIZENS: I have listened with great attention to the remarks you have just heard, and it gives me much pleasure to say, I mainly agree with them. On behalf of the citizens of southern Kansas, I thank the Chief Magistrate of our distracted land, for the spirit of justice by which he seems to be actuated. All the free state party desires is *justice*. It has been a *stranger* to it a long time, and will hail this fair and honorable agreement with delight. That part of the agreement which refers to myself is particularly pleasing. In the last seven months I have not been at home as much as a fortnight, and a return will give me sincere pleasure. It has not been *choice* that has kept me away, but *necessity*. While my country needed my services, I could not leave the field, however great the temptation to do so. To-day, three hundred men follow, when needed, the banners and fortunes of Montgomery. When the Governor redeems his pledges given to-day, I will disband these men and retire to my cabin home, there to remain. As long as the Governor and his friends respect their side of the treaty, I and my party will respect ours."

The Governor addressed the citizens at Fort Scott in

64

about the same spirit as quoted above. The stipulations of the treaty effected between the parties there for the pacification of difficulties were, that the civil organization of Bourbon county and the townships therein should be perfected; that all past offenses against the laws should be referred to the grand juries; that both parties should refrain from prosecutions and vexatious arrests for petty and imaginary offenses; that they pledge themselves to do all in their power to bring offenders to justice, by having them arrested for offenses hereafter committed, and for all others upon which indictments should or might be found, by a legally constituted grand jury; that all questions growing out of claim titles should be referred to the legal tribunals for settlement; that the troops should be withdrawn from Fort Scott at an early day.

Although not so stated in the treaty, it was the distinct understanding that "by-gones should be by-gones," and that no arrests should be made for past offenses, and that a free state Marshal should be appointed in that district. This was the solemn pledge of the Governor, made at Raysville, upon which Montgomery and his men retired to their homes, and which were termed the "Secret Articles." But the peace thus established proved of short duration, as will soon appear.

Although the object of this Convention was peace, still, when the Jayhawkers and Border Ruffians were thus brought together, it came near breaking up in a general fight.

Governor Ransom, instead of seeking to quiet the fury of passion and advising conciliation in his speech, began to arraign the Jayhawkers before the Convention as robbers and assassins, whereupon Judge Wright called him to order. Words not polite to ears refined passed between them, and they rushed towards each other. Friends interfered however, and prevented a display of their pugilistic powers upon the stage. Had they clenched, doubtless the fight would have become general.

CHAPTER XLVII.

POLITICAL PARTIES.

From the first advent of Governor Walker political elements had been undergoing a change. The two great and hostile parties which had fought the battles of '55 and '56, began to disintegrate and divide, as an immediate consequence of the new policy of the Governor and, for a time, of the administration.

The scheme of Walker for settling the vexed question in Kansas was a move of the conservative wing of the Democratic party, endorsed by Douglas and his followers, to avert what they really believed would be the final result of forcing the Lecompton Constitution upon the people. It was at that time evident and incontrovertable that slavery could not be fastened upon Kansas by fair means and equally plain that the use of unfair means to effect this object would be attended with civil war and a disruption of the Federal Government.

The policy of Governor Walker contemplated the abandonment of the attempt to make Kansas a slave State; and, instead thereof, to so shape and mould political elements in the Territory as to make it a Democratic State. The motto of Governor Walker was, "Yield justice to Kansas in order to save the Union, annex Cuba and make slave States out of the South-western Indian Territory, to secure the final triumph of slavery." Says he to the President:

"The extremists are trying your nerves and mine, but what can they say when the convention submits the cnstitution to the people and the vote is given by them? But we must have a slave State out of the South-western Indian Territory, and then a calm will follow; Cuba be acquired with the acquiescence of the North, and your administration having in reality settled the slavery question, will be regarded in all time to come as a resigning and resealing the Constitution." "Cuba! Cuba! (and Porto Rico, if possible), should be the countersign of your administration, and it will close in a blaze of glory."

Governor Walker, upon his arrival in the Territory, at once applied himself to break up the two great Territorial parties, and gather together all the Democrats he could into one organization. With this end in view, he prepared his inaugural, which took the ground that climate forever precluded slavery from Kansas, and hence, it was folly to continue the contest about a matter already settled by the unalterable laws of nature. The mass of the pro-slavery party, who never had been pecuniarly interested in making Kansas a slave State, readily abandoned the contest and became the followers of Walker. The more rabid, however, and ultra, who did not care a fig for the Union, and who were in constant communication with the traitors at Washington, soon became bitter opponents of the Governor, and favored forcing slavery upon the new State by injustice and fraud, regardless of the consequences.

This is a very important point, not only in the history of Kansas as making the beginning of the overthrow of slavery in the Territory, but also in the history of our common country, in clearly revealing the designs of subverting the Union by the slave propagandists, who pressed the Lecompton measure, all the more zealous, as it tended to involve the whole country in war and destroy the general Government. We shall have occasion to notice with what pertinacity they urged the measure in Congress when we reach that period of time.

The pro-slavery party in Kansas, almost *en mass*, at first manifested a disposition to fall in with Governor Walker's plan, even the most rabid remaining quiet though not altogether relishing his views. At the convention, held on the 3d of July, 1867, at Lecompton, the policy of Walker was endorsed, and a resolution to sustain the constitution, whether submitted to the people, or not, was tabled by a vote of 41 yeas, to 1 nay.

But as quick as the Lecompton scheme was manufactured at Washington and transmitted to the Territory, the radical pro-slavery men became loud in their denunciations of the Governor, as is shown by the convention on the 7th of December, whose action we have before narrated. It was then that this scheme of forcing slavery upon the people by fraud was clerely developed. This faction remained inconsiderable, as shown by their vote for State officers and, after the defeat of their darling project, affiliated with the Democrats.

Political factions seldom survive a war of their own waging. The free state party, which had presented such a solid and unbroken front to its adversaries, and so victoriously repelled armed invasion and aggression, that stood so united and firm against the combined forces of legislation, force and Federal authority, was not an exception to this rule, but perished in the hour of triumph. Disintegration in it can be traced to the time when Governor Walker declared that the October election should be conducted fairly and justly, not under Territorial legislation but under the act of Congress, organizing the Territory. Though a division of opinion arose, with regard to contesting certain elections, still it preserved itself almost intact until after the October and January elections, which it carried with strong majorities.

The cause of division among the free state men was not in the ends to be attained; for all desired to make Kansas a free State; but it was in regard to the best means for accomplishing that result. A few had held, from the time the question was first raised, that it was too humiliating, and inconsistent with former resolutions and acts, to recognize in any way the Territorial authority. Others admitted that it was humiliating, but believed that by taking possession of the Territorial Legislature, they would disarm their enemies, and could turn their effective battery upon them; that success was what they sought, and hence were willing to humble themselves that they might be exalted; that having taken possession of the Territorial Government, they would more likely and easily accomplish the object of the Topeka State organization.

When the Territorial Legislature met at Lawrence strong efforts were made by the firm adherents to the State movement to prevail upon that body to remove legal obstructions in the way of the full and practical establishment of the Topeka State Government, and to co-operate in upholding and maintaining it. But the Territorial Legislature, though strongly free state, declined to run the risk of supplanting itself—a legal body—by one not so recognized by the Federal Government.

The State Legislature adjourned, after remaining in session about ten days, with the understanding that it would re-assemble at Topeka on the 4th of March, then and there to complete and perfect the State Government, if the Territorial Legislature should open up the way. But the Legislature had made different provisions, and public opinion with reference to the Topeka Government had continued to change. It was now generally conceded that the Topeka Constitution was but a temporary expedient to afford a rallying point and shelter to free state men while contending against slavery and oppression; that the emergency for which it had been framed, was past, and it had better be abandoned, as a more regular and unobjectionable course could be pursued in order to attain the same object.

The Territorial Legislature, therefore, instead of putting

forward the Topeka Government, provided for a convention to frame a new constitution, with all the safe-guards and regularities of law. Thus, it was thought, that the objections to the Topeka and Lecompton Constitutions would be obviated, and a speedy and safe admission of Kansas into the Union secured.

There was also much prejudice entertained against the Topeka Constitution by the free State Democrats, who regarded it as irregular and partisan in its formation. By calling a new convention these prejudices would be removed and all free state men united in supporting and pushing forward a State Government.

A few still clung to the Topeka State organization and, hence, when the time arrived for the Legislature to convene, according to the provisions of the constitution, on the 4th of March, these few assembled at Topeka. But the leading men of its originators had deserted it, and were not present. No quorum presenting themselves, those present appointed a committee to prepare an address to the people, and adjourned. Thus ended the Topeka free state government—deserted and abandoned by those who originated it. It never had any vitality, nor was it designed to have, until Congress should impart it by a recognition of it, as embodying the will and wish of the people of Kansas, or until it was ascertained that all peaceable remedies had failed, and forcible resistance furnish a prospect of success in ridding themselves of the foreign legislature, fraudently thrust upon them. It can scarcely be termed a government; for it never had more than a passive existence. Its originators were neither revolutionists nor traitors, but freemen, who had resorted to it as a measure to throw off oppression. They held the Topeka Constitution up before Congress, and asked that body to clothe it with authority and power, When the difficulties, which it was designed to meet, were removed, it was wisely abandoned.

The delegates (101 in number) to the Constitutional Convention were elected by about 9,000 votes. No great interest was manifested in the matter, as considerable doubt was thrown upon the legality of the act creating the convention. The bill was sent to the Governor, who retained it without sending in his objections. The House at the expiration of the time given him to retain it, as was supposed, passed action upon it again and adjourned. But upon a more thorough investigation of the length of a legal day, it was found that they had adjourned before the expiration of the time allowed the Governor to return the bill.

The convention assembled at Mineola on the 23d of March, and on the second day adjourned to Leavenworth. It was in session eleven days, and adopted a constitution similar to the one framed at Topeka, leaving out some of its objectionable features. It was characterized by a more radical and liberal spirit. The rights of women in property were better protected; all male citizens over twenty-one years of age were entitled to vote; schools were to be thrown open to all colors. The constitution was to be submitted to the people for their ratification or rejection, on the third Thursday of May, and an election held at the same time for State officers under it. A copy of it was to be forwarded to Congress upon its ratification, and if Kansas was admitted as a State under it, the State Government was to go into immediate effect.

According to the call of the "Concentrated Committee," a convention was held at Topeka on the 28th of April to nominate candidates for State offices. The following ticket was framed: Governor, H. J. Adams; Lieutenant Governor, C. K. Holliday; Secretary of State, E. P. Bancroft; Treasurer, J. B. Wheeler; Auditor, G. S. Hillyer; Attorney General, C. A. Foster; Representative in Congress, M. F. Conway; Superintendent of Public Instruction, J. M. Walden. The convention passed a resolution to the effect that if Kansas should be admitted into the Union under the Lecompton Constitution, then pending before

Congress, without a condition precedent, that said constitution, at a fair election, shall receive the ratification of the people of the Territory, then they should put the Leavenworth Constitution and Government under it into active operation and support, and defend the same at all hazards.

They instructed the people to vote for or against negro suffrage, and mixed schools of colored and white children, assuring them that such an action would operate as instruction to the first Legislature, to provide for the constitution in that respect.

The nominees of this convention, of course, were elected. The constitution was adopted. But the vote was exceedingly slim, as a great many free state men either did not interest themselves in the matter, or threw their influence against it. There were about 3,000 votes for it and 1,000 against it. The cause of this indifference was the doubts about its legality, the objections many had against it, and election on the English bill which engrossed the attention of the public. Before the Constitutional Convention adjourned at Leavenworth, advices from Washington assured the free state men that there was no hope in Congress for the success of the constitution thus framed, from the fact that there had been no enabling act passed by that body authorizing the call for the Constitutional Convention. It was in consequence of this assurance that the movement was treated with such indifference; but the Leavenworth Constitution lingered along, and finally reached the Senate of the United States. It was presented to that body with a petition asking the admission of Kansas under it, on the 6th of January, 1859, and found a grave in the Committee on Territories.

On the 2d of August, 1858, the election on the Lecompton Constitution as proposed in the English bill, was held. A general interest was manifested and the people, irrespective of party, cast their votes against it. The proposition was rejected by 11,300 to 1,788 votes, making a majority against it of 9,512. Thus was this insulting proposition made by Congress, to bribe the people of Kansas and control their action, indignantly cast beneath their feet.

The previous Legislature, among the many oversights of which it was guilty, failed to make any new apportionment ot representatives in their body. Efforts were made to remedy this, by inducing the Governor to make a new apportionment himself, or call an extra session of the Legislature for that purpose. He replied that he had no authority to make the apportionment himself, nor would he call an extra session of the Legislature, as he would have no guarantee that they would attend to the matter when assembled. Accordingly the election was held under the old unfair and unjust apportionment. The free state party, including the Republicans, who had not formally separated from it, carried the election with large majorities.

The disintegration of the two great conflicting parties, which had been going on for more than a year, was completed this fall. The pro-slavery party really became defunct in the fall of '57, but the radical element of it continued to cherish a hope from the Lecompton Constitution. When it was hurried beneath the ballots of an outraged people, the last light of the pro-slavery party, which had kept the nation in commotion for four years, was extinguished. Its members, after the party itself became inactive, lavored with free state Democrats.

Immediately after the October election, (1857), a call was made by the Chairman of the Central Committee for a free state delegate convention, to be held at Lawrence on the 11th of November, "to discuss various questions connected with the present political organization of the Territory, and to determine the true policy of the party;" "to consider the question of the speedy admission of Kansas into the Union as a free State." It seems not to have been generally attended, but developed clearly the design and wish of partisans to organize the Republican party. On the other hand, there was a large portion of the free state men opposed to its organization, consisting of two classes—those desiring the preservation of the free state organization until Kansas should be admitted into the Union, and those who were formerly Democrats, and were opposed to Republicanism on national issues. All sincerely desired Kansas to be a free State, but all felt there was no question as to that result. The point of difference arose in the desire for individual advancement and party renown. Some wished the "Old Free State Party" to remain a unit until the question was fully decided by the admission of Kansas into the Union, and thus let it have the honor of triumph. On the other hand, a great number declared that the question had already been decided, the contest was over, and the results would come in due time, and being in a majority, Republicans, favored the organization of that party, while outside influence was brought to bear to accomplish the same object.

As an offset to this effort to organize the Republican party an attempt was made to reconstruct the Democratic party in such a way as to engraft the Democratic element of the free state party upon the conservative trunk of the pro-slavery party of Kansas. It was claimed that slavery was no longer an issue, and that the most radical had abandoned their efforts to make Kansas a slave State; that by organizing under the ensign of Democracy, and upon the basis of the old pro-slavery party, which had always possessed the ear of the Administration and influenced its action, they—the conservative Democrats of Kansas—could thus retain all the influence of the defunct pro-slavery party, and control the politics and elections of Kansas, despite the Republicans. This all seemed very satisfactory, but it was with great difficulty that a platform was constructed upon which such incongruous elements could unite, at a convention held for that purpose at Leavenworth, on the 24th of November, 1857. The platform was rather a non-committal affair, favored excluding free negroes from the State, and denied the sovereign power of Congress over the Territories. The movement, like the effort to organize the Republican party, was a failure, the free state men regarding it as an effort on the part of the pro-slavery men to retain their power and control. But, nevertheless, like the Republican effort, it gave direction to public sentiment and around its ensign, around which had rallied the Ruffians of '55 and '56, rallied the free State Democrats of '58.

But these primary attempts to reorganize the old national parties in the Territory, gave shape to public sentiment. New comers arriving, knew nothing about the old organizations, and readily fell in with the new. In fact, by the spring of '58 there were more new emigrants than than those who were here during the troubles.

In the spring, therefore, the people were ready for the organization of these two great national factions. A strong effort was made by some to preserve the unity of the free state party. A convention was held at Big Springs on the 12th of May, 1859, and an attempt made to rally to its standard free state men, and reorganize the other forces of old party. They passed a resolution that it was the duty of all free state men, as in '55, to eschew minor diffierences and political distinctions, and unite upon the broad platform of laboring together to make Kansas a free State. But the effort was vain. The free state party, like the Topeka Constitution, was buried in the place of its birth. It had been a power in its day, but, having served the purpose for which it was created, it was abandoned.

It is worth observing that those who most strongly condemned the adherents to the Topeka Constitution were themselves the tenacious adherents to the free state party. While, on the other hand, those who favored putting the Topeka government in advance of the Territorial Legislature, on failing in this object, endorsed the Leavenworth Constitution, failing again, triumphed in organizing the Republican party.

The Democratic party, composed chiefly of those who affiliated with the pro-slavery party, perfected its organization at Lecompton on the 11th of May, 1859. They neither endorsed nor condemned the Administration, but adopted the principles of their party as enunciated by Jefferson and Jackson. They denounced the Lecompton Convention movement, were for excluding free negroes, &c.

The Republican party was fully organized at Osawatomie the 19th of May. Horace Greeley was present and made a speech. The convention adopted resolutions condemning the Administration and opposing the extension of slavery, but did not assume the radical and partisan character which Mr. Greeley desired.

There was but little difference in the platforms of the different parties. The slavery issue—the great national issue—was not at all applicable to Kansas politics, as it had long before given up the contest. The organization of these parties was the inauguration of that confusion and personal bitterness that has always characterized Kansas politics. Her early troubles attracted to her soil men of talent and ambition. Never could a new Territory boast of so many able and enthusiastic young men. The troubles had made them querulous; when these had subsided each one was ready to cast everything aside that stood in the way of his aspirations. No party nor principle could carry them through, for there was little distinction in parties; they were but in their infancy. Office-seeking, therefore, became a personal strife, an individual contest between men of equal merit and ability.

The Territorial Legislature convened at Lecompton on the 3d of January, 1859, and on the following day adjourned to Lawrence. A. Larzalere was elected Speaker of the House, and C. W. Babcock President of the Council. This body was composed of more experienced and efficient men than its predecessor. They applied themselves knowingly and earnestly to their work. A committee was appointed to codify the laws, who reported from time to time during the session for the action of the Legislature. In their final report they say: "The enactments of 1855, known as the 'Bogus Statutes,' have been supplied, and are ready for repeal—a consummation long looked for and earnestly desired by a large portion of the people of the Territory. The general laws of 1857 are ready for the same fate. The laws of 1858, to which we were confined as a basis, have been revised and supplied. The code of civil procedure remains substantially the same."

On account of the treaty made by General Denver at Fort Scott in the spring, he became unpopular with the Democratic party, and in consequence of this, the Administration being unable or unwilling to sustain him, he resigned in October.

In December, Samuel Medary was appointed Governor. He was a native of Ohio, and formerly editor of the "Ohio Statesman." On the accession of Mr. Buchanan to the Presidency, he was appointed Governor of the Territory of Minnesota, which position he filled until it was admitted into the Union as a State. He was then made postmaster at Columbus, Ohio, from which he was transferred to the Governorship of this Territory. He was a man of ordinary ability, and a devoted follower of the Administration. He remained Governor until after the State was admitted into the Union, and resigned a short time before the State Government went into effect.

CHAPTER XLVIII.

TROUBLES IN SOUTH-EASTERN KANSAS.

The difficulties in south-eastern Kansas continued, notwithstanding the treaty effected by Governor Denver. Personal encounters, neighborhood broils, thieving and robbing were in no way abated. It would require a volume larger than this to contain a full account of the many frightful rencounters, horrid outrages, and shocking murders that belong to the history of that part of the Territory. I can only give a brief sketch of leading items of a general character, and leave the others for the writers of biography and romance. From the fall of 1856 the whole of south-eastern Kansas was in constant state of excitement, overrun by predatory bands oppressing free state men, who would rise in mass at times, and retaliate upon pro-slavery settlements for harboring the Ruffians. This would be followed by other acts of retaliation, and thus a continued tumult, or civil war, prevailed.

Soon after the treaty, two free state men who had some horses stolen by a party of maurading Missourians went over into Missouri in hope of recovering them, and when near Papinsville were taken prisoners, led into the woods and shot. They were left for dead, but one, though badly wounded, finally reached his home in the Territory. The settlement on the Little Osage was visited by a second foray of Missourians and plundered, shortly after the above occurrence. Secret societies were formed among the pro-slavery men for the purpose of assassinating the leading characters whom they feared. In accordance with this plan, Montgomery's house was assailed by about thirty men. They secreted themselves near the cabin, and when the door was opened, fired a volley of buck-shot into the room, some of which burried themselves in a bed on which was lying Mrs. Montgomery and her child, while others specked the surrounding walls, but fortunately injuring no one. The door was instantly closed, lights extinguished, Montgomery and Kegai flew to their arms and stood by the port-holes of the cabin, eagerly peering out into the darkness for the enemy. The Ruffians dared not show themselves, and judging from the silent darkness of the room that Montgomery was prepared for them, they evidently thought best to retire. After various attempts of this kind, Captain Montgomery gave his boys privilege to operate against the enemy in their own way, who soon cleared the country of these roving bands, and in some instances severely chastised them, although he himself remained at home, still observing the terms of the treaty.

Next followed the arrest of Marshall, one of Montgomery's men, *on an old writ* issued before the treaty. This highly incensed his neighbors, who reported the affair to Montgomery, and solicited his interference. He immediately wrote to Marshal Campbell that this act was a breach of faith, demanded the release of Marshall, and intimated the consequence in case of a refusal. The prisoner was instantly raleased.

During the summer, emigrants arrived in vast numbers from the free States, and prosperity began to dawn upon this unhappy people. Comparative quiet reigned, with the exception of some robbing and stealing, though hostile feelings still rankled in the breasts of many settlers.

Slavery clung to south-eastern Kansas with a tenacious grasp, in order to preserve for its heritage the broad and fertile lands included in the Indian Territory. Whenever it should be thrown open to settlement, slavery would again be defeated. In November, a free state man by the name of Rice was arrested, for an offense committed early in the spring, during the troubles, and thrust into the jail at Fort Scott. Montgomery, regarding this as his neighbors did—a violation of the treaty—made a demand for his release, which was defiantly refused. A few gentlemen on the Osage, apprehending a renewal of difficulties, interceded to prevent the threatened calamity, and, at their instance, a convention was called at Raysville, with a view of bringing about a reconciliation. At this meeting, the Fort Scott gentry repudiated what was termed the secret article of the treaty, viz: that no indictments nor arrests should be made for past offenses. There was, therefore, no compromise effected, but the convention broke up with every indication of a brewing storm.

John Brown, with his party of men, had fortified themselves in a log house not far from Montgomery's, and on his claim. They had come down in the spring to assist the free state men, and, after the treaty, had retired to this fort to await developments, giving their neighbors the assurance that they had settled there to be peaceable or to fight, just as they were treated. Brown had around him the same men that accompanied him to Harper's Ferry, who, like their leader, were brave, fearless and determined; but unlike him, were actuated by the love of adventure instead of a heavenly calling.

As Montgomery was returning from the Convention, he was informed that Brown's fort had been menaced with destruction. He hurriedly collected fifty men, claimed the log house as his property, and proposed to defend it as such. The following day McDaniel, with four hundred men, came to Montgomery's, and solicited a conference, for the purpose of seizing him. Montgomery and his men were in the house, prepared for an an attack, but did not go out. His wife, who was in the yard, to whom McDaniel had directed his remarks, replied that she presumed if he would come in a civil manner, without an armed band, that her husband would readily comply with his request; but, as it was, if he wished to see her husband, he would have to enter the house. McDaniel, viewing the dark port-holes of the fort-like constructed cabin, and fearing that it was filled with the contents of the Trojan horse, had not the courage to approach the door, so he retired with his force.

It is proper to remark that McDaniel was a free state Democrat, belonging to that party which was organized at Leavenworth, the members of which, together with those who adhered to the Old Free State Party, were opposed to Montgomery with as much hostility as the pro-slavery men. They slandered and abused him and his men in public prints, representing them as thieves, robbers and assassins, and sought their destruction more from political animosity than personal grievances. The Republicans warmly endorsed Montgomery and his associates in all their actions, with few exceptions.

The free state Democrats, seeing that they could not destroy Montgomery, whose influence in that section of the Territory was unbounded, concluded it best to win him over to their favor. McDaniel, accordingly, returned the next day alone, and was at once admitted to an interview. He assured Montgomery that the free state Democrats had agreed to endorse his conduct, proposed a public covention for that purpose and invited him to attend.

Meantime, Brown drew up a series of resolutions that should serve as a basis of affiliation. These were presented at the meeting and adopted. The most important one provided that "those violent pro-slavery men who had been forcibly expelled from the country, should be forever kept away, as a just punishment for their many aggravated crimes." The convention fully endorsed Montgomery and his men, and received them into fellowship.

Montgomery, having not yet abandoned the resolution to

release Rice, remained quiet a short time, that the gentry at Fort Scott might be off their guard. On the night of the 15th of December, he and sixty-eight men, with one piece of artillery, through darkness, snow and ice, wended their way to that village, and arrived on its outskirts about sunrise. Here he halted, separated the men into three divisions, and assigned them their respective duties. The first was to seize the prominent citizens and hold them prisoners; the second was to form around the hotel; and the third was to enter and release Mr. Rice. It had been reported by the Ruffians that they had forty men in the hotel, guarding the prisoner, who could fire twenty times a piece without stopping to reload. Every division performed its part most perfectly. Captain Montgomery, who had been previously informed of the prisoner's position, through a gentleman who had been permitted to carry an exchange of clothing to him, headed the party which entered the building. The doors were easily kicked open, except the one opening into the prisoner's room, which was beaten down by a bed railing. The prisoner was found, and the staple holding his chains was loosed with an ax. The party and prisoner safely descended to the street.

Meantime, the other divisions were performing their work. J. H. Little had opened his store door and fired at the free state men, wounding Captain Seaman. The shot was instantly returned, the ball lodging in a volume of the Kansas bogus statutes. The store was then surrounded. Little, while peeping from a transom window, was killed by a shot in the forehead, scattering his brains on the floor —just one year from the day he attempted to capture the free state court. The assailants had determined, in case any resistance was offered, to burn the town. Accordingly, order was given for the store to be set on fire, and the torch was applied. But, on the second thought, Montgomery concluded, as his men were in needy circumstances, and, knowing that the store-room contained some good clothing, thought it best to first supply them with a new suit, so the fire was extinguished. It not being safe to enter the house by the door, the cannon was brought to batter the building down. But at the intercession of Dr. Little, and some women in the house, the piece was not fired. The inmates were ordered to abandon the building, which they did. The boys then entered the house, helped themselves to clothing, but the money in the safe was not touched, at the request of Montgomery.

Captain Brown had accompanied the expedition on the first part of the journey; but when within a few miles of Fort Scott he asked Montgomery what was his plan of attack, to which the reply was given, that he had none; he refused to go any further, having no faith in the project without a well arranged plan of operating. Upon the return of Montgomery and his men, he congratulated them on their success, praising the mode in which the assault was conducted. Montgomery seldom arranged his plan of attack in detail, leaving himself to shape his action as occasion might demand.

Brown and his party then retired to Little Osage, where three days afterwards a fugitive slave stumbled upon their encampment, and immediately made known a tale of woe and sorrow, stating that "he, together with his wife, two children, and another negro man was to be sold within a day or two, and he begged for help to get away." On the following night Brown and his party went over to Missouri, liberated fourteen slaves, and returned with them and their effects to Kansas. In this foray one pro-slavery man was killed.

This occurrence produced a wonderful excitement all over the country. The Governor of Missouri offered a reward of $3,000, and the President of the United States $250, for the apprehension of Brown. Great fears were experienced lest the Missourians would cross over and retaliate upon free state men. Brown acted the part worthy of a hero, sending the negroes on to Osawattomie, while he placed himself and men on the Border, to shield his friends from the danger which he had occasioned. There he remained and watched until the storm blew over. He then proceeded to Osawattomie, took charge of his train and set out for Canada. At Holton forty-two pro-slavery men made a charge upon him, but were badly routed and four taken prisoner, who were detained five days, not allowed to swear, and compelled to say their prayers every morning and evening.

The following is an extract from a highly partisan letter, written by Judge Williams to Governor Medary, immediately after the occurrences above noticed, and will show the state of feeling in Fort Scott at the time:

"We are here with all the public records of the courts, the land offices, as well as the private property of our citizens at the mercy of these outlaws and desperadoes. We have mustered some seventy men, partly armed; with these we keep watch day and night. Our women and children, many of them both from town and neighborhood, have gone for safety to Missouri. Night before last, our guard was fired upon by some of these bandits. We have been expecting another attack since the murder of Little, on the 16th inst., as these miscreants have been seen in small bodies hovering around us. They do not pretend to secresy of their designs. They openly avow them. They are about completing the last of these forts. We received information on yesterday, that Montgomery and Brown had forty men engaged in finishing the fort on Osage, so as to defy the United States troops, should they be put into requisition to capture them. On the night before last, the same men attacked Brownville, quite a clever town, on the military road, about twelve miles from this place, and literally cleaned it out, both of inhabitants and property, leaving but one man in it unharmed, and robbing, of the last article, the store of Mr. Chance. Now I wish one thing to be noted as a fact indispensable. It is this; that during last fall, winter and spring, and now this winter, there has been *no instance* of these outlaws troubling the many *towns and cities* laid out, and owned by the members and agents of the "Massachusetts Emigrant Aid Society," and they drive out of the Territory and rob none but pro-slavery men and national Democrats. These facts clearly show a systematic programme, made up by and emanating from headquarters. Before this fall Montgomery and Brown were the only head bandits; now we have Osawattomie Brown and the man styled Rev. M. Brockman. Instead of two, making four companies of murderers, robbers numbering about 200, oath bound to bloody purpose. This fall in accordance with Mr. Seward's Rochester speech, the institution of slavery has been boldly attacked in the States where it exists, by invading Missouri, murdering one of its citizens, carrying off some twelve slaves, robbing some five or six families and driving them from their homes with notice not to return on pain of death. This is the small domestic army familiarly talked of by Judge Conway, Mr. Wighman and their Massachusetts friends, in their correspondence of last fall, when they sent for more money, &c. The men composing these companies are nearly all young men, evidently sent to Kansas to do the work in which they are engaged. They are well armed with Sharp's rifles, and two revolvers each. They do not pretend to work or have homes. In a word they are in a position of a standing or ready army, so that they boldly condemn the civil law. We have tried to execute writs, but so many are the sympathizers of these men, while others are held in fear, that, although about 100 writs have been issued on informations and indictments, not one can be executed. What, then, remains for the people of this region? It is for you to say, sir. I am clearly of the opinion that nothing but martial law carried out by the strong force of the United States can save this part of Kansas from utter prostration and ruin."

The difficulties in southern Kansas early engaged the attention of the Legislature, at whose request the Governor presented a pro-slavery version of them. To remedy the evils in that part of the country, the jurisdiction of Douglas county was first extended over the infected district, and the prisoners ordered to be brought to Lawrence for trial, away from the scene of strife. Montgomery went to Lawrence and gave himself up for trial, while the Marshal was sent to arrest his men and bring witnesses. But it soon became apparent that this measure would avail little in restoring peace and tranquility, and a general amnesty act was soon passed by the Legislature, to the following effect:

> "SECTION 1. That no criminal offenses heretofore committed in the counties of Lykin, Linn, Bourbon, McGee, Allen and Anderson, growing out of any political difference of opinion, shall be subject to any prosecution on complaint or indictment in any court whatsoever in this Territory.
>
> "SECTION 2. That all actions now commenced growing out of political differences of opinion shall be dismissed."

This act taking effect immediately after its passage, pardoned and liberated the prisoners then in custody. Considerable excitement prevailed on the following day, by the advent of Captain John A. Hamilton, in charge of sixteen free state prisoners. He was supported by an armed guard. He had not heard of the amnesty act, and was returning prisoners according to the directions of the Court. As they entered town, the cry was raised that this was Captain Hamilton, who committed the murders at Choetau's Trading Post, whereupon a crowd collected and assaulted the new comers. The guard was disarmed, the prisoners rescued and taken to the blacksmith shop, where their chains were cut off and they set at liberty. A general cry was made for Hamilton, and the whole town was, for a short time, filled with commotion. Several shots were fired, but fortunately no one was hurt. Quiet was however soon restored, by its being explained that this was not the murderer Hamilton, but a stanch free state man of the same name. The arms taken from the guard were never restored.

In presenting the troubles of south-eastern Kansas, I have traced the operations and movements of Captain Jas. Montgomery, as the best method to give a clear and consecutive view of events. It should be remembered that others operated in that section of the country, such as Captains Jennison and Bayne, who are frequently leaders of bands against the Ruffians. Many others performed individual exploits, met with frightful rencounters—in short, everybody, every settler, was a soldier, and waged war on his own hook. It would, therefore, be impossible, in a book of this size, to narrate all the personal incidents of importance and interest connected with this subject. Captain Montgomery was the Chief of Jayhawkers, and did more than all others in this mode of warfare, and whose movements are really historical.

CHAPTER XLIX.

VARIOUS ITEMS.

The first Legislature at its second session in 1857, passed an act providing for the auditing of claims, "for moneys actually expended for the purpose of maintaining, and carrying into effect, the laws of the Territory, or for the purpose of suppressing any rebellion or insurrection, whether sustaining the militia, or any other posse of the Marshal, or Sheriff of any county of the Territory;" for "the loss of property, or consequent expenses at and time since the passage of the act organizing the Territory," growing out of political difficulties.

"The act provided for the taking of testimony in support of such claims, collections, and certificates of vouchers, and making a true and correct statement in duplicate of such accounts, and to be laid before the next Congress of the United States, and the other before the next Legislative assembly of Kansas Territory, to the end that proper and united effort might be made to obtain from Congress compensation and indemnity for the losses, expenses and damages incurred by the citizens of the Territory, without distinction of party."

Hon. Wilson Shannon was first appointed to audit these claims, but declining to serve, Hon. H. J. Strickler was chosen to fill his place. Having given proper notice to

67

claimants, he held sessions to hear and receive testimony, and audited claims in various localities in the Territory during the month of September, October and November. "Accordingly, three hundred and fifty claims were presented under oath, with corroborating testimony of two or more witnesses." The amount claimed by this report was $301,-225, and $254,279 28 were allowed, Thirty-eight thousand nine hundred and forty-two dollars and ninety cents of this were of the public class, and the remainder of a private character.

This report was submitted to the Legislature in 1859, and ordered to be printed. The report, though impartially made, was imperfect, from causes over which the commissioner had no control. Many had no faith in the plan of indemnification; others were politically hostile to the commissioner, and would not appear before him; no provisions were made to compel the attendance of witnesses and consequently the proof rested on interested testimony. The Legislature, therefore, determined to provide for ascertaining more fully and correctly the losses sustained by the settlers during the troubles in the Territory.

An act was accordingly passed providing for the appointment of three commissioners, one by the Governor, one by the Council, and the third by the House of Representatives of the Territorial Legislature, whose duty should be "to audit and certify all claims for the loss of property taken or destroyed, and damages resulting therefrom, during the disorders which prevailed in this Territory from November 1, 1855, to December 1, 1856." They should fix the times and places of holding their sessions, prescribe such rules and regulations concerning the taking of testimony as they should deem proper, were empowered to appoint clerks and enforce the attendance of witnesses. They were required to take an oath to support the Constitution of the United States, the organic act, and to faithfully discharge their duties. They were required to examine the evidence taken by the former commissioner, and adopt or reject it, as they should deem just and right. The provisions of this act applied only to those who were settlers at the time the losses occurred.

"Upon the completion of the testimony and the recording of the award in each case, the commissioners shall, upon the demand of the claimant, deliver to him a certificate of such decision or award. And on or before the first day of September, 1854, said commissioners shall close their proceedings under this act, and make up and file in duplicate in the office of the Secretary and in the office of the Auditor of the Territory, a statement of all claims presented, and the amount, if any allowed thereon; and they shall also file in the office of the Secretary of the Territory, all testimony, vouchers, papers and documents pertaining to their investigations."

It was made the duty of the Constitutional Convention afterwards to assemble to make suitable provisions for the payment of these claims, by the Federal Government, by incorporating in the ordinance to be submitted with the Constitution, a provision to that effect. By a supplementary act an attorney was to be appointed by the Legislature to attend the commissioner to assist in the investigation.

Accordingly the Council elected H. J. Adams; the House, S. A. Kingman, and Edward Hoagland was appointed by the Governor, as the three commissioners. On the recommendation of Governor Medary, William McKay was elected attorney by the joint votes of the Legislature.

This committee faithfully and fully discharged their duties. They examined witnesses, received testimony and passed judgment upon four hundred and eighty-seven claims. Only one hundred and ninety-six of those audited by Mr. Strickler were presented to this Board. The mass of testimony, fully revealing the private designs and workings of individuals, and the fearful character and extent of the troubles in Kansas, through two of the most boisterous years, was published by order of Congress, making two large octavo volumes, of eight hundred and ninety-two pages each. It furnishes valuable material to the historian in forming a correct conception of the Kansas wars. The testimony was taken when the issue which caused the troubles no longer existed, and political excitement had died out. It was prepared by three gentlemen well qualified for the work—noted for their exactness, magnaminity, and justice. Mr. Hoagland has since died, Mr. Kingman has become Judge of the Supreme Court of Kansas, and Mr. H. J. Adams has occupied various positions of public trust.

According to this report, losses were claimed by the settlers to the amount of $479,973.92; and the Commissioners awarded, and issued certificates for $454,001.70. Of this allowance there was $37,349.71 for crops destroyed; seventy-eight buildings were burned or torn down; three hundred and sixty-eight horses, and five hundred and thirty-three cattle were taken or killed. Out of $412,978.03 of this property destroyed, $77,198.99 were owned by pro-slavery men, and $335,779.04 by free state men. The amount of property taken or destroyed by pro-slavery men was $318,718.63; that taken or destroyed by free state men was $94,529.40. Thus it will be seen that each party took, or destroyed, property in an inverse proportion to the amount lost and the amount owned. The pro-slavery men did not own quite one-fourth as much as the free state men, and destroyed almost four times as much. The free state men lost more than four times as much as the pro-slavery men, whereas, they only destroyed a little more than one-third as much.

The Commissioners calculated that fifty thousand dollars more would cover the losses of all whose claims might thereafter be established. Then the total amount of property, proven to be destroyed during the Kansas troubles, would have reached the neighborhood of five hundred thousand dollars.

This report accompanied the Wyandotte Constitution to Congress, with the request that Congress "appropriate five hundred thousand dollars, or in lieu thereof, five hundred thousand acres of land, for the payment of the claims awarded the settlers of Kansas, by the Claim Commissioners." But Congress refused to make this appropriation, and thus the people of Kansas Territory not only suffered from anxiety, privation, oppression and outrage, through the inactivity of the general Government, which was then acting the part of a guardian towards her, but also the loss of five hundred thousand dollars worth of property.

According to the provisions of the act providing for the adjustment and payment of these claims, making it "the duty of the Auditor of the Territory, upon the delivery to him of any certificate of award given by the said Commissioners, to draw his warrants on the Treasurer of the Territory in such sums as may be required, for the amount therein named, in favor of the party to whom such award has been made, or to his order, and deliver the same on demand."

The Auditor issued warrants of the above character to the amount of $349,933,63. The Treasurer, agreeable with an act providing for the funding of the Territorial debt, issued Territorial bonds on the face of the warrants, to the amount of $95,700 00, the law limiting the amount of debt to be thus funded to $100,000,00. These should bear interest, payable annually, and the principal should be paid in 1864, in New York.

But it seems not to have been the design of the legislators or a majority of them, in any way to saddle this debt upon the Territory, and make it responsible for the payment of the same, in the event that Congress did not assume it. Hence, matters became very embarrassing by the action of the Territorial officers, whereby almost one hundred thousand dollars of this debt was taken up in bonds, for the payment of which the faith of the Territory was pledged. The subject engaged the attention of the Legislature in 1860, which failed to take any action upon it. The last Territorial Legislature appointed a committee to investigate the whole matter, which reported adverse to the payment of the bonds, and the Legislature passed an act in accordance with the report, but which failed to become a law, in consequence of the Governor's veto and the admission of the State into the Union, while the subject was under consideration. But the same act became a law the March following, by the action of the State Legislature.

This was not the only sacrifice made by the free state men of Kansas Territory. There was the State Government inaugurated in 1855, passively sustained and upheld for two years, costing days of hard labor, expense of traveling and loss of time. The old Executive Committee was authorized to issue script to the amount of $25,000,00, and $15,265,90 was thus employed in organizing the free state government. The constitution empowered the State authorities to issue script, the full amount of which cannot be determined. The fate of that State Government was pledged, but it perished insolvent, and to-day can be found in many a Kansas cabin relics of its "departed worth." Conventions or elections were held almost every month; the Territory was canvassed, arms and ammunition procured, defenses constructed and soldiers maintained. Crops were not tended, stock fared no better fate. The people of Kansas, after having spent all they had, appealed to friends in the States, who generously responded.

In accordance with the provisions of the English Bill, the Legislature passed an act for calling a convention to frame a constitution. To ascertain whether the people wished a State Government, an election was held on the fourth Monday in March. At this election, 5,306 votes were cast in favor of it, and 1,425 against it, making a majority in favor of a constitution and State Government of 3,881. Being but little division of public sentiment upon the matter, there was no contest at the polls, which will account for the smallness of the vote.

In pursuance with an act calling the convention the Governor announced this result, and issued his proclamation calling for an election on the first Tuesday of June for fifty-two delegates to the Constitutional Convention. At this election the highest number of votes was cast that ever was polled before in the Territory—about 14,000.

These delegates met, in conformity with the law, at Wyandotte on the 5th of July. The following officers were elected: J. M. Winchell, President; J. A. Martin, Secretary; J. L. Blanchard, Assistant Secretary; G. F. Warren, Sergeant-at-Arms; Ariel Draper, Reporter; Rev. M. R. Davis, Chaplain.

The following list of committees was appointed: Preamble and Bill of Rights, Hutchingson, Lillie, Hanway, Perry, John Wright; Executive Department, Greer, Porter, Dutton, McDowell, Hubbard; Legislative Department, Thatcher, Arthur, N. C. Blood, McClelland, Brown; Militia, Blunt, May, T. S. Wright, Hubbard, J. Wright; Judicial Department, Kingman, Thatcher, Burress, Greer, Blunt, Lillie, Perry, Slough, Stinson, Parks, Wrigley; Electors and Elections, Townsend, Porter, May, Palmer, Arthur, Slough, Wrigley; Schedule, Burress, Middleton, Ritchey, Hanway, Williams, Ingalls, McCullock, McDowell, Hipple; Apportionment, Preston, McCullock, Graham, Palmer, Thatcher, Arthur, Moore, Crockett, Ritchey, Hoffman, Ross, McDowell, Stiarwalt; Corporations and Banking, Graham, Burress, J. Blood, Lamb, Middleton, Stolks, Blunt, Crocker, Burnet, Griffith, Slough, Barton, Perry; Education and Public Instruction, Griffith, Middleton, Stolks, Houston, May, McClelland, Hipple; County and Township Organizations, Ritchey, L. S. Wright, Preeston, McCullock, Moore, Simpson, Brown; Ordinance and Public Debt, J. Blood, Dutton, Kingman, Hangman, Hanway, Hoffman, Burnet, Hutchingson, Lamb, Preston, N. C. Blood, Graham, Stinson, McCune; Finance and Taxation, Simpson, N. C. Blood, Crocker, Hutchingson, Palmer, Signer, Lamb, Hoffman, Porter, Stinson, Foster; Amendments and Miscellaneous, Houston, Ross, Ingalls, Signer, Williams, Burnet, Forman; Federal Relations, T. S. Wright, Hodson, Stinson, Palmer, Forman; Phraseology and Arrangement, Ingalls, Ross, Kingman, Stolks, Dutton, Porter, Townsend, Griffith, Lillie, Stiarwalt, Barton, Perry, Foster, McCune, Parks.

This is a very important assembly in the history of Kansas, as it laid the foundation of the State Government. It was composed of talented and experienced men of both parties.

The rights and privileges of women and negroes called out considerable discussion. Petitions were received by the convention from ladies of various localities in the Territory, asking that no distinction should be made in the rights and privileges of the sexes, which were referred to the Committees on Judiciary and Elective Franchise. The following is the report upon the subject by these committees, submitted by Judge Kingman:

"Your Committee concede the point in the petition, upon which the right is claimed 'that the women of the State have, individually, an evident common interest with its men in the protection of life, liberty, property and intelligent culture;' and are not disposed to deny that sex 'involves them in greater and more complicated responsibilities.' But the Committee are compelled to dissent from the conclusion of the petitioners. They think the rights of women are safe in present hands—the proof that they are so, is found in the growing disposition on the part of different Legislatures to extend and protect the rights of property, and in the enlightened, progressive spirit of the age, which quietly but efficiently has its effect upon the legislation of the day. Such rights as are natural are now enjoyed as fully by women as by men. Such rights and duties as are merely political in their character, they should be relieved from, that they may have more time to attend to those 'greater and more complicated responsibilities,' which petitioners claim and your committee admit, devolve upon women.

"The theological view of this question, your committee will not consider."

When the subject of elective franchise came up, a feeble and ineffectual effort was made to strike out the word "male." There were but few in the Convention who favored women's rights.

The negro occasioned considerable jarring in the Convention. Two attempts were made to exclude him from the Territory, but such motions were tabled, first by 26 yeas to 21 nays; and the second time by 28 yeas to 20 nays. Mr. Blunt, who voted in the negative, did so, not because he favored the measure, but desired it brought before the people. The vote on excluding negroes from the public schools stood as follows:

Yeas—Brown, Barton, Foster, Forman, Greer, Hipple, Hubbard, Kingman, Moor, McDowell, McCune, McClelland, Parks, Porter, Slough, Stinson, Stiarwalt, J. Wright, Wrigley, T. S. Wright—20.

Nays—Arthur, Burnet, Blunt, Burriss, J. Blood, N. C. Blood, Cracker, Dutton, Graham, Griffith, Hutchinson, Hanway, Hoffman, Houston, Ingalls, Little, Lamb, Middleton, McCullough, Preston, Palmer, Ritchie, Ross, Signor, Stokes, Simpson, Thatcher, Townsend, Williams—29.

Upon a resolution, endorsing the Fugitive Slave Law, the vote stood the same way, except Messrs. Kingman, Porter and T. S. Wright, voted in the negative. On motion to strike out the word "white" from the clause on the qualification of electors but three voted in the affirmative, Hutchingson, Ritchie and Stokes. But one voted against the clause prohibiting slavery in the State—Mr. Forman, of Atchison.

Strong efforts were made to extend the northern boundary of Kansas, so as to include all that portion of Nebraska south of the Platte River. A delegation, representing the people of southern Nebraska, attended the convention and strongly urged the measure. The proposition was rejected by about the same votes which controlled the action on the exclusion of the negro.

The question of locating the temporary seat of government, engaged a good share of the attention of the convention. Strong electioneering was practiced. According to a resolution passed, as the roll was called, each one named the place of his preference for the capital, and the four which received the highest number of votes were to be the only nominations. But afterwards, by general consent, the number was restricted to three, Topeka, Lawrence and Atchison. The roll being called again, Topeka received twenty-six votes; Lawrence, 14; Atchison, 6. Thus Topeka was made the temporary seat of Government. It was required by an article among the miscellaneous that the first Legislature should provide by law for submitting the question of the permanent location of the capital to a popular vote.

The schedule provided that the constitution and the clause preventing a homestead from a forced sale should be submitted to the ratification or rejection of the people at an election on the first Tuesday of October, and in case the constitution was duly adopted by the majority, an election should be held on the first Tuesday in December for all the State, District and County officers, provided for in that instrument.

The convention completed its labors on the 28th ot July, and the constitution was adopted as a whole, by a Republican majority—the Democrats voting against it. The debates and full proceedings of this body were published, making a small octavo of over four hundred pages.

The constitution was duly ratified on the 4th of October by the following popular vote: For the constitution, 10,421;

against the constitution, 5,530; for the Homestead clause, 8,788; against Homestead, 4,772.

Both parties held their conventions and nominated candidates for the elections of officers on the 6th of December, under the constitution. The following is the result of that election for all State officers, the Democrats with a star before their names, the others being Republicans:

Candidate	Votes
GOVERNOR.	
C. Robinson	7,908
*S. Medary	5,395
SECRETARY OF STATE.	
J. W. Robinson	7,864
*A. P. Walker	5,396
AUDITOR.	
G. S. Hillyer	7,856
*J. K. Goodin	5,365
CHIEF JUSTICE.	
Thomas Ewing, jr	8,010
*Joseph Williams	5,301
ADJUTANT GENERAL.	
B. F. Simpson	7,880
*Orlin Thurston	5,372
LIEUTENANT GOVERNOR.	
Joseph P. Root	7,893
*John P. Slough	5,392
TREASURER.	
Wm. Tholan	7,937
*R. L. Pease	5,348
SUPERINTENDENT OF PUBLIC INSTRUCTION.	
W. R. Griffith	7,598
*J. S. McGill	5,287
ASSOCIATE JUSTICES.	
S. A. Kingman	7,895
*S. A. Stinson	5,396
L. D. Bailey	7,721
*R. B. Mitchell	5,492
MEMBER OF CONGRESS.	
M. F. Conway	7,674
*J. A. Halderman	5,567

For members of the State Legislature the political result stood as follows: In the Senate twenty-two Republicans and three Democrats; in the House of Representatives fourteen Republicans and eleven Democrats.

Persons having been appointed to take the census who were rather unfavorable to the admission of Kansas, and there being no funds to defray expenses, it followed that the provisions for taking the census were not fully carried out, and the enumeration in many counties very imperfectly, or not at all, taken. The consequence was that the report of the census returns showed a population of only 69,950 whites, 406 blacks and 21,628 voters, whereas the committee appointed by the Council at the next session of the Legislature to investigate the matter, were of the opinion that the population was about 97,570. This furnished a pretext for the Democracy to oppose the admission of Kansas and to keep her out of the Union one year longer.

CHAPTER L.

THE DROUTH.

The Territorial Legislature assembled at Lecompton on the 2d of January, 1860, and on the 6th adjourned to Lawrence, which occasioned a rupture between that body and the Executive. The Governor remained at Lecompton, to await the decision of the Attorney General upon the legality of this action of the Legislature, and the Secretary of the Territory refused to furnish the members, upon their reaching Lawrence, with papers, documents, stationery, printing, &c. In view of these facts, both branches of the Legislature passed a concurrent resolution on the 18th day of January, to adjourn *sine die*, without having accomplished anything in the way of Legislation.

The Governor immediately issued his proclamation, call- the Legislature to convene at Lecompton the following day, "then and there to consider and perform such duties as are demanded by the interests and necessities of the people." The Legislature re-assembled pursuant to the call, but again adjourned to Lawrence, where it remained in session until the 27th of February, and faithfully performed its work, enacting many salutary and much needed laws.

The year of 1860 is remarkable for an unprecedented drouth, which occasioned what is generally termed the "Kansas famine." The facts in the case are briefly stated. From the 19th of June, 1859, to November, 1860, there was not a shower of rain fell at any one time, to wet the earth two inches in depth. During the intervening winter, there were two slight snows, neither of which concealed the ground from view. The roads were never muddy, during the whole period, and during the summer, the ground would break open in great cracks, embarrassing the rolling of wagons, while the winds blew with a burning and parching sirocco's blast from the south, and with the hot beams of an unclouded sun, parched the soil and burned up vegetation.

Such was the frightful character of the drouth, which it becomes faithful history to record. The consequence was, that the crops in the Territory were almost an entire failure. Fall wheat, induced by the snow and frost of winter, shot forth in the spring, but withered and died when that moisture was exhausted. Spring wheat, of which there was little sown, fared no better. Out of 4,000 acres of good land sown in Shawnee county, not five hundred bushels were raised—less than one-eighth of a bushel to the acre. Other counties did some better, but most of them did not harvest a bushel. Esculent vegetables were a perfect failure everywhere; not a cabbage, bean, radish, onion or anything of the kind was raised. Potatoes and turnips—the next things to the staff of life—were likewise failures. From the carefully prepared statistics of Shawnee county, it is shown that two hundred and seventy-nine acres of potatoes were planted, and only ten bushels raised; seventy-six acres of beans produced but ten bushels; from two hundred and twenty-four acres of Hungarian grass, only ten tons were mowed; while buckwheat, turnips and garden vegetables were utter failures. Corn fared some better. The low bottom lands, where properly tilled, averaged almost one-third of a crop, and the high lands and ridges produced no grain whatever—only dry fodder. From the above statistical table it is shown, that from 3,319 acres of corn planted, only 5,187 bushels were raised, or about one bushel and two-thirds to an acre. Other places did better than this, or at least particular fields, which were low lands and well tilled: they averaged about ten bushels to the acre, and some produced as high as fifteen or twenty—a few still more. Timothy and clover hay was a total failure. From the excellent Government Farm at Fort Leavenworth, which usually yielded about 1,100 tons, not a bushel was secured.

The prairie grass furnished the chief support of the people. It grew and flourished nicely until about the middle of June or the 1st of July, when it parched and died on all the uplands. Along the ravines and creeks, and in the "pockets" it remained green still later, furnishing hay for winter. The wild grass, though not so abundant as usual, still was of such a superior quality that it kept the cattle fat all summer and fall. The sap having dried up, left it very nutritive, and stock ate it with as much relish as though it had been green. Some difficulty in places was experienced in procuring hay, there being no grass long enough to mow, except in some of the low lands and along creeks and rivers. Farmers went in a few instances, as far as forty miles to procure hay for their cattle. Stock, which would otherwise have famished, fed upon the spontaneous growth of grass on the prairies during the summer, fall and winter.

To add to the already distressed condition of the country, the wells, springs and brooks dried up. Very few held out during the year. Families on the prairies were compelled, in many instances, to haul their water several miles, and would even thus procure a very inferior quality. They had neglected to dig wells, depending on creeks and brooks for water, so that when these were dried up they were left destitute.

The drouth in some localities of Kansas was not as bad as

above described. Along the Missouri River and in the north-eastern portion, a sufficient was raised to feed the population of that region. In the Kaw Valley, where properly tilled, the land yielded a two-thirds crop of corn. But elsewhere throughout the Territory the drouth was fully as alarming as we have shown above.

The drouth of 1860 was not confined to Kansas alone. It extended over southern Missouri, Arkansas, western Tennessee, and a portion of Kentucky, almost, if not quite as great as in this Territory. As little was raised, according to the amount planted, in those States, as in Kansas.

But the people of this Territory were illy prepared for this universal dearth of crops. Their granaries were generally exhausted before the summer months arrived, at which time not one-half the farmers in Kansas had a bushel of corn on hand. It being a good price at the Border towns the fall previous, and the roads being excellent all winter they had sold in market all the surplus corn they supposed they would have after June set in, trusting to the grass from the prairies for feed. So with wheat; all those that had raised more than their own consumption would demand, had disposed of it at what they supposed was a good price, and appropriated the money to supply the wants of their families. By the fall of 1860 there was scarcely any corn or wheat in the Territory; not six thousand bushels of either in each county.

Furthermore, the people here were poor and scanty of pecuniary means. Many of them had suffered heavy losses in '55, '56 and '57, by not being able to attend to their crops, having lost much of their time, and spending much of their money in feeding and clothing their families, and in attending conventions, traveling, buying arms and ammunition, &c. They had, during the years of '58 and '59, put their claims in repair, and were making ready for full and rich harvest gatherings. Many were new comers, whose condition, in some instances, was more deplorable than the older settlers, from the fact they had expended all their means upon their new homes, and trusted entirely to their crops for a livelihood.

The result was that thirty thousand settlers left the Territory and returned to their friends and to provision in the States. It looked at the time as though the whole country would be depopulated and left a barren and uninhabited waste. Claims, with their improvements, houses, fences, &c., were abandoned and stood dreary and alone upon the prairies. Long trains of covered wagons, drawn by lean horses, with woe-begone looking inmates, in mournful procession crossed the Border.

Thirty thousand more would have left, but they had no means with which to get away. They had not a sufficient amount of clothing and provisions to last them half the winter, and Famine, with all his grim and ghastly features, stood sentinel at their doors. It was plain that they must perish from starvation, unless that Father who supplies the birds of the air with food would bring deliverance to their homes. They were the industrious poor of Kansas, who had come here to rear themselves homes upon the wide extended prairies by hard toil, and had no hope of supplies only what they gathered from the fields. They had no rich friends in the East to lend a helping hand, nothing on earth could meet their necessities but the Spirit of Benevolence.

The other forty thousand of the population in Kansas were in a condition to withstand the famine, but could do nothing towards alleviating the wants of others. With the provision and clothing they had, and with that which they had money to procure, together with the assistance of friends from abroad, they could manage to live themselves.

The painful fact stared the people of Kansas in the face, that want and starvation were before them. There was no evading or overcoming it, notwithstanding its admission would militate against the character of the new and growing country. The alarming rumor reached the East, and at once touched the kind and sympathetic hearts of the numerous friends of Kansas. Thadyus Hyatt, of New York, who had always taken an active interest in Kansas, was the first to move in relief of the destitute. He came to the Territory himself, visited numerous counties, acquainted himself with the actual state of affairs, and gathered statistics. Being satisfied that the necessities for relief were urgent, he had the counties to organize and appoint their committees, and constituted S. C. Pomeroy, general agent of northern Kansas, and W. F. Arny, of southern Kansas, who should receive and distribute money and provision for the suffering. Mr. Hyatt returned East, petitioned the President for assistance, in behalf of the destitute in Kansas, and published to the world his statistics and facts of personal observation, with an appeal for an immediate response for the relief of the sufferers.

The movement thus inaugurated, continued its operations until the spring of 1861, and contributed vastly towards the relief of the deestitute, as the following figures will show. Contributions in clothing and provisions were received, packed in boxes and sent to Atchison for delivery, while the remittances in money were applied to defraying the expenses of freighting and boxes. On its reception at Atchison, it was distributed out among the different counties.

According to the report of this Committee, the total receipts of provision for distribution up to March the 15th, 1861, were 8,090,951 pounds. Total distribution at Atchison, exclusive of branch depots, 6,736,424 pounds. At Wyandotte and Leavenworth, the Committee distributed 437,190 pounds of provisions of various kinds. These statements do not include clothing and garden seeds, of which large quantities were received and distributed. As early as the first of January, 1861, 2,200 garments of various kinds, 262 pairs of boots and shoes, and 550 yards of cloth, were received and distributed. By the first of March, 1861,

2,500 bushels of seed wheat were received and distributed among the different counties.

The whole amount of cash received by the Committee, was $83,869,52, which was chiefly expended on bagging, boxing and freight. But little or no money was distributed among the settlers.

The Committee and all their agents labored gratuitously, never receiving a cent for their time.

Besides the relief furnished by this Committee, contributions flowed into the Territory through other channels. Churches, individuals and communities operated independently, and for certain persons or localities. It would be impossible to arrive at any just estimate of the amount thus furnished. Much of that sent through the General Relief Committee had special assignments, and was designed for certain neighborhoods or settlements.

The State of New York deserves a special mention in connection with the relief movement, for generously appropriating $50,000 towards purchasing and shipping seed wheat to Kansas. The Legislature of Wisconsin extended a similar favor; while the citizens of Indiana, Illinois and Ohio made liberal donations in seed grains of various kinds.

Such efforts as these greatly relieved the people of their wants, without which not only would hundreds have perished during the winter, but still more would have been unable to plant their fields in the spring, and consequently unable to better their condition. But notwithstanding the vast amount of remittances from the East, the people of Kansas, in many instances, experienced all the effects of destitution and privation.

The evil effects of this drouth were not confined entirely to the personal sufferings it occasioned, but threw the Territory back in her march of progress, not only by diminishing her population one-third, but by deterring emigration to the present day. Ever since this great calamity, Kansas has generally been regarded abroad as subject to drouth, and with it the idea of famine has been associated. Thousands have been prevented from emigrating to the State, from the popular conviction that this country is periodically visited by such appalling misfortunes as that of 1860. In justice therefore to the Territory whose history we are writing, it behooves us to examine into the facts bearing upon this subject, which will amply show that Kansas is no more liable to drouth, and no more affected by it, than any other State of similar latitude.

The following table was taken from Dr. Sink's report to the Governor upon the climate of Kansas, which was arranged from the records of all observations made at the military posts within the State, extending to the year 1865:

MEAN PRECIPITATION OF RAIN, CALCULATED FOR SEASONS AND YEARS.

Place of Observation.	Spring......	Summer ...	Autumn....	Winter	Year.........	No. Years.
Fort Leavenworth	7 32	13 03	7 57	3 42	31 34	30
Fort Riley	5 62	10 68	5 87	2 72	24 90	5
Fort Scott	12 57	16 37	8 39	4 79	42 12	10
Fort Larned	5 36	8 45	4 01	81	8 63	4
Fort Kearney	6 80	10 62	4 85	1 50	23 77	13
St. Louis	12 39	14 14	8 94	6 94	42 32	19
Cincinnati	12 14	13 70	9 90	11 15	46 89	20
Pittsburg	9 38	9 87	8 23	7 48	34 96	18
Athens, Illinois	12 20	13 30	9 20	7 10	41 80	10

"The measure of moisture, precipitated in rain and snow, for the entire year, in Kansas, is very considerably below that for the other States represented in the table. By comparing the measurements for the spring, summer and autumn months, however, it will be found that the difference is very slight.

"The winter months show a great dimunition in the relative amount, but as the deficiency occurs during the absence of vegetation, it is of no practical importance. As a consequence, the roads during this season are usually dry and in splendid condition for travel, thereby rendering transportation easy at the very time the farmer desires to send his heavy produce to market."

"The precipitation of rain for the month of March shows a small increase over the winter months. The quantities are doubled in April, and again doubled in May. The mean maximum occurs in June, and the mean minimum in January.

"The greatest amount in one year ever observed at Fort Leavenworth was 59 inches, in 1858; the least amount was 16 inches, in 1843. The greatest at Fort Scott was 52½ inches, in 1844; the least was 29 inches, in 1838. No records were kept at Fort Scott during the year of 1860, but the amount for the summer months was undoubtedly less than at Fort Leavenworth, as was evidenced by vegetation. The deficiency of rain at Fort Leavenworth in 1843 must have been local, as the records at Fort Scott for the same year show a measurement of 44 inches. Besides, the Indians living in the Territory at that time have no recollection of a drought of a general character. The amount of snow that falls during the winter is usually very slight, and it remains on the ground but a short time.

"Taking the records at Forts Leavenworth, Riley and Scott, as a basis for calculation, the mean annual precipitation of rain for the eastern half of the State in 32 78-100 inches. The mean for the western half is about 24 inches. The mean for Minnesota is 30 inches, for Wisconsin, 32 inches, and for Michigan, 30 inches.

"In 1860, the relative deficiency of rain was quite as great as in southern Missouri, Arkansas and western Tennessee as in Kansas. In 1854 a general drought prevailed in all the Central States, from the Missouri River to the Atlantic coast.

"The following tabular statement will give a better expression of its extent and character than if made in general terms. The statistics are for the summer months only, as this is the period of greater importance in the supply of rain. The drought, however, continued throughout the autumn months, in most of the localities.

	Summer of 1854—inches.	Average for Sum—inches.		Summer of 1854--inches.	Average for Sum--inches.
Fort Leavenworth	5 7	13 0	Pittsburg	4 7	9 8
Fort Riley	2 7	10 6	Washington	4 8	12 0
Fort Smith, Ark	4 1	13 9	Norfolk, Va	3 5	15 1
St. Louis	5 4	14 1	New York	5 1	11 5
Cincinnati	6 6	13 7	Burlington, Vt	5 1	10 8

"A drought so widely extended as that of 1854, is a rare occurrence in this climate. They are usually confined to a much smaller compass, and, at such times, the neighboring districts are supplied with an excess of rain. While a drought is by no means a desirable occurrence, an excess of rain is equally injurious. The general proposition, that the whole Mississippi valley is more damaged in its grain and root crops by an excess of rain than from a deficency, will scarcely be questioned."

CHAPTER LI.

VARIOUS ITEMS.

There were several events of interest occurred this year, which we will briefly narrate, though not connected with the general history of the Territory.

In the winter of 1859 and '60, Dr. John Doy, of Lawrence, set out to conduct thirteen negroes, by way of Iowa, to Canada. They had fled from slavery to that city. This was a common thing in those days for the negroes of Missouri. On their arrival they always found friends and help in effecting their escape. As he was passing through the northern part of the Territory, fifty miles from the eastern boundary, he was suddenly captured by Missourians and carried to St. Joseph, where he was tried on the charge of enticing away slaves, a crime punishable with death according to the statutes of that State. The Kansas Legislature appropriated one thousand dollars to employ counsel for Doy at his trial. Though he was charged with an offense as having been committed in Platte County, and though the prosecution was unable to prove that Doy had been within thirty miles of that State, the Jury at the first term of Court failed to agree, but at the next he was convicted and sentenced to the penitentiary for life.

But Doy had friends in Kansas who cared but little whether he was sentenced or not, knowing well that they could effect his deliverance. A company from Lawrence and vicinity, under the leadership of Stewart, the fighting preacher whom we have before noticed, one dark Saturday night, crossed the Missouri River a little below the ferry, and soon stood before the jail at St. Joseph. It so happened that a storm came up about the same time and a torrent of rain was pouring down upon them. The jailor was awakened, called out and asked to allow them to secure a prisoner until Monday morning in jail, whom they had caught on the charge of horse stealing. They represented there was no doubt of his guilt, that they were tired and it was late to wake up the Justice of the Peace that night for an examination of the criminal. The jailor with reluctance consented and conducted them into the building. No sooner had they entered than they shut the door, and with a cocked revolver before the jailor's heart, bid him not move or give the alarm at the risk of his life. They told him their purpose was to release Doy, and demanded the keys of the building. Having obtained these they next compelled the poor jailor to lead them to Doy's cell, which they unlocked, and the prisoner walked out. They then told the jailor that he should remain in the jail, mute and still, until daylight, that they would post guards around the house, and if he made a noise they would rush in and assassinate him on the spot.

They passed out, locked the door after them, and proceeded towards the river. Just at that time a fire broke out on one of the principal streets; the fire bell rang the alarm sound, and every body hurried pell mell to the burning building. In the midst of this confusion and excitement, Stewart and his party made their escape to their boats and crossed the river in safety. There were two happy coincidents connected with this rescue, seemingly providential—the rising of the storm and the breaking out of the fire.

The last Territorial Legislature assembled at Lecompton on the 7th of January, 1861, and adjourned soon after to

Lawrence, where it remained in session until the second of February. According to the Auditor's report, the following table exhibits the amount of revenue annually received by the Treasurer, and the amount of warrants annually issued by the Auditor, during the Territorial existence of Kansas:

	Revenue.	Warrants.
1856	$ 1,811,88	$5,211,48
1857	3 383,09	11,604.47
1858	681.12	4,502,93
1859	26,544,06	64,400,26
1860	3,197,53	41.234,14
Total	$35,617,48	$124.962,28

According to this report, the total amount of warrants on the treasury outstanding at that time was $89,344,80. Before the first State Legislature convened, this was diminished by in-coming revenue to $87,390,84, which was the amount assumed by the State. These warrants have been paid from year to year, until there remains now of them only $9,288,57.

The free state men never paid a cent of the Territorial tax levied by the authority of what was called the bogus Legislature. It remains charged against the respective counties, constantly accumulating by interest, until the Legislature of 1867 canceled it out.

In the spring of this year an effort was made to revive the old difficulties of 1855 and 1856, by the attempt on the part of the United States Deputy Marshal, Leonard Arns, to arrest John Ritchie, of Topeka, upon an old indictment growing out of the early troubles, which Governor Walker declared "should be by-gones." In 1856, Mr. Ritchie had been arrested upon a trumped-up charge of mail robbery, and, with other fellow-townsmen, taken to Lecompton, there retained in close confinement for three months, when he made his escape. It was upon the same charge that Marshal Arns sought to re-arrest him, on the 20th of April, without the least show of writ or authority. As he was advancing upon Mr. Ritchie with a drawn revolver, the latter, protesting against arrest and warning him to come no further, shot him dead. Mr. Ritchie gave himself up for trial, at which he was acquitted, on the ground that the homicide was an act of self-defence.

Old feuds in south-eastern Kansas had not yet been healed, and threatened to break out afresh this summer and fall. Bad characters had returned to the Missouri Border, who, with other kindred spirits, began to harrass the free state men, across the line in Kansas. Many free negroes had found homes in the Territory. These the Ruffians would kidnap, hurry them South, and sell them at good prices. They would also induce slaves in Missouri to run off from their masters, by presenting to them flattering prospects of freedom. When the master would offer a reward for the apprehension and restoration of the absconded negro, these pretended liberators, knowing the whereabouts of the slave, would seize him and thrust him back into bondage. In other instances they would decoy the slaves away, and secrete them until the reward should be offered; then take them back and claim their money. This was a heavy business, and carried on with great profit all summer.

The free state men finally determined to make a stand against this iniquitous practice of man stealing, and began to give protection to the abused fugitives. Whenever runaway slaves came into that vicinity they were either guarded or conveyed to other places.

Foremost among these man-stealers was a Ruffian by the name of Hines. The free state men determined to catch him if they could, and hang him, but he, for a long time thwarted all their efforts to secure his person. Finally it was reported that Hines and others were coming to attack Montgomery and get possession of a slave the latter harbored. A company of free state men gathered together and set out to meet Hines, and shortly came upon him. Feigning to be in hunt of runaway slaves, they induced Hines and his party to join them. While in company with him they obtained his confidence, and ascertained all about his misdeeds and plans. At a favorable opportunity the Kansans seized the Ruffians, disarmed them, and held them for trial. They gave them a drum-head trial, liberated all except Hines, whom they found clearly guilty of man-stealing, and, in accordance with the Hebrew code, sentenced him to death. A paper with the words, "Hung by the people of Kansas, for man-stealing," written upon it in large letters, was pinned to his shirt bosom. He was placed upon a horse, (November 16,) one end of the rope attached to his neck, the other to a swinging limb of a tree above, the horse led from under him, and he left dangling in the air.

This event was immediately followed by the hanging of two free state men, Guthrie and Catlan as horse thieves, but really because they were abolitionists. Others were killed by the secret order, called the Dark Lantern Committee, a band of Ruffians that had their headquarters at Barnsville, Missouri. One day John Denter, while standing in the door of a grocery, near that place, was shot dead by a passing horseman.

Bands of cut-throats from Texas and Arkansas, infested southern Missouri, were drilling, in anticipation of the coming war, and threatened to inaugurate the bloody drama of mobbing, killing and robbing free state men, which they had just been carrying on in the above mentioned States.

According to the treaty of peace, which, it will be recollected, was written by Old John Brown, in Southern Kansas, all Border Ruffians were prohibited from returning on pain of death. Accordingly when some of these ventured to make their appearance this year and engage in their former outrages, the free state men suddenly seized one, hung him to a tree with the inscription on his body, "Hung as a returned Border Ruffian." The free state men organized a secret society, which they called "Wide-a-Wake," pretended to have immediate connection with the vast host of

"Wide-a-Wakes" in the Northern States, made all the display they could, thus spreading terror among the Border Ruffians.

A great outrage was committed by the agent of the Federal Government this fall upon the settlers on the Neutral Lands. According to a treaty made with the Seneca Indians, of New York, they held a strip of land eight miles wide in the vicinity of Fort Scott, the boundaries of which were not definitely established. Immediately south of this and between it and the Cherokee possessions were 800,000 acres, which, according to a treaty with the latter tribe, was closed to settlement by any class of emigrants, and was called the Neutral Land. When Kansas was thrown open to settlement, Squatters made claims upon the New York Indian lands, presuming that they would soon come into market.

But when the survey of the Neutral Lands was made in the summer of 1859, it was found that their northern boundary extended some distance above what the Squatters supposed it did. In this way a large and thrifty neighborhood, called the Dry Wood settlement, numbering 1,527 souls, fell in the Neutral Land. They had improved their claims, built fences, barns and dwelling houses, and were every way in a flourishing condition.

The order was first given by the Commissioner of Indian Affairs, in the spring of 1860, for the removal of the settlers; still no forcible measures were employed to effect this object until the following November. The agent suddenly appeared among them with a strong force of United States troops and began driving the families from their homes, dashing their furniture out of the houses and firing them. In this way seventy-four families were turned out upon the chilly and open prairies—homeless.

The New York Indian lands were offered for sale, this fall, on the 3d and 15th of December. Great excitement prevailed among the settlers, in consequence of the treatment towards the squatters upon the Neutral Lands. On account of the drouth, few were able to purchase their claims—even at government prices, and it was feared that if speculators did not come in and bid off the lands, the government would withdraw the sales, and remove the squatters by force.

By this time the people in southern Kansas had learned to take care of themselves, and resist oppression, no matter from whom it came. They organized, armed themselves, and attended the sales, where it was generally understood that if any one sought to bid off another's claim, he should pay the forfeit with his life. But one person sought to do this, and he had scarcely left the town before he was seized by a party, who would have taken his llfe had he not begged so earnestly, and offered to deed over the land in fee simple to the original claimant. They finally let him go. They thus preserved and held their homes, the Government not seeking to interfere with them.

The troubles and feuds in south-eastern Kansas continued until the breaking out of the national conflict, when they assumed a destructive character, and did not subside until the close of the rebellion.

The Wyandotte Constitution was presented in the Senate on the 14th of February, 1860, and referred to the Committee on Territories, together with a bill for the admission of Kansas. The Committee, unable to agree among themselves, finally reported without any recommendation on the subject.

The same Constitution was laid before the House, on the 10th of February, and on the 15th, Mr. Grow, of Pennsylvania, introduced a bill for the admission of Kansas into the Union, which was read the first and second times, and referred to the Committee on Territories. This bill was reported back favorably from that Committee, and, on the 11th ot April, passed the House by 134 yeas to 73 nays. The Senate stubbornly refused to take it up, and adjourned, leaving Kansas still a Territory, though two years previous that body had warmly favored her admission, under a constitution which had its origin in fraud and outrage. Thus Kansas was deprived of taking any part in the Presidential election of 1860, and kept out of the Union for another year, though every way qualified for admission.

The pretexts for opposing the admission of Kansas, employed by opponents, were that her inhabitants were inadequate, and that the provisions of the English bill had not been fully observed.

At the next session of Congress the application for the admission of Kansas was again renewed, and, on motion of Governor Seward, the House bill which had been passed at the former occasion, was called up in the Senate, in which, on the 31st of January, after some slight amendments it was passed by a vote of 36 yeas, to 16 nays. On the 21st of the same month it was taken up out of regular order, on motion of Mr. Grow, of Pennsylvania, and passed with the Senate's amendments, by 119 yeas to 42 nays.

On the same day Kansas was admitted, Messrs. Jefferson Davis, Clement C. Clay, Fitzpatrick, Mallory, and others, abandoned their seats in Congress to take part in the southern rebellion. Thus the conflict, inaugurated by the repeal of the Missouri compromise, and fought upon the principles of Squatter Sovereignty, ended, making the first defeat of slavery, and the first triumph of free labor, in our national history.

The struggle in Kansas, though not marked by great battles or frightful carnage, was none the less fierce and powerful. It was a contest in which patient endurance, inflexible courage and prudent management were more essential to success than military strength and valor, requiring not only the qualifications of a soldier, but of a statesman, a martyr and a philanthropist. Not only had the enemy to be met with cool determination and with force, but public sentiment abroad had to be considered, a conflict with the

Federal Government avoided, and yet a government upheld and maintained, in opposition to the one recognized by the Federal authority, means raised without taxation, and subsistance and arms procured. Still, so prudently, skillfully and successfully were things managed by the free state men, that throughout the long protracted trouble there can be but little found in their conduct to censure or condemn.

The soil of Kansas is historic ground for fifty miles in width. Along its eastern border, there is scarcely an acre but has been the scene of some daring rencounter, battle or event, connected with the difficulties in the Territory. Old settlers, as they ride along, will here and there call the attention of the stranger to the spot where some one was killed, a house burnt, a skirmish between the opposing parties took place, or where a convention was held, which resolved to resist oppression. Along her ravines free state men have skirted or found a hiding place, to elude the pursuit of their enemies, and over her prairies the fiery chase has often passed.

APPENDIX.

TOPEKA CONSTITUTION IN CONGRESS.

[The following matter should have followed the 302d page, but by an accident, the copy was mislaid until after the time it should have been set up, and, consequently, it is inserted here.]

The Topeka Constitution did not reach Congress until the spring of 1856. On the 24th of March it was presented in the Senate by Lewis Cass, and referred to the Committee on Territories. In the House it was presented by Mr. Mace, on the 7th of April. Agreeable with the petition accompanying the document, a bill was introduced by Mr. Grow, of Pennsylvania, on the 25th of June, admitting Kansas into the Union, and passed the House on the 3d of July, by a vote of 99 yeas to 97 nays. Upon going to the Senate it was referred to the Committee on Territories, from which it was reported back on the 8th of July, with the recommendation that the bill be amended by striking out the preamble, and also the whole of the bill after the enacting clause, and insert in lieu thereof the Senate bill, which had passed that body, authorizing the people of Kansas to frame a constitution and apply for admission into the Union. The bill thus changed to almost a new one, was passed by 30 yeas to 13 nays; while it was pending efforts were made to amend it still further by a clause declaring the Territorial laws framed at Shawnee Mission invalid, but failed by a vote of 32 nays to 12 yeas, A bill was then introduced into the House and passed, reorganizing the Territory of Kansas, but on going to the Senate was lost. Attention was again called, in connection with the Lecompton fraud, to the Topeka Constitution by the minority report, but no action was ever again taken upon it.

WORKS CONSULTED IN COMPILING THIS VOLUME, AND A BRIEF NOTICE OF THE TERRITORIAL LITERATURE OF KANSAS.

It would be tedious and useless to give all the sources of information that have been resorted to in writing this book. The authorities have been so various and numerous, that the author has not mentioned them in foot notes, to avoid increasing the size and cost of the volume. Much has been gathered from living witnesses, and participants in events—much that has never before been published of a secret and party character. The following have been the author's chief references:

HISTORY OF LOUISIANA.

French's Historical Collection, from French writers upon the early history of Louisiana Bruer's History of Louisiana, Stoddard's Sketches of the West, Martin's Louisiana, Peck's Annals of the West, Bancroft's United States, Dillon's Indiana, Gregg's Commerce of the Prairies, Sparks' Biographies of Marquette, De Soto and La Salle, Hildreth's United States.

ON SLAVERY AND CONGRESSIONAL.

Bancroft's United States, Greeley's American Conflict, Annals of Congress, Colonial Histories of New England and other Colonies, Benton's Thirty Year's View, Congressional Globe, American State Papers, Madison's Writings, Life of Clay, of Calhoun, &c.

KANSAS TROUBLES—OFFICIAL.

Report of the Investigation Committee of the United States House of Representatives, Report of the Commissioners to Audit Claims, Executive Minutes, Journals and Acts of the Territorial Legislature, Executive Documents of the United States and the Congressional Globe, Covode Investigation of 1860, Journal of Topeka State Legislature, Report of the Speeches and proceedings of the Wyandotte Constitutional Convention.

HISTORICAL.

Hale's History of Kansas and Nebraska, published in 1854, before Kansas had much history. It is valuable for matter relative to N. E. Emigrant Aid Society.

Bruerton's "War in Kansas," published in the spring of 1854, is valuable in giving particulars, and is very truthful in point of fact.

Mrs. Robinson's "History of Kansas" is very accurate upon all it treats, but is limited and on the diary style. Published in the fall of 1856.

Wm. Phillip's "Conquest of Kansas" is a very interesting and reliable book, but contains discrepancies. It is a valuable addition however, to Kansas histories; published in the fall of 1856. Mr. Phillips has always been one of Kansas' true friends.

"Three Years on the Border," by an Episcopal clergyman, shows the state of feeling in Western Missouri, before and after the repeal of Missouri Compromise.

"Geary and Kansas," by Dr. Gihon, treats chiefly of Governor Geary's administration, and is valuable, though faulty in many respects. He evidently was a friend of the Governor.

"The Englishman in Kansas," by Mr. Gladstone, consists of personal observations in traveling up the Missouri and in the Territory.

Redpath's "Life of John Brown" is indispensable to a writer on Kansas history, though it must be used with care. But his "Roving Editor" has but little application to Kansas.

"Kansas in 1858," by Thomalson, proposes to give an account of the difficulties in south-eastern Kansas, but treats of only a few incidents in a transposed and disconnected manner.

"The Kansas Annual Register," published in 1864, is a singularly constructed work, containing much valuable local matter, &c., &c.

JOURNALISTIC.

"The Herald of Freedom" was an excellent paper, and indispensable to one writing the history of Kansas. The first number was issued in Pennsylvania, October, 1854, and the second on the 6th of January, 1855, at Lawrence, under the editorship of G. W. Brown. It was the ablest edited and largest free state paper in the Territory, and continued until 1860, when it was superseded by the "Tribune." In 1857, the editors published in its columns a complete history of the Territory, up to that time.

Foremost among the pro-slavery papers was the "Squatter Sovereign," published at Atchison, and edited by Dr. Stringfellow and Kelly. It was very ultra, and bitterly opposed to free state men, and was the semi-official organ of the Border Chieftains. It was first published at Liberty, Missouri, by the name of the "Democratic Platform," where it warmly supported Atchison and opposed Benton. In the fall of 1854, Mr. Kelly moved his press to Atchison, where he was joined by Dr. Stringfellow in the publication of "The Squatter Sovereign," the first number of which was issued on the 3d of February, 1855. It was thus issued until the spring of 1857, when it was published by Hon. S. C. Pomeroy and others, and as it changed hands, changed name and politics.

In September, 1854, before a single building was completed at Leavenworth, the "Kansas Weekly Herald," was issued under an old elm tree, near the corner of Cherokee Street, and the levee, under the management of Osborn & Adams, the former of whom was soon superseded by L. J. Eastin. Its tone at first was upright and manly, but it soon gave way to party pressure, and became very ultra and bitterly partisan. It was the first paper published in the Territory. In 1859 it became a daily, and in 1861 its existence terminated by the death of its then proprietor.

The "Kansas Territorial Register," first issued in July, 1855, and destroyed in December of the same year, was edited by Hon. M. A. Delahay.

The "Topeka Tribune" was first published at Lawrence in October, 1854, by John Speer, the present editor of the "Lawrence Tribune." The following spring it was moved to Topeka, and edited by Speer & Ross. In December, 1856, Speer sold out to W. W. & E. G. Ross, and returned to Lawrence. He has been editor in Kansas longer than any other man, always true to the principles of freedom.

The "Kansas Freeman," edited by E. C. K. Garvey, and published at Topeka, is valuable, as it contains the proceedings of the Constitutional Convention and State Legislatures.

The "Lawrence Republican" was established in 1857, and edited by Mr. Dwight Thatcher. It strongly favored the organization of the Republican party.

The Kansas "Free State" was a well conducted paper, under the editorship of Elliott and Miller. It was destroyed at the sacking of Lawrence, and never revived at that place.

The "Kickapoo Pioneer," published at Doniphan, was the second pro-slavery paper in the Territory in point of ultraism and hostility to free state men.

There were several other small papers published in the Territory, but the above mentioned were the principal ones, all of which the author has had before him while writing this book.

Besides the above, much has been gathered from the newspapers in the northern and southern States, which are too numerous to mention.